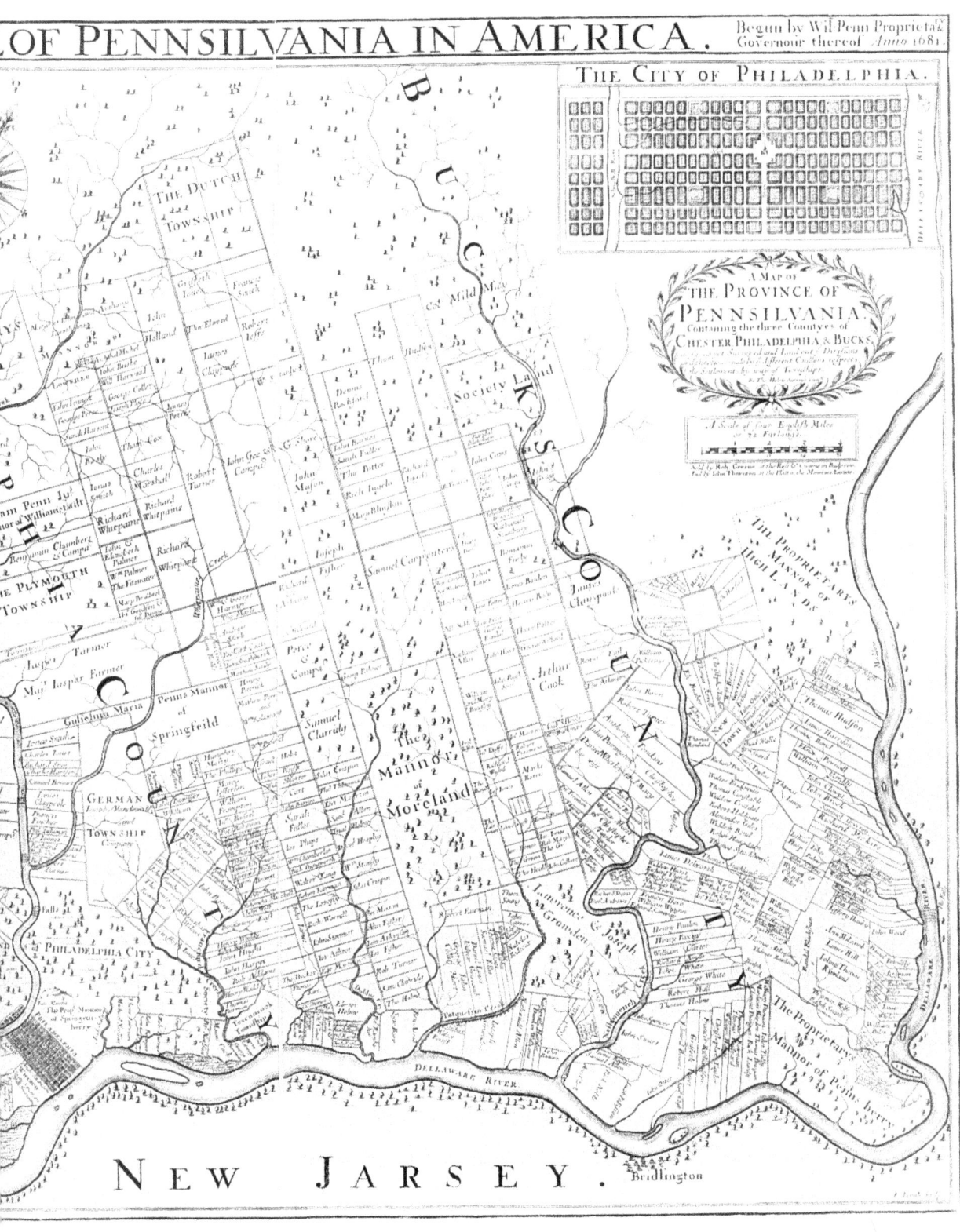

Thomas Holme
1624–1695
Surveyor General of Pennsylvania

Thomas Holme
1624–1695
Surveyor General of Pennsylvania

Irma (Wilma Abigail) Corcoran, B.V.M.

MEMOIRS OF THE
AMERICAN PHILOSOPHICAL SOCIETY
Held at Philadelphia
For Promoting Useful Knowledge
Volume 200

Copyright © 1992 by The American Philosophical Society for its *Memoirs* series.
Publication of this book is subsidized in part by the John Frederick Lewis Fund of the American Philosophical Society.
Library of Congress Catalog Card Number: 91-76987
International Standard Book Number 0-87169-200-7
US ISSN 0065-9738
End papers: Thomas Holme's map of the Province of Pennsylvania, 1681.
Used with permission of Philadelphia Museum of Art.

To
Ann Ida Gannon, B.V.M.

CONTENTS

Illustrations, Documents, and Maps	ix
Abbreviations and Short Titles	xi
Introduction	xiii
Prologue	xvii
Part One: The Yeoman's Son	**1**
1 A Boy in Lancashire	3
Part Two: The Soldier	**11**
2 The Civil Wars	13
3 The Conquest of Ireland	25
Part Three: His Own Man	**33**
4 The Surveyor	35
5 The Religious Activist	47
Part Four: The Governor's Man	**73**
6 The Long Voyage	75
7 Initiation	89
8 Inauguration	109
9 Foundation	135
10 The Home Front	155
11 A Presence in the Delaware Valley	173
12 Watershed	201
13 Politics	223
14 Serendipity	245

15 The Cartographer	257
16 The Wayfarer	283
Epilogue	297
Works Consulted	299
Glossary	307
Index	311

List of Illustrations

Fig. 1. Thomas Holme desk carving in grammar school at Hawkshead.   9
Fig. 2. Grammar School, Hawshead.   10
Fig. 3. George Fox.   19
Fig. 4. Marriage record of Thomas and Sarah Holme.   22
Fig. 5. Title page from Leybourn's *The Compleat Surveyor.*   41
Fig. 6. Holme's seal.   42
Fig. 7. House alleged to be Holme residence, Wexford.   52
Fig. 8. Title page of Holme's tract on suffering.   55
Fig. 9. A young William Penn.   64
Fig. 10. Record of deaths of Sarah Holme and some of the Holme children.   69
Fig. 11. Commission from William Penn to Thomas Holme.   82
Fig. 12. Portion of Robert Morden's map showing placement of Philadelphia.   84
Fig. 13. George Calvert, third Lord Baltimore.   90
Fig. 14. William Penn's letter to the Indians with Holme's signature.   95
Fig. 15. Thomas Holme's map of the city of Philadelphia, "Portraiture of the City of Philadelphia."   Between 116–117
Fig. 16. Drawing of William Penn in Middle Age by Francis Place.   119
Fig. 17. Detail of 1687 map with apportionments next to Liberty Lands.   132
Fig. 18. Holme's letter to William Penn on the day of his son's burial.   170

List of Illustrations

Fig. 19a. Further detail of 1687 map showing German tract. 185

Fig. 19b. Further detail showing first group of Welsh settlers. 185

Fig. 20. New Castle area. 200

Fig. 21. Original version of 1687 map with Growden property and intrusion of Johnson and Walker. 262

Fig. 22. Revised version of 1687 map with Gray portion. 263

Fig. 23. Pickering holdings near Penn's Manor of Gilberts 282

Abbreviations and Short Titles

Abbott: William Cortez Abbott, *The Writings and Speeches of Oliver Cromwell*
ACM: Albert Cook Myers Collection, Library of the Chester County Historical Society, West Chester, Pennsylvania
ACMI: Albert Cook Myers, *Immigration of the Irish Quakers Into Pennsylvania*
ACMN: Albert Cook Myers, *Narratives of Early Pennsylvania, New Jersey, and Delaware*
AD: Autograph document, not signed
ADS: Autograph document, signed
AL: Autograph letter, not signed
ALS: Autograph letter, signed
Annals: Samuel Hazard, *Annals of Pennsylvania*
APS: American Philosophical Society
Ashley: Maurice Ashley, *Great Britain to 1688*
C: Contemporary copy
Campbell: Mildred Campbell, *The English Yeoman Under Elizabeth and the Early Stuarts*
CSPC: Great Britain, *Calendar of State Papers, Colonial: America and West Indies*
CSPD: ————, *Calendar of State Papers, Domestic*
CSPI: ————, *Calendar of State Papers, Ireland*
DAB: *Dictionary of American Biography*
DNB: *Dictionary of National Biography*
Firth: C. H. Firth, *Cromwell's Army*
FLD: Library of the Society of Friends, Dublin
FLL: Library of the Society of Friends, London
Gilbert: John T. Gilbert, *A History or Brief Chronicle of the Chief Matters of the Irish Warres . . .* (1650)

GSP: Genealogical Society of Pennsylvania
HMC: Historical Manuscripts Commission
HSP: Historical Society of Pennsylvania
LS: Letter in the hand of another, signed by the author
MdA: *Archives of Maryland*
Micro.: Unless otherwise identified, Microfilm of the Papers of William Penn, HSP, 1975. References are to reel and frame.
MPC: *Minutes of the Provincial Council of Pennsylvania* (1938)
Nash: Gary B. Nash, "The Free Society of Traders and Early Politics in Pennsylvania," *PMHB* 89 (1965): 147–173
OUD: *Oxford Universal Dictionary*, 3d edition
OR: Selected list of Old Rights surveys, *PA* 3, 2:662–770
PGM: *Pennsylvania Genealogical Magazine*
Planting: Hannah Benner Roach, "The Planting of Philadelphia . . . ," *PMHB* 92 (1968), nos. 1 and 2
PMHB: *Pennsylvania Magazine of History and Biography*
PRC: *The Earliest Registers of the Parish of Coniston*
PRH: *The Earliest Registers of the Parish of Hawkshead*
PTL: Philip Theodore Lehnmann
PWP: *The Papers of William Penn*, 5 vols., ed. Mary Maples Dunn and Richard S. Dunn
Richeson: A. W. Richeson, *English Land Measuring to 1800*
Sprigge: Joshua Sprigge, *Anglia Rediviva*, MSS and printed vol., 1649
Twenty-three Ships: Marion Balderston, "William Penn's Twenty-three Ships," *PGM* 23 (1963), 27–67
Votes: *Votes and Proceedings of the House of Representatives of the Province of Pennsylvania*, PA, 8th series, vol. 1
Wx: *Wexford Friends' Register . . .* , FLD

Introduction

Originally this book was to be called *The Governor's Man: Thomas Holme, 1624–1695*, but as research progressed Thomas Holme emerged as a hard-headed, hard-thinking, hard-working middle-class Englishman who had lived nearly sixty meaningful years before he threw in his lot with thirty-six-year-old William Penn. As part of the circle of the most active Friends in Ireland he had known William Penn for at least a dozen years, but in Pennsylvania he always addressed him as "Governour" and referred to him as "the Governour." Their relationship on the whole seems to have been characterized by mutual affection and respect, and Holme was a zealous champion of the governor's interests; but he was, in modern terminology, "his own man."

In the pages which follow I have endeavored to present him as his actions show him to have been, not a perfect but a greatly striving man. His was a commission that could have absorbed all his time and effort, yet he was immersed, with a relatively small circle of others, in the shaping of the government, Indian affairs, and other tangential matters. He had a weakness that could have been, but was not, disastrous.

Articles about Thomas Holme and books and articles which give some space to his accomplishments are more abundant than accurate. I have not cited them because I did not find them helpful, and most of them are misleading in one or more respects. The matter of his descendants, apart from the Crispin family, is beyond the scope of this book.

Relatively little of what appears to have been a fairly voluminous and important body of Thomas Holme's correspondence with William Penn is extant. In letters that survive there are references to lost letters and messages, and sometimes replies to matters discussed in lost missives supply valuable information.

In quoting from documents and early publications I have adhered to originals as closely as possible except in the expansion of abbreviations such as the tailed *P* (per, par, etc.), words in which y, representing the Anglo-Saxon thorn, was used with superscript letters (that, the) and similar combinations in which superscripts appear. For these entire words or common abbreviations are substituted. The long *s* is modernized, but idiosyncrasies of spelling and idiom have been retained, even to Thomas Holme's use of *contagious* for *contiguous*. Because in England during Thomas Holme's lifetime the new year commenced on 25 March, and the preceding January and February bore the date of the year before, I have indicated dates where this calendar was observed by including both years, e.g., 1683/84, and when the Quaker practice of numbering months and days of the week in order to avoid names of pagan origin is followed and clarification seemed desirable I have inserted the customary name in brackets.

It would be impossible for me to set down a complete record of my indebtedness to librarians, archivists, and unofficial but helpful volunteers to whom I am grateful for assistance during the many years of intermittent research that unearthed and enabled me to gather into these pages some account of the life of Thomas Holme. Three of these benefactors head the list: Ann Ida Gannon, B.V.M., as president of Mundelein College, prompted me to commence the project and recommended the year's leave from the classroom that gave time for the original investigations. The American Association of University Women and the American Philosophical Society through grants made possible the use of that time for research abroad.

Basic to the search for Thomas Holme's life in Pennsylvania were the riches of the library of the Historical Society of Pennsylvania, in which I had the advantage of being for a year and a half assistant preparator of the Papers of William Penn for the microfilm released in 1975—a position I enjoyed at the invitation of the late Hannah Benner Roach, with the concurrence of the late Nicholas B. Wainwright, then executive director of the society, and his successor, James E. Mooney. The assistance of Linda Stanley during her time as assistant and, finally manuscripts librarian was invaluable. During the preparation of the magnificent five-volume edition of the *Papers of William Penn* published by the University of Pennsylvania Press I enjoyed consultation with the general editors, Richard S. Dunn and

Mary Maples Dunn, and the editors of the individual volumes, for which I am most grateful.

Among the many librarians and archivists of the Pennsylvania area to whom I am indebted are the late Miss Ogilvie of the Arch Street Friends' Library; the late Frederick B. Tolles and the staff of the Friends' National Library at Swarthmore; Bart Anderson and Dorothy Lapp emeriti librarian and assistant librarian and to the present librarian, Rosemary B. Philips of the library of the Chester County Historical Society at West Chester, the staff of the Library Company of Philadelphia, successive manuscripts librarians of the American Philosophical Society, and the curators of the Philadelphia Archives and of the Pennsylvania State Archives at Harrisburg, particularly Martha Simonetti and the late Genevieve Blatt. To Edward L. Pearce I owe access to the early records of Bucks County.

To the librarians of the general reading room, the Map Room, and the Students' Room of the British Library and to those of the Round Room of the Public Record Office in London I am most grateful, as also to the staff of the Bodleian Library. Archivists R. Sharpe France of the Library of the County of Lancaster at Preston, England, and I. E. Gray, Records Officer of Gloucestershire at Gloucester, England, were most helpful. To the successors of Thomas Holme's first neighbors I am also deeply indebted, especially to the late Mary Coward, and to Amy Parks, curator of the Hawkshead Grammar School.

To the librarians of the National Archives of Ireland and the officials of the National Library of Ireland I am deeply indebted, as also to Mr. Sullivan, Manuscripts Librarian of Trinity College, Dublin. To two successive rectors of St. Peter's College, Wexford, I am grateful for the use of the papers of Francis and Philip Hore, authors of the six-volume history of County Wexford, and to faculty member Seamas S. de Val, who arranged for an enlightening tour of the then intact but unrestored John's Castle at Limerick. I am grateful also to Michael Kehoe of County Wexford, for an extensive tour of the lands once owned by Thomas Holme and Robert Cuppage, a visit to a house in which the Thomas Holme family may have lived, and a wealth of local history. To Edward Milligan, then librarian of the Library of the Society of Friends in London, and especially to Mrs. Olive Goodbody, librarian of the Society of Friends in Dublin I owe familiarity with significant portions of the early history of the Society of Friends.

I have had daily cause to be grateful to the members of my religious community, who have been tolerant of my enthusiasms and laments and generous with offers of assistance, especially to Ann Leone Graham for obtaining after-thought materials in England, and to the coordinators of the Mundelein College Computer Center and their staff, who entered the manuscript on the microcomputer. Thanks are due also to Raymond Baumhart, S.J., President of Loyola University and Caroline Farrell, BVM, Vice-President for Mundelein College of Loyola University for the use of a choice office, telephone and fax facility that made possible the completion of this project.

Finally, I am deeply indebted to Carole N. Le Faivre and Susan M. Babbitt of the Publications Office of the American Philosophical Society, without whose patient entertainment of my long distance queries and explanations (in addition to the services of a nameless editor) the Thomas Holme revealed here would not have come to light.

It is a pleasure to express my gratitude to these benefactors and to a host of volunteers who have made work a joy.

Prologue

On the top of a hill overlooking northeastern Philadelphia stands a modest obelisk bearing on each of its four sides an inscription:

In memory of Thomas Holme, d. 1695, aged seventy-one, Surveyor General of William Penn. He drafted the plan and laid out the city of Philadelphia.

He became the proprietor of 1600 acres of land in one tract by grant of Penn in 1683 named his "Well Spring Plantation" of which this ground is a part.

In lieu of a donation in his will for school purposes, his heirs gave the land on which Lower Dublin Academy is located.

This stone was erected in 1863–64 by the following named Trustees of the Lower Dublin Academy, as a mark of respect to the memory of the originator of the School. Benjamin Crispin, George W. Holme, Isaac Pierson, George Fox, Henry Dewees, Samuel Willits, Charles T. Harrison, George Wagner, Alfred Enoch, Thomas Shalcross, Firman D. Holme.

The man so commemorated is said to have selected the site himself. One may well believe that he frequented the spot in life, looking about him at his beloved plantation, and, as far as he could see, at the vast tracts of rolling land that he had surveyed or caused to be surveyed and had mapped for "The Governour." Far away to the southwest, where Delaware turns sharply south from its southwesterly course, lay the city whose "portraiture" he had drawn before it was laid down in the two-mile span of rich Pennsylvania earth between the Delaware and the Schuylkill. The prospect was not unlike that of his native northern Lancashire, nor was the quality of the man much different from that of the generations of yeomen from whom he sprung.

Thomas Holme had come a long way from his early haunts. He had fought in three wars and had engaged in allegedly peaceful protests; he had won and lost prestige and property; he had suffered still more personal defeats and disappointments. With all his faults and frustrations, he had contributed to the planting of a new land. He died and was buried on his hilltop. His work remains, an ineradicable part of Pennsylvania history.

An attempt has been made in the following pages to set in this history a "portraiture" of Thomas Holme himself, who remained throughout the ups and downs of the more than quarter-century of their friendship, not subserviently but militantly loyally, "The Governour's Man."

Part One

The Yeoman's Son

Chapter 1

A Boy in Lancashire

The people of upper Lancashire were tall, hardy, opinionated, and obstinate. Tenaciously religious and political, Catholics and Anglicans were usually Royalists; and Protestants, Parliamentarians. Descendants of beneficiaries of the closing of the monasteries under the heavy hand of Henry VIII, they had inherited considerable economic know-how, usually supporting themselves directly by the products of their own land, and disposing of surplus at a local market. Campbell states that the picture of yeomen presented by legal documents is

> that of a group of ambitious, aggressive, small capitalists, aware that they had not enough surplus to take great risks, mindful that the gain is often as much in the saving as in the spending, but determined to take advantage of every opportunity, whatever its origin, for increasing their profits.[1]

---

[1] Unless otherwise stated, information concerning births, marriages, and burials is from *The Oldest Register Book of the Parish at Hawkshead in Lancashire, 1568–1704*, ed. H. S. Cowper (London: Benrose & Sons, 1897) For accounts of Thomas Holme's early milieu see H. S. Cowper, introduction to *PRH*; Samuel Lewis, *Topographical Dictionary of England*, 7th ed., 1849, 1: 680; William Farrar and J. Brownbill, eds., *Victoria History of the County of Lancaster* (London, 1914), vol. 8; Cory, *Transactions* of the Cumberland and Westmorland Antiquarian Society 4: 28; and Mildred Campbell, *The English Yeoman Under Elizabeth and the Early Stuarts* (Yale University Press, 1942). For more intimate knowledge of the Hawkshead-Coniston area the author is indebted to conversations with inhabitants, particularly with the late Mrs. Mary Coward, who introduced her to the slate-fronted house at the Waterhead, which she was convinced was originally a yeoman's house dating from the early 1600s, and with Miss Amy Parks, curator of the Hawkshead Grammar School, who joined in the search for Thomas's name on the desk and, in fact, found it. Because as a Quaker Thomas abjured baptism, he recorded his birth in *Wx 3*, 1 November, rather than his baptismal date, 3 November, which appears, in *PRH*.

Thomas Holme's family inhabited a land of fertile valleys overshadowed by hills that were not quite mountains, but a little too aggressive to constitute a gently rolling countryside. Their stock was strong, the sheep clothed in long wool that was soft and heat-holding next to the skin, but coarse and tough on the outside, able to shed rain and snow. Buried under snow, they could survive for two or three weeks. There was iron in the hills, with mines and a foundry owned by the Sawreys, who employed neighbors in the mines and the foundry or as wood cutters to fell trees to fire the furnaces. Slate was abundant in the hills, and by the first quarter of the seventeenth century, when freeholders and yeomen were replacing dark cottages with one and even two-story houses, they faced and roofed them with slate shingles. Their fields were surrounded by dry-stone fences, and one of the signs of the coming of spring was neighboring farmers "walking the bounds" to assess the damage done by the frosts of winter. For the rest of the year trees, grass, crops, wild flowers, and bracken were lush. Intensely cold, clear streams powered mills, transported travelers, watered stock, augmented well water, and offered year-round recreation.

Into this milieu, at the head of Coniston Water, on 1 November 1624, was born Thomas, son of George and Alice Holme of Waterhead.

His was a very old name. Most of those bearing it in the great oval of counties that swings north from Yorkshire to southern Scotland and downward through Westmorland, Lancashire, and Cheshire are said to have sprung from a common ancestor, one John of Stockholme, retainer of William the Conqueror, who in the distribution of prizes following the Conquest, was settled on a substantial estate in Yorkshire. The name, shortened to Holme, in time took various forms, including Home, Hume, Holmes and Hulme, although Holme remained a distinctive spelling in the area in which Thomas Holme lived.

A few generations from the first John Holme one of his descendants is said to have become embroiled in difficulties with King John, from whom, in 1209, he and his family fled from their ancestral seat to Mardale, a secluded valley beside Hawes Water in upper Westmorland.[2] From there it was easy for the fugitive's descendants to cross a mile or so of hills to High Street—the old Roman road that runs north towards Scotland and south half a dozen miles to the Lower Lake District. It seems likely that the Holme families of upper Lancashire

---

[2] Joseph Whiteside, "The Holmes of Mardale," *Transactions* of the Cumberland-Westmorland Archeological Society n. s. 2 (1902): 146–150.

stem from this family. The given names in the Hawkshead and Coniston parish registers echo those in the Shap register: William, George, Christopher, Reginald, John, Thomas, Ann, Ellen, Agnes, and Isabel recurring frequently. Although it is true that these names are too common to be of much value to the genealogist, the family names of southern Lancashire follow a somewhat different pattern.

Lords, knights, craftsmen, and husbandmen bore the surname Holme, but the greater number of them were freemen or yeomen, with numerous gentlemen in Yorkshire and mid-Lancashire. If Thomas Holme had any ancestral claim to distinction it may have been through relationship to the Huntington, Yorkshire, family, whose arms, a field argent with chevron azure between three chaplets gules, appear in the seal he used when his official positions made personal authentication desirable. He enclosed the field in a bordure of ten rondules to show the degree of kinship, but there is no record of his having had a claim to arms confirmed.

The earliest identifiable forebears of Thomas Holme are his paternal great-grandfathers, Michael Holme, whose will was proved in 1600, and Myles Sawrey, who lived until 1613. The wills of both survive in the Lancaster County Library at Preston, as does that of Michael's son George. Both great-grandfathers were yeomen of considerable means. Michael left to his son George, grandfather of Thomas, his revenue at Skelwith Bridge; all his tenements, and other property, at Yewdall, with rent of Mr. Fleming; the Almshouse; and, with his widow, Agnes, all the meal in "the great Arke, the Arke to remain to George"; as well as a share with two other "sons" (sons-in-law) in three mills, in addition to numerous smaller bequests. He left a legacy including cash to George, "my son George's oldest son [Thomas Holme's grandfather]." His stipulation that John Hodgson and Alexander Holme or "Ellen my daughter to have no benefit by this my will" gives to the closing lines of the document a tone of irascibility not infrequent among Holme papers.[3]

Myles Sawrey, who outlived not only his daughter Ann's father-in-law Michael Holme, but also, it may be inferred, two of his daughters and his son-in-law George Holme, seems to have been a substantial

---

[3] *A List of the Lancashire Wills Proved within the Archdiocese of Richmond*, ed. Fishwick (Record Society, Lancashire and Cheshire, 1884). According to *PRH*, an Elline Holme, presumably Michael's daughter, was baptized on 26 November 1581; and a girl of that name married Jeffery Tyson on 15 January 1597/98. That Michael's animus was not shared by his son George appears from the latter's legacy to Jeffery in his will of 2 December 1602. Unless otherwise noted, subsequent references to parish register material will be to this volume, abbreviated *PRH*. The combination of class, chronological, and alphabetical arrangement makes page numbers superfluous.

citizen. He was able to leave to his sons tenements and farmholds at the Waterhead and elsewhere in the parish of Hawkshead, along with grounds in "farre Coniston" on the west side of Coniston Water, with other bequests to the children of sons-in-law Jopson, Hodgson, and Holme. The overseer of his will was his "beloved friend in Christ Mr. Edwin Sandys," the son or, more probably, a nephew of a Hawkshead celebrity of the same name, Archbishop of York and founder of Hawkshead Grammar School.[4]

Michael Holme's son George and Myles Sawrey's daughter Ann were married in their late teens—George was eighteen and Ann a year younger—and George died at thirty-five, leaving Ann with four living children, of whom the eldest was eleven. George's inheritance seems to have shrunk somewhat during these sixteen years, since the only possessions mentioned in his last will and testament, dated 2 December 1602, are the tenement (dwelling) and farmhold at Waterhead bequeathed him by his father. These he left to his son George, who, on reaching twenty-one, was to pay each of his three sisters her share of the estate at marriage or her twenty-first birthday.

That the children lost no time in collecting their legacies is evinced by the four marriages contracted within the year of George's attainment of the specified age: George, who was twenty-one in April, 1613, married Alice Whiteside in Coniston on 18 May; Elizabeth and Reginald Holme were married on 1 August; Agnes and Richard Burrey on 4 September; and Mabell and Thomas Hodgson on 27 October. Elizabeth was twenty and Mabell fourteen; the baptismal date of Agnes does not appear in the registers of the Hawkshead and Coniston parishes. Since no notice of the baptism of an Ann Holme of suitable age nor of the death of "vid. Geo. Holme" appears in local registers, it is likely that the Ann Holme who married William Middlefell on 27 November, slightly more than six months after the burial of George Holme on 10 May 1603, was his widow. There is no further mention of her in local records.

Alice Whiteside, the wife of young George Holme of Waterhead, was a newcomer to her husband's neighborhood. There are scattered references to her surname in other portions of Lancashire, but it is not native to the Hawkshead-Coniston region. Whitesides were most

---

[4] The archbishop, whose family seat was at Grisedale in Hawkshead Parish, died in 1587/88 after a somewhat stormy career. His son Edwin entered the Middle Temple in February, 1589/90, and may have been a friend of Anthony Sawrey of Hawkshead, apparently a nephew of Miles, who matriculated in November, 1590. The Edwin Sandys to whom Sawrey refers is most likely the gentleman of that name who appears in *PRH* as the father of Ann Sands, baptized on 23 July 1602. He was buried in the "quire" of the church at Hawkshead on 16 June 1625. The Middle Temple entry appears in H.A.C. Sturgiss, *Register of Admissions . . .* 1: 604.

numerous in Poulton le Fylde, near Blackpool. Alice was a common name among them, and the Alice who married George Holme may have been the otherwise unaccounted for daughter of William of Poulton and his wife, Agnes Smith, who was baptized on 21 April 1598.[5]

Since George Holme of Waterhead was the first of three of the name in the Hawkshead-Coniston vicinity to be married between 18 May 1613 and 12 December 1619, only a few of Thomas Holme's siblings can be identified with any certainty: Ealse, who was baptized on 30 April 1614; Mary, baptized on 13 September 1627 and named specifically as the child of George of Waterhead; and Michael, baptized on 27 October 1628.

Thomas Holme's first six years were like those of other children in the Monk Coniston area. His days were filled with games, small chores, sparring with older siblings and watching over younger ones. Lessons at home or at a dame school taught him basic arithmetic, reading, spelling, and writing. The reading, based on Scripture and accompanied by memorizing of biblical passages, was also an exercise in memory. When he had reached what was considered acceptable proficiency in his elementary studies he went on to grammar school.

He had scarcely embarked on his educational career and had only recently been deemed old enough to tramp about the fields inspecting the stone fences with his father, when the rhythm of his life was broken by his father's death. George Holme of Waterhead died at the age of thirty-eight. Since he seems to have died intestate it is probable that his death was sudden, perhaps the result of one of the accidents recorded from time to time in the parish registers, drowning when a boat capsized in the rapids or being crushed by a falling tree. He was buried *in templo*—in consecrated ground—at Hawkshead on 17 December 1630. Thomas Holme became the responsible big brother of three-year-old Mary and two-year-old Michael.

After a year of caring alone for the family and for the property at Waterhead, Alice Holme married William Collyer at Hawkshead. The introduction of a stepfather into the household must have made some impact on seven-year-old Thomas, although probably William Collyer was at least accepted philosophically, since the remarriage of a bereaved spouse was normally to be taken for granted. The daily life of the Holme-Collyer family would go on very much as before.

---

[5] We know Alice's identity from her son's autobiographical summary, the original of which is Item 9 in Register F 3 for County Wexford, hereafter cited as *Wx 3*, at Friends' Library, Dublin. For records of the Whiteside family see William Edward Robinson, ed., *The Registers of the Parish Church of Poulton-le-Fylde*, Lancashire Parish Record Society (Wigan, 1907), 19: 14. The marriage of George Holme and Alice Whiteside is recorded in *PRC* 30: 42.

When his dame-school days were over, Thomas was fortunate in the accessibility of the excellent school at Hawkshead that had been founded and endowed by the distinguished, though controversial, local prelate, Bishop Edwin Sandys, to provide "grammar and the principles of the Greek tongue with other sciences necessary to be taught in grammar school." It was notable, too, for the spirit of the founder, a friend of Queen Elizabeth, who was about as radically independent as he could be and yet remain within the Anglican communion.

A man of independent judgment, Sandys was an outspoken defender of freedom of conscience and a militant opponent of all remnants of Catholic liturgical practices, from the wearing of vestments to the use of the sign of the cross in baptism. Well educated himself—he held three degrees from Cambridge University—he was concerned for the development of all capable young people. Like all educators of his time, he was familiar with the theories of Richard Mulcaster, master of the prestigious Merchant Taylors' School in London, whose influence was being felt throughout England. Mulcaster insisted that pupils should master English before commencing the study of Latin, and that the study of music and drawing should be required of all children to the age of twelve. The first headmaster of the Hawkshead school was Peter Magson, M.A., who was succeeded by his son Francis, both of whom must have been acceptable to the founder.[6]

The only evidence of Thomas's "small Latin" is a proverb in one of his letters to William Penn, and he gave no sign of exposure to Greek. His first plan of Philadelphia, carefully laid out on now tattered vellum preserved in the State Archives of Pennsylvania, shows more than necessary care in the illustration of parks and houses, and a ship in full sail on the Delaware.

At the end of his career at Hawkshead Thomas took out his well-sharpened knife and cut his name, deeply and squarely, among the others that were already vying for space on the top of the long desk that he shared with a row of other students. If one wishes to believe that he carved also the medallion of mountain scenery below his name, there is no one to gainsay it.

What Thomas did after he left grammar school is anyone's guess. Many options were open. He may have stayed with his mother and stepfather, helping to operate the hereditary property at the Water-

---

[6] Thomas Habinton, "Statutes for Hawkshead Grammar School," in his *Antiquities of the Cathedral Church of Worcester*, 163–169.

Fig. 1. Thomas Holme desk carving in grammar school at Hawkshead. Photograph by author.

Fig. 2. Grammar School, Hawkshead. Photograph by author.

head, or he may have apprenticed himself to a tradesman or followed the example of relatives who had gone from grammar school to Oxford or Cambridge or to one of the Inns of Court. His name does not appear on the fragmentary surviving rolls of any of these institutions. His writing and other accomplishments in later life show him to have been intelligent, practical, and literate; they do not suggest a legal or university education. In any event, the grammar school at Hawkshead was capable of providing an education adequate to his future responsibilities.

Part Two

The Soldier

Chapter 2

The Civil Wars

Whatever Thomas Holme's plans for his future may have been, they could scarcely have encompassed the actual events. By the time he was seventeen the economic, political, and religious tensions that had been mounting from the beginning of the Stuart regime—a year before he was born—were nearing the breaking point. That point arrived during the summer before he was eighteen. By 22 August, when King Charles I, by setting up his standard at Nottingham, issued the traditional call to arms, all parts of England were psychologically aware of the state of war. It is said that in Lancashire men enlisted at once in the parliamentary army to escape conscription by the local Royalist leader, the Earl of Derby.[1] Thomas Holme probably acted upon this expedient. We lack details of his service, but we know from his own account that he was a veteran when hostilities ceased in England.[2]

Both Royalists and Parliamentarians regarded themselves as on the right side of a holy war. The conflict was inescapable. If you were in the army, you fought. The holiness, too, was assumed; but the channels of grace were somewhat confused.

Thomas Holme found himself at once in a war marked at first by a certain vagueness and sometimes divisiveness of command. In the spring of 1645 the fragmented forces were molded by Cromwell into

---

[1] Maurice Ashley, *Great Britain to 1688* (Ann Arbor, 1961), 348.
[2] *Wx 3*. The term *English Army* signified veteran standing.

the New Model army, and action proceeded decisively. It grew also in physical hardship and horror. What branch of service Thomas Holme was in we do not know. The "Captain Holmes" who replaced the Captain Franklin slain at Exeter may have been either Thomas Holme or Abraham, later Major, Holme, who served under Lilburne in the "traine," or engineering service.[3] Later assignments suggest that Thomas Holme had some engineering experience. On the other hand, he may have been a member of the dragoons, the mounted infantry that traveled with the cavalry but fought with the infantry.

Yeomen frequently brought to military service horses and something in the way of weapons, and wound up in a troop of dragoons. These and the cavalry, to a greater extent than infantry, were involved in the Civil War in the West, and Cromwell's own regiment, composed of cavalry and dragoons, was made up of Lancashire men. It is likely that Thomas Holme was among them.[4]

The soldiers were, on the whole, hard-headed and realistic, protesting vigorously the rigors of their life and the uncertainty and inadequacy of pay. On these scores they had ample cause for complaint. According to Sprigge, marches varied in length from one to thirty-two miles, frequently with intervening stops for only one night. When a section of the army moved, it did not settle down again, unless required by military exigencies to do so, within seven miles for infantry and ten for cavalry.

Fighting, in a countryside whose thick woods and copses and many ditches, hedges, walls, and hills obscured the view and made advance or retreat difficult and perilous, was a sore tax on men encumbered with clumsy weapons and armor that, even when stripped to essentials, was burdensome. Setting up bridges and storming fortified houses and towns under the conditions of seventeenth-century warfare were terrifying. When such work had to be prosecuted on an inadequate diet, it was inevitable that both discipline and the local populace should suffer. Sometimes meat was so scarce that horses had to be protected at night from hungry marauders.[5] Pay, when it came, was small. To motivate troops and enhance discipline a number of books for distribution to the army were published early in the conflict.

Perhaps the most potent of these was an instrument of indoctrination called *The Souldiers Catechism*, produced in 1644 "for the Incour-

---

[3] Joshua Sprigge, *Anglia Rediviva* (London, 1649), 328; MS, BL.
[4] C. H. Firth, *Cromwell's Army*, 3d ed. (London: Methuen & Co., Ltd., 1962), 123–28.
[5] [Robert Ram], *The Souldiers Catechism*, 1644. Firth notes that a facsimile reprint of this volume edited by Reverend Walter Begley was published in 1900. The quotations here are from the original edition.

agement and Instruction of all that have taken up Armes in this Cause of God and His People; especially the Common Souldiers." Opening on a mild and pious note, it grows in vehemence, presenting scriptural justification for war in a good cause, then assuring the readers that their current cause is of the approved sort.

In the course of a few questions the author assumes that the king is lower than "the meanest court in the land," that those about him are plotting to deliver the country into the hands of Rome, and that it is therefore the religious duty of all to fight against his faction. As for fighting against their fellow countrymen, they were not to think of them as countrymen, relatives, or fellow-Protestants, but "as enemies of God and our Religion." The "authors, and occasioners of the unnaturall Warre," were, "The Jesuites, with all the Popish party, and the [Anglican] Bishops, and the rotten Clergie, with all the Prelaticall party." It may be said that, for a not very ecumenical age, conspiracy made strange bedfellows. Two elements of this indoctrination that impressed themselves particularly strongly on young combatants were the rights of the individual and the wickedness of the clergy.

Anyone who fought against the Royalists and their leader or who completed the demolition of idolatrous ornaments in churches not already despoiled by zealous predecessors rendered service to God. The soldiers prosecuted their duty in this regard with the mixture of motives to which human nature is prone.

When the long day's fighting or marching was over, the first concerns of most of the men were rest and food and their overdue pay.

Discipline in the army was regulated according to *Laws and Ordinances of War established for the better conduct of the Army*, issued by Essex on 8 September 1642,[6] with a few later accretions as experience dictated. In a negative way, these *Articles of War* are eloquent of military life in England during nearly a decade of strife. They embrace duties of every category and prescribe punishments, ranging from boring the tongue with a red hot iron to death, for what often seem to be minor lapses on the part of the common soldier. The army became suitably hardened against temptations toward mercy.[7] Inevitably young, often idealistic, survivors of forces schooled in such experience, the *Catechism*, and the *Laws and Ordinances of War* were either broken or very tough indeed. Throughout their lives many of them labored under the paradoxical obligations of righteousness and mercy.

---

[6] Firth, appendix: 400–410.
[7] The devastation of this magnificent house and the slaughter or capture of its garrison and many refugees was a Cromwellian triumph. See Sprigge, 151, quoted by Firth, 192.

For combatants convinced that they were fighting a bloody war because such was the will of God, clarifying their relation to God was a corollary necessity. Thomas Holme and most of his peers had never before been confronted with choices in this regard. Their families belonged to the local Protestant church and brought up their children according to its creed. Now they encountered a mixture of creeds and customs. Protestant elements of the population found the Anglican hierarchy as distasteful to them as the Catholic one had been and were apprehensive of a return to popery. Many of them had risen appreciably on the economic scale through the dissolution of the monasteries, and so had material as well as spiritual interest in maintaining maximum freedom from governmental interference by either church or state.

The largest single group in the army during the early stages of the war was the Presbyterians. The church was governed by a general assembly, beneath which were the individual presbyteries, with individual congregations governed by their own sessions of elders forming the base of the pyramid. Absolutely speaking, all elders were of equal rank. The government of the church may have been democratic, but no freedom of opinion as to belief or forms of worship was permitted.

The sermon took precedence over any remnants of liturgy. The Bible was the sole arbiter of faith and conduct, and acceptance of the Calvinist doctrines of the depravity of post-lapsarian man and the absolute predestination of the individual to salvation or damnation—allegedly discoverable in the Bible—was mandatory.

More acceptable to most of the rank and file were the principles of Congregationalists, or Independents, who upheld the autonomy of each local congregation. Corollary to this theory was the practice of lay preaching, which had been carried on sporadically for many decades, particularly in central and northeastern England, including Cromwell's home county of Huntingdon.

Robert Browne, who had given his name to an early congregational sect, gave some coherence to it by his promotion of "gathered churches" bound under God by covenant but free of governmental direction. It was to Browne's group that the term *separatists* was first applied, although it was soon extended to include all those who had detached themselves from the Anglican communion. Indeed, the term *Independents* seems to have included in time any Protestant of any shade of belief exclusive of Catholicism, Anglicanism, or Presbyterianism.

More suspect than most separatists because more turbulent were the Fifth Monarchy faction, who not only expected Christ to return to found a fifth world monarchy, but seemed bent on hastening the event by disrupting government here and now. It was to this group that William Crispin, the husband of William Penn's cousin, Rebecca Bradshaw, belonged, at least after the Hispaniola fracas. Abraham Holme, originally an Anabaptist, also became a leader of this sect.[8] On these hardy souls, so long as they promoted the zeal and did not undermine the discipline of the army, Cromwell at first looked with approbation. The carrying of these principles of independence and democracy into the realms of civil and military government was a different matter.

When, in 1647, the liberal elements of the army, under the leadership of John Lilburne, prosecuted their aims so forcibly that there was no longer any way of ignoring them, they were permitted to form a "Council of the Army" consisting of two non-commissioned officers, or "agitators" elected, and two officers appointed, for each regiment, who attempted to wrest from Parliament what they considered their rights. The upshot of their activities was greatly increased power in Parliament and accession of numbers in the army, so that the Levellers, as they had been dubbed by the Royalists, became overweeningly arrogant corporately and individually. Cromwell himself found them getting out of hand. Although they were a political rather than a religious faction, they invoked the principles of the rights and dignity of the individual espoused by the dissenting religious groups.

Their ambitions were well defined. They demanded not only the abolition of kingship, but complete freedom in religion, together with universal manhood suffrage. Lilburne urged the dissolution of Parliament and its reestablishment on democratic lines.

An offshoot of the Levellers was the group called the Diggers, founded by George Everard and Gerard Winstanley in 1649. Like the Brownists, they believed in communal ownership of land and in what they considered to be a scriptural principle, that man was to earn his bread literally by cultivating the soil—in this case crown property and commons—with the spade. So it was that passersby along a Surrey road in April 1649 were astonished on lifting their eyes to the hills to see on one of them a group of solemn Englishmen digging away. They explained their beliefs and assured interrogators that their number would increase to four thousand.

Arrested and hailed before General Fairfax, they expounded their doctrines, prophesying that these would be vindicated by the elimination of poverty, idleness, and oppression. They were peaceable men,

---

[8] *Clark Papers*, vol. 1, Camden Society Publications, n. s. 49: 436.

whose resistance to evil would be nonviolent and, obviously, obdurate. As though this were not frustrating enough, they further exasperated officials by keeping their hats on.

In a letter to the Council of State, Winstanley declared that "If the Norman power [i.e., feudal] is still upheld we have lost by sticking to the Parliament." Those who had relied on their promises of free land claimed "freedom to enjoy the common lands, bought by our money and blood."[9]

If Thomas Holme was involved in any of these sects he was not so conspicuously active as to be commemorated in print. Nevertheless, these groups prompted widespread consideration of the forms and functions of government. Ideas and practices of all of them had seeped through an army made up largely of men brought up in, but dissatisfied with, the establishment and the various sects, and resentful of their present condition. Many of them were ripe for conversion to a spiritual system that would have strong appeal to war-weary men. A sect that embodied elements of most of these sects was taking shape in England under the leadership of an itinerant lay preacher who had already begun to attract throngs of followers when the first war ended in 1646.

The life of George Fox was almost exactly co-extensive with that of Thomas Holme. Like Thomas Holme, he came from a comfortable but not affluent environment, from which he departed at the age of nineteen to wander about as a lay preacher and "seeker"—one of a fairly large number of persons who, repelled by the dogmatism of most sects, sought religious significance in subjective consideration of themselves and all things. Like the Anabaptists, Fox relied for guidance on an inner light and sought the freedom and conversion of the people by urging them, too, to "wait upon the Lord" and to resist by non-violent means coercion of any sort toward customs of which they did not approve.

As Fox grew increasingly sure of himself he became a truly magnetic preacher, attracting thousands of listeners in upper Lancashire and Cumberland. The name Holme is prominent among his converts in the deanery of Furness, in which Hawkshead, the Conistons, and other villages and farmlands were situated.

Since they opposed the payment of tithes, the "Friends of Truth" and "Children of Light," as they called themselves, incurred the en-

---

[9] Gerard Winstanley, *Letter to the Council of State*. For his creed, see also his *The Saint's Paradise: Or the Father's Teaching the Only Satisfaction to Waiting Souls*, cited by Lewis H. Berens, *The Digger Movement* (London, 1961).

Fig. 3. George Fox. Used with the permission of the Newberry Library.

mity of the church. Their conviction that all persons were equal under God and that God manifested Himself by inspiration as an inner light further antagonized other religious organizations, since it led them to protest the exhortations of ordained ministers and the teaching of any dogmatic religion. Like the Levellers, they refused to acknowledge the authority of one man over others by doffing their hats to officials—a practice about as popular with seventeenth-century magistrates as refusal to salute commissioned officers would be in a twentieth-century army. Many "seekers" and "waiters" joined their number.

At first Fox's society was largely civilian in character, but as its fame and influence spread—and it was an actively proselytizing sect—it infiltrated the army and gathered large numbers there. Diggers and Levellers, among them John Lilburne, who thereupon wrote *The Resurrection of John Lilburne*, and Fifth Monarchy men swelled their ranks, intensifying corporate opposition to what they regarded, often rightly, as injustice and oppression. The world was taking note of them by 1647, when they were first referred to as "Quakers," and it was not long before they, with the Levellers and Fifth Monarchy men, were regarded as potentially seditious elements in the army. The Levellers fomented mutinies that interfered with recruitment and movement of the army for Ireland.

Expedience apart, the Diggers and the Quakers were a source of scandal to many sincere believers in more conventional sects. Since the followers of Fox displayed more organizational ability and evangelical zeal than the other dissidents they quickly gained the ascendancy. Although Thomas Holme must have been familiar with all of these sects, it is only after the end of the conquest of Ireland that we see the fruit of the religious foment maturing in his own life.

Concerning Thomas Holme's exact whereabouts during most of the first Civil War we can only make an educated guess. We know that by the summer of 1649 he was in Tewkesbury, from which it may be assumed that after the wars he was with the garrison of that town. He may have been in the regiment detached from Fairfax's forces and sent to the garrison under Massey at Gloucester. If, as seems likely, he served in the New Model Army under Cromwell, he reached the West by a more circuitous route. In that event he would have been with Cromwell when, after taking Blechington House in April 1645, he "marched privately towards Witney . . . [and] forced the enemy into Bampton Bush."[10] There he might well have seen in the eastern window of ancient Minster Lovell near Witney the Holme arms which

---

[10] Sprigge, 12.

he was later to display.[11] The indications are, also, that he would have been a dragoon or cavalryman, since Cromwell is said to have had no infantry with him in that engagement.[12] Given the pattern of the war from this point it is probable that he was garrisoned in Tewkesbury until the Irish campaign. From 1644 Tewkesbury, mid-point between enemy forces, was alternately under the control of Royalists and Roundheads.

In the various actions in the West, names of some interest with relation to Holme abound. Second in command of one Roundhead contingent was a Sir Edwin Sands, who seems to have been more valiant than wise. Sir Hardress Waller, in whose regiment Thomas Holme would serve in Ireland, participated in battles in this region, as did Henry Ingoldsby, with whom Thomas Holme later waged a private war in Limerick. A *Letter printed for John Wright in the Old Bailey, April 17, 1643*, declared that "the taking and keeping Tewkesbury is of great consequence to these parts."

In 1648, according to Bennett, an additional troop of horse belonging to Parliament was quartered upon the parish, and in the following year a petition to the government from the corporation asserted, in substance, "that the town was a parliamentarian garrison, that the inhabitants generally were faithful friends to the parliament, and that most of them were provided with arms in their houses."

It is during the year of the Tewkesbury petition that we again establish positive connection with Thomas Holme. According to his cumulative record in the Wexford Register of Births, Marriages, and Burials, 1640–1720, it was on 5 August 1649 that he married Sarah, daughter of William and Maudlin Croft, in Tewkesbury, and "seventh months following [September] went to Ireland with the English Army."

The Irish campaign had been in the making for some time, and the centuries-old enmity between England and Ireland had been aggravated by the troubles of the past half century. As early as 1647, Captain Henry Ingoldsby had volunteered for Ireland, but his regiment had refused to go. Scroope's regiment of horse, one of those chosen by lot on 20 April 1649, also mutinied and was disbanded. The troubles of the summer of 1649 seem to have been sparked by the Levellers, one of whom had been shot in London for his part in fomenting the mutiny. Ingoldsby's men in Oxford revolted, taking over New College for their garrison; but they were soon chastened.

---

[11] Bristol and Gloucester Archeological Society Publications, 34: 24. The arms are chevron azure between three chaplets gules. Thomas surrounded these with ten rondules to indicate the degree of relationship—approximately the number of generations since the descendants of John of Stockholme had taken refuge in Mardale.

[12] Alfred Burne and Peter Young, *The Great Civil War* (London, 1959), 19.

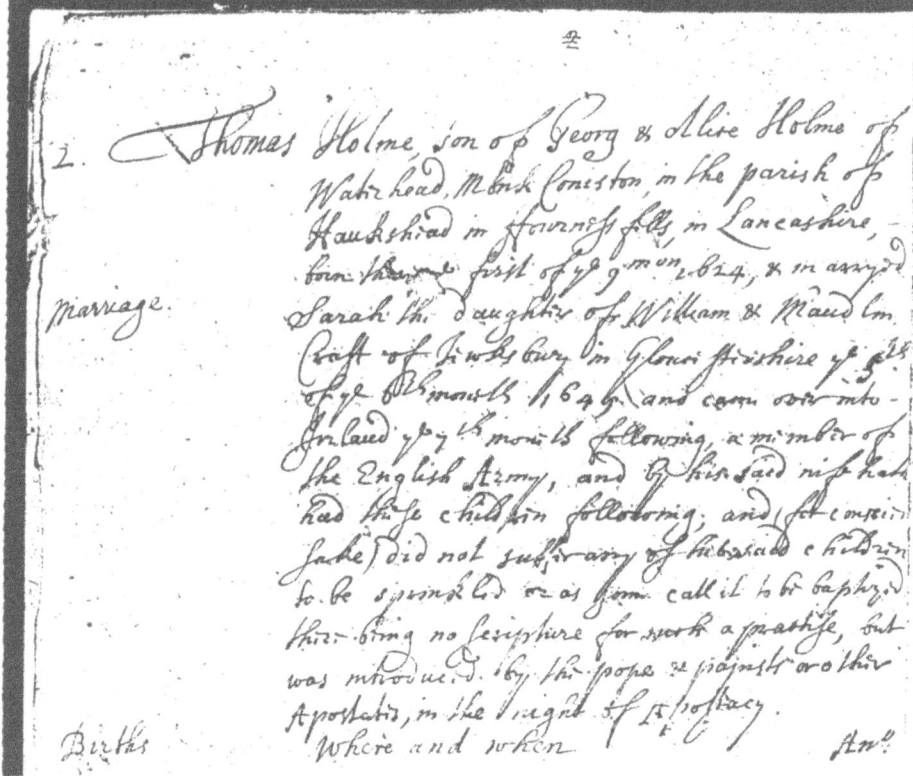

Fig. 4. Marriage record of Thomas and Sarah Holme. Used with permission of Wexford Registry, Friends Library House, Dublin.

Cromwell was severely tried. He had refused to accept the lieutenancy—won over Presbyterian Waller and the Independent Lambert—until he was guaranteed pay and transportation to Ireland for his twelve thousand men. Now he was forced to bribe, cajole, or force numbers among them to remain in service. Thomas Holme was one of the contingent that agreed to go.

On 13 August, Cromwell embarked for Ireland with thirty-two ships, followed in two days by Ireton with forty-two ships and Hugh Peter with twenty. Peter made a second trip, and on 15 September wrote that at last the whole army for Ireland had been transferred there.[13] It was in this final lot that Thomas and Sarah Holme sailed.

---

[13] John T. Gilbert, *A Contemporary History of Affairs in Ireland from 1641 to 1652* . . . , 3: appendix, "A History or brief chronicle of the chief matters of the Irish warres . . . from Wednesday, the first of August, 1649, to this present July, 1650." Published by authority (London, 1650), 157. Actually, "stragglers" were sent over in groups of forty under the direction of Whaley as they assembled, but the date in *Wx 3* indicates that Thomas and Sarah were with Peter's second crossing.

Throughout the disorders and uncertainties of the first weeks of their marriage, Thomas and Sarah had remained in Tewkesbury, knowing only that they would be going to what was regarded on their side of the Irish Sea as a rebellious, uncivilized, and perilous country that was to be subdued and converted. Now, in the company of the flamboyant shipmaster-chaplain Peter, they crossed the narrow but rough strip of water to an alien land that would be their home as long as Sarah lived.

Thomas Holme would again be part of a tumultuous army, a large part of which was fired by fanatical zeal to intensely personal interpretations of the will of the Lord that were quite capable of splitting them from the official body of the Independents and driving them to martyrdom. Sarah would take her place with other wives and sweethearts of soldiers, to care for the sick and wounded.[14]

---

[14] Firth, 298.

Chapter 3

The Conquest of Ireland

The war in Ireland, insofar as Thomas Holme was involved in it, was of more than two years' duration and about as bloody as war can be. Cromwell arrived in Dublin shortly after the middle of August, with some seventeen thousand men. Since advance attempts to secure the south coast had failed, he planned an orderly sweep of the east coast, from Dundalk to Waterford, and systematic taking of strategic points from there to Limerick.

For the time being he established himself in a house at the corner of Werberg and Castle Streets, with the horses of his troop conveniently stabled in St. Patrick's Cathedral.[1] Here, too, his Independent soldiery harangued congregations in churches not required by the horses.

Thomas Holme had not yet arrived in Dublin when he mustered a dozen regiments of picked men and, on 1 September, set out for the seaport of Drogheda, or Tredagh, as the English called it, covering twenty miles in one day and stopping within three miles of the walls. He reduced the town with a violence that set the tone for the rest of the campaign. With all the piety of the *Souldier's Catechism* he reported the action to Speaker of the Parliament Lenthall: "It was set upon some of our hearts that a great thing should be done, not by power or might, but by the Spirit of God."[2] When one considers that the defense had rested upon a garrison of two thousand foot soldiers in the

---

[1] *Dublin Penny Journal* 3 (1835), 274, cited by Denis Murphy, *Cromwell in Ireland* (Dublin, 1883), 81.
[2] Abbott, 2: 124.

face of the lieutenant general's seventeen thousand mounted veterans, it must be admitted that the Spirit of God received considerable support from power and might. If the reduction of Basing House had shown the English Royalists what was to be expected of the parliamentary army in England, Drogheda demonstrated the fury that any defenders of Irish ground would have to face.

Leaving the ruins of Drogheda behind him, Cromwell subdued Dundalk and then returned to Dublin. There he was joined by what Whitelock refers to as "stragglers" of the army—one of whom was Thomas Holme—brought over by Hugh Peter.

Even in a modern ship the Irish Sea is likely to be no smooth thoroughfare in September. The new arrivals can hardly have regretted the respite they enjoyed in Dublin while Cromwell and his forces were making their way down from Drogheda. It would be the last rest they would have before the fall of Limerick two years later. With only slight delay the four regiments of horse, four of dragoons, and eight of foot, supported by a very limited train of artillery, marched from their rendezvous at Donnybrook without the lieutenant general, who remained in Dublin to recuperate from an indisposition, retaining horse and foot for a personal guard. He would overtake the army before the major encounter at Wexford.

It would be both tedious and superfluous to recount the details of the expedition. The official summary reads like the journal of a triumphant monarch.[3] It was not all triumph. Many of the men suffered from the country sickness and were weak, miserable, and irascible. It was true that, badly outnumbered, under-provisioned, and appalled by the story of Drogheda that had rolled down the coast ahead of the army, some Irish garrisons gave up at a first summons or fled before the army confronted the walls. This was the case at Arklow, where Major Sankey, with a party of the lord lieutenant's own division and four troops of dragoons went ahead to find a passage across the river for the army and to summon the town, but as a parliamentary diarist put it, "Before their coming up the enemy had blowen up of the castle and fired the rest and so departed."[4]

For the Irish this was a sorry decision. They lost the city, and the English gained a large supply of food and other provisions and some powder. It was here, too, that Cromwell overtook the army, reinforcements came in by sea, and the shipping for Wexford passed. Despite

---

[3] Gilbert, *History or brief chronicle of the chief matters of the Irish warres . . . from Wednesday, the first of August, 1649, to the treaty sixth of this present July, 1650* (London, 1650), appendix, 159.
[4] Johanus in Lymerick, MS diary, Trinity College, Dublin, fols. 218–224.

the loss of horse and supplies in an ambush attack by Brian MacPhelim O'Bryne,[5] they proceeded with better heart through slightly easier terrain toward Wexford. On the way they took the castle at Fernes, an ancient relic then in usable condition, the lower masonry of which is said by the townspeople to go back to the days of Dermott, and the upper portion to have been rebuilt by Henry II for Eleanor of Aquitaine.

On the following day the castle at Enniscorthy fell easily into their hands, although it was well provisioned and enjoyed an advantageous position on a high steep hill, the windows and gun-slits in its massive walls commanding a wide view in all directions. The capitulation after a slight resistance seems to have been expedited by the captain's having been at Drogheda two days before it was stormed.[6] Greatly coveted by both sides, this castle was to change hands twice again before the war was over.

Coming down from Arklow to Enniscorthy the army had followed what remains the main-traveled route, but it veered a little to the west at this point, quartering at Kereight, on higher ground than that along the River Slaney. From there it moved southeast to Wexford. At night the citizens of the town could see the campfires of the approaching army.

Rough and perilous as the long march from Dublin had been, the terrain resembled that of the Coniston-Hawkshead landscape. Although he probably did not anticipate returning to this land once it was conquered, Thomas Holme passed directly by the plot of Corlican where, a little more than a quarter-century later, he would bring Sarah's body to the laurel-enclosed circular ground for burial, and he could have seen from the line of march the townland of Holmestown, over which they were to look in years to come from the yard of their house at Bregurteen.

On Monday, 1 October, the army arrived, John of Limerick records, before Wexford, a port city of major importance to the conquest and later significant to the life of Thomas Holme.

Cromwell dispatched Lieutenant General Michael Jones with a troop of dragoons to take the castle at Rosslare, the principal guardian of the harbor ten miles below Wexford. The garrison fled to their frigate in the harbor, only to be caught between the fort they had deserted and the incoming parliamentary supply ships. Cromwell summoned the town in writing, opening a series of exchanges between

---

[5] *Aphorismus Discovery* 2: 54.
[6] Murphy, 164 ff.

himself and the governor. These commenced as frigid civilities but, fluctuating with the hopes of the governor as the tenuous assistance appeared, they deteriorated quickly into outrageous demands on Sinnott's part and outraged denials on Cromwell's. Eventually, Stafford, the captain of the castle, put an end to negotiations by succumbing to Cromwell's "fair treatment" for himself and surrendering the castle, which was at once manned by the enemy.

When their own guns were turned against the town the incredulous defenders left the walls and fled inward, colliding with the civilian populace as they poured into the streets to learn what had happened. People flocked to the churches and, according to local tradition, some three hundred, largely women, children, and aged persons, gathered around the great cross in the old Norman bull ring near the northern end of the town. The slaughter that ensued rivaled that of Drogheda.

Churches were violated and those who had fled to them for safety were slain; houses were looted, and if the owners escaped with their lives it was because they were fast on their feet or their belongings held the attention of the invaders. Monasteries and churches were special targets. Friars were shot, hanged, or otherwise murdered. The names of some of the most distinguished victims were shared by both the defending captain and the alleged betrayer of the town—Sinnott and Stafford—so that valor was enhanced and disgrace was balanced by martyrdom. As was common in seventeenth-century reporting of any disaster, prodigies were recorded. Bullets were said to have rolled harmlessly from the cowls of friars destined for execution, and soldiers who cavorted in the habits of religious were said to have come to bad ends or to have become converted and given up their evil ways.

When relative quiet fell at last on Wexford, the general effect was that of a ghost town. Cromwell wrote to Lenthall on 14 October,

> When they were come into the market-place, the enemy making a stiff resistance, our forces brake them, and then put all to the sword that came in their way. Two boatfulls of the enemy seeking to escape . . . sank whereby were drowned near three-hundred of them. I believe, in all, there was lost of the enemy not many less than two-thousand; and I believe not twenty of yours killed from first to last of the siege.[7]

He regrets the prevailing ruin that would make the town less valuable to the government than he had hoped, but there were compensations, for "the soldiers got a very good booty in this place." After enumerat-

---

[7] Abbott, 142.

ing many items of official booty, from tallow to a frigate of twenty guns under construction in the shipyards, he continues, "This town is now so in your power that [of] the former inhabitants, I believe scarce one in twenty can challenge any property in their houses." He hopes that "an honest people would come and plant here where are very good houses, and other accommodation fitted to their hands." He adds that "the town is pleasantly seated and strong, having a rampart of earth within the wall, near fifteen foot thick." He was wise to note the thickness of the defense, since any Englishman settling there in future was to need all the protection he could get.

Cromwell settled down briefly at Wexford in a castellated house at 29 Main Street. It had been Sinnott's residence, and it remained occupied for more than three centuries, a substantial house with shops on the ground floor and living quarters above. In St. Bride's Lane another sturdy stone house belonging to a Mr. Reade was used as a jail, which was later transferred to Stafford's former dwelling. Thomas and Sarah Holme were later to become familiar with the facilities of these establishments.

From Wexford parties went out to gain or regain local objectives. When other administrative duties had been performed, Cromwell himself issued forth with all but the forces necessary to garrison the town. The ill and many wounded were glad of the opportunity to recuperate before starting on toward Waterford.

Fame of the reduction of Wexford, following by only a month that of Drogheda, expedited the conquest of the rest of the country. Even so, it would take nearly two more years to reduce Ireland to a state of restless and menacing captivity. Ross resisted but was quickly overcome. Waterford was difficult, withstanding a brief siege at the end of November and continuing intermittent assaults. Here, too, the army suffered widespread incapacitating illness. The city did not capitulate until August 1650. Waterford would also figure importantly in Thomas Holme's life after the death of Sarah, his wife, in 1676.

After a brief respite following the fall of the city the army pushed on to Cahir, Cashel, where Thomas Holme would meet a personal defeat a few years later, and Kilkenny, where Ormonde had reigned in all but regal pomp and power. The ordeal would be extremely precarious for Sarah Holme, whose pregnancy would be imperiled by the further hardships of wartime conditions. It was therefore decided that she should return to her family in Tewkesbury until the birth of her baby in early summer. She may have traveled with the company of Cromwell, who, after the taking of Clonmel, named his son-in-law Ireton lieutenant general of the forces in Ireland and returned to London.

At any rate, Sarah was in England during part of this time, for it was in her native town of Tewkesbury that she gave birth to her first son, Thomas, on 19 June 1651.[8]

It was about this time also that the army in Ireland sat down before the gates of Limerick, which would be the great parliamentary stronghold of the south, and would cause the most trouble. During the long siege, city, civil, military, and ecclesiastical leaders argued passionately about the best course to follow. Townspeople and garrison in great numbers were dying of plague and famine. From the walls and towers of King John's Castle the garrison looked for miles at the broad placid waters of the Shannon and thought of the Cromwellian genius for crossing unbridged streams. To guard the bridge at the castle was one thing, but to defend a town that was not altogether convinced of the advisability of defense and that was almost as much exposed as protected by the great river was another. The city fell in late October. Accounts of the capture of the vast fortress are still burning with grief and anger and dark allegations of treachery.

Thomas Holme was nearly twenty-seven when Limerick fell. With only a brief interval, England had been at war since he was seventeen. Some of his companions were dispatched to aid in the siege of Galloway, the last Irish stronghold. This final action would draw out through a bleak winter until the following March. Otherwise the army was in somewhat dubious control throughout the land. There was constant harassment from pockets of die-hard Irish outside the cities; food was scarce; the men were debilitated from sickness and fatigue, and resentful of long overdue pay. In Limerick a strong garrison, of which Thomas Holme remained a member, settled down to a peace for which nearly a decade of hostile peregrination was not the best preparative, but the actual hostilities were over.

Although he would not be demobilized for another five years, Thomas Holme was able to face the future with some optimism. Sarah would soon return from Tewkesbury with his namesake son. He acquired a stone house in Limerick in the region of John's Gate, with Captain Hartwell and Messrs. Ternell, Gafen, and Bennett as neighbors.[9] Their adjoining gardens formed a tract that was still to be

---

[8] *Commons Journals*, vi, 428, cited by Firth, *Cromwell's Army*, 39.
[9] Irish Manuscripts Commission, *The Civil Survey, A. D. 1654–1656*, ed. Robert G. Symington, Vol. 4: *The County of Limerick* (Dublin, 1938), 415. So sturdy were the small houses in this area that many of them were still serviceable halfway through the twentieth century.

known as "the Gardens" more than three centuries later, although by that time they had deteriorated into a weedy parking lot behind three tall dilapidated stone houses that may well have been the dwellings of Thomas Holme and his neighbors. Here he and Sarah, in the third year of their marriage, would be able for the first time to establish a home.

Part Three

His Own Man

Chapter 4

The Surveyor

Despite the horrors of the war through which it had passed, Limerick was still a beautiful city. It was, moreover, the hub of much of the activity of reconstruction. The soldiers, no longer occupied in siege or battle, nevertheless were busy. Castles and fortified houses at strategic points were selected for repair, and the demolition of others was completed. Thomas Holme was sent to repair Core Castle, for which service he received seventy pounds, fifteen shillings—more than seven thousand dollars in today's buying power.[1] That he was in charge of this project suggests that he had had some engineering experience, although had he been in the "traine" (artillery), to which engineers were attached, he would have received his lands in Limerick rather than in Wexford County. Moreover, Prendergast places him explicitly in Waller's regiment at this time.[2] Such experience as he had picked up during his years of soldiering stood him in good stead in this assignment, and the money was doubly acceptable because of his growing family. This appointment came near the arrival of Sarah's namesake on 4 September 1653.

---

[1] Johnson Westropp, "Cromwellian Account Books, Limerick," *Journal of the Royal Society of Antiquaries of Ireland*, Paper and Proceedings 2.

[2] John P. Prendergast, *The Cromwellian Settlement*, 2d ed. (Dublin, 1875), 216. Waller, who had come to Dublin some weeks later than Thomas Holme, was at this time major general of the foot in Ireland (Firth, *Regimental History* 2: 445). Although it is possible that Thomas had been in such a company from the first, Cromwell's predilection for Lancashire men makes it more likely that he had been in one of the companies of cavalry or dragoons of the general himself.

Assignments such as this were special plums; the soldiers on the whole were not so fortunate. To compensate the men for their services and at the same time to promote the complete subjugation of Ireland, it was decided to expand a program of resettlement of the country that had been advocated as early as the reign of Henry VII, attempted during the reign of James I, and discussed sporadically since. All literate Irish landholders with an income of ten or more pounds a year would be forced to go into exile or to move to the poorest section of the country (the traditional phrasing of the alternatives was "to hell or to Connaught"), and their property would be distributed to the army in lieu of cash.

No one had any illusions about the difficulties involved in this procedure, but even the most pessimistic probably underestimated the task. For one thing, it must be accomplished with all possible speed. The rank and file of the army were disillusioned. They were resentful of Cromwell's nepotism, the enormous wealth he had accumulated, and the progressive degrees of affluence throughout the upper echelons of military and civil government. They were veterans of active and violent campaigns, now reduced to relative inactivity; they had not received just compensation for their labors; and many of them were hungry. They could see no prospect of having more to say about their own government, or more economic opportunity and social prestige, or more religious liberty than they had had under the monarchy. There was danger of widespread revolt that might very well be successful.

The proposed resettlement would involve a prodigious amount of work. The first step would be a comprehensive survey of the bounds and resources to be distributed—Ulster, Leinster, and Munster. The actual labor would have to be carried out in the face of persistent ambush and general interference by all of the Irish who would have been competent to help. A large number of surveyors would be required, and surveying was traditionally a highly specialized art that demanded mathematical acumen and fine draftsmanship. Furthermore, the whole project would have to be financed.

Captain Thomas Holme was going to be affected by all this in many ways. As an officer and a veteran of long standing he would be entitled to a fairly large share in the Commonwealth's plundered goods. He would be responsible for collecting his subordinates' share of the funds that would finance the project; he would be able to take up his residence far from the detested Ingoldsby; and, although he could not foresee such an effect, he would learn much of the craft that would open a new career to him at an age at which not a few men of his time were preparing to retire.

In the spring of 1653 steps toward the surveys were taken. The Act for the Satisfaction of Adventurers and Soldiers was ratified on 26 September, and a commission was appointed to oversee the distribution of land. This group included Lieutenant-General of the Army in Ireland Charles Fleetwood; Lieutenant-General of the Horse Edmund Ludlow; Miles Corbet; and John Jones; three of whom constituted the Parliament's Commission for the Civil Government of Ireland. They were instructed to cause three surveys to be made: one by *inquisition* (an estimate of the extent, boundaries, and qualities of the lands, with identification of the current incumbents, obtained through interviews with the longest established inhabitants of the area being surveyed), one by admeasurement, and one a "Gross Survey" or "measurement of the surround of whole baronies."[3]

The Gross Survey was undertaken immediately, but was abandoned in 1654 because the results did not warrant continuation of it. Benjamin Worsley, the surveyor general, was then instructed to implement the other two surveys. The first, which was known as the Civil Survey, was to be executed by the local commissioners for revenue and their assistants, and to cover most of Ireland, with the exception of Connaught, for which the Strafford survey of the time of James I was deemed adequate. Commissions for the surveys of individual counties were issued in order of predetermined priorities, the first ten being for the Adventurers and Soldiers. These were begun at once, and the last seems to have been concluded by 1656. In 1654 Thomas Holme was one of those commissioned to conduct the Civil Survey of county Kerry, where he was commissioned also "for examining the Delinquency of the Irish &c in Order to distinguishing of their qualification."[4]

Thomas Holme's friend Robert Cuppage was the recipient of a number of commissions during this time of reconstruction: the survey of Cork, 26 November 1653, and, on 11 April 1665, with others, "to see that any Irish exempted from transplantation be not allowed to live scatteringly but be gathered together into townships and villages for defense." Previously the commissioner for the high court of justice had ordered that Cuppage and others join the commissioners to erect and appoint a high court of justice "for the Tryal of all murders,

---

[3] For description of the Civil and Crown Surveys, see Prendergast, 201–206.
[4] BL, Add. MSS, Egerton 1762, fol. 132103. Thomas Holme's co-workers in the Civil Survey of Kerry were John Wilson, John Balaverhassett, Henry Wheeler, Richard Ousley, Whitall Brown, William Hall, and James Beverell Esq.

Massacres of any English and Protestants bearing date at Kilkenny, the 11th of October 1652. . . ."[5] Other prominent surveyors were Richard and Henry Osborne. Assignments such as these were not of the sort to endear their recipients to the remaining Irish inhabitants.

According to Crispin family tradition, the year that followed Thomas Holme's work in county Kerry found him in a totally foreign situation. The legend varies slightly in form, but all versions of it seem to go back to the same source, the reminiscence of a great-grandson of both William Crispin and Thomas Holme in 1792. This fourth-generation William Crispin stated that Thomas Holme was a midshipman in the expedition of Admiral Penn in the West Indies at the time of his appointment to succeed William Crispin—twenty-six years before Pennsylvania was founded, and while the first William Crispin not only was still alive, but was commanding the vessel in the expedition on which Thomas Holme was said to have served.[6] He appears to have confused the surveyor and friend of William Penn with the ensign Thomas Holme who, with a Lieutenant Galbois, entered a petition with reference to a company of foot to be raised on the Isle of Wight for General Venables.[7] It is just possible to fit the period of the Hispaniola expedition of Admiral Sir William Penn and General Venables—late December 1654, to September 1655—into the chronology of Thomas Holme of Limerick, but in light of his known activities, the dissatisfaction of Venables at not being able to obtain Irish veterans, and the fact that Rear Admiral Sir Robert Holme was governor of the Isle of Wight from which the expedition departed, and probably was the father of Ensign Thomas, it seems improbable that Thomas Holme of Limerick was engaged in the expedition.

As the necessity for accuracy and detail in the surveys became more obvious, misgivings concerning the possibility of executing them within a reasonable time increased. Some estimated that the work would take twenty years for completion. Worsley's estimate was thirteen years. To do the man justice, it must be conceded that he considered perfection.

The relatively simple instruments and procedures that had sufficed for land measurement during the Middle Ages did not satisfy the demands of a newly property-hungry populace. Enclosure of common land accelerated the development of a fool-proof system of surveying.

---

[5] BL, Add. MSS, Egerton 1762, fol. 128:95; Fol. 159.

[6] This misidentification is referred to by Hough and stated as fact in *Some Account of the Crispin Family . . . Written by William Crispin in 1792*, ed. William Frost Crispin, et al.

[7] CSPC, 1657–1676, addenda, 1574–1674; Chatham Miscellany 4 (1872): 4; *Narrative of General Venables*, xxii, 5–6, 91, 100.

The simple cord or rod marked in some generally accepted lengths for linear measure, a magnetic compass, a quadrant, another astronomical instrument such as the astrolabe or the azimuth compass for ascertaining directions and measuring angles and the plane table for recording observations, had by Worsley's time been augmented or superseded by far more complicated and, it must be admitted, more accurate systems. Geometry and trigonometry were introduced into the university curriculum, and logarithms were discovered early in the century; and teachers of mathematics were expected to be able to teach surveying, with practice in nearby fields. The catalogue of surveyor's instruments now included not only the protractor and those already mentioned but also the circumferentor—a flat brass circular plate with sights at the ends and a round brass box marked with a graduated circle over which swung a magnetic needle, and a theodolite, consisting of a planisphere, which was a round brass plate, the circumference bearing 360° markings, with an alidad, or index, with sights, for measuring horizontal angles. In order to adjust the measurement of the actual surface of a tract, a level, and a micrometer or vernier, both of which subdivided the already available degrees for the measurement of angles, were used, as were vertical instruments utilized in navigation, or adaptations of them, as in the astrolabe and the azimuth compass for surveying heights. In an attempt to simplify the surveying process by combining all the necessary instruments in a highly complicated structure, surveyor Arthur Hopton in 1611 introduced his *topographical glasses*.[8] This appears to have been too complicated for even the most meticulous practitioners, and was not extensively used.

To Worsley a survey meant the degree-perfect determination of both the bounds and the content of a tract to be surveyed, and he was obdurate in his estimate of the time the surveying of the greater part of Ireland would require.

At this point a man of astonishing genius volunteered to engineer its accomplishment in thirteen months, provided he would receive additional funds to take care of special expenses and the large staff he would need. He was a brilliant and efficient opportunist, Dr. William Petty, a physician with the army who, commencing his independent career as an impecunious yeoman's son, by daring and judicious trading had jockeyed himself into a substantial financial position and had obtained through schooling and private study a solid education in mathematics, economics, and law. This, coupled with an extraordinarily keen practical sense, was to bring any accomplishment he fancied

---

[8] Richeson, 95.

within his reach.[9] The survey situation presented the combination of opportunity and challenge to which he responded with an alacrity that in a less competent man would have been rashness.

He made a quick, efficient estimate of the scope of the project and the needed—and available—manpower and presented his estimate to the government. By 11 December 1654, after considerable deliberation and over the angry protests of Worsley, the Commission of Affairs for Ireland was ready to sign Petty's contract, and the army had taken upon itself to supply, by taxing the soldiers themselves, the extra funds required. With this, Petty set about to revolutionize surveying.

Coming fresh to the profession of surveying, he was not hampered by the accumulation of materials and procedures that appeared requisite to Worsley. His procedure probably was based on William Leybourn's recently published (1653) *The Compleat Surveyor.*

Petty's methods of recruitment and division of labor were revolutionary, and opened the way for a relatively large influx of competent though only moderately well educated surveyors into what had hitherto been an exclusive company. He enlisted practitioners of many crafts in the preparation of chains, magnetic needles and their pins, and other small items. Other precision tools—"tyme scales, protractors, and compass-cards"—were prepared by experts in London, and from London, also, he ordered such necessaries as "a magazin of royall paper, mouth-glew, pencils, &c."[10] When "a perfect forme of a ffeeild book" was decided on, uniform books for all the surveyors were prepared and sheets of paper five or six feet square were glued together and divided into ten-acre areas plotted to uniform scale, while others were ruled in single-acre sections. He provided portable tables, boxes, rulers and other necessary items, as well as "small Ffrench tents . . . to enable the measurers to doe any businesses without house or harbour, it being expected that into such wasted countreyes they must at some tymes come." He secured also practical, relatively simple textbooks, almost certainly that of Leybourn, who suggests that the use of the theodolite and the circumferentor suffices for large surveys and the plane table for small. So much for the accoutrements of the surveyors. No means of expediting and insuring the accuracy of the survey were overlooked.

While the tools were being prepared books were made containing

---

[9] Sir William Petty, *The History of the Down Survey, A. D. 1655–1656*, ed. Thomas Aiken Larcom, for the Irish Archeological Society (Dublin, 1851). Reprinted, 1967, by Augustus M. Kelley, Publishers. Unless otherwise stated, further information concerning the Down Survey is quoted or abstracted from this volume.
[10] Paper measuring 24 X 20 inches for printing, 24 X 19 inches for writing (*OUD*).

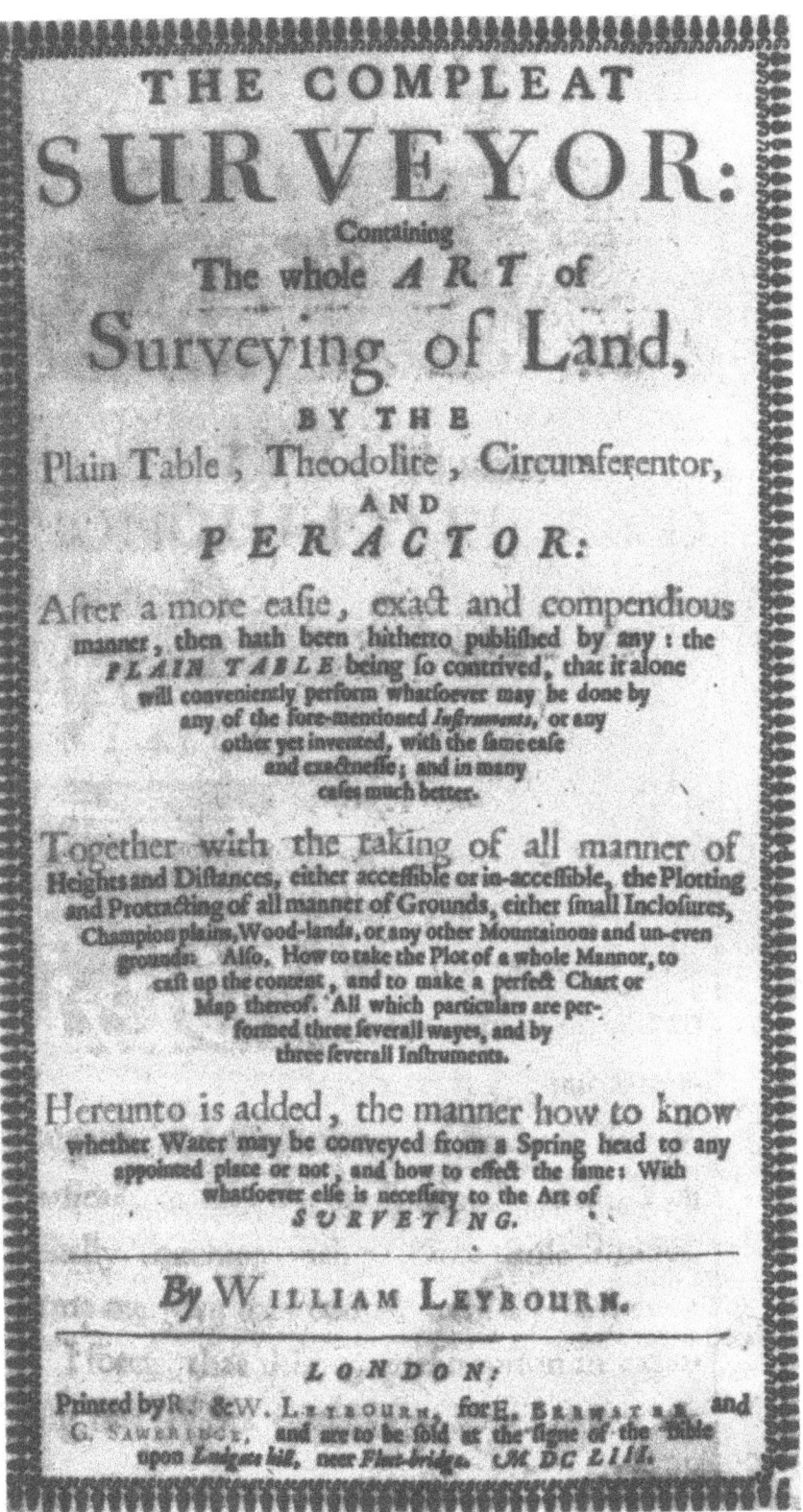

Fig. 5. Title page from Leybourn's *The Compleat Surveyor*. Used with permission of the Newberry Library.

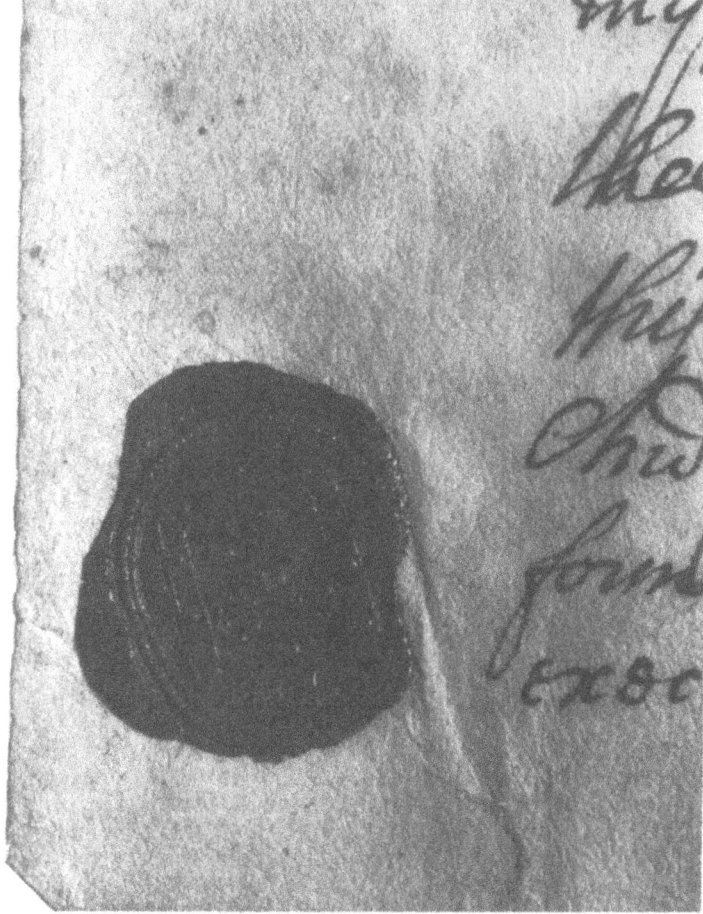

Fig. 6. Holme's seal. Used with the permission of the Historical Society of Pennsylvania.

the names of all the lands to be measured and of their "ould proprietors," and "guesse-plotts made of most of them," which would tell the surveyors how to begin and would also enable Petty "to apportion unto each measurer such scope of land to work upon, as he might be able to finish within any assigned time." To be noted also were the bounds of each piece of land, important topographical features, the position of garrisons for defense, and persons who could be relied upon to keep an eye on the surveyors. As events proved, this last was also a judicious step, and might well have been taken a quarter-century later in Pennsylvania.

In place of an elite, specially trained crew, Petty scandalized officialdom by utilizing in the admeasurement of land the field experience of the soldiers themselves, who were hardened to endurance of heat and cold, poor lodgings and bad food, who "could leape hedge and ditch, and could alsoe ruffle with the severall rude persons in the country, from whome they might expect to be often crossed and opposed." Many came from tradespeople and were able to read and write. These, "if they were but headfull and steddy minded, though not of the nimblest wits," were taught how to use survey instruments, taking the bearings of lines, and using chains, especially in hilly territory, and other skills. Others, especially those who had been "of trades into which payntinge, drawinge, or any other kind of designinge is necessary," were taught protraction, the drafting of plots, and the estimation of the territory "comprehended within every surround."

In addition to admeasurers and protractors, two other classes of surveyors were employed by Petty. One group was responsible for "reducing barrony plots . . . within the compass of a cheet of royal paper" so that the maps would be of uniform size for binding, and "[s]ome hands that were imployed in the said reducements did, for the most parte, performe the colouringe and other ornament of the worke." The final group, being "a few of the most nasute [*sic*] and sagacious persons," who were thoroughly acquainted with all the details of surveying, was responsible for checking every previous operation and totaling the linear surveys of all the admeasurers.

Detailed instructions were laid down for every procedure. For admeasurers Petty drew heavily on the foot soldiers, some of whom may have worked before on "grosse surrounds," and "others who had wrought on former surveyes, and also such as had been more lately instructed and exercised in that faculty."

Following the leads provided by the terriers of the Civil Survey, his staff set to work. The kind of assistance to be derived from these documents is evident from the one cited above to locate the house of Thomas Holme in Limerick. Rural areas were less explicitly described. They were located, the quality and potential of the land estimated, the annual value as of 1640 recorded, and the bounds given. The Civil Survey was neither suited, nor intended, to be a basis for actual distribution of land, but it was valuable as a preliminary guide, and those who participated in it were enlisted in the final survey. Because the names of admeasurers and protractors were not preserved, some maps were unsigned, and the listed signatures are from the final versions of maps made by professionals in the higher offices, it is impossible to know the identity of the greater number of surveyors and the first cartographers, but it is logical to suppose that when

Thomas Holme advanced to work on the Down Survey that followed the Civil Survey, it was as a cartographer.

Certainly Thomas Holme's childhood in upper Lancashire and his life in the army were enough to qualify him for the work of an admeasurer, to which his familiarity with a great part of the land to be distributed would be an added advantage. Further capability had been fostered by sound early education. Was the carved landscape near his name on the desk at Hawkshead indicative of early interest in pictorial design? He had studied drawing in the grammar school at Hawkshead. His repair of a castle must have necessitated some kind of design and mathematical ability, and his later writings and maps, particularly in color and illustration, show him to have been considerably more than literate.

Such evidence of his skill in writing and draftsmanship as we have today strike one as being the products of a mind and hand whose natural aptitude was developed pragmatically rather than in the more theoretical and sophisticated environment of a London school, but it was developed to a degree beyond what might have been expected from such records of his early life as have survived. He would have been well qualified to learn protraction, drafting, and estimation of quantities of land, and, further, the reduction of field maps to uniform pages and addition of color and ornament—in short, to master the skills required by the middle or higher echelon of surveyors. The Down Survey must have been the school in which Thomas Holme received the experience that many years later would produce the first map of Pennsylvania and the "Portraiture" of the capital city.

It would be difficult to overestimate the variety of problems encountered by the survey. Even the astute Petty had underestimated the fringe difficulties. He found it necessary to extend the time by two months and to stipulate the allowance of an additional year for unforeseen adjustments after the completion of the work.

The devastation of the country has already been noted. With the decrease of human population, wolves had multiplied. As in England, no amount of persecution had succeeded in eliminating the Catholic clergy. While these for the most part refrained from violence, they may have engaged in sabotage; and certainly the English contention that they persisted in what the army and the foreign government considered "superstitious practices" and helped maintain the spirit of the native Irish. The Tories were a constant menace. One of them, "Blind Donough" O'Derrick, with a small party, kidnapped, tried, and hanged eight surveyors "as accessories to a gigantic scheme of ruthless robbery" in a wood in Kildare.¹¹ From Cromwell's arrival in August 1649, to November 1656, "monies . . . paid for the public service in Ireland" included sums:

Paid for killing wolves	3,847.5s.0d.
Paid for taking and apprehending Popish priests, etc.	756. 3.3.
Paid for apprehending notorious rebels and Tories	2,149.12.4.¹²

All of these enemies lurked in woods, bogs, ravines, and caverns, which, like every rod of open ground, had to be traversed by the surveyors. There may have been some truth in the allegations of Petty's opponents that the soldiers he employed for surveying were a "drunken, blasphemous, thieving crew"; but no one could deny their courage.

As the surveys of the various counties were completed, lots were drawn for the settlement of the regiments assigned to them. On Friday, 7 November 1656, six days after Thomas Holme's thirtieth birthday, the lots for Sir Hardress Waller's regiment, of which Thomas Holme was a member, were drawn by Lord Henry Cromwell, Lord Lieutenant of Ireland, himself.¹³ Another disbandment mentioned at this time was that of Captain Croft's company, following a blank line reserved for "Wm. Croft: Pet." Was this Sarah's brother from Tewkesbury?

The uneasiness of Ingoldsby at this time is evinced by his letter to Henry Cromwell requesting additional funds to carry out Cromwell's order "to keep the forces in the precinct [of Limerick] in a watchful posture."¹⁴ This order kept the Holmes in Limerick until the following spring.

Thomas's last reported contribution to army service is recorded in Petty's account book under the date of 16 October 1656. Reporting the returns from agents of troops and companies for amounts deducted from army pay to finance the survey, he records, "Recd. of Mr. Robert Short monye for which I have as not yet given no particular receipt

---

¹¹ Prendergast, 206.
¹² Robert Dunlop, *Ireland Under the Commonwealth*, Manchester University Publication, Historical Series 17, 18: 638. In this volume Cromwell is said to have arrived in Ireland on 6 July 1649.
¹³ BL, Add. MSS 35, 102: *Act of Trustees for Army Arrears in Ireland*, 1656–59, Phillips MS 6466, fol. 16: 25, and fol. 43.
¹⁴ BL MSS, Lansdowne, 822, fol. 256.

and which were discounted as followeth . . . [among sums ranging from £1.7.2 to £15] Capt. Holme—6.13.9."[15]

Ultimately Thomas Holme acquired over four thousand acres of land in Wexford with an annual total rent value of 15.15.5 1/4. It is possible that not all of this was included in his allotment; many soldiers, either because of their desperate financial straits or because they had already more of Ireland than they wanted, sold their debentures to their officers for as little as two-fifths of their value[16]. Thomas was not blind to a bargain.

---

[15] *Sir William Petty's Account Book*, Manuscript Library, Trinity College, Dublin, press mark n. 1. 4a, p. 13.
[16] Prendergast, 222.

Chapter 5

The Religious Activist

Thomas Holme's various public duties were carried on against a backdrop of personal joys and sorrows of domestic life and religious exhilaration. Sarah's daughter Sarah was born on 4 September 1653. Like her brother Thomas, she was a healthy baby, and her birth in this first home seemed a special blessing on the family. Two more babies were born in Limerick. They were less fortunate. Esther, born on 8 February 1654/55, lived only a little more than a year, dying less than two weeks after the birth of a third daughter, Mary, on 10 May 1656. Mary died in September of the same year. Both infants were buried in Limerick. Thomas Holme's employment with the repair of Core Castle and with surveys had kept him away from home during part of this time, so that Sarah had to cope alone with the care of the children and with loneliness and anxiety. Sometime during this interim while Thomas Holme was a member of a garrison at peace, he and Sarah became involved in another kind of warfare: they became members of the Society of Friends.

It is difficult to associate anyone who had been so much a man of action as Thomas Holme with quietistic elements of Quakerism, but it must be remembered that the sect was characterized by a spiritual militancy that was anything but passive.

Once the fighting was over, a restless spirit might well be attracted to the combination of peace and spiritual warfare that the Friends represented. Gloucestershire was an early and fruitful ground for proselytizing Friends, and it is possible that when Sarah Holme returned from Tewkesbury with their infant son in 1651 she had adopted their faith. On the other hand, she and her husband may have been convinced together during the spiritual campaign of 1654.

Certainly both public and private affairs converged during the early fifties to make Thomas and Sarah Holme receptive to the tenets of the Friends. The years of bloodshed and physical exhaustion, now that the excitement of the conflict was over, must have left them a legacy of disgust and horror of war, however convinced they were of the righteousness of the cause. The cause itself seemed to have deteriorated during its prosecution. At thirty it was time to live with peace, to have a cause beyond themselves to live for. What greater cause could there be than peace, social and political, and, most of all, peace of heart?

They did not find this under the yoke of any of the hard-driving religious sects they had encountered. The simple ministers of the Friends spoke from a peace and gentleness that could come only from an inner light.

At the meetings for worship, silence was broken only when someone felt impelled to share a light received from this indwelling spirit with the others. They would suffer for this cause as they had for the other, but this was a cause of infinitely greater importance.

Sometimes this spirit of peace gave way to urgency to convert the entire populace to its pursuit. In England Quakers had become an obstreperous minority. The Thurloe State Papers bear witness to their widespread activity.[1] Not only were Diggers, Levellers, Fifth Monarchy Men, and less spectacular Protestant sects vulnerable to the Quakers' preaching, but even the ranks of the Franciscans had been broached. Major General Worsley wrote that there was much trouble with the Quakers in Lancashire. Here they were thrown into the dungeon of Lancaster Castle, and a William Holme, possibly a brother of Thomas, died of the ill treatment he received there.

In January Major General Gaffe reported from Winchester that George Fox, the founder of the sect, and two other eminent northern Quakers were in the city, "doing much work for the devil." On 27 June 1656 Major General Haynes stated that "all the Fifth Monarchy party are at present as quiet as lambs and seeme to repent of what was done; yet I'll not promise for them." The Anabaptists and Quakers, he declared, made work for all the rest. Colonel Daniel wrote back to Monck that the Quakers were troublemakers in the army.

---

[1] *A Collection of the State Papers of John Thurloe*, ed. Thomas Birch (1742), 3: 94, 123, 117; 4: 333, 408; 5: 166, 188; 6: 167.

These, patently, were voices not merely of prejudice, but of fear. The Quakers, on the other hand, were convinced of their mission to deflect the world from what they saw as its headlong rush to perdition. Some persons from all ranks of society were converted, but with the majority there was no communication.

Understandably, the arrival of the Quakers in Ireland alarmed authorities who were already beleaguered by hostile natives. Never violent, the Quakers were nevertheless disruptive. Forbidden the use of public halls, they obstructed traffic by meeting in the streets. If they attended religious services, it was only to interrupt the minister with contradictions and reproaches. They would not pay tithes to the churches, and, in what seemed to be the most infuriating non-gesture of all, they refused to doff their hats to officials. Exasperated, officers ordered wholesale arrests and imprisonment. Lord Lieutenant Henry Cromwell wrote to Thurloe:

> Our worst enemy now are the Quakers, who begin to grow in some reputation in the County of Cork, their meetings being attended frequently by col. Phaier, major Waller, & moste of the chief officers thereabouts. Some of our souldiers have been perverted by them, & amongst the rest his highness's cornet to his own troop is a professed Q. and hath written to me in their stile . . I thinke their principles & practices are not very consistent with civil government, much less the discipline of an army. . . .

On 12 February 1655 Thurloe wrote back to Cromwell that this was the first mention in England of Quakers in Ireland.[2]

Our first references to Thomas Holme as a Quaker are dated 1655, but the sect had appeared in Ireland at least a year prior to that date. According to Quaker historian Thomas Wight, William Edmundson, also a veteran, was "first of the ministering friends to come out of England with the Truth."[3] He established the first Friends' meeting in Ireland at Jurgan in 1654.

It was about this time, too, that Elizabeth Fletcher, one of the most revered of the early Quakers, came to Ireland. Wight states that she and Elizabeth Smith came and were imprisoned at Newgate in Dublin for speaking at a Baptist meeting. They held a meeting at the room of Richard Fowkes, a tailor, near Polegate and went from there to Youghall on the south coast, where Captain James Sicklemore and

---

[2] Thurloe, 4: 508, 530. Eventually Mayor Haddon's wife and, finally, he himself "went that way." (Various records of sufferings.)

[3] Thomas Wight, *A History of the Rise and Progress of the People Called Quakers, in Ireland, from the year 1653 to 1700*, ed. John Rutty, 4th ed. (1811), 73.

others whom Wight does not name were convinced. A slightly later group of convincements included Samuel Claridge, a friend of Thomas Holme during the years of his later delegacy to the half-yearly meeting in Dublin. It is quite possible that Thomas owed his convincement to Elizabeth Fletcher, who may have been a relative.[4]

Finally, in 1656, four years after the official end of the war, Thomas Holme was demobilized. He and Sarah with their small family stayed on in Limerick through the winter of 1656.

One of Thomas's first acts as a civilian was to circulate a petition to Henry Cromwell against Colonel Ingoldsby's abuse of the Irish Society of Friends. This document seems to have vanished, but we can judge of its contents by the Colonel's vituperative apologia.

Zealous for the welfare of the Children of Light, Thomas and Sarah Holme opened their home for meetings. At one of these, when Friends had assembled for worship, the door burst open and soldiers swarmed into the room. Thomas Holme and co-author Abraham Fuller in their *Compendious View of some extraordinary Sufferings of the People Called Quakers*, later described the taking of one of the guests: "James Sicklemore, being peaceably in Thomas Holme's house in Limerick, was seized . . . and committed to prison, and banished the City, by order of Colonel Ingoldsby."[5] Another historian who mentions the raid states that Lieutenant Waller had resisted the soldiers sent to break up the meeting.[6] Sicklemore seems to have been the only one abused, but books and papers were ransacked and some were carried. The effect on the Holme children of four, two, and under one year must have been traumatic. The youngest of the three and the infant with whom Sarah was pregnant at the time died within the year.

The banishment of Sicklemore is understable in the light of Ingoldsby's letter to Henry Cromwell on 31 March 1656. Quakers he

---

[4] John Fletcher, who accompanied Thomas to Pennsylvania, is identified by Thomas in his will as a relative. A clue to the relationship may be the fact that on 28 April 1651, the will of Edward Vallens of Carsington, County Derby, was proved by his niece, Elizabeth Fletcher, alias Holmes. *Alias* was sometimes used to indicate the maiden name of a married woman. This Elizabeth could have been mother or aunt of the Quaker minister. For further accounts of Elizabeth see Wight, 92 and 139.

[5] *A Compendious View of some extraordinary Sufferings of the people called Quakers . . . in the Kingdom of Ireland, from the Year 1655 to the End of the Reign of King George the First. . . . In three parts*, part 2: 51. An earlier volume, *A Brief Relation Of some part of the Sufferings of the True Christians, The People of God (in scorn called Quakers) in Ireland For the last Eleven Years, viz. from 1660, until 1671. . . .* Collected by T[homas] H[olme] and A[braham] F[uller], published in 1671, contains a statement of the tenets and program of the Friends.

[6] Lieutenant Waller is introduced by St. John D. Seymour in *The Puritans in Ireland, 1647–1661*, (Oxford:, Clarendon Press, 1921), 135. Ingoldsby's letter is in BL, Lansdowne MSS.

described as a "wild yett subtill and designeinge Generation of people." Nevertheless, "For the Quakers that are the growth off the towne, vipers bred in or bosomes, they have the Liberty to meete amongst themselvs wthout disturbance," but not to "entertayne Strandge Quakers or Irish Papists a night in theire houses wthout first acquaynting the present Govr therewith." Admittedly, he had "banged" a "Sarjeant Quaker" for giving him "base Languadge." As proof of his diligence he recounts the disruption of the meeting at Thomas Holme's house. Having been informed of the meeting, he felt it incumbent upon himself to break it up, "but when the officer of the guard came to see the occasions off such a Meetinge in the garrison the dore was kept agst him, till he broake itt up with his guard." He continues.

> The chiefe Quakers that wee have off this towne are Capt Holmes. Mr. Phelps, & Mr. Peirce, that are starke mad att mee, that I give not all Quakers strandgers as well as others liberty to meete in this Garrison. . . Me thinks iff theire devotion weare soe hott for that wch I dare not call a religion ye country att Lardge should Serve there turne to bee in, for the Exercise of itt; but noe place will please them but this.[7] Whatever conscience might do to others, it did not make cowards of the Quakers.

Harsh as Ingoldsby's measures were, there is something pitiable about his desperation. He was at this time mayor of Limerick, and he was under orders to suppress any elements threatening the still unsteady peace. Of these elements, whether justifiably or not, the Quakers were generally considered the most ominous. They were jailed on the slightest pretext. When one Friend went to prison, others went, too; when a group went, others flocked in great numbers to visit them, so that everyone was upset.

In the spring Thomas and Sarah Holme, who were then expecting their fifth child, and their two living children—six-year-old Thomas and Sarah, who was three and a half—moved to their new home in the townland of Dongeare in county Wexford. In the selection of the homestead Thomas had had many possible sites from which to choose. Among them were half the town and the lands of Taghmon, the birth-

---

[7] Ingoldsby's letter is in BL, Landsdowne *MSS. Registers of Tewkesbury Abbey*, Shire Hall, Gloucester. There is some question regarding the name or title of the Tewkesbury Susanna's father. The record keeper interprets the first letter as *N* on the ground that *Nester* would have been in keeping with the common practice of giving classical names to children, and that *Mester* would have implied a university relationship. However, the initial in question functions also as *M* (see, for example, Tannenbaum's *Handwriting of the Renaissance*) and is identical with the capital *M* used by Sprigge in his *Diary of the Civil War in the West*; it could identify the person concerned as ship's master. Could not this have been Thomas's brother Michael, and the infant Susanna, Thomas Holme's niece, the future wife of ship's master John James?

Fig. 7. House alleged to be Holme residence, Wexford. Photograph by author.

place of the philosopher Dun Scotus, which might have distressed Thomas had he known it. This tract comprised 986 acres, including the town where the road from Wexford branched out toward Waterford and Rosse, and had "in the midst of it a faire and strong stone Castle indifferent well in repair." From its high rock in another part of his land in the parish of Taghmon, the remains of Browne's Castle looked down on the rapids of the Pill, where for generations a mill had served the people of the neighborhood. This "smale Pile of stone out of repaire" was the ruins of the medieval castle of Sir Nicholas le Brune, blown up in 1650 by its Royalist defenders at the cost of the lives of two hundred of Thomas Holme's companions in arms. In this area, too, was his townland of Forest, eighty acres of not very good soil in a pleasant location, upon which the first Friends' Meeting House in Shelmalier Barony would be built. Nearby was Lambstown, the property of Thomas Holme's friend, Robert Cuppage.

In the Civil Survey Dungeare was rated among the best areas in the Barony, having 130 acres of arable land, twenty acres of wood, and thirty of moor and pasture. Possibly the most desirable dwelling stood within its limits, and possibly the castle was habitable, though generally these picturesque structures were better suited to defense than to gracious living. A little to the north, between Dungeare and Bregurteen, lies Harristowne, of which 267 acres were allocated to Thomas.

Dungeare was to remain the home of the family for three years. Thomas Holme and his son traversed the land as he had gone about the land around Coniston Waterhead when he was six. The first important event of their life in their new home was the birth of Susanna on 19 July. Curiously, another Susanna, daughter of "Mester and Sarah Hulme," was christened on 1 August of that year in Tewkesbury. *Hulme*, as is noted above, is an alternate spelling for *Holme*, and may have represented here a brother of Thomas, a ship's master, Michael.[7] A little more than a year later, on 20 September 1658, a second son, Samuel, was born in Dungeare.

In 1657 there occurred an event of perhaps greater importance to Thomas Holme's life than his move to county Wexford and the birth of Susanna. Thomas Loe, a member of the Society of Friends who had been convinced during the previous year and who would come to be regarded with reverence second only to that accorded the founder, George Fox, came to Ireland. Enjoying greater freedom for service now that he was out of the army, Thomas joined Loe in his visits to Friends' meetings throughout southern Ireland. As Thomas would relate some years later in his "book of sufferings," the journeys were sometimes perilous. On one occasion, Thomas Loe, Thomas Holme, and others were seized at a meeting in Cashel, and

> were violently (by soldiers) turned out of the Town, & the Gates kept against them though it was near Night, and a dangerous Time for Englishmen to be out of the Garrison, because of the Tories and Robbers, and thereby exposed to the Hazard of their lives.[8]

In contrast to the disappointment and suffering at Cashel was a comforting meeting near Cork. Admiral Sir William Penn, as his son and namesake would relate many years later, invited the wayfaring Quakers to his castle at Macroom for the edification—or entertainment?—of his guests. Unexpectedly these were moved to tears by the simplicity and sincerity of the group, and particularly by the speech of Thomas Loe.

Among the audience was the admiral's thirteen-year-old son, William. Later he was to attribute the beginning of his convincement to the movements of grace he experienced during this period of his life. It is reasonable to suppose that Thomas Holme was still in the company of Thomas Loe on this occasion, and that the meeting was re-

---

[8] Fuller and Holme, 53. The surname of the leader of this group also appears as *Low*. Mrs. Olive Goodbody, Librarian of the Friends' Library in Dublin, states that the meeting was in the house of Major Robert Cuppage, a personal friend of Thomas Holme. Lieutenant Howard, lieutenant to Colonel Hunt, was also present.

called by Thomas and William when they met in Dublin a little more than a decade later.[9]

Not always were Friends so graciously received, nor were they as visitors uniformly gentle. Everywhere members of the group were being beaten, robbed, thrown out of the town, and imprisoned for their faith; but hardships were not permitted to interfere with their apostolic labors.

Wight recounts a story that no subsequent historian has been able to resist retelling. At one point in the early years of the Quaker ministry in Ireland, when Robert Wilkinson, a captain in the army, was speaking at a Protestant meeting, Abraham Newbold of Waterford rose up and commanded in a loud voice, "Serpent, be silent." Wilkinson attempted to continue but was so discomposed that he could not, and was carried out of the meeting. On the next meeting day he was "so disordered that he was taken out of the meeting fainting and from this time ceased preaching any more, and become foolish in the latter end of his days."[10] His collapse evidently vindicated Newbold's attack.

It would be understandable if during these early years as a civilian Thomas Holme's first concern was the establishment of material security for his young family. As a native of Monk Coniston he turned to milling and agriculture rather than to a business establishment in Taghmon or Wexford.

This is not to say that he did not continue to concern himself with the affairs of the Friends. In 1659 he was the signer and perhaps the author of a long epistle entitled *A Narrative of the Cruel Sufferings of the People of God in the Nation of Ireland Called Quakers Addressed to the Parliament of London.*[11]

Both ministry and sufferings continued. At the order of Mayor of Dublin Robert Dee, Thomas, Robert Turner, Samuel Claridge, and others—seventeen men and six women, according to the book of sufferings—were taken by soldiers from a meeting for worship and imprisoned, "first in the Main-Guard then Newgate, for several days." Released, they continued to be consumed by religious zeal. Politics concerned them only as it related to themselves.

Oliver Cromwell died on 3 September 1658 and was succeeded by his ineffectual son Richard. His resignation on 25 May 1659 inspired

---

[9] William Penn to William Burroughs, in which Penn states that from the age of thirteen [1657] he has been "a pursuer of religion." HSP, Penn Papers, no. 487 (n.d. 1674?). Printed in *PWP* 1: 302–303.
[10] Wight, *History*, 86.
[11] Besse, *Narratives of the Cruel Sufferings*, BL #31344: 118–124.

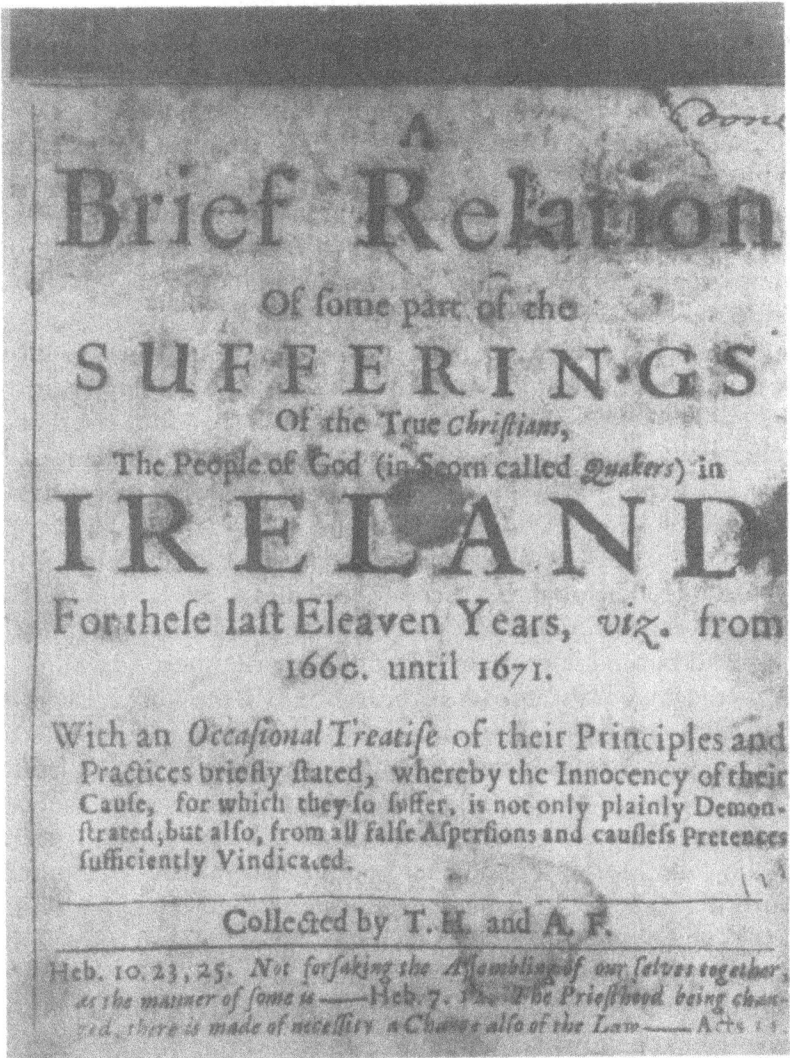

Fig. 8. Title page of Holme's tract on suffering. Used with permission of the Newberry Library.

fresh hopes in the never inactive Royalists and increased the doubts of some of the erstwhile republicans. The state of the government went from bad to worse until, on 8 May 1660, Charles II was proclaimed King. He was welcomed to London on 29 May. Although his return must have stirred some misgivings among those who had fought against his father, the Act of Indemnity was reassuring to those who were not actually regicides.

The Quakers in Ireland welcomed Charles II with "A Brief Roll

Presented to the King of England" that listed in seven long pages the sufferings of the Irish Friends under the Commonwealth and Protectorate. It contains particulars of Thomas Holme's three trials, one of which is the Cashel eviction already described. The other two, undated, seem to belong, respectively, to his Wexford and Limerick residence. The other event, presumably, antedates the first mentioned, since it concerns Thomas's relations with Ingoldsby, by whose orders "the saudiers rivelled . . . Thomas Holme his house and took of what they pleased."[12] This apparently refers to the raid already described.

From this point on, sufferings for tithes, for non-swearing, for absence from the established worship, and for presence at their own meetings for worship escalated with a regularity that dulls the reader's apprehension but must have been a constant, painful irritant to the persons involved; yet nothing could stem their zeal or rouse them to retaliation.

Merely to meet in Dublin seemed to be asking for trouble. In 1660 and again in 1661 Robert Turner and Thomas Holme, with as many as eighteen others, men and women, were taken from meetings for worship and put in Newgate by order of Mayor Hubert Adrian.[13] The dates of the meetings are not recorded, but if they occurred at the time usually favored by the spring half-yearly meeting, the second one followed shortly upon the birth of another daughter to the Holmes on 27 April 1661. Thomas and Sarah Holme gave this child the name of the infant Hester who had died at Limerick.

By the time Hester arrived, her parents had moved to another of their townlands somewhat nearer Wexford: Bregurteen, the "hill of the little plowed fields." Local historians believe that they may have lived in the very respectable old farmhouse, known to have been used by an English landlord in the eighteenth century as a hunting lodge, that overlooks the townland of Holmestown—a territory whose name may have attracted Thomas even before he received his land in county Wexford. The modest two-story stone house looks somewhat imposing on its hilltop, and the walled garden in front and the farm buildings, modern but built on the old foundations that form a courtyard at one side and the rear, are characteristic of the defensive architecture of the beleaguered Anglo-Irish farmstead.

From the house at Bregurteen Thomas and Sarah Holme continued the active life of the Friends. In 1662 Sarah suffered her one recorded incarceration, when she was shut up in Wexford prison. She had laid

---

[12] CSP, 1669–70, addenda, 1625–70.
[13] For this and subsequent sufferings, see the chronological lists in *A Brief Relation* . . . and *A Compendious View* . . . and Besse, 2: 466 and passim.

herself open to convenient arrest by going there to visit other Quakers, among whom may have been her husband. With her were Thomas Loe, to whose preaching and example some time later William Penn attributed his convincement, and his wife, Mary. In Dublin that year Robert Turner, who would figure largely in Thomas Holme's life in America, was again imprisoned, and with him Samuel Claridge, also a friend of Thomas.

Life continued at Bregurteen a little more comfortably, perhaps, than at Dungeare. There were at the time of the census of 1659 two English and four Irish households in the townland. These included the family of Thomas Holme, named in the same document *Titulado* (Sir William Petty's term for principal inhabitant) of Bregurteen and Harristown. The other English family may have been that of Thomas's brother Michael, which is known to have lived in county Wexford. The Irish families were probably husbandmen, although they may have been among the few landholders who, because of age or decrepitude, were exempt from transplanting. Many English settlers had petitioned and received permission to keep penniless and illiterate Irish peasants on the land as servants and farm laborers. Some of these, it is said, were actually members of the landed gentry in disguise who were willing to undergo temporary ignominy for the sake of an eventual opportunity to regain something of what they had lost. Not unusually tradespeople were permitted to continue in the new community. In some localities these circumstances led to a slight easing of tension between the two groups of inhabitants.

One of the satisfactions of Thomas Holme's life at Bregurteen was his greater proximity to his friend Robert Cuppage at Lambstown, a few miles to the northwest. This land had been the scene of one of the fiercest battles of the late war, called by the English "the Bloody Gap"—a title repudiated by the local Irish. One cannot but wonder what memories stirred as they looked out over the hills, and what impressions were forced back into the invisible matrix that would help mold much of future thought and action.

In April of 1663 a third son was born to the Holmes. They named him Tryall, perhaps in commemoration of the trials they had weathered during the years just passed, or perhaps on the inspiration of William Edmundson, who named a son Tryal and a daughter Hindrance. Yet another son arrived just short of three years later—William, born on 5 March 1665/66.

One would like to think of this growing family leading an idyllic life on their high hill, surrounded by friends, materially secure in land whose large acreage compensated for the poor quality of some of the soil. The parents were literate and, like Friends everywhere, zealous for the education of their children and competent to initiate it. Young Thomas was fourteen now, and Susanna nearly twelve—old enough to give assistance and companionship to their parents and to help care for the younger children.

From a distance of three hundred years the prospect appears bright, yet it was not entirely so. Ten years had not accomplished what hundreds had failed to do. Political as well as religious hazards abounded. Not all of the Irish aristocrats had gone to hell, Connaught, or Spain. The woods, cliffs and caverns along the River Slaney less than a half-dozen miles away harbored Tories who emerged at unpredictable intervals to destroy or take back by force as much as they could of what had been taken by force from them, or to seize compensation for what had been looted from their own and their neighbors' property.

On the night of 11 March 1665 Robert Cuppage was the victim of such a raid. Word was brought to Thomas Holme at once, and the next morning he wrote a full report of the attack to the custodian of lands in Wexford, Sir Richard Clifton. Clifton immediately enclosed it in a letter of his own to the Duke of Ormonde, Lord Lieutenant of Ireland, among whose papers it remains today. Thomas wrote:

> S: R: C. The last night about 8°. clocke, Major Rob: Cuppage was robbed of even all he had with him in his house. He being at supper there came to his house about 6. lusty young men, and with pistolls & their swords drawne, calling him dogge rogue & bad words, demanded his moneys, & presently they fell to robbing, and in short they tooke away his moneys, plate, lynnen, woolen, ripped open some of the bolsters & bedding, & let the feathers about the roome, broke up the chests, and trunks, &c, and so, in about an hours time they made an end, and went away; it seems they had even about 30 horses, & they said themselfes at their first coming into the house, that they were discont'ed gentlemen: they spake Irish to one another, and would take no flesh, but did take bread and cheese's. It was the majors desire, that this should be made known to thee, and also represented to the Duke and Councill, that so, they may see in what danger Englishmen in the Countrey are in; & how easy they may (in ordinary houses) be stripped of all; it seems, that of late, there have been several English, in the County of Corke, robbed and fired; I suppose Major Cuppage, have lost to the value of 300$^l.$ ^{bs} Thus much at present
> from
>
> Bregurteen   12th march 1665   Thy friend,
> Tho: Holme[14]

---

[14] NLI, MS Letters of James, Duke of Ormonde, 1: 213, 215. The letters of both Thomas Holme and Clifton are printed in the Calendar of the MSS of the Marquis of Ormonde, n.s. 3: 209–210.

Such depredations were shocking to the English, now firmly established because of the success of their own violence against the original owners of the land. Probably neither Thomas nor Robert remembered the Wexford of October, 1649, of which Cromwell wrote, "I believe scarce one in twenty can challenge any property in their houses." Native Wexfordians could not be credited with so short a memory. Thomas Holme's reference to Cork suggests the part, already noted, that Cuppage had played in reducing that county and others to the order of the Commonwealth and Protectorate. It is more than likely that the Irish knew the names of officials accessible to them, and that Cuppage and Thomas Holme, among others, had an uncomfortable feeling of being marked men.

Clifton, too, was uneasy. In the cover letter with which he forwarded Thomas's letter to Ormonde he took occasion to press for the repair of the castle at Enniscorthy, whose walls were defective in three places. He felt sure the repairs would be willingly undertaken by the town and county, some of whom, "at least such that have not as yet bowed their knees to Baall," might be trusted if occasion arose. The repairs could be made for about thirty-five pounds, and a few carbines would aid in the defense of the countryside.

For the first few years of the restored monarchy the Adventurers and soldiers continued to enjoy the land granted them under the Cromwellian Settlement. Soon, however, the claim of the "innocent" dispossessed—those Irish who could satisfy investigators that they had not borne arms against the king or given aid to the Commomwealth—commenced to bear fruit. In 1663 Thomas Holme lost six hundred acres of his choicest booty—his part of the town and much of the surrounding land of Taghmon—to William Hore, "innocent Protestant," and the crown. Other previous owners of his land who were declared innocent and were restored to part of their property were John Roche, William Browne, and John Cheevers of the Barony of Forth, from whose original holding Thomas Holme retained a total of about eighty acres. The official record of the restoration of Hore's land recounts that of the 986 acres set out to Thomas Holme in the parish of Taghmon in 1655 and enjoyed by him until June 1663, William Hore esq., "upon a decree of innocency as a protestant in the court of claymes, recovered 400 of the said lands," with common pasture on all the rest, and that in 1666 Thomas Holme "past letters patent of 349 acres thereof." The remaining 237 acres went to the crown, always saving the common pasture rights to Hore and "also saveing, unto Daniell Gahan esq. his right and title to the said 237 acres, if any he hath."[15]

The Subsidy Roll for 1666 lists Thomas Holme's assessment for his remaining property at 26s. 8d. among others ranging from 10s. to 50s.[16] Those holding the land of Catholic claimants were, for the most part, more fortunate, since the greater number of Catholics had resisted previous royal attempts at confiscation of their property and interference with the practice of their religion as fiercely as they had fought Cromwell, and so were subject to penalties from both sides. They had been victims of aggression. Now the aggressors themselves were sucked into the vicious circle. In this land, substantially all the soldiers' pay for two to ten years of horror and hardship was at stake.

Having lost much, Thomas Holme set about salvaging what he could. Among the deeds recorded during the reign of Charles II is an indenture made 19 July 1667, "between Thomas Holmes of Bragurteen, Co. Wexford, Gent., & Danial Gahan of Dublin Esq.," explaining that although by indenture between them dated 28 February 1665,

> it was agreed that Holmes should exhibit his Claim for severall Messuages & Tenements, then in his Possession . . . should obtain their Certificate, & should after permit the said Gahan to pass patent thereof in his own Name, [now] for avoiding all Differences, & for the sum of 211 pounds,

he sold this property, containing 349 acres, to Gahan at the quit rent of 7.1.2. The indenture was enrolled 6 February 1667/68.[17] He had seen the handwriting on the wall and pocketed the £211 with relief. At the same time, Gahan himself probably felt that, whether he could regain his 237 acres or not, being able to "sit down" on 349 acres of his own estate was worth the price.

Matters of money and freedom of conscience were not all that plagued Thomas Holme during the sixties. Now his brother Michael, a disbanded Royalist from whom he had been separated by the exigencies of civil war, introduced himself to Ormonde, mentioning Thomas as one of two channels of aid in his own embarrassment. He addressed a petition

---

[15] PRO, Dublin, *Inrollment of the Decrees of Innocents: Restorees, Charles II. Inquisitionum in Officio Rotulorum cancellariae Hiberniae asservatarum Reportorium* 1 (1826): 10, Car. 2, *Wx*, 15 January, thirtieth year (1678).

[16] Subsidy Roll (I H No. 25), PRO D [Copy], Philip Hore, *Hist. Wx* 5: 424. The original document was destroyed in the fire of 1922.

[17] PROD, Ch. 2, 1: 216.

To his grace James of Ormonde. The humble petition of Capt. Michael Holme. That your petitioner hath ever faithfully served his late Majesty in England and his Majesty that now is with your Grace in this kingdom and beyond Seas after the yeare 1650 as hath been formerly certified by your grace and now seeing your petitioner and his servant being mustered supernumeraries by particular order from the late lords Justices and now dismissed the service since the 29th of July last by your Graces general order and having ever since with much want and expense attended your Grace's promise and pleasure for satisfaction of arrears and employment in his Majestie's service, which is the whole dependence for your petitioner's livelihood and through want there-of having not present subsistence is with his poor wife exposed to extreme want and misery

Most humbly prays

That it may therefore please your Grace in tender sentiment and sympathie of the petitioner's present condition, and his many past years of adversities, to grant him your Grace's particular warrant to receive the seasonable comfort of his and his servants stated arrears out of his Majestie's treasury at Dublin or by way of assignment on his brother in the county of Wexford towards the comfortable life and support of the petitioner until your Grace shall with opportunity dispose of the petitioner putt on list for his future employment in his Majestie's service.

And he shall ever praye &c.

Dublin Castle, 11 Nov. 1662

Ormonde, who was not remarkable for tender sentiment and sympathy, endorsed the petition: "If the arreares above mentioned be within the rule prescribed for payment, the master generall is to state the same, and to prepare a warrant for the payment thereof and present it unto us for signature. Ormonde."[18] How or when Michael Holme served as captain does not appear.

Being in such straits, he probably made a direct appeal also to his brother Thomas. His distress seems eventually to have been relieved through other channels, if he is the Captain-Lieutenant Michael Holme admitted to Lord Caulfield's troop on 10 March 1664/65.

It was also during the decade of the sixties that three events of especial importance to the Irish Quakers occurred. The first of these was the visit of the founder. George Fox visited most of the Friends' meetings in Ireland, and his journeys were accompanied by extraordinary manifestations of grace and zeal. In one of the insertions from Ellwood's edition of his journal Thomas Holme makes a brief appearance. On leaving Dublin Fox reviewed his meditations of the love of

---

[18] Ormonde, 27: 209, NLI, Dublin. See HMC, app. to 4th report; HMC, 9th report of RCHM part 2, appendix (London, 1884), 161.

God and His attributes of life and power, "and soe all passed away, & we came on, onley two friends Thomas Holmes, & a friende of Dublin would see us over the watter, & soe came over the watter into England with us."[19]

Fox's estimate of the Dublin meeting is in keeping with the spirit the Quakers of Ireland would show in Pennsylvania: "And a gallant visitation they had, & there is gallant spirit in them, worthy to be visited." Thomas Holme and his companion demonstrated some of this gallantry on their return to Dublin, when the master of the ship, returned from Liverpool, circulated a tale that George Fox had spent the night drinking in a tavern: "& friends heareing of it, two of which were eminent men & came over with G: ff: & knew that he did not stay above a quarter of an houre in that towne, soe they made him to repent of his slander, where he had slandered him. . . ." It would be interesting to know who Thomas Holme's friend was on this occasion. It does not require much imagination to picture the retribution visited on the miscreant by veterans of several wars and of the penal actions of the Anglo-Irish government.

Thomas Holme played a less romantic but more substantial role in the community in their establishment of a national center for the Quakers of Ireland. The evidence was discovered approximately three centuries later, used as the binding of a minute book. It is an indenture dated 12 May 1669 between William Mayne, carpenter of Dublin, and nine representatives of various labors and locations, including Robert Turner, linen draper; Samuel Claridge, merchant, both of London; William Edmundson of Rosenallis, Queen's County, husbandman; Abraham Fuller, yeoman; and Thomas Holme of Bregurteen, County Wexford, yeoman, "by which said William Mayne leased lands known as Baron's Inn Garden, Bride Street, suburbs of Dublin with liberty of ingress for all Friends (called Quakers) and liberty to build thereon to the above Trustees."[20] This is the land on which the first house of the Society of Friends was built in Dublin, at the corner of Bride Street and Bride Alley.

The third major event of 1669 would lead a dozen years later to the final and greatest period of Thomas Holme's life. The thoughtful thirteen-year-old of Macroom had become a thoughtful and independent-spirited young man. For some time young William Penn had been torn between the enticing possibilities set before him by his

---

[19] *The Journal of George Fox*, ed. Norman Penney, with an introduction by T. Edmund Harvey (New York: Octagon Books, 1973), 148.

[20] Olive C. Goodbody, *Guide to Irish Quaker Records, 1654–1860* (Dublin, Stationery Office, 1967), 158, no. 211.

father and the attraction of the despised sect. Now he was sent down from Oxford in disgrace because of his association with them.

His father, the admiral, distressed, had sent him to France, where he hoped that William would develop an appetite for more glamorous life, and now to Ireland to act as his deputy. William was twenty-two, and competent enough to win Ormonde's praise for his part in quelling the mutiny of troops at Carrigfergus. He went on to Dublin, and from there to Cork. It was at Cork that he reestablished connections with Thomas Loe and was finally convinced by him.

William's sincerity was soon to be tested. In November of that year he and eighteen other Friends were taken forcibly from a meeting for worship and thrown into jail by order of Mayor Christopher Rye. He was soon released, but he was there long enough to know the price the ordinary Quaker paid for the faith. The tradition lingers in county Wexford that William Penn spent a winter with Robert Cuppage at Lambstown, and it may have been this time. If so, he cannot have failed to become better acquainted with Thomas Holme.[21]

The year following Penn's convincement was to be marked by bereavement for both Penn and Thomas Holme. Thomas's eldest son and namesake had died at the age of seventeen, at Bregurteen, on a day not named by his father in the Friends' record, and "was buried in the burying place of the people of God at Corlecan, 1668." Now Thomas Loe, a close personal friend of both men, died in London. Penn, back in England by this time, delivered a moving tribute at Loe's obsequies.

On his return to Ireland in 1669, Penn at once joined in the activities of the Friends and used in their behalf his influence with more powerful persons to whom they had less direct access. The half-yearly meeting had been established the year before, and when Penn came it convened at his lodging on 5 November. "The sufferings of friends came before us," he wrote in his journal. The accounts from Leinster and Munster seem to have been fairly full, but it was thought necessary to send letters to all provincial men's meetings to remind them to be more punctual in depositing records of sufferings with the half-yearly meeting.

After calling on Lord Drogheda and receiving his promise to give what assistance he could to the Friends, Penn had a long visit with Sir William Petty. Was he even at this time contemplating applying for a grant of land in America? Petty's part in the Cromwellian Settlement would make him a valuable adviser in such an endeavor. During this

---

[21] William Penn, *The Irish Journal*, printed in *PWP* 1: 106; MS, HSP.

Fig. 9. A young William Penn. Used with permission of the Historical Society of Pennsylvania.

week in Dublin, Friends, including T.H. [Thomas Holme?] met with him at his lodging. His visit was an inspiration to an already active Society.

By 1671 the affairs of the Society in Ireland were being organized and administrative procedures set up. At the half-yearly meeting at Dublin in May of that year Thomas Holme, George Gregson, and Thomas Randall, with the consent of the rest of the Friends, signed a decision to keep records of birth, death, and marriage. The reports of sufferings were to be brought first to the monthly meetings, then to the half-yearly meeting in Dublin "in order to be recorded and some of them printed and others put before rulers. . . ." Abraham Fuller, the future collaborator with Thomas Holme, was, with Robert Turner, responsible for the transmission of records of suffering in Leinster.

Thomas and Sarah Holme had been in county Wexford for fourteen years now. Six of their children had been born during their years here. The youngest, William, was six years old; the eldest, Thomas, had died three years before. In this summer of 1671, fourteen-year-old Susanna died and was buried at Corlecane. Perhaps it was the memory of her that gave Thomas a special solicitude for his niece, Susanna James, in later years.

Meanwhile the Holmes' religious activities continued. The book of sufferings by Thomas Holme and Abraham Fuller that was published in 1672, *A Brief Relation of some part of the suffering of the True Christians, the People of God (in scorn, called Quakers) in Ireland, for these Last Eleven Years, Viz. from 1660 until 1671*, recounts many inconveniences, often real hardships, endured at the hands of civil, military, and ecclesiastical authorities. One of these was the loss by Thomas Holme himself of £200 due him from Captain Robert Thornhill. Thomas had obtained legal judgment in common law for the debt, but Thornhill, knowing that, as a Quaker, Thomas Holme would not take an oath, hailed him into chancery and so escaped payment. Because of the great change in monetary values over three centuries it is difficult to estimate accurately the modern equivalent of that sum, but according to a reliable authority it would amount to about $20,000 in purchasing power today.

Thomas's antagonist on this occasion was a fellow officer who had amassed a large estate in county Wexford. Hore supplies an extensive dossier on him. It records Thornhill's unacknowledged debts to Dublin for "£200 wool etc." and £1000 owed to the Lord Protector as one of the sureties for the Receiver of Assessments etc. He seems to have kept on hand some "creditable tidbits" to palliate disaffected authority. After he was called to account in March 1658, for the destruction of woods, he came up with a petition for the disposal of popish priests whose example interfered with the conversion of the Irish to Protestantism. When he was accused before the commissioners of several misdeeds, he produced a set of proposals for the elimination of wolves. Among the misdemeanors urged against him "which (if they be true) will incapacitate him to continue the command of the Militia Troop in the County of Wexford" were "His being cashiered the Army for cheating and other misdemeanors, His being ejected the Anabaptists church . . . which undoubtedly was not without some great offense," and "His being a Comen Lyar."[22]

Thomas was concerned regularly with reports of sufferings, distribution of books, the tracing of missing shipments or orders of payment for them, the allocation of books and bequests, relief of afflicted Friends, investigation of alleged misbehavior. When at the half-year's men's meeting that opened in Dublin on 6 May 1672 a system was devised for the collection of accounts of sufferings, he was one of the Leinster representatives responsible for notifying all the meetings of Leinster of the desire of the meeting then in session at Dublin that all such materials should be presented in good form by a specific deadline with a view to their being printed. In 1673 he was one of twelve to sign a report condemning the ideas of Muggleton.[23]

At the half-yearly meeting opening on 5 November 1673 Thomas Holme was named one of a committee "to mind the concerns of friends deeds of Gift, or wills, buriall places or the like for the Service of Truth." With Francis Randall, William Blanch, and William Wright, he was appointed to speak to Alice Atherton and to know her mind and intent of giving £100 in general or particular, and to make a deed of gift to A.B.C. "in Consideration of love and affection, without mentioning the uses and trusts." It may have been the need for this inquiry that prompted the directive to Thomas Holme and William Edmundson to write to the London meeting to learn "about presidents for Wills gifts, buying Buriall places, &c. So as they may be secured & the ends answered, &c."[24]

By this time Thomas Holme, like other Friends, had acquired property in Dublin. The Hearth Tax Rolls for 25 March 1666–25 March 1667 list Samuel Claridge's tax in St. Nicholas Without at 2s.4d., Mr. Turner's of St. Bride's, 3s.6d., and Thomas Holme's at 6s. with one oven at 14d. Robert Turner also paid 4s.8d. in St. Warberg's Parish.[25]

---

[22] Hore MSS, *Wexfordiana* 9: A 17.18, St. Peter's College, Wexford.
[23] *National Meeting Procedure*, 1673, 21.
[24] *NMP*, 1671–1688, 23.
[25] Hearth Tax, City of Dublin, ACM, 147 (Box 47), CCHS.

A further important charge to Thomas Holme, this time with Francis Rogers, was to write to England for a good teacher for a school to be established in the Castledermont area. Education would remain a prominent concern of the Society. At the half-yearly meeting of 1681 there was a report of the schoolmaster's meeting to read a letter from Christopher Taylor on methods of teaching children and on the best textbooks for Latin and spelling. The paths of Thomas Holme and Christopher Taylor would cross again very shortly.

During the 1670s the houses of Thomas and Sarah Holme at Bregurteen and Robert and Mary Cuppage at Lambstown emerge as centers of Quaker activity in rural Wexford, with both families participating in meetings at the home of Jonas Newton. John Tottenham and his second wife, Ann Clark, were married at Bregurteen on 30 July 1671; Henry Hillary and Mary Fuller on 17 September 1675, with Elinor Holme replacing her mother as witness; and Jane Newton and John Ellis, with Thomas and Sarah Holme again as witnesses, on 17 October 1675.[26] Francis Randall was a frequent associate of Thomas Holme in the affairs of the half-yearly meeting at Dublin. 16 March 1675 also saw Thomas Holme enlarging his economic scope to include the export of calves' skins to the continent.[27]

On 12 September 1672 had occurred what to the Holme family was the most important ceremony of all: the marriage of the young Sarah Holme to Richard Holcomb of Dulverton in Somerset, England. The wedding took place at the home of the Cuppages at Lambstown. The wedding certificate was signed by the young couple with suitable flourishes, and by Sarah's parents, the Cuppages, and a large number of other neighbors, including Randall and Tottenham. Sarah was a week past her nineteenth birthday, the only one of the four children born at Limerick to survive. She and her husband now left to establish their new home in Richard's native town.

Perhaps Sarah senior's absence from the marriage of Henry and Mary Hillary in September of 1675 was a warning of failing health. Otherwise there is no indication of weakness on her part. Less than a year later, however, Thomas Holme suffered an almost shattering blow. Sarah, the wife who as a bride had accompanied him on a long and painful military campaign, who had borne him ten children, who had lived more than a quarter-century in this ever-perilous foreign country and had been an indefatigable co-worker for the faith they

---

[26] For this and subsequent records of marriages, see *Wexford Marriage Certificates*, 1671–1681, FRW, 27.
[27] PRO, London, E 190, 63/4.

shared, sickened and died on 10 April 1676. Thomas buried her beside two of their children, Thomas and Susanna, in the laurel-enclosed circle at Corlicane.

A little more than three months later, Samuel, the eldest of Thomas Holme's remaining children, also died. The fact that there is no mention of his ever having participated in his parents' religious activities suggests that he may have been physically or mentally unable to do so. According to the reckoning of their time, the two remaining daughters were adults, Elinor at seventeen and Hester, fifteen. Fortunately for their father, they were able to take over management of the household. The two boys were at a more difficult age. Tryall was thirteen, and William eleven.

Apparently for the first time since it was founded, Thomas Holme was absent from the spring half-yearly meeting in Dublin, which convened less than a week after Sarah's burial. It is possible that when the members who were present assigned Thomas Starkey to write to Thomas Holme about eleven-odd pounds due Ellis Hooks of London for books "which he hath taken upon him to receive the money that he speedily remit it to Robert Turner in order to be sent to Ellis Hooks because he hath written this meeting about it,"[28] they had not yet heard of his bereavement. One may in charity assume that it was conflicting duties rather than carelessness that had caused his delay in this matter.

The family at Bregurteen was now reduced to five. After the list of Friends' marriages witnessed by Thomas and Sarah Holme and their neighbors, the name Thomas Holme as the only official witness of the marriage of Robert Fairbanks and Sarah Leonard at Robert Cuppage's house of 27 August has a lonely ring. In November Thomas Holme was back in Dublin as an official representative of Leinster at the half-yearly meeting. He was then one of six Friends engaged in the interests of the imprisoned John Goodbody.

Sometime within the year that followed, Thomas Holme left Bregurteen. He was present at the half-yearly meeting in May of 1677, but was not listed as a delegate from Leinster; and in November he appeared as a representative of Munster.[29] Although Bregurteen remained his legal address in personal business matters to the end of his stay in Ireland, Thomas Holme lived in Waterford, in the house of William Penn's cousin, William Crispin, who was on duty at Kinsale.

Perhaps because a new generation that had suffered less than its

---

[28] *NMP*, 33.
[29] *NMP*, 34.

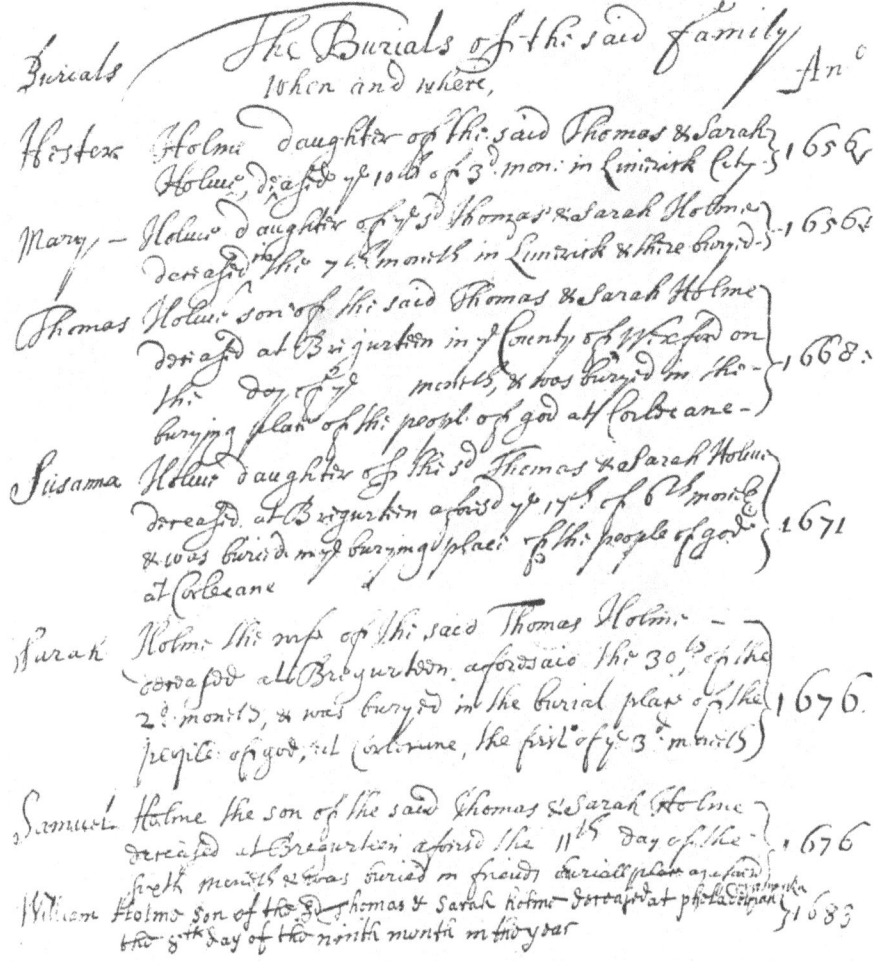

Fig. 10. Record of deaths of Sarah Holme and some of the children.

elders and so had not quite so solemn a view of life was growing up, and perhaps, too, because the Society was expanding beyond the original fairly homogeneous group, the half-yearly meeting at Dublin in the fall of 1671 found it necessary to appoint "devout and regular observers" to visit "all those who have entered into the world's fashions." The resolution introducing this practice was signed by Thomas Holme and a large number of other members, including Fuller, Claridge, and Randall, all of whom were later associated with Thomas in various ways.

From this time forth these matters would be objects of concern.

From Cork in 1671 came an exhortation against extremes in women's dress, which Thomas and others at the meeting signed. In 1681 an emphatic warning against "levity and finery at weddings" was issued, with a directive to tailors to "make clothes plain." William Penn himself was privately criticized for having had a wig made when the unhealthful conditions of his imprisonment robbed him of his own hair.[30]

A different sort of vanity is evident in a case referred to a committee of which Thomas was a member. They were assigned to investigate a report of a young lady who was quoted as saying that "a young man dyed for love of her." The committee reported that she had said it in sorrow, not boasting.[31] Their decision is particularly gratifying, inasmuch as her father had had the optimism to name her Grace in contrast to the names Tryal and Hindrance bestowed on her brother and sister.

A more serious problem was that of personal sexual morality. At the May half-yearly meeting in 1677 Samuel Claridge, a frequent associate of Thomas Holme in Friends' interests, was censured for adultery. Claridge was an active member of the society, and had suffered imprisonment and considerable loss of property for the faith. Although many of those present signed the censure, Thomas abstained. Abraham Fuller signed the paper when it was first circulated but abstained on the second round.[32] The erring Friend acknowledged his fault straightforwardly and humbly and was charitably reinstated. Thomas's abstention from censure on this occasion and his charitable report concerning Grace Edmundson seem to have been in line with a tendency toward mercy.

Admonitions concerning all vanity and frivolity recurred at successive meetings. Young people were warned against too great familiarity before marriage, indicating that, like the rest of the world, these people who were trying valiantly to follow the straight and narrow road were sometimes enticed by primrosed by-paths. A year after his censure as an adulterer, Claridge was involved in a financial controversy. This time the Friends, including Thomas Holme, signed a report of the sum due from him to a man named Dawson and agreed to pay it in order to put an end to the unpleasantness. Later Claridge would come to the aid of Thomas in his purchase of a second five-thousand-acre lot of land in Pennsylvania.

Greater anxiety was caused by indications of falling off from the early religious beliefs of the Friends, and of free association with non-

---

[30] *Irish Journal*, 25 November 1669, 108, *PWP* 1: 101–131, 108. *NMP*, 21.
[31] MS Minutes of the Meeting of Leinster Province 1: 19, cited by ACM, Box 61.
[32] *NMP*, 8 May 1677, 56.

Quakers. Carpenters were to have nothing to do with the making or installing of altars in churches or images in ships. In trades only Quaker apprentices were to be accepted, and children were to be put only to Quaker masters. Midwives were instructed to avoid baptizing and baptismal observances. The seriousness with which the injunction against baptism was regarded is evidenced in Thomas Holme's declaration in his summary of family history in the Wexford register that he "(for conscience sake) did not suffer any of his said children to be sprinkled or as some call it, baptized, there being no Scripture for such a practise, but was introduced by the pope & papists or other Apostates, in the night of Apostacy." In 1680 a special exhortation against mixed marriages was prepared and signed, like most of the documents, by Thomas Holme and others.

Thomas Holme was a representative of Munster again at the half-yearly meeting in 1679 and 1681, and his signature appears on a document of the meeting in 1680; but his apparently consistent absence from the November meetings of 1678–1681 suggests that he had assumed business or other commitments that kept him occupied at that time. The last remaining evidence of the Holme family's participation in the activities of the Wexford Friends is the signatures of Tryal, William, and Elinor on the marriage record of Benjamin Green and Elizabeth Mortons of Balliwidder at the house of Robert Cuppage, on 3 June 1680. Conceivably Elinor, now eighteen, had been left at Bregurteen in charge of her young brothers, with Hester keeping house for her father in Waterford. In that city, where he was identified as a merchant, Thomas Holme had become involved in shipping merchandise to both New England and the Continent.

Port books carry evidence of shipments by Thomas Holme during 1681 and early 1682. Three were for New England: on 17 March 1680/81, in the *Edward and Ann*, wrought silk, men's worsted hose, and bound books; in the *Elvis and Mary*, 3 August 1681, wrought silk, men's worsted hose, cheese, glass bowls, iron, steel, flannel, saddles; and on 14 April 1682, wrought silk. The goods for America were largely what might be considered luxury items—silk, glass bowls, worsted hose—while the bulk of continental shipping consisted of horne plates and iron. One shipment for "Deep" [Dieppe] was in the *Harp*, which Thomas would encounter later under different circumstances.

Other than shipping, the last records of Thomas Holme as a resident of Ireland are concerned with real estate. There are two of them, both dealing with grants of land in Shelmalier Barony to Charles Collins, under the Act of Settlement and Explanation in 1667. These were in addition to the two parcels retained in his own name in the Barony of Forth.

In consideration of £400 the use of these had been conveyed to Thomas Holme in 1678, with the understanding that he would reconvey them to Francis Randall and John Tottenham, for whom they had been acquired in the first place. Tottenham thus acquired the land of Ballyloskeran, adjoining Bregurteen, on 17 May 1680, and the patent was enrolled four days later, reserving "a parcel of land . . . lying between the Place where the Killgarven Water runs into the new Mill-Race, and the old Watercourse on the Side, being about half an Acre, . . . in the Possession of Holme, and to hold to him and their heirs. . . ." [33] This bit of land would seem adequate only for a mill, although the settlement mentions a new mill close by belonging to Tottenham.

On 6 January 1681/82 almost on the eve of the reception of his leaving certificate from the Friends in Waterford, before his immigration to Pennsylvania, Thomas "sold and conveyed to Randall the Lands of Clonmore," a townland along the Slaney at the northernmost tip of the Barony of Shelmalier.

Again, there is no record of Thomas Holme's presence in Ireland between May of 1681 and January of 1681/82. Is it implausible that he had joined other Friends in the combined commercial and ministerial traffic with Barbados?

---

[33] PRO, SPD, Charles II, I App. 219; 2: 82, 181.

Part Four

The Governor's Man

Chapter 6

The Long Voyage

However Thomas Holme was occupied between May of 1681 and the sixth of January 1681/82, he certainly knew of the project undertaken by William Penn. To recover the debts, financial and otherwise, of the Stuarts to his father, Admiral Sir William Penn, William Penn had succeeded in obtaining from Charles II a large tract of land along the west side of the Delaware River, which had belonged alternately to the Swedes, the Dutch, and the English. Memorials of these successive ownerships remained in the few scattered villages and plantations that dotted the territory, but the land above the fortieth parallel was ceded to William Penn with the provision that already established settlers would be persuaded to sell their holdings and go elsewhere or remain where they were as peaceable and taxpaying residents of the new province.[1]

The king's formal declaration of the patent, which had been signed on 4 March 1680/81, was dated 12 April 1681. Penn at once commissioned his cousin William Markham as deputy governor and dispatched him to the province. In October he commissioned another cousin, Thomas Holme's friend and current landlord, William Crispin, assistant to Markham, chief justice "to keep the seal, court, and ses-

---

[1] *CEB* 76: 105, and 93: 164. Accounts of the consideration of "Mr. Penn's Patent" by the Lords of Trade and Plantations appear in *CEB* 106: 218, 249, and 253, and in 97: 130. For abstracts of these and other pertinent documents relating to the grant, including the controversy over boundaries with references to the originals in the PRO, see *CSPC, A* and *WI*, 1681, the charter and other documents reprinted in the *MPC*, ed. Samuel Hazard (1838), vol. 1 and *MdA* 7: *Calvert Papers*.

sions, accountable to William Penn, and have the profits thereof," and to serve as one of four land commissioners. Markham, Penn added, was to "treat him with respect."[2] In addition to these responsibilities, according to Crispin tradition, he was to be surveyor general, although no commission naming him to this office is extant. The other land commissioners were John Bezar, Nathaniel Allen, and William Haige. Bezar and Allen embarked on the *Bristol Factor* from Bristol in late October 1681, and arrived at New Castle on 15 December. Crispin and Haige, on the other hand, left from London on the smaller *John and Sarah* which encountered severe storms and serious health problems.[3]

Thomas Holme himself was considering buying land and immigrating to America. William Penn had set up machinery requisite for sales, with Philip Ford and Thomas Rudyard as agents, and there were already purchasers. The prospect was inviting. The land was said to be fertile, the climate benign. There would be no tithes, no harassment by a hostile government; and there would be opportunity for new and challenging commercial enterprise. Thomas Holme had sent modest cargoes from Wexford and on moving to Waterford had entered into a more extensive market. As already mentioned, on 3 August he shipped a varied and valuable cargo to New England by the *Elvis and Mary*, Elisha Bennet master, for which he paid £7.14.6 duty.[4]

The *Elvis and Mary* is of more than passing interest for a number of reasons. It seems to have been the ship on which the sister-in-law of James Claypoole sailed, as appeared from the correspondence of Claypoole and his brother Norton, the "ship from New England" that

---

[2] William Markham was the son of Sir William Penn's sister Rebecca Penn Markham, and William Crispin was the husband of Rebecca Bradshaw, the daughter of his sister Rachel Penn Bradshaw (HSP, *Genealogical Notes* 29: 5). The commissions of Crispin and his fellow officers are dated 25 October 1681–1800, in the Division of Public Records, State Library, Harrisburg (Hazard, *Annals*, 1609–1682, 1850: 637). For Penn's letter to Markham concerning Crispin, see HSP, *Dreer*, 5.

[3] Marion Balderston, "William Penn's Twenty-three Ships," *PGM* 23 (1963), 27–67, hereinafter referred to as "Twenty-three Ships." Unless otherwise noted, further information concerning ship movements is drawn from this article.

[4] For Thomas's shipping, see PRO, *London Port Books* E 109: 63/64, and E 190: 109, passim. On 14 July 1682 James Claypoole wrote to his brother Norton at New Deal near New Castle that he was glad to have learned by Norton's letters of 16 and 29 December 1681/82, received 19 April 1682, that Norton's wife had arrived safe after the delay and inconvenience of having been "put to shore" so far away. The lady had refused to go directly with Thomas Arnold, but "minded more the counsel of the other master [Elisha Bennett]" (*CLB*, 133). Richard Lundy, who later married Elizabeth, daughter of William Bennet, may reasonably be assumed to have received command of the ship during the long interim in New York before proceeding to Pennsylvania (*Port Book* E 190.108; *CLB* 34, n.14). Balderson assumed that the *Amity* came by way of Barbados, although Claypoole patently expected it to go directly to the Delaware.

arrived "for the river [Delaware] the 19th of the 3d Mo [May] 1682." Finally, the length of the voyage, allowing a month or more to complete loading the vessel, suggests that, in keeping with common practice, it went by way of Barbados. If this was true, Thomas Holme was likely one of the Quakers who carried on in Barbados a flourishing enterprise combining trade and religion. If so, he probably accompanied his cargo as far as Barbados.

If he was at Barbados in the fall of 1681 he witnessed the arrival of the storm-battered *John and Sarah* with its company of desperately ill passengers. William Crispin was one of the victims. The ship lay in for repairs and then went on to Pennsylvania with Commissioner Haige and the other survivors. Someone at Barbados returned to England by the next ship, bringing the news of Crispin's death to William Penn. Was Thomas Holme the messenger? If so, it could well be that Penn was thus inspired in the emergency to choose Thomas Holme, Friend, merchant, experienced surveyor, as a partial replacement for his cousin.

Except for his age—he was in his fifty-eighth year, twenty years older than the Proprietor—Thomas Holme was a likely choice: a veteran of the complications of the Cromwellian Settlement, including the surveys; physically hardened by many years of soldiering followed by strenuous rural life and many travels; accustomed to dealing with persons of widely varied walks of life; old enough to be free from the emotional hazards that might beset younger men in the wilderness; a Friend of proven fidelity. His family were old enough to be of assistance and relish the challenges and opportunities the new land had to offer. Moreover, Thomas Holme was a merchant. He would be useful in another capacity. Not only had the province at large taken shape in Penn's mind; he envisioned also a chosen band of businessmen whose enlightened self-interest would insure the speedy establishment of commerce.

The Proprietor lost no time in enlisting the nucleus of such a group, which consisted of his steward, Philip Ford; James Claypoole, friend and business correspondent of Thomas Holme's friend Claridge; and Nicholas More, a well-to-do London physician.

Thomas Holme became involved in the Pennsylvania Company, as it was first called, during its formative stages. His interest was probably directly solicited by William Penn. He, Robert Turner, and Samuel Claridge had owned property in the same neighborhood in Dublin and had shared imprisonment and other hardships for their Quaker faith. He had had business dealings with Francis Rogers of Cork, and his acquaintance with Penn went back at least a dozen years. These men were his friends. After the death of Sarah and four of their children and the loss of a great part of the land he had amassed, the prospect of starting over in a new country in association with them and with others who, for the most part, shared not only his economic interests but his devotion to Penn and his religious convictions as well, was enticing indeed. With them he invested in five thousand acres of William Penn's new land.[5]

By the first week of January at the latest he had decided to emigrate. He concluded his business commitment with Randall on 7 January 1681/82. On 29 January he obtained his leaving certificate from the monthly meeting of the Society of Friends at Waterford. On 23 March he witnessed the deeds of William Penn to Samuel Clancy of Dublin and Francis Rogers. On 28 March he was loading his merchant's cargo on the *Amity*.[6]

If he felt any apprehension it was overbalanced by a certain relish for this final adventure as he saw on board his "6 cwt. lead; 10 cwt. iron, 12 cwt. nails; 6 smal 2 great sadles; 80 lbs. shoos; 1 doz. bridles; 1/2 Chald. grindle stones; 1/2 cwt. of gunpower; 10 horse collers; 1 doz. shood shovels."[7] Between his departure from Waterford at the end of January and his sailing on the *Amity* three months later, Thomas Holme was busy not only in assembling his cargo but in participating in the foundation of the Pennsylvania Company, which became the Free Society of Traders.

James Claypoole, who was one of the most enthusiastic and influential organizers of the group, reported the progress of the company in letters to various business correspondents, some of whom were also acquaintances of Thomas Holme, among them Francis and George Rogers.[8]

By the first of April he informed Samuel Claridge that the book of articles for the company was printed, "and I did intend to send thee one this day, but Thomas Holme told me he purposed to send 2 to Dublin, one to thee, and one to another." In the same letter Claypoole suggests that Claridge ask Thomas Holme to arbitrate a dispute he was having in one of his business involvements. "Thomas," he wrote, "may be a very fit man [to help solve the problem], being honest and of good understanding." Claypoole was soliciting subscriptions to the

---

[5] HSP, *Penn-Ford Accounts, 1681 Monies Received for Land in Pennsylvania.*
[6] ACM, *Arrivals.*
[7] PRO, *London Port Book* E 190/132/1. *Collector's Book* E 190, 192/1 and *Surveyor's Book* 112/1 show slight variations. The ship here is called the *Unity* but is more frequently called *Amity.*
[8] *CLB*, 100. Claypoole was a well-to-do Quaker merchant, brother of Cromwell's son-in-law John Claypoole and business associate of Samuel Claridge.

Society from various business associates and looking forward to an important position in its administration. He wrote to his brother Edward in Barbados that he had "bought 5000 acres of land of William Penn, and we are endeavoring to settle a society for trade," of which he expected to be one of the chief officers.

Thomas Holme was more than a month on his way to Pennsylvania when, on 29 May, the elections of the Society were held. As he probably had learned before the *Amity* sailed, he was named one of the committee of twelve appointed to live permanently in Pennsylvania, serving the interests of the Society. Claypoole had won the post he coveted, that of treasurer. Writing to John Spread on 30 May he said that the company had subscribed between five and six thousand pounds and would continue to accumulate funds for another month, when they would acquire and fit out a ship to arrive in the province before winter. Nicholas More was president of the Society; John Simcock deputy; himself, treasurer. An agent and six factors were chosen for the London officials, and twelve for Pennsylvania, among whom were Robert Turner, Thomas Holme, and William Haige. Three members of the committee, John Bezar, Nathaniel Allen, who had come on the *Bristol Factor*, and William Haige, who had come on the *John and Sarah*, were already in Pennsylvania when Thomas arrived. Griffith Jones would be a fellow passenger on the *Amity*. James Harrison was on the storm-battered *Submission*, which discharged its passengers at Choptank on Chesapeake Bay on 2 November 1682, leaving them to make their way to Pennsylvania as best they could. Among other passengers were Harrison's son-in-law Phineas Pemberton, who would be one of the most devoted of Penn's followers in the province, and Allis Dickinson, servant of Phineas, who married Thomas Holme's indentured servant, Edmund McVeagh.[9]

The *Amity* was to sail towards the end of April. By mid-April at latest Thomas Holme had been officially appointed surveyor general, although he probably had been told of his selection for the office some time earlier. On 15 April James Claypoole wrote again to the Rogers brothers, announcing that "my son John is to embark next week for Pennsylvania with Thomas Holme, to assist him in surveying the country," and on the eighteenth he repeated the news to Samuel Claridge, this time expecting the sailing "this week." Finally, on 20 April, he wrote jubilantly to his brother Edward, a merchant in Barbados,

---

[9] "Twenty-three Ships."

I have been at Gravesend with my son John, who is gone on the *Amity* . . . of Pennsylvania to be assisting the general surveyor, whose name is Thomas Holme, a very honest, ingenious, worthy man. . . . his employment is very creditable and if he be diligent and sober may come in a few years time to be profitable. However, it will be a present maintenance and keep him from ill company.

Whether Thomas Holme was flattered or irritated at having this young man specially commissioned as his assistant depends upon the degree of communication between the English Cromwellian remnant (James Claypoole was a brother-in-law of Cromwell's favorite daughter, Elizabeth) and the Irish ex-military Friends. Since seventeenth-century society was not immune to gossip, Thomas Holme may have suspected that this problem son might be difficult when beyond parental reach.

The inadequately dated account of "William Penn Esq. D^r. to Thomas Rudyard and Herbert Springett and al."[10] reveals much of the activity that preceded the *Amity* voyage. Here we find listed among many other items headed Trinity, 1662, fees for commissions in "vellom" to Charles Ashcom, Richard Noble, William Crispin, [John] Bezar, [Nathaniel] Allen, and [William] Haige. Ashcom and Noble, commissioned and established in Pennsylvania before Thomas Holme, later were among his deputies—a fact that would have varied significance for him later. Other items on this list relative to Thomas Holme's later history are statements for making and engrossing a catalogue of "all purchasers, two large skins, sent with the first ship and two fair copies thereof," for a total of £4, "expenses at Gravesend Besides Mark's charges of 12^d.: to write things to go in the ship, 12s," and "A bill of Sale of the Ship Amity to Wm Penn—0:2:0." A second column on the last full page of this account is headed: "mad: on bd and all Catallogs for Pss [passengers] at sevrall times—" includes a number of other items pertinent to Thomas Holme's work:

A 2^d. List wth. a Commission to sett out Land sent by Rich^d. Diamond . . . ffaire cop: thereof . . . Ingd [engrossed] Chart in Vellom 2 sets near 2 large skins each . . . A list of all Purchas^{es}. fro beginning new methodz [methodized (alphabetized)] and ingd wch. was sent aft. Tho: Holme . . . A Small Aditionall List—Methodizing . . . and Ingd . . . Cop: of the whole . . . A List of all the purchasers from the beginning for P . . . the same remade . . . to Pennsylvania Leases and Releases sent to B: ff. boxes for Seales and for carriage. . . .

---
[10] HSP, *Penn MSS, Private Correspondence* 1: 49.

In addition to his merchant's cargo Thomas Holme must have had on board also the basic instruments of his profession and a text book for the guidance of himself and his deputies, perhaps relics of the Down Survey. If "On board" refers to the *Amity*, patently the last list of purchasers was completed later, as is consistent with the heading of the column.

Laden and ready for departure, the *Amity* lay at Gravesend for at least a week awaiting favorable winds. During the last three weeks before they came, Penn was busy transacting further business related to the establishment of the province. On 18 April he conferred on Thomas Holme the commission that made him ultimately responsible for surveys of all the land of the province of Pennsylvania "for and during his natural life, he behaving himself honestly and faithfully in the said Office Trust and employment." He continued with a clause which Thomas Holme later found necessary to invoke in court: "And I hereby grant to the said Thomas Holme to take, receive and to his own use enjoy all and every such proffits and benefits for the Survey and advancement of the said Province or any part thereof. . . ." Three days after this commission was signed Penn issued another:

> To Cap[t]. Thomas Holmes Greeting. Reposing Special Trust and Confidence in thy integrity and Ability I do hereby Constitute and Appoint thee First Assistant to my cousin William Markham Deputy Goveno[r]. of Pennsylvania with him for me and in my name to act in all things relating to the good of the Province and also my own private affairs: for which this shall be thy Sufficient Warrant. Given under my hand and Seal at Gravesend the one and twentieth day of the Second Month in the year One Thousand and Six hundred Eighty and Two. William Penn.[11]

Thomas Holme was already to some extent prepared for the work of a surveyor general; being assistant to a deputy governor who stood in need of considerable assistance was not a simple assignment.

On 23 April the long-awaited good wind came, and the *Amity*'s sails billowed out, under the mastership of Richard Diamond, a bridegroom of three months and purchaser of land in Bucks County; and Thomas Holme was on his way to a new world.

For everyone on board except, perhaps, some of the crew, this was a voyage into an almost unknown world of brown-skinned people,

---

[11] *Patent Book* A-1, 1, Department of Community Affairs, Bureau of Land Records, Harrisburg, Pennsylvania. The original of the warrant is a parchment manuscript in the library of the New York Historical Society, cited by ACM 23: 12. It is printed in the *Magazine of American History* 8 (1882): 849.

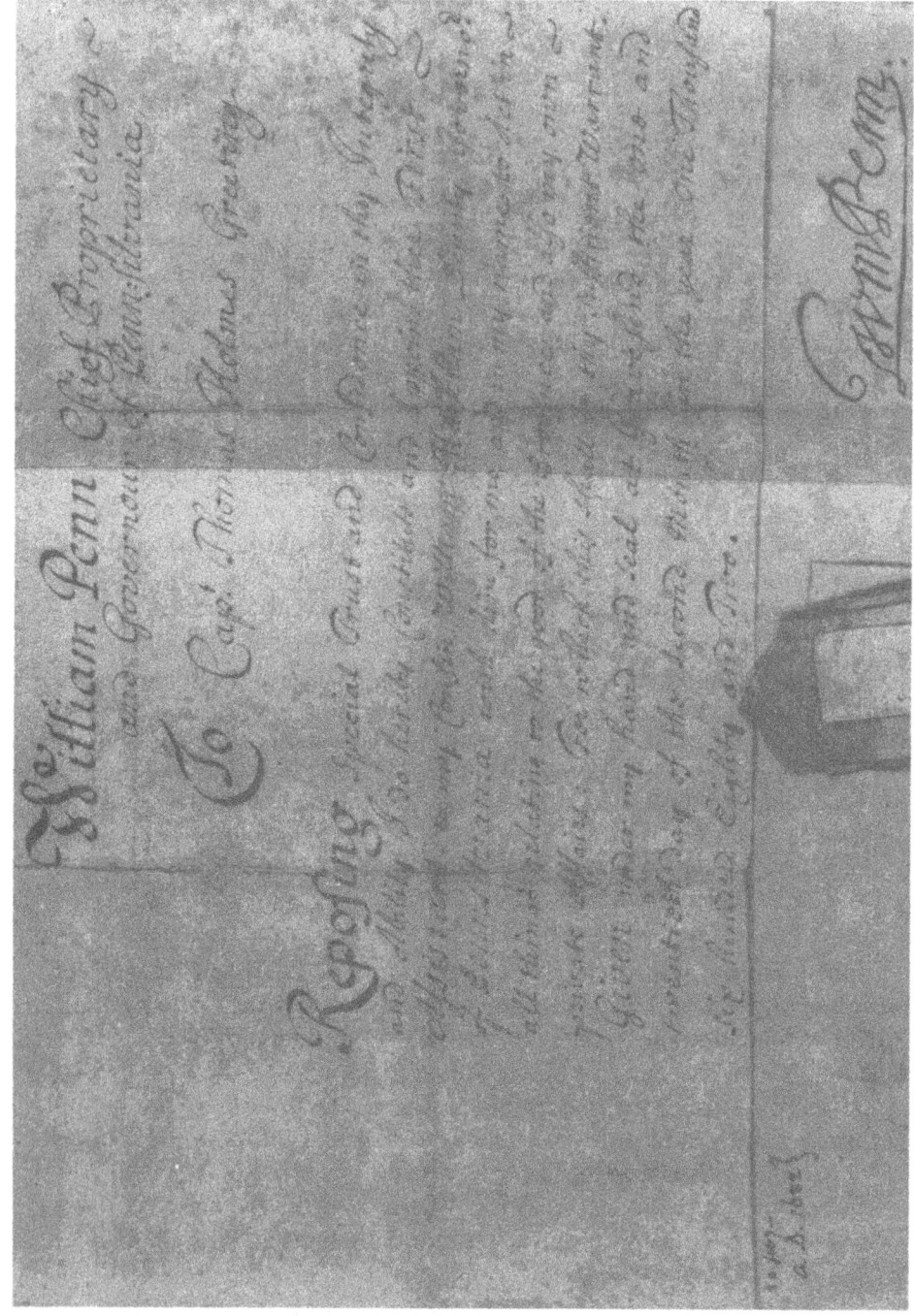

Fig. 11. Commission from William Penn to Thomas Holme.

exotic fruits, and strange birds and beasts reported by earlier voyagers, and the opportunity to build a new home on his own land. For Thomas in particular it would be a fresh start, after many losses and disappointments, as a great official in the province of William Penn.

The *Amity* had a long voyage. For at least the greater part of fourteen weeks Thomas paced the deck, saw to it that his children did likewise, dined on food chosen to stay edible on a long journey, pored over his map, and laid plans for the weeks ahead. He drilled Tryall and William in mathematics and surveying procedures and insisted that Hester and Elinor spend part of each day in reading and study, principally in Scripture and in Friends' devotional literature and memorials of their history. These must have included the books their father and Abraham Fuller had written.

As surveyor general Thomas Holme familiarized himself as far as possible with the territory for which he would bear heavy responsibility. Since there was no adequate map, he had to rely, like Penn himself, on maps made well before Pennsylvania came into being, sufficiently revised to show the expanse of the province along the western side of the Delaware. Watson suggests that Thomas Holme himself may have made the hybrid map used by Penn in 1681/82, which appears to have been a composite of the upper portion of the *Map of Virginia and Maryland* drafted for Lord Baltimore and published in 1670, and, apparently, "*A Mapp of Virginia, Maryland, New Jersey, New York, & New England*, [sold] by John Thornton at the Sundyall in the Minories and by Robert Greene att the Rose and Crowne in Belgrave. London." Robert Morden's *Map of Some of the South and East Bounds of Pennsylvania in America, Being Partly Inhabited*, sold by John Thornton at the Signe of England and Scotland and Ireland in the Minories, and by John Seller at his shop in Popeshead Alley in Cornhill, London, placed Philadelphia at the Schuylkill side of the angle at the juncture of the Schuylkill and the Delaware.[12]

Chesapeake and Delaware Bays and the lower part of the Delaware with their multitudinous tributaries spread like tangled fronds of bracken on the map, unlike the neat lines of Conniston Water and the Slaney. The southern place names and some of the personal names were already familiar to him. Robert Wade was what Sir William Petty would call titulado of Upland (Chester). Ephraim Hermann of New Castle, important in local government, also a surveyor, was the son of Augustine Hermann, the map maker, Baltimore's chief surveyor. Richard Noble, chief surveyor of Upland, with property in the north-

---

[12] *Annals*, 581; CLB, 132.

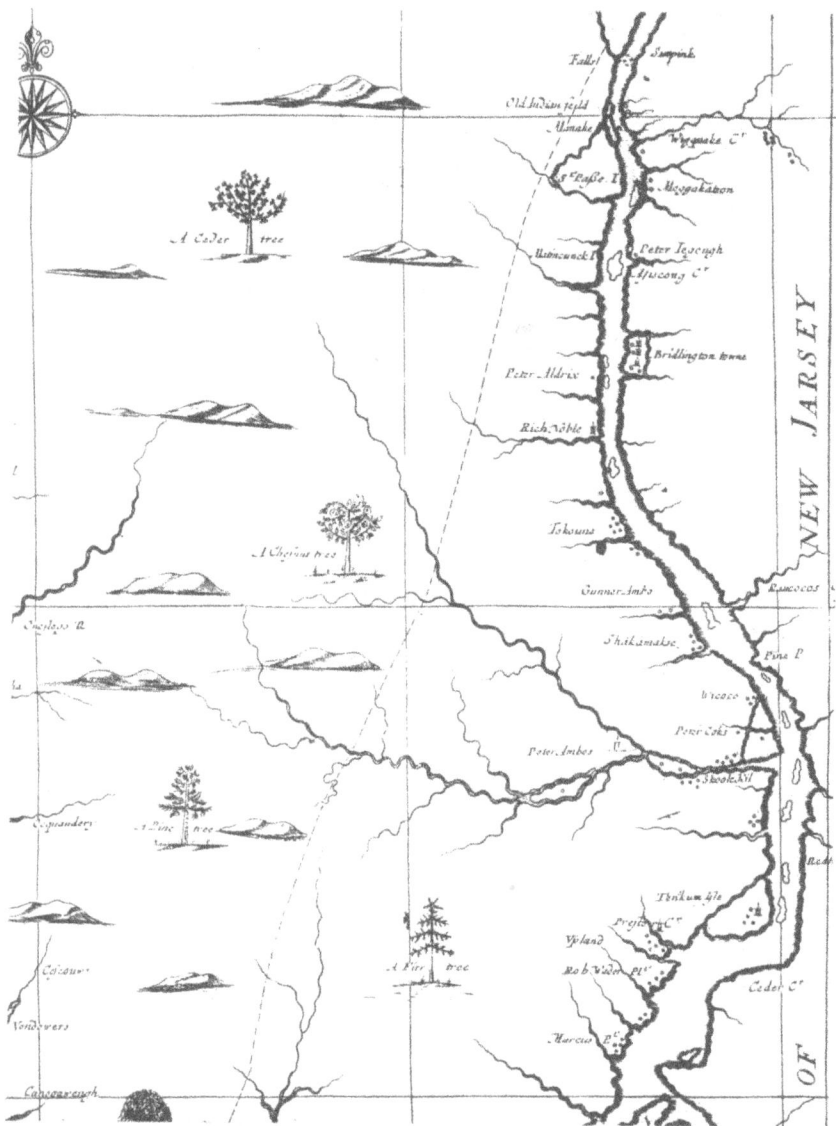

Fig. 12. Portion of Robert Morden's map showing placement of Philadelphia. Used with the permission of the Historical Society of Pennsylvania.

ern area, had come to Pennsylvania via New Jersey.[13] Names like Tenekum, Wicaco, and Shakamakse invoked mysterious images of the race he had yet to meet.

The map both intrigued and frustrated him. He tried to envision the sort of land that lay enclosed by these minor streams and water-

---

[13] *NJA* 1, 21: 555, 575. Cited by Roach, *PMHB* 92 (1968), 23.

ways and to estimate unknown distances from a few that were known. The next map—the first real map of the province of Pennsylvania—would be the work of his own hands.

Thomas Holme planned his agenda for the weeks that would intervene before the governor's arrival. At the head of the list of things to be done would be a briefing by Markham on the present state of affairs, particularly the matter of the boundary between the province of Pennsylvania and Maryland, the demesne of Charles Calvert Lord Baltimore. Probably next in urgency was the location of the capital city, also apparently entrusted to William Markham and other commissioners. He regretted that Markham was not a Friend, but he was the governor's cousin, and that in itself was sufficient recommendation. And Penn had entrusted him with the deputy governorship. Nevertheless, Thomas had an uneasy feeling that when Penn named him first assistant to Markham he heard an unspoken undertone that implied, "Take care of him."

Silas Crispin, too, would be able to tell him something about the situation in the province. Silas was a responsible, well-balanced young man. Thomas was not the only one of his party who looked forward to seeing Silas Crispin again. Hester had been surprisingly ready to say goodby to her friends in Wexford and Waterford and set out on this grand adventure.[14]

Why the voyage took so long is not recorded. No cargo had been designated for Barbados, and Claypoole assumed when writing to his brother Norton on 14 July that "they be safe at port long before this." Nevertheless, on other transatlantic voyages the *Amity* stopped at both Barbados and New York, and the same route may have been taken on this first crossing. The fact that these ports are not mentioned in the port books for this voyage does not preclude passengers having been delivered to them, since the books were concerned only with outgoing cargo.

Reverting to the reminiscences of the eighteenth-century William Crispin referred to earlier, we find his account of the *Amity*'s having sailed for Pennsylvania in the fall of 1681 and being blown off course during violent storms, finally arriving at Pennsylvania in the spring of

---

[14] Contrary to the Crispin tradition referred to above, Silas did not sail on the *Amity* with the Holme family. Balderston cites a reference to him in Chester County Court Records, 15, as a juror at Upland on 13 June 1682, from which she deduces that he sailed on the *John and Sarah*, which had arrived sometime late in 1681/82. Further evidence of his presence in Pennsylvania at this time is his signature on a memorandum of an Indian deed printed in *William Penn's Own Account of the Lenni Lenape or Delaware Indians*, revised ed., ed. ACM with a foreword by John E. Pomfret, 79.

1682. As Balderston points out, this was impossible, since William Penn's *Amity* was loading in England in February.

At this point a mystery ship, which Balderston dismissed as "wholly imaginary," enters into consideration. In a letter to an inquiring relative, John ap John, or John Jones, relates the story of his father's coming to Pennsylvania on a ship that left London under the auspices of William Penn (not, as Balderston states, *named* William Penn) in October, 1681, enduring a stormy passage, first, it appears, to Barbados and then to within sight of the coast of Delaware. There, with sails torn and rudder badly damaged, it turned back to Barbados. After the expenditure of three weeks and a large sum of money for repairs it returned without further trouble to the Delaware and reached Pennsylvania on 16 April 1682.[15]

The lading of such a ship for Pennsylvania is not listed in extant London port books, although its destination may have been given as Barbados or, as a mere supplement to preceding ships, it may have carried no commercial cargo. The only ship recorded as arriving at Upland in the spring of 1682 is the *John and Sarah*, which docked early enough for William Haige to have taken observations at New Castle before 9 March, but this does not preclude the arrival of another ship.

Balderston admits that, even allowing for the fallibility of memory, John ap John's story has the ring of truth. The ship on which Thomas John Evan sailed may well have been the smaller *Amity*, possibly utilized for the transportation of accumulating impatient passengers, perhaps following the *John and Sarah* and caught in the same storm, and afterward returned to its customary traffic with the continent. The *Amity* on which Thomas Holme embarked was a 240–300 ton vessel known also as the *Unity* and the *Adventure*, although the bill of sale of the ship *Amity* to William Penn written at Gravesend leaves no doubt as to its official title. Apparently it had sailed under the other names before it was acquired by Penn.

As the *Amity* sailed up the bay into the mouth of the great river, the passengers tried to identify inlets and creeks noted on the map. At last they sighted New Castle, the largest town that many of them would see until their own was established. Largely because of its good port and key situation it would be a source of bitter contention between the Penns and the Calverts for many years to come.

---

[15] CCHS, ACM, Box 41, *Works of William Penn* 123, *Selections from Port Books*, PRO, CO 13, no. 6: Ship *Amity* of London, 240 tons, from New York, Richard Diamond . . . entered Barbados 21 October 1682.

Although New Castle was the first port of call for vessels arriving from Europe, it was to the village of Upland a few miles up the river that the company turned its attention. The site of the capital city of the new province was still an open question when the *Amity* left England, but Upland was regarded as the almost certain choice. Thomas Holme looked out over the little group of buildings and down at the gathering of people waiting anxiously for news from England and for arriving new settlers, possibly for William Penn himself. Behind him pressed his own party—Elinor and Hester, Tryall and William, Edmund McVeagh, John Fletcher, John Osborne, perhaps John Claypoole, some of the members of the Free Society of Traders.[16]

They saw a small, unprepossessing village. A few buildings had the look of business or governmental headquarters; the rest apparently were dwellings on a rather modest scale. All the land visible from their vantage point aboard ship seemed already to be occupied. The commissioners had been directed by Penn to see to the accommodations of the settlers who had embarked with them until they could secure their own. Thomas Holme hoped that their commission extended to his shipmates and the increasing numbers following close behind. He hoped also that Penn had not been too sanguine when he assured prospective emigrants that the already established inhabitants, "Sweads, Dutch, English . . . are capable of giving entertainment to New Comers, till they can provide for themselves."[17]

---

[16] CCHS, ACM, vol. 119. Printed in ACM, *Narratives*, 455, n. 4. For Balderston's comment and the story of the *Amity* and on John ap John's letter, see "Twenty-three Ships," 65–67. For the arrival of the *John and Sarah* and Haige's activities, see p. 33. On the matter of nomenclature, see *London Port Book* E 190/109/1, the *Collector's Book*, in which lading is listed as taking place on 22 February and 24 March 1682, in *Unity*; on 24 March in *Adventure*; and on 27 and 28 in *Amity*, all Richard Diamond for Pennsylvania; and, among other entries, in *Amity*, Michael Holmes, for Danzig (modern Gdańsk) and other continental ports. For the letter of John Jones, 1725, see *Narratives*, 453. While Balderston's article was in progress a mutual acquaintance mentioned a suspicion that young John Claypoole had jumped ship and completed the voyage later. His father's surprise at not hearing of his arrival from John, Thomas Holme, or anyone else, then having heard that someone had seen a letter from Barbados, apparently in John's writing, and annoyance with the Rogers brothers for having retained John's belongings from the sea, and, finally, his relief at learning that John at last was active in surveying (all in CLB).

[17] "Address to the Reader," printed below the map of 1681.

Chapter 7

Initiation

Markham or, if he was not present, the official he had appointed to meet any ship that came, was waiting to see Diamond, the master, and Thomas Holme, assistant to the deputy governor and surveyor general of the province. The first ship to arrive since May had been eagerly awaited. Probably the Holme family was temporarily installed in the house that Markham had secured for the use of Penn.[1] Markham himself had moved some distance up river to the estate of Thomas Fairman, also a surveyor of note from New Jersey and a member of Markham's council.

For Thomas Holme after he had been introduced to the townspeople, a briefing by Markham, Haige, and the other commissioners was first in order, since Markham's report had not reached Penn before the *Amity* sailed. One of the first things he learned was that the Wicaco area rather than Upland would be the site of the city. And there was much more.

After a year in Pennsylvania, including two summers that he had found debilitating, Markham was more realistic than romantic about land problems. In an unwarranted spirit of optimism King Charles had written to Lord Baltimore, proprietor of Maryland, in April of 1681,

---

[1] For the history of this transaction see "Planting," 23, n. 33. In estimating the times of Markham's and Holme's moves to Shackamaxon it is assumed that Fairman entered them chronologically in his account given to Penn. (See Release, Fairman to Penn, Philadelphia Deed Book D-13, 274, cited in "Planting," 23, n. 33, and reprinted in Westcott, *History*, 81.) This statement also describes exploratory trips and Fairman's assistance to Markham and Holme on various occasions.

Fig. 13. George Calvert, third Lord Baltimore. Used with permission of the Enoch Pratt Free Library, Baltimore.

apprizing him of Penn's grant and commending him to Baltimore's neighborliness in defining the line between their holdings and all other matters of joint concern. He had urged the same solicitude on the part of Penn. Markham had been the bearer of both of the king's letters.

Both proprietors wanted the boundary settled as soon as possible, and both were in good faith in placing the line at the fortieth parallel. The difficulty lay in the wide discrepancy between their conceptions of the location of that meridian. Penn, relying on the opinion of Quaker residents, was under the misapprehension that it lay below Poole's Island in Chesapeake Bay, which would have given him the outlet to the ocean that he deemed essential to the province. Baltimore was convinced that it lay at Wade's property at Upland. Markham, having arrived at Upland in June, toward the end of August had gone to Maryland to confer with Baltimore concerning the boundary. There he was overcome by the heat, and the autumn passed in recurrent illnesses and conflicting calendars, until finally the project was postponed until spring. When Haige arrived about the end of February or early in March, his first move was to take observations at the head of Chesapeake Bay. The results of these were more favorable to Baltimore than to Penn, since they tended to confirm the calculations of Baltimore's surveyor, Augustine Hermann.[2]

Baltimore had opened negotiations again in May. He appointed a four-man commission to sail as soon as weather permitted to Hermann's house, to contact Penn's representatives, and to proceed at once to establish the precise location of the fortieth parallel. The attempt was fruitless. Markham had been understandably reluctant to confront Baltimore with contradictions unsupported by evidence, especially when the instruments he had lent to Hermann—the small one supplied by Penn and the large "sextile" [sextant?] he had borrowed from Col. Lewis Morris of New York—went against the decision he was expected by Penn to produce. They agreed to meet again in September. This time Thomas Holme would be present.

Meanwhile, conscious of the size of the task before him, Thomas Holme grew restive during the week's delay in the unloading of the *Amity* and the two ships, the *Freeman* and the *Hester and Hannah*, that had followed within a week. Markham left on a business trip to the Falls of the Delaware, deputing Ralph Smith to receive the goods.[3]

---

[2] *Letters of Lord Baltimore*, MdA 4 (1887): 348, 375. For full account of Penn-Baltimore proceedings, see *MdA*, vols. 5 and 17.
[3] Markham to Phillip Ford, *Lenni Lenape*, 70.

Thomas Holme in the meantime talked with the townspeople, made the acquaintance of surveyors who would be his deputies, and learned what he could through conversations and short excursions into the surrounding territory about this world in which he had committed himself to live for the rest of his life.

Eventually Smith saw to the unloading of the ships, and the wharf was stacked with trunks, barrels, crates, and boxes, and thronged with owners trying to collect their possessions. In time the *Amity* was relieved of her cargo and sailed away to New York, There she would pick up another cargo for Barbados, and thence go on to London.[4] She left behind a distressed erstwhile passenger, John Martin, whose belongings had vanished before he could retrieve them. Thomas Holme picked up his own goods and deposited them in such space as he could acquire for the time being.

Markham returned. The briefings continued, often during exploratory expeditions. For all the differences in age and background—Markham was ten years younger than Thomas Holme—the two men formed an amicable working team that was to last through many years of loyal service to the Founder. Now they set about to accomplish as much as possible before William Penn arrived.

The choice of site for the capital city was of paramount importance.

Markham and Fairman had followed the Proprietor's instructions to take soundings along the Delaware. These, as they and Thomas Holme reviewed them, were encouraging, indicating as they did that large ships could sail far up the river, thus leaving open various options for the site. Commissioners Nathaniel Allen and John Bezer had arrived in December 1681, and had been able to observe to some extent the amount of land occupied along the river and navigable creeks. From the start Upland, originally favored by Penn, was out of the question as a capital city, already extensively settled as its environs were and, what made it a precarious choice, apparently dangerously near the edge of the Proprietor's grant. Fairman had taken soundings on the Schuylkill and, according to his own account, had placed Philadelphia "upon Delaware River."

Markham and the commissioners had at first tentatively chosen the general area of the angle between the two great rivers, the Schuylkill and the Delaware. Their announcement of this choice did not reach Penn until after the *Amity* had sailed, but arrived in such time that

---

[4] CCHS, ACM, Box 41, *Works of William Penn*, vol. 123, *Selections from Port Books*, PRO, CO 13. No. 6: Ship *Amity* of London, 240 tons, from New York, Richard Diamond . . . entered Barbados 21 October 1682.

James Claypoole, apparently relying on Morden's map, had been able to write to his brother Norton at Deal on 14 July that he had "a 100 acres where our capital city is to be upon the river, near Schuylkill and Peter Cock's."

A few miles upstream they had discovered a more promising location, the most important feature of which was a cove large enough to admit small vessels, with two tributaries that would accommodate lesser craft. Beyond this, conveniently high banks rose above a channel deep enough for large ships. The river frontage and land reaching westward comprised some three hundred acres. Thomas Fairman was appointed to negotiate for it with the Swansons, major landholders in the area. By early autumn 1682, they had agreed to Penn's offer of a larger quantity of land elsewhere for release of territory needed for the city, and the first soil for the capital was secured.

Pleased though he was with the purchase, Thomas nevertheless looked with misgivings at the initial sketch of this small wedge-shaped tract and again at Penn's stipulations for the laying out of the capital. The city itself was to be surrounded by ten thousand acres of liberty land; beyond that lay a vast territory to be surveyed for individual purchasers and companies. Obviously, the tract secured from the Swansons would not accommodate the generous proportions of the city and liberty land that William Penn envisioned.

Among the many concerns that awaited Thomas Holme, one had a special quality of initiation about it: his first communication with the Indians. Before the original commissioners had embarked for America in October of 1681 William Penn had composed a letter to the Indians, which he asked to be read to them at an early date. No mention of such a reading is extant, however, perhaps because the document had been entrusted to the unfortunate Crispin. In his instructions to the commissioners Penn had admonished them to be "tender of offending" the Indians: "Be grave," he wrote; "they love not to be smiled on," and to learn, "by honest spies," of any attempt to subvert them from cooperation with him and the Province.

Before the *Amity* sailed the following April, Penn delivered into the hands of his newly commissioned surveyor general a second letter to the Indians, dated 21 April 1682. It was meant to greet and reassure the natives. As soon as he became familiar with his surroundings, therefore, Thomas Holme got in touch with an interpreter, probably Lasse Cock, one of Markham's councillors, who served most frequently in that capacity, and sent messages to the local kings, inviting them to meet and hear the letter of the great white chieftain and friend who would come soon to meet them.

Thomas Holme had already met some of the Indians who visited the white settlements along the rivers, bartering game and goods to the advantage of both. The Indians on their part had been familiar for a generation with the settlers. They had even sold land to individuals and small groups of newcomers. This invitation, however, was a new and dignified approach to them as the original landholders of the area. They came, these chieftains and their chosen followers, and stood silent before this tall bearded man with a face brown and leathery from a long summer at sea, with companions whom they already knew as important members of the great new settlement.

If he was a trifle shaken as he stood before the assemblage of reputed savages, Thomas Holme did not show his feelings. He greeted the assembly gravely. Then he opened the letter he had practiced reading many times and read in a loud voice still reminiscent of Lancashire, pausing phrase by phrase as his interpreter translated into the Lenni Lenape language. The letter opens with a prayer that "the great God, who is the power and wisdom that made you and me" may incline the hearts of the Indians to "righteousness, love, and peace," and with the assurance that he himself "seeks nothing but the honor of His name, and that we, who are His workmanship, may do that which is well-pleasing to Him." He concludes with the practical reassurances.

> The man which delivers this unto you is my special friend, sober, wise, and loving: you may believe him. I have already taken care that none of my people wrong you, by good laws I have provided for that purpose; nor will I ever allow any of my people to sell rum, to make your people drunk. If anything should be out of order, expect, when I come it shall be mended, and I shall bring you some things of our country that are useful and pleasing to you. So I rest in the love of our God that made us.
> I am your loving Friend.
> England, 21st of second month, 1682 William Penn.[5]

After the ceremonial presentation of Penn's gifts and expressions of mutual respect and hope for the blessing of God upon the relations between the Indians and Penn's English followers, the Indians with-

---

[5] CCHS, ACM, *Penn MSS*, Box 2, 1: 14 October 1681; Hazard, *Annals*, 258. A corrected draft of the first letter to the Indians dated 18 September 1681, is included in the HSP *Penn-Forbes Collection* 1: 48. See also Hazard, *Annals*, 532. The original of this letter is in HSDA; printed, *PMHB* 19 (1895): 413.

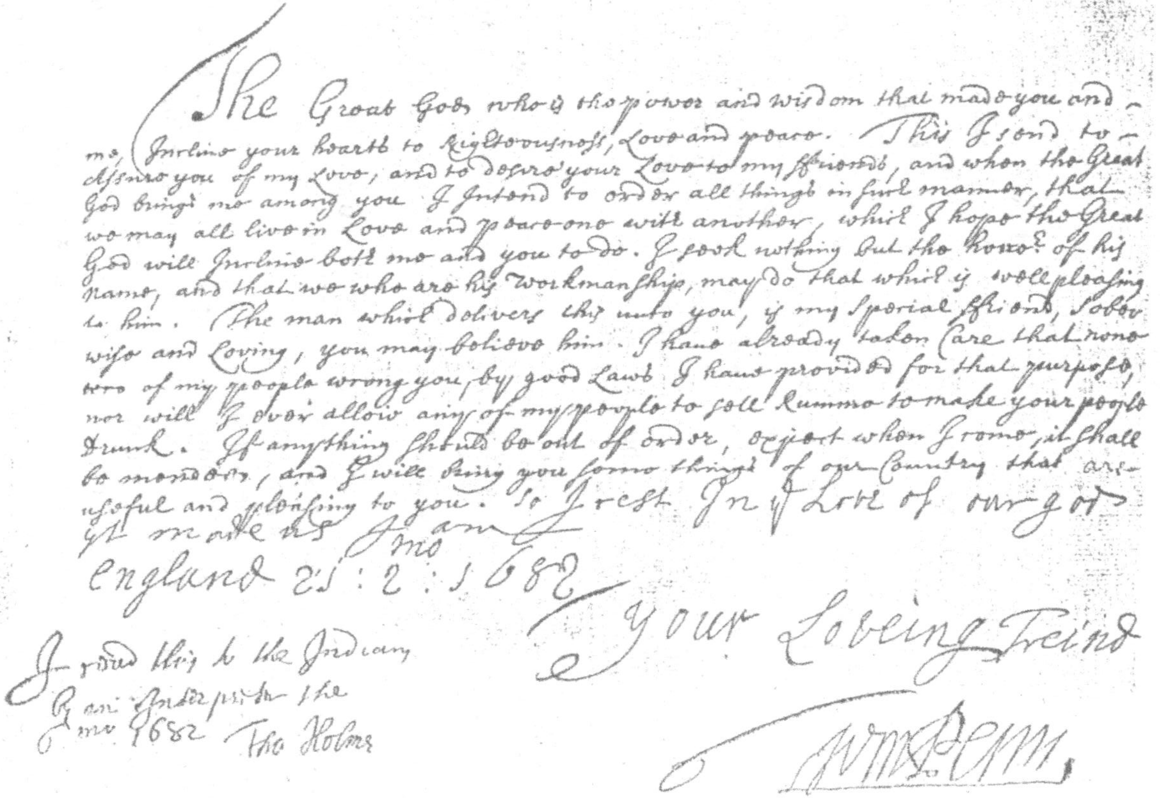

The Great God who hath the power and wisdom that made you and me, Inclines your hearts to Righteousnes, Love and peace. This I sent to assure you of my love, and to desire your Love to my friends, and when the Great God brings me among you, I intend to order all things in such manner, that wee may all live in Love and peace one with another, which I hope the Great God will Incline both me and you to do. I seek nothing but the honor of his name, and that wee who are by birth mankind, may do that which is well pleasing to him. The man which delivers this unto you, if my special friend, sober wise and Loving, you may believe him. I have already taken care that none of my people wrong you, by good Laws I have provided for that purpose, nor will I ever allow any of my people to sell Rumme to make your people drunck. If anything should be out of order, expect when I come it shall be mended, and I will bring you some things of our Country that are useful and pleasing to you. So I rest in ye Love of ye great god that made us all

England 21: 2: 1682   Your Loveing freind

                                          WILL PENN

To: ye Kings of the Indians
Capt Gould deliver the
   for 8682 / Tho Holme

Fig. 14. William Penn's letter to the Indians with Holme's signature. With permission of FLL.

drew into the forest. Thomas Holme looked after them until they disappeared. They had been grave, and, with no abrogation of their own dignity, respectful to the representative of the great man whose coming they anticipated.

Thomas Holme was relieved when the session was over. Nearly six hundred thousand acres of the Indians' land had been sold, and he was responsible for seeing it laid out in peace to the satisfaction of hundreds of strangers. Being human, he was nonetheless eager to be about the business for the reason that five thousand of those acres belonged to him, with the purchase of another five thousand already arranged for. This, with what he had salvaged in Ireland, would amount to approximately what he had received as back pay for his military service, and it spoke only of peace and security for him and his family. Back at his desk Thomas Holme sat looking for a moment at the document he had just read, then dipped his quill and wrote at the bottom of it, "I read this to the Indians, by an interpreter, the sixth month [August], 1682—Thomas Holme." It was his first official act in Pennsylvania.

With the terms of his commission before him, "to enter into, survey, and admeasure, or cause to be entered into, surveyed, and admeasured, (with all resonable expedition,) all the said province of Pennsylvania," Thomas Holme was acutely aware of his mission. He gathered together such facts as he knew about this land. There were settlements along the Delaware and the Schuylkill, but most of it was not measured nor even explored. He did not know how large it was or how far away were the sources of the streams. The Schuylkill, he had already learned, was a much more significant stream than it appeared on the map, and its course less regular. What were pictured as short, wide, almost evenly placed tributaries of the Delaware would have to be examined, since access to water, particularly to navigable streams or rapids good for mills, was important to settlers.

Ships that had taken advantage of spring and summer weather for the long voyage to Pennsylvania were arriving with immigrants and promises of more to come. After the *Freeman* and the *Hester and Hannah* already mentioned came the *Lyon* on 13 August, with a contingent of Welsh settlers who would give rise to extra problems for some time. The next day the *Friendship* arrived, and the day after that the *Mary*. In spite of the fact that the liberties were not yet determined, Penn and the commissioners were giving warrants for land in all three areas concerned—city lots, liberty land, and country at large. One more ship, the *Society*, arrived on an unspecified day late in the month, and the initial *Agreements Made in England* had in themselves been declared warrant for surveys.

With a shrewd and appreciative eye Thomas Holme studied the quality and variety of unoccupied land along the Delaware above the site of the capital, and the courses, depth, and currents of its most important streams. Borrowing horses from Fairman and sometimes accompanied by the surveyor himself, he rode a few miles into the interior. On 17 August, two weeks to the day after his arrival in the country, he ordered his deputies "By order and direction from the Governour and Commissioners for Setting out Lands to the purchasers in Pennsylvania,"

> to survey and lay out for my own use the quantity of 500 acres of land contagious to Capt. Wm. Markham upon the lower or western side of the Delaware river, and unto William Haig and Thomas Rudyard 750 acres next unto mine and 500 acres unto Silas Crispin next contagious, observing to allow but 20 pole or perch to the river side for each hundred acres and to return to me a true duplicate of the original field work and protracted figure, which are to remain in my office. Date 17-6-1682. Thomas Holme, Surveyor General, to Richard Noble, Thomas Fairman, Charles Ashcomb, or any of them.[6]

Except for the order for 247 acres to be laid out to William Cecil on 11 August, these seem to have been the earliest of Thomas Holme's orders to deputies. The area was prestigious, with only Markham's tract between it and the Proprietor's Manor of Pennsbury, and the recipients were men of consequence at the beginning of the province.

The tracts would be relatively easy to survey. Their five hundred-acre tracts entitled Thomas Holme and Silas Crispin to one hundred pole (rods) or 1,650 feet—the equivalent of two and a half standard city blocks each—of frontage on the Delaware River, and Haige and Rudyard to 2,475 pole, or approximately three and three-quarters block equivalents each. It would then be only a matter of simple arithmetic to determine the length of the third side of each tract—each of which would be two and a half miles. The angle of this third line could be easily determined by a protractor or any of a variety of simple instruments. Leybourn had favored simplicity of both instruments and techniques, and no doubt whenever possible Thomas Holme followed his judgment. There were not sufficiently significant elevations here to require more sophisticated devices for measuring hills in order to include such extra land as they would contribute to the simple total.

---

[6] Department of Community Affairs, BLR, Hbg. *Dept. of Surveys Order Book*, 1682–1693, 87.

The diagonal drift of the river, however, gave to the interior boundary of these tracts a saw tooth edge, as illustrated in the map of 1687. It is possible that these surveys were made entirely with the use of the chain and the plane table.

On 12 September Thomas Holme gave further orders to lay out land to Haige and Rudyard. Two days later, on warrants from Markham, two more pieces of land were laid out to Thomas Holme, and a tract later described as "lying Southwest of Susquehanna Street and marked Hannah Salters on Holme's map," which joined the first tract on the southwest. This came to be his Well Spring Plantation. On 27 September six hundred acres were ordered laid out to Thomas Holme in right of Samuel Claridge. This was a beautifully situated triangle of land lying in the bend of Poquessing Creek and bounded on the south by a fine tributary of the creek. This Thomas Holme called his Shaftesberrie Plantation, which he later sold to Nicholas Rideout. Claridge, who received payment for six hundred acres through John Tottenham on 6 August, seems to have purchased his five thousand acres to accommodate Thomas, who eventually purchased the entire amount.

The complications that might arise over the settling of large tracts had been foreshadowed in September, when Penn's attorney, Thomas Rudyard, a prominent and aggressive New Jerseyite, presented his warrant and received his land, only to have his possession of it challenged by John Bowman, who a few days later presented a warrant from William Penn for what he believed to be the same tract. Both men blamed Thomas Holme for the confusion, and took the matter to the justices of the peace for decision. The verdict was that Thomas Holme had legally issued the order for the survey to Rudyard, who had rightful possession of the land. On the map of the province published in 1687 the two contestants are seated on the same tract.

Thomas Holme looked with some satisfaction at this expanse of property held by Penn's cousin and deputy, Markham; himself, the surveyor general; Rudyard, Penn's attorney; and Silas Crispin, Penn's cousin and his own son-in-law apparent.

If he was complacent about the arrangment his enjoyment of it was short-lived. Less than a month later he received Penn's warrant to lay out land between the tract of Markham and himself to Thomas Bowman. Markham and the commissioners, who issued the warrant, must have known that the tract was already occupied by Rudyard, but they were not up to challenging the Proprietor's order, or were more than willing to replace the somewhat irascible Rudyard. Thomas Holme could only say:

I have given warrant for other lands to be laid out there, but lest they may come to hand in time enough, thou art to observe to begin at Samuel Clifts and so lay out to Griffith Jones 500 acres next to Silas Crispin, 500 acres next to myself, and the remainder betwixt that and Capt. Markham's bounds to lay out and divide equally between Thos. Rudyard and Will Haigs, so that Th. Rudyard be laid out next to mine.[7]

On 26 October Thomas Bowman obtained a warrant for survey, apparently in the same area, which instigated a disagreement that William Penn himself was called upon to arbitrate nearly two years later. He referred the matter to a committee, who on 31 July decided that

the subsequent warrant & said purchase for Thomas Bowman could not directly operate to lay out the tract of land for Thomas Bowman because the same contents were particularly included in the prior warrants to Thomas Rudyard & surveyed in effect as being signally & especially bounded by the warrants thereof, as lying between the land of Capt. Markham & mine (said Sur. Gen.).[8]

According to what is allegedly the earliest printed version of the map sent by Thomas Holme to William Penn in the spring or summer of 1687, it appears that part of the solution of the problem was Thomas Holme's and Silas Crispin's abandonment of their share of the riverfront property in favor of choice tracts elsewhere. Markham had moved; the lion and the lamb lay down peacefully beside the river.

The map shows property on the Delaware, beginning with the lower line of "The Proprietary manor of Penns-berry" and extending to the island just above "Bridlington" (Burlington), belonging to William Dungan, John Tully, Mordecai Bowden, Thomas Dungan, Clement Dundan, and Richard Lundy on one large tract, Thomas Bowman and Thomas Rudyard on an adjoining tract, William Haige on a smaller tract, and Christopher Taylor, Francis Richardson, and Griffith Jones, each occupying a tract the size of Haige's. A tract of the same size below theirs is divided between Edmond Bennet and Samuel Clifts.

Above this battery of surveys, its lower margin saw-toothed by their irregular projection but with an even northeastern line and approximately half a mile on Neshaminy Creek lies a large tract bearing Thomas Holme's name. The smooth upper line of this property was of obvious advantage to surveyors, who were plagued by accusations

---

[7] CCHS, ACM, Box 41, *Works of William Penn*, vol. 123.
[8] CCHS, ACM, Box 331.

of having made surveys that were irregular in either the figurative or the literal sense of the word. The jagged lower edge would give them practice in triangulation.

This was not the last difficulty Thomas Holme would have with overlapping surveys, usually because of warrants issued by different sources. They demonstrate the pertinacity of the purchasers and the endurance of the surveyor general who had to issue the orders.

Within this period of surveys for important and enterprising early warrantees Thomas Holme was introduced into another initiatory experience: his first encounter with Lord Baltimore. Encouraged perhaps by the presence of an official assistant, surveyor, and senior citizen who enjoyed the full confidence of his exacting cousin, Markham again acceded to the pushing of Penn and the pulling of Baltimore. With Thomas Holme, Haige, and others, he set out for the meeting that was, according to Baltimore, to have taken place at the head of Chesapeake Bay. The report of the meeting from Lord Baltimore's viewpoint, although delivered with some bias in the *Archives of Maryland*, is probably factually accurate. It reads, in part:

> . . . in September 1682, his L^{opp} with the same Comm^{rs} went up the Bay; of which Capt Markham . . . gave assurance of his readinesse to attend; But instead of that Markham goes to the head of Delaware, and there keepes out of the way untill the fireing of some Gunns in Delaware gave Markham some confidence to beleeve the L B was return'd from New Castle, where his L^{opp} was forct to goe to find the Gentleman, as also to Upland, where Markham came at last, not imagineing to find his L^{opp} there; But there to his great Confusion he mett the L. B.: Tho' noe business was don. . . .

Baltimore, furious at Markham's elusiveness, attributes it to Penn's orders. After further complicated moves of pursuit and evasion narrated in detail, Baltimore's secretary concludes this portion of his account by stating that

> at the water side at Upland just afore his taking leave of Markham, Major Homes and Mr William Haige, and many more Quakers, he spoke thus to Capt Markham. S^r you know that by a Private observation taken here yesterday, this very spott Lies about twelve miles due South from the Degree of 40 North Latitude and that therefore this plantation of Robert Wades is soe many miles within the North Bound of my Charter. Accordingly he claimed the land and taxes it would produce.[9]

---

[9] *MdA* 17: 156, 159.

From the official account of the meeting preserved among the British *State Papers, Colonial,* and reprinted in Volume 5 of the *Archives of Maryland* we learn the dates of Markham's and, presumably, Thomas Holme's peregrinations at this time. These lasted from shortly after Markham wrote to Baltimore on 8 September until the twenty-fourth of the month. They included a trip to East New Jersey, from which Markham returned with "such a disordered countenance and odd behaviour as was easily perceived by all the Company."[10] The report would seem to justify Penn's anxieties about his cousin's reliability.

There was no gainsaying the results of the observations of both parties: the fortieth parallel lay far north of what William Penn considered the necessary lower limit of his grant.

On 27 September Baltimore returned to Hermann's to await a further meeting with Markham. Instead, he received a letter stating that the "persons most concerned for the Government" would not consent to the meeting because the Quakers objected to Baltimore's claiming Chichester, a few miles south of Upland. Thomas Holme, as assistant to the deputy governor and still the assertive Quaker of Irish days, must have been one of these. The contestants agreed to meet again in the spring.

If the conference with Lord Baltimore had accomplished anything at all, it had worsened the problem of the boundary. It was one with which Penn himself, and only he, could cope. Markham and Holme could only return to headquarters and make what preparations they could for the arrival of the Proprietor.

The whole affair was a jarring one for Thomas Holme. It presaged the persistent tension he would experience between the integrity of his office and the interests of his employer and longtime friend, and it revealed something of the nature of his office as assistant to the deputy governor.

Markham's task was a difficult one to which, perhaps, he was not altogether suited. Penn himself had some doubts about his appointment. In a letter of 18 October 1681 he had offered his cousin an alternative: "Now I shall tell thee, that if thy inclinations rather run to a sea life, I shall putt thee in Command of a vessel to carry People & goods betwixt this country and that . . . the profit is more, & I think the credit not less. . . . "[11] Markham may have considered the

---

[10] *MdA*, vol. 5.

[11] There may have been a touch of irony here. Markham does not strike one as being exactly of the sea-going sort. Later, writing from Kensington, Penn asks Harrison to see that Markham "do not dishonour me, nor himself, by idleness and prodigality, he was promised me very fair" (CCHS, ACM, 27, 283: 4).

deputyship the lesser of two evils. His health was poor, and, although he had successfully negotiated land purchases with the Indians, he appears generally, when confronted with superior adversaries, to have preferred discretion to valor. In the present situation all the evidence was against the decision he was expected to produce. Baltimore, with generations of aristocracy behind him and almost royal status in his own province, was a formidable adversary, and Markham was not only inexperienced in diplomacy but lacking in authority (if he possessed the judgment) to make and enforce decisions. Thomas Holme had met Markham apparently for the first time only a little more than a month before and had had no previous experience with Baltimore. He was nevertheless committed to supporting and, probably, in Penn's mind, advising this superior officer who was ten years his junior. In his capacity as surveyor general he would be at times a buffer between the Proprietor and dissatisfied settlers. If he had experienced a certain élan at his appointment a little of the radiance was dissipated by this trip.

Meanwhile, on the horizon was the matter of the Free Society of Traders. Every ship brought some subscribers. Fortunately they were eager enough to make at least temporary arrangements for themselves that they were willing to await the arrival of the officers of the society and the Proprietor himself for any concerted action.

There had been a merciful interval of three weeks without new ship arrivals. Now traffic picked up again with the coming of the *Golden Hind* and the *Samuel* on 18 September, the latter probably bearing Penn's additional list of purchasers, earmarked "to be sent after Thomas Holme" in Rudyard and Springett's statement alluded to above. The *Friends' Adventure* and the *Providence* arrived a little over a week later, on 27 and 29 September, and the *Hopewell* on 3 or 4 October. On 22 October the *Lamb* reached Upland. Each ship brought fresh expectation of the longed-for coming of the Proprietor himself on the *Welcome*, which was loading in London in July, and of the Society's ship, the *Jeffrey*.

It was a busy, sometimes exasperating, fall. Hordes of settlers had arrived, credentials in hand, expecting to have their land set out at once or to build ships and home factories before winter. They had to be pacified, and temporary shelter had to be found for them. Some were able to rent from earlier settlers. Some necessary procedures had to await Penn's arrival.

In the meantime the surveyor general and his colleagues continued to explore sections of the hundreds of thousands of acres for the surveying of which he would be responsible and show and order surveys for tracts for purchasers prepared to commence clearing space and building houses at once. With an eye to the necessity of expanding the plot already secured for the capital, Thomas Holme gave special attention to the area that lay behind it to the west. About two miles distant the Schuylkill ran nearly parallel to the Delaware for a mile or so. The land between was reasonably high, especially at the center, with a few streams and marshes in the eastern part and tributaries working their way through land that was for the most part low and marshy to the Schuylkill on the west. Except along the rivers the tract was a jungle of vines, underbrush, and tall trees, inhabited by snakes and wild animals and frequented by Indians. Only hardy settlers desperate to establish themselves could make their individual allotments habitable before winter.[12]

Tracts in the liberty lands were in demand as being nearest to the capital city and small enough to be at least partially cleared before the weather changed. The date of the final decision about the extent of the city and the bounds of the liberties seems not to have been reached until Penn arrived. In general, apart from the already almost fully occupied river fronts, the liberties would comprise the land between Frankford Creek on the northeast and Mill Creek, a large tributary of Darby Creek, on the west. Beyond the as yet undetermined upper limit of this area it was possible to lay out larger holdings.

Thomas Holme looked from the list of land sales to the mysterious hills and forests and streams, gathering such information as he could, conscious of the apprehension of previous settlers and the grudging observation of some of the already practicing surveyors, chief among whom would be his host for the winter, Thomas Fairman, perhaps also to the budding rivalry among the First Purchasers themselves. To these considerations was added the perfectly understandable eagerness of all the arrivals to be settled. This was a far cry from the surveying of Ireland, most of which had been traversed before the surveyors set out, as equals and under direction, aided by preliminary descriptions of the land, to lay down its portraiture for Sir William Petty's big maps. And could he, despite the reassurances of William Penn and the formal friendliness of his initial experience with them, rely upon the Indians to be less hostile than the dispossessed Irish?

Insecure though he may have felt at times, Thomas Holme's explo-

---

[12] For a description of the uncleared land see the abstract of a letter of Thomas Peskell [Paschall] of Pennsylvania to his friends J. J. of Chippenham (ACM, *Narratives*, 250). Paschall arrived on the *Society* in August, and the returns on Surveys of two five-hundred-acre tracts in his name were recorded on 19 September 1682 (PA, OR, 3, 11).

rations were not all hardship. The man from Monk Coniston could not but enjoy the flaming autumn hillsides, the smoky ridges, the intensely blue rivers, the "cricks" with their borders of lush weeds and russet bracken. Bregurteen had commanded a wide prospect, but there was a harshness about the furze and the gnarled trees of the upper Wexford landscape that was all too consonant with the human hostility of the Englishman's life in Ireland. Here, Thomas Holme was on genuinely English soil again, in a setting that, except for its tangle of trees and vines, might have been a gentler version of the fells of Furness.

Despite the pressures of his position, things were looking up for Thomas Holme, Gentleman, or Captain Thomas Holme, as he was variously called. Of the eleven thousand acres he had now purchased, enough remained for the claiming of choice tracts in other areas. He was in a position to help his daughters to good marriages, and his two young sons were just arrived at an age to aid him in his duties and to establish themselves in peaceful and profitable pursuits far different from his own initiation into adulthood in a civil war. William, seventeen now, was helping in his father's office, proudly signing records, "intra per Wm. Holme." Tryall, nineteen, was getting actual surveying experience with Charles Ashcom in Chester County.

Surveying was impeded by the necessity of settling claims of previous inhabitants or laying out new estates without cutting into their property. Although the total acreage of occupied land was relatively small, particularly in the upper area of Penn's claim, it naturally embraced some of the most desirable land. An example of this was the 2,800-acre tract of Andrew Carr on the northwest side of the Delaware, between Pennypack and Neshaminy creeks, which had been surveyed in October, 1671, by Walter Wharton. Numerous smaller tracts also had been settled in what would be Philadelphia, Bucks, and Chester Counties. In his instructions to his commissioners Penn had directed that if land chosen for the city was already taken up in larger quantities than would make a city plan practicable and was not already improved, they should try to persuade the holders to give it up. They were to "allow no old patents. They have forfeited them by not planting according to the Law of the place."[13] Those who had already planted in the country were to be persuaded, if possible, to exchange it for property elsewhere.

The inconvenience of patches of already occupied land notwithstanding, a slowly increasing number of other First Purchasers were

---

[13] WP, Instructions to the Commissioners, Hazard, *Annals*, 528.

being seated. Between 6 August and 28 October returns were filed for over thirty surveys, and at least eighteen more orders for surveys had been issued, with a backlog of warrants for surveys not yet assigned. One group of settlers of special concern to Penn was those who could pay for passage for themselves and their families but had no money left to buy land. For their encouragement and protection he ruled that they be allowed to take up fifty acres at a penny an acre in perpetuity, "which the Surveyor of the Country shall set out as soon as the said person comes to take it up." The quitrent for this property was to be only two shillings a year forever, the payment of which gave the owner the status of a freeholder in the country. By September nine returns of surveys of such head rights had already been made for Bezer and Company. On 13 September Markham and Haige issued an order to Thomas Holme to survey land to poor persons "already arrived his province . . . [who] are or may be unable to stay until all ye purchasers be first satisfied, & so their selves and familys be Exposed to penury and ruine. . . ."[14]

An early applicant for his larger tract was Thomas Serey, or Cerey, of Oxford, a fellow passenger of Thomas Holme on the *Amity*, who had purchased five hundred acres. The survey was duly made and recorded on 19 August. Another prompt applicant was Thomas Holme's probable relative-in-law, James Croft, who had arrived on the *Society* from Bristol sometime near the end of the month and received and had entered his survey on 19 September. One of the most enterprising of the August arrivals was Thomas Brassie, who had come on the *Freeman* of Liverpool only two or three days after Thomas Holme himself had arrived. Like Thomas Holme he was a First Purchaser and a member—the head, in fact—of the Committee of Twelve engaged to live permanently in Pennsylvania. He brought with him a various merchant's cargo of

> 6 casks, 2 chests, 1 pann[equin], qty. 60 lbs. woolen cloth; 15 lbs. Norwich stuffs; 60 ells English linen; 6 doz. plain sheep leather gloves; 4 ordinary saddles; 2 cwt. cheese; 6 lbs. leather manufactured; 1/2 cwt. brass manufactured . . . 6 cwt. wrought iron; 3 cwt. nails . . . 13 pigs [blocks of lead, not livestock], qty. 15 cwt. lead; per post, 5 cwt. lead . . . 2 mill stone value £5.

Cerey lost no time in applying for surveys for part of his land, and on October he saw returns made on two tracts in Philadelphia County,

---

[14] Department of Community Affairs, BLR, Dept. Sur. OB D-85–81, 98.

one for three hundred, and one for six hundred, acres. All in all, more than seven thousand acres were surveyed and returns made during Thomas Holme's first month in Pennsylvania—not an impressive amount, perhaps, until one considers the task of measuring boundaries and establishing landmarks where visibility was poor, and unevenness of terrain impeded progress.

There were a few commissions beyond possibility of fulfillment. How could the best intentioned surveyor lay out roads connecting "cities" that could not be located until the land was charted and surveyed? Obviously, also, it would be impossible to survey city lots before a true plat of the city was laid out. And there were other problems, not directly connected with the surveyorship.

If Thomas Holme was surveyor general, he must also, as assistant to the deputy governor, bear his share of the duty toward arriving ships, with greeting of shipmasters and immigrants, reception of mail and messages, and the orderly disposition of cargo. The necessity of care with regard to cargo was borne in upon him by Martin's mishap, already referred to. The vanished possessions were never recovered, and Martin sued Richard Diamond, master of the *Amity*, for their value. Diamond and the *Amity* had sailed, and Thomas Holme undertook to defend Diamond. The record of the Chester County Courts of 12 September 1682 names Thomas Holme as attorney for Richard Diamond in the suit of "John Martin plain^r, Richd Dymon Def^t." At the instigation of the suit, the record reveals, "The def. by Mr. Thomas Holme appears & desires a reference which the pl. yields to & so the accon. rests." When the case was next called, "the def. did not appear." By this time the defendant must have been at least as far as New York on the way to Barbados, and Thomas Holme was with Markham, eluding Lord Baltimore.

When the case was tried during a later session, the boatswain, apparently either disassociated from the *Amity* or summoned from New York, testified that Martin's goods had been set ashore, but he did not know what became of them. He admitted that he did not think they went to Martin. Whoever was to blame for their disappearance, Diamond was required to make good the loss to the sum of £12, and Thomas Holme's first recorded venture as attorney proved unsuccessful.[15]

With every new company of settlers the necessity for at least a symbol of orderly establishment grew. Those who had secured their land put up hastily constructed houses. Some families rented accom-

---

[15] *Records of the Courts of Chester County . . . 1681-1697* (Colonial Society of Pennsylvania, 1910), 21, 24.

modations outside the bounds of the city from earlier residents, but a number of others obtained limited but legal possession of, or merely appropriated, space on the river front for temporary cave dwellings. Not actual caves, these were more properly huts, cut to a few feet into the bank above the narrow beach and built up above ground with sod, a mixture of branches and mud, or wood. Some of these were rendered fairly comfortable, with furnishings brought from England. Other were frankly makeshift stopping places that spurred the enterprising to seek their own lots and build houses as soon as possible, or eroded the pride and energy of the less ambitious. Merchants and craftsmen, of whom there were many, were particularly eager for some sort of town settlement in which they could build combination residences and shops.

William Markham, Thomas Holme, and the commissioners knew that it was imperative that a semblance of city establishment be made, although under the circumstances it would have to be a temporary one. As we have seen, according to William Penn's directives land apportionment was to be made on the basis of the five-thousand-acre shares of the five hundred thousand acres of land reserved for First Purchasers. Each such share entitled the holder to a 2 percent, or one-hundred-acre, tract of liberty land, "if the land would bear it," and, at first, ten acres in the city—an allotment soon reduced to two acres. On the basis of one hundred five-hundred-acre shares, the tract purchased from the Swansons might be adequate for the city of 1682, but would not leave room for expansion.

Thomas Holme, the deputy governor, and the commissioners did all that could be done at this point. Thomas Holme set down a tentative plat for the beginning of the city, neater than the tract purchased actually was, with four streets: Second Steet, Broad Street, Fourth Street, and Dock Street. These were marked off into fifty-four numbered lots each. On 19 September Markham and Holme, witnessed by Haige and Griffith Jones, drew the lots, by streets, each of the shareholders represented having, in all, four lots.[16] Many of those to whom lots were assigned had not yet arrived, and some would never come. The drawing could not be implemented for a variety of reasons, but at least it was a beginning. The Proprietor was expected shortly, and he would see for himself the problems that arose and would consider the solution.

For the time being, Thomas ordered surveys warranted for land outside the town, continued his explorations, and brooded over Fairman's reports on populated areas and the land between the rivers.

---

[16] Hazard, *Annals*, 642–643. Cited by Roach, "Planting," 29.

Chapter 8

Inauguration

Thomas Holme, Deputy Governor William Markham, and other dignitaries were on the dock to greet William Penn when the *Welcome* dropped anchor at New Castle on 27 October. If they had planned to entertain the Proprietor with a good dinner and exchange of news, they were disappointed. The Proprietor had his own agenda.

William Penn's first act was to summon on board John Moll, chief commissioner of the New Castle grant, and Ephraim Hermann, who had been appointed by James, Duke of York, co-attorneys to deliver the fort of New Castle with the twelve-mile circle around it to William Penn. Hermann was out of town, but Moll and other commissioners were prompt to comply with Penn's request. He showed them his two deeds of feoffment, one for New Castle and the twelve-mile circle, the other for the territory from twelve miles below New Castle to Cape Henlopen. He agreed to postpone the official reception for twenty-four hours, pending Hermann's return. Despite his eagerness, the night's reprieve must have been welcome to the man who had just crossed the Atlantic on a sailing vessel. The following day, Moll recorded,

> We did give and surrender, in the Name of his Royal Highness, Unto the said William Penn Esqr Actual & peaceable Possession of the Fort at New Castle, by Givinge him the key thereof, to Lock upon himself alone the dore, which beinge opened by Him againe, We did deliver also unto Him one turf with a twig upon it, & a parringer with River Water (and soile,)

In part of all what was Specified in the said Indenture or Deed of Infeofm^r. from his Royall Highness. . . .

The official memorandum was signed by Thomas Holme, William Markham, Arnoldus de la Grange, George Forman, James Graham, Samuel Land, Richard Tugels, Joseph Curles, and John Smith. The ceremony was followed by the signing of a pledge of obedience to Penn in the name of New Castle by members of the Council.[1] All this, it must be remembered, took place several miles below what surveys by both Baltimore's and Penn's surveyors had observed to be the fortieth parallel, the designated boundary between the two provinces. Penn considered the proceedings legitimate because he had come fortified with the indenture from the Duke of York. The difficulty lay in the fact that at this time New Castle and vicinity were not the Duke's to give.[2] Baltimore's claim was also questionable, in that the Calvert grant contained a stipulation that it did not include land already occupied by Christians. Swedish, Dutch, and English settlers had dotted the area for some time. That they had been there at the time of the original Calvert grant was probably true but not documented. The burden of proof was on Penn.

Thomas Holme, Markham, and their assistants had a strenuous week. Two more ships arrived about the time of the *Welcome*: the *Bristol Factor*, completing her second voyage to Pennsylvania, and the *Jeffrey*, a very large vessel—Claypoole estimated it to be a five-hundred-ton ship—bringing Nicholas More, president of the Free Society of Traders, and many other members, with sixty or seventy servants, supplies, merchandise, and, to Thomas Holme, deeds for paid property from Philip Ford, which entitled their holders to prompt survey of their land.[3] Somehow in the midst of other business the passengers and their goods had to be taken care of.

Meanwhile the Proprietor appointed justices of the peace and issued orders to county sheriffs to call meetings on 20 November for the election of representatives to the assembly and the council. Whether he visited the proposed site of his capital city during the initial rush of activity following his arrival is uncertain. A letter attributed to him written home from Upland on 1 November declares: "The

---

[1] HSP, DS, *Chew Family Papers* (Micro. 3: 615). PA 2, 16: 368; Hazard, *Annals* 1: 607, 507; PWP 2: 305.

[2] These deeds were dated 24 August 1682, although the patent for the territory, ceded to the Duke orally in 1664, was not officially granted until 22 March 1683, when the Lords of Trade and Plantations held it inoperable until the dispute would be settled. SPC, 1681–1696, 408, no. 1011.

[3] HSP, Hough Papers, Philip Ford to TH, 17 September 1682.

city of Philadelphia is laid out and begun. Many pretty houses are run up of late above the River and backwards, that do very well. An house for William Penn is a building. . . ."[4] Since this quotation is from a single source, its authenticity is open to doubt. If Penn had actually made the approximately thirty-mile round trip to the "city," any pretty houses he saw must have been those of earlier settlers. The first house, probably that of George Guest, was said to have been begun on 22 September at the south end of the cove, and such as were built between that date and William Penn's arrival were hastily constructed to meet immediate needs. The Swedes were experts in swift construction and were credited with having set the model for the basic pattern of a structure, usually thirty feet long, divided approximately in the center, with one end again divided to provide three rooms in all, sometimes enlarged by the construction of a loft.

On 2 November Penn convened a court at New Castle, to which he had summoned local officials "for settling jurisdiction of these and your parts." Present were the Proprietor, "Major" Thomas Holme, council members William Haige, John Simcock, and Thomas Brassie, and justices of the peace John Moll, John de Haes, William Simpill, Arnoldus de la Grange, and John Cann.[5]

For the Proprietor this initial court was a hard-working session. After again producing his royal credentials, he "willed and desired" of the assemblage that at the next court at New Castle they bring in "all patents, surveys, grants, and claims which they had to their lands, livings, tenements and possessions," in order to confirm legitimate titles and make proper adjustments for others. He also asked them to examine their town plots to see if they might have space to accommodate newcomers. Until laws for Pennsylvania could be provided, they would follow the pattern of the laws for New York.

Anyone having questions or requests on any juridical matter was invited to present them at the assembly which would convene at Upland on the first Monday of the next month, 4 December. A court would be held at Upland 6 December to consult with the Proprietor "for the common good of the inhabitants of that province."

The session over, William Penn and Thomas Holme departed for the site that had been chosen for the city, leaving William Markham, in his capacity of deputy governor, to receive in Penn's name the lower counties and, with the justices of the peace, to set up arrangements for

---

[4] CCHS, ACM, Box 331.
[5] For an English adaptation see James Claypoole, *Letter Book*, 223.

a market on Saturday, 18 November, and all succeeding Saturdays. Traditionally Penn and Holme are believed to have arrived by boat at the cove, near the Blue Anchor tavern and George Guest's house.[6] If so, they went on by land to Thomas Fairman's house at Shackamaxon. According to the minutes of the Abington Meeting,

> At this time Governor William Penn and a multitude of friends arrived here and Erected a City Called Philadelphia about a half mile from Shackamaxon where meetings were Established. . . . Thomas Fairman at the request of the Governor removed himself and his family to Tackony where there was also a meeting appointed to be kept, and the antient Meeting of Shackamaxon removed to Philadelphia from which Meeting all other meetings were reappointed in the Province of Pennsylvania.

Thomas Fairman was delegated to provide a book for the Meeting. A log meeting house would be built on land given by him in Oxford Township.

The meeting was followed by the ceremony of which Penn had dreamed for many months. On 28 October 1681, exactly a year before he disembarked at New Castle, he had written, "I doe Call the City to be layed out by the Name of Philadelphia, and soe I will have it Called."[7] Now, although it was little more than a prophecy of what it would become, Philadelphia, an expanse of woods and weeds and wild things, with a narrow fringe of caves and small houses, would be erected a city by the Proprietor of the province. The title of Philadelphia not only expressed what Penn had hoped his capital would be, a city of brotherly love, but was the name of the only one of the seven cities addressed in the Book of *Revelations* that was not rebuked. Parts of the letter seemed to embody his own feelings for the gathering of his people in:

> Here is the message of the holy and faithful one who had the key of David, so that when he opens, nobody can close, and when he closes, nobody can open: I know all about you; and now I have opened in front of you a door that nobody will be able to close—and I know that though you are not very strong, you have kept my commandments and not disowned my name. . . . Because you have kept my commandment to endure trials, I will keep you safe in the time of trial. . . . Soon I shall be with you: hold firmly to what you already have, and let nobody take your prize away from you. Those who prove virtuous I will make into pillars of the sanctuary of

---

[6] *Records of the Court at New Castle* 2: 23; Hazard, *Annals*, 600–602.
[7] HSP, Gen. Coll., *Abstract of the Records of the Abington Monthly Meeting*, 2; Watson, *Annals* 3: 42.

my God in the name of the city of my God, the new Jerusalem which comes down from my God in heaven, and my own new name as well. If anyone has ears to hear, let him listen to what the spirit is saying in the churches.[8]

Many of the inhabitants of the city-to-be, it must be recalled, had suffered material deprivation and imprisonment for their religious faith and a number of them had shared in meetings of worship with William Penn in England and with Thomas Holme in Ireland.

For Thomas Holme the meeting was of urgent importance. The drawing of names for city lots on 19 September had been merely a token action. Now, accompanied by Fairman, he rode with Penn through the forest to the Schuylkill and along the river fronts west and east of an area more in keeping with the size of the projected city than the inadequate triangle purchased of the Swansons. It was the judgment of all concerned that this should be the base of the capital.

The most necessary preliminaries over, Penn proceeded on the first of two diplomatically expedient journeys: he set out to visit the governor of New York, with side visits to the Friends' Meeting on Long Island and to New Jersey, with whose destinies he had been involved well before he obtained his grant of Pennsylvania. That this trip taken "to pay his duty to the duke by visiting his colony" may have been more than a pleasant courtesy is suggested by the later emergence of rivalries and jurisdictional disagreements between Penn and his neighbor regarding boundaries, Indian affairs, and mutual defense.

Although the Proprietor had taken over the issuing of warrants for surveys, the purchase of property before embarking for the province had been declared sufficient warrant for laying out of land, which many wished to acquire as soon as possible. Thomas Holme had an ever-increasing backlog of warrants for surveys of land to lay out in territory that was still not adequately defined. The bounds of the city must be staked out and, beyond them, the outline of the liberty lands beyond it. The survey of the liberty land tract was entrusted to Richard Noble. Negotiations for occupied land along the rivers were still going on, but it was possible to estimate approximately the bounds of the liberty land so that Thomas Holme could order tracts to be laid

---

[8] CCHS, ACM, Memorandum of Additional Instructions to Wm Markham & Wm Crispin & John Bezer, 28 October 1681. Transcript from c.c. by Samuel Carpenter, now lost, CCHS, ACM (Micro. 3: 360). For further suggestions concerning the name of the city see *PWP* 2: 30, n. 4.

out well beyond the estimated line of the liberties; but it was the city itself to which he now gave his concentrated attention.

A faint idea of the task confronting him can be gained by contemplating a densely wooded modern forest preserve of roughly two thousand acres to be measured and reduced at once to a town with an orderly pattern of staked-out streets. With Fairman, Thomas Holme again examined the land between the rivers, making careful preliminary observations. He appointed deputies to survey the straight outer bounds from the Delaware to the Schuylkill that would enclose the city, while he proceeded to the drafting of a workable plan for the city. From the outer bounds the deputies would mark out four streets, the modern Walnut, Chestnut, Market, and Arch streets. The central north-south, or Broad, Street and the central east-west, or Market Street were probably marked following the laying out of the bounds. The other east-west streets may have been indicated from the Delaware as far as Broad Street and the center square before the rest of the streets on the Schuylkill side of the city, since most of the early surveys were for the Delaware side.

The streets originating on the Delaware side were both the most urgently needed and the most difficult to plan because of the incursions of the cove at the south end of the tract, and a dry gut and Coaquannock Creek on the north. These would affect the apportionment of some of the lots between the river and Second Street. The Proprietor's specifications appear somewhat confusing. "Be sure to settle the figure of the Towne," he wrote,

> so as that the Streets hereafter may be uniforme down to the Water from the Country bounds; let the place for the Store [house] be on the middle of the Key [quay], which will yet serve for Market and State houses too. . . . let the Houses built be in a line. . . .

This is clear enough as far as it goes, but the order continues with what seems to be a conflicting turn:

> Pitch upon the very middle of the Platt where the Towne or line of Houses is to be laid or run facing the Harbour and great River for the Scituation of my house, and let it be not the tenth part of the Towne, as the Conditions say . . . But I shall be contented with lesse than a thirtyeth part, to witt, Three Hundred Acres, whereas severall will have Two by purchasing Two shares, that is, Ten Thousand Acres and it may be fitting for me to exceed a little.[9]

---

[9] *Jerusalem Bible*, Reader's Ed. (1968), 323.

Clearly Penn is here referring to the allotment of liberty land. However he perceived the future city, two points he emphasized: each house should be a minimum of two hundred paces from the stream or harbor to allow room for building of streets along the water front, and should be "in the middle of the plot as to the breadth way of it, that so there may be ground on each side, for Gardens or Orchards or fields," that it may be a "green Country Town which will never be burnt, and always be wholesome." He seems to have envisioned the residential green country town as facing one river, with houses, even, perhaps, mansions, spread along it, separated from the river bank by wide straight streets. The logistics of plot and plan were patently irreconcilable, as the Proprietor himself was quick to see.

With the original specifications in mind, almost symmetrical territory to work with, and a combination of creative imagination and practical perception, Thomas Holme superimposed on the two square miles of wilderness his famous *Portraiture of the City of Philadelphia*.

Much fruitless speculation has been expended on the inspiration of the design of the city. Babylon, Jerusalem, Londonderry, Roman and medieval cities, and Burlington, New Jersey, among others, have been nominated for prototypes. Thomas Jefferson's comment persists, "They are none of them comparable to the old Babylon, revived in Philadelphia, and exemplified."[10] A further suggestion is the seventeenth-century English army camp, of which Thomas had ample experience. He knew well also Wexford, Waterford, Cork, and Limerick—all of them waterside cities. But no one has remarked the simple fact that a one-by-two mile tract to be laid out in graduated but regular lots, invited a grid.

Probably the most practical suggestion he received came from the plan for the rebuilding of London after the great fire of 1666, presented by Richard Newcourt. Both Thomas Holme and William Penn remembered the tragedy of the burning city and were determined that Philadelphia should never suffer a similar trial. At the same time, it should be a city for people, taking into account the need for communication and recreation and the aesthetic aspects of what would become a great capital. As Roach points out, "the chief elements in Newcourt's plan—a grand central square at the intersection of axial streets . . . symmetrically placed subordinate squares, and the grid pattern formed by intersecting streets—were all incorporated in Holme's Por-

---

[10] HSP, DS, Penn MSS, Misc. (Micro. 3: 310), Instructions to My Commissioners . . . 30 September 1681.

traiture."[11] With the challenging task of laying out a city in almost virgin territory before him, Thomas Holme considered everything he knew from the theory and practice of others and his own experience. The result of his endeavors was a basic draft substantially the same as that believed to be his original drawing on vellum which survives in a dilapidated state in the library of the Historical and Museum Commission at Harrisburg. Variations from this drawing and the printed versions of it are chiefly such as would have been made by the professional to whom it was given for making the official copy.

The topography of the plot is slightly simplified. Three creeks are depicted on the Delaware side of the city. The Coaquannock on the north arises near the center of the northern portion of the tract and proceeds in a northeasterly direction to enter the Delaware at the extreme corner of the uninterrupted strip of land accorded William Penn. Two lesser creeks empty into the small cove called the Dock in the southern quarter of the tract. The smaller of these streams, only a few rods in length, flows directly east into the southwest corner of the Dock. The larger one is depicted as flowing from Third Street a little above what is now Walnut to the northwest corner of the Dock, although actually, according to Watson it rose much farther to the northwest and was augmented by springs that formed pools and marshy spots along the way.[12]

Two-thirds of the Schuylkill margin of the map has been lost, but what remains shows four streams, one of which arises near the center of the northern part of the city, and the other nearly as far, pursuing a crooked course from the present Walnut Street to High Street and then westerly to the Schuylkill.

The only streets named are High Street, reaching from river to river, and Broad Street, intersecting High Street at right angles in the middle of the plot. The intersection is interrupted by a large central square, and four small squares embellished by pleasantly realistic drawings of trees stand symmetrically two squares north and south of

---

[11] Cited by Lingelbach, "William Penn and City Planning," *PMHB* 68 (1934), 403. Among many discussions of the origins of the plan of Philadelphia, see Anthony N. B. Garvan, "Proprietary Philadelphia as Artifact," in Oscar Handlin and John Burchard, ed., *The Historian and the City* (Cambridge, Massachusetts, 1963), and John W. Reps, *The Making of Urban America* (Princeton, 1965), both cited by Roach, whose "Planting" may be regarded as definitive. It should be noted that both Garvin and Reps follow Watson's inaccurate supposition that TH arrived in Pennsylvania in June, 1682. Since Watson wrote, Markham's letter dating the arrival of the *Amity* on 3 August has appeared.

[12] PHMC, DPR, Harrisburg, MS Group 11, Map Collection, no. 165. The map is entitled, *A Portraiture of the City of Philadelphia in the Province of Pennsylvania by Thomas Holme Surveyor General*. Although it bears no printed date, it is assigned to 1683. It is a drawing in color on vellum, now somewhat tattered, with some slight irregularities, notably at street intersections and Washington and Franklin Squares, obviously the basis of the familiar printed version.

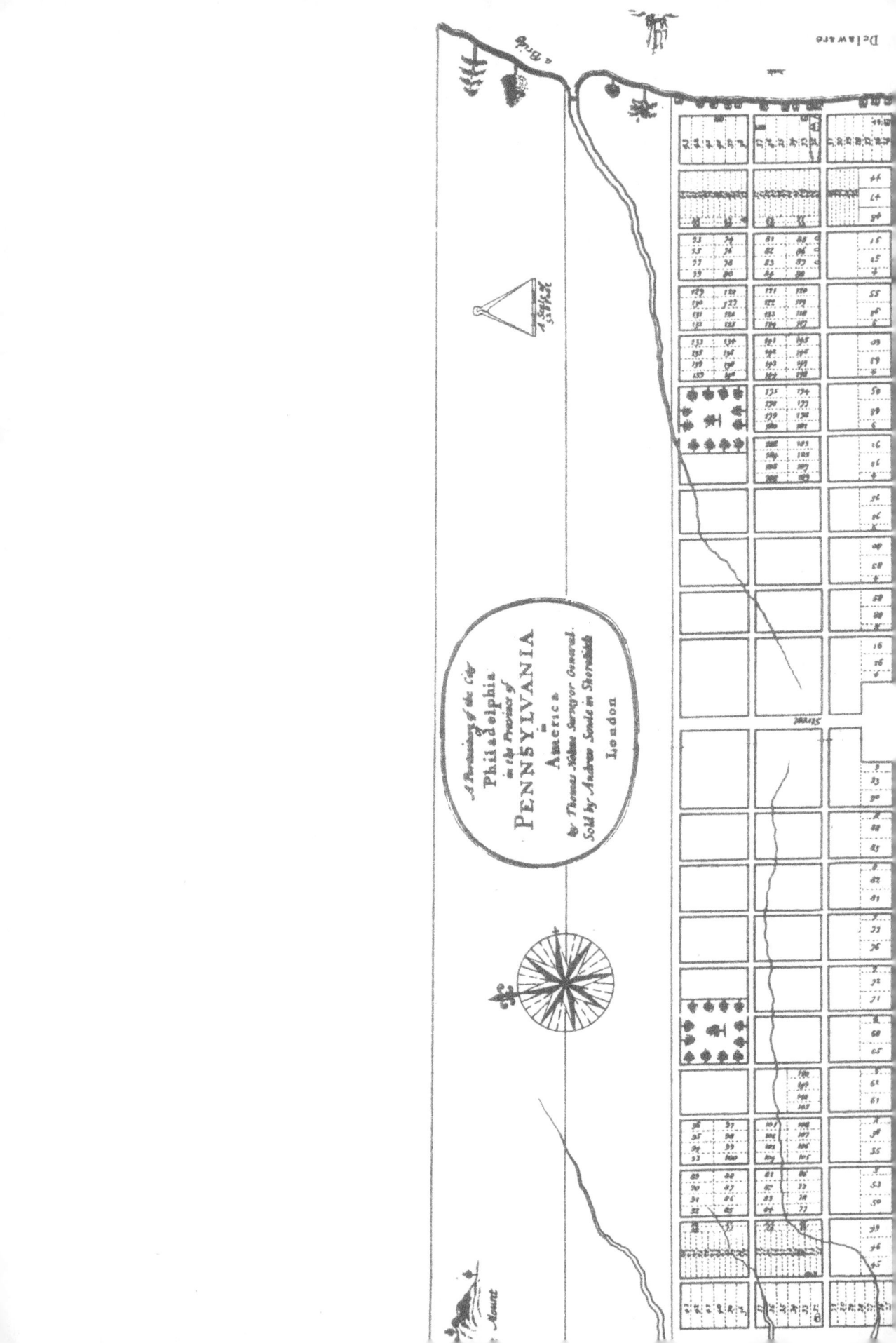

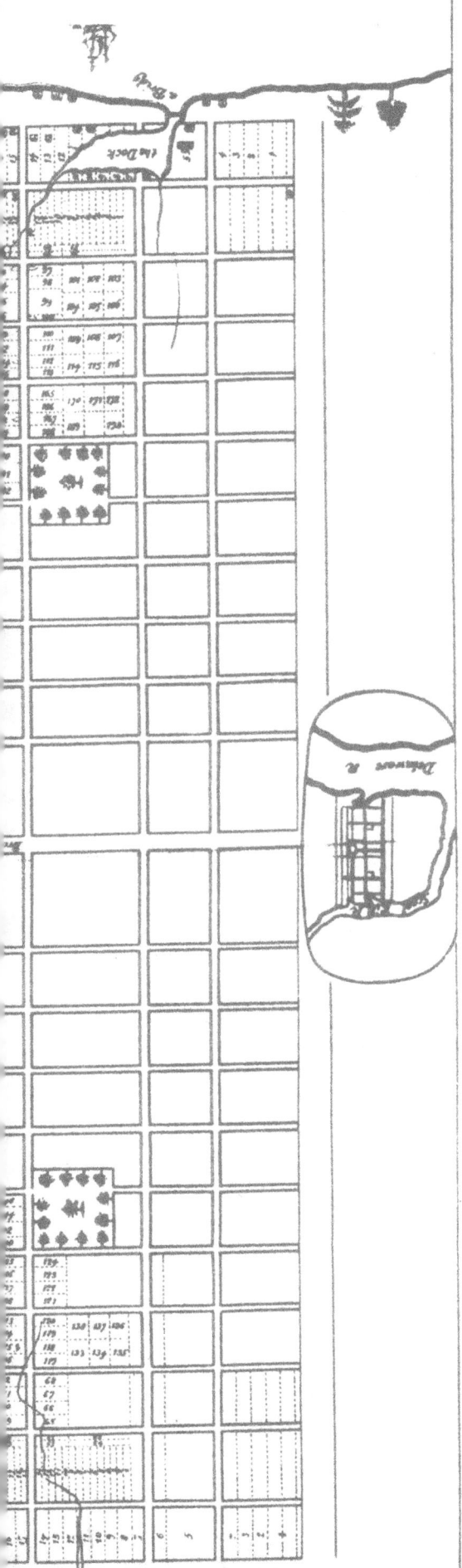

HOLME'S PORTRAITURE OF PHILADELPHIA

Fig. 15. Thomas Holme's map of the city of Philadelphia, "Portraiture of the City of Philadelphia."

High Street and beginning at Fifth Street from each side of the plot. A "bridg" is indicated at the mouth of the cove and another near the mouth of the Coaquannock, and a large sailing ship rides near the mouth of the creek.

This basic platform is given a grid pattern by three streets running from the Delaware to the Schuylkill parallel with and north of High Street, and four similarly placed streets to the south, crossed by eleven streets on either side of and parallel to Broad Street. Roach's analysis of the uncharacteristic variation of distances demonstrates the skill with which Thomas Holme integrated topographical irregularities and economic priorities into an otherwise regular grid.

In "The Nefarious Philadelphia Plan and Urban America: A Reconsideration," Thomas R. Winpenny reviews the attacks on the platform of the city and defends the rationale of straight streets that simplify the construction of ever-increasing numbers of one-family houses and ease of movement about the city. Even he overlooks the fact that Thomas Holme and his mentor in no way considered the plan inimical to friendly neighborly converse. Society officials and large contributors were for the most part seated in the area that to this day is known as Society Hill, and acquaintances frequently found accommodation near each other. Moreover, Thomas Holme explicitly called attention to the squares that in each quarter of the city were to be left open for public concerns. The large center square was intended for public buildings and especially for a meeting house where the entire Quaker community would assemble for worship and business—a plan that proved not to be feasible because of distance and lack of transportation.

In preparation for individual surveys, Thomas Holme divided more than enough squares to satisfy immediate demands into lots, the largest lots for the largest purchasers in preferred locations, between Front and Second streets and along High Street, with smaller lots in less choice streets. These he numbered for convenience in recording purchasers' names. The resultant whole was a masterly reconciliation of the aesthetic and the pragmatic. It must be remembered that however obnoxious the grid may be to modern sensibilities, to the pre-romantic eye of the seventeenth-century it bespoke the tranquillity of order. Thomas was ready thus far with the plan of the city when the Proprietor returned from New York.

Penn's visit to New York was not unduly prolonged. At Upland on 13 November he had issued a warrant for head right land to Jeffrey

Hawkins and warrants for other settlers, and he was back in Upland by the twenty-eighth, writing to Thomas Holme:

> Pray make hast to me, & I wish President [Nicholas More, president of the Free Society] would come too, about public business: This Frd. John Bowen desires about 1000 Acres, he will look out behind some [of] ye waterside Lotts in Philadelphia [County] or Bucks, let him chuse, but 500 Acres in a place is enough. no more but my love
>
> Thy true Frd / Wm Penn

To this communication Thomas Holme added a postscript and a true copy of a memorandum dated 2 November:

> Chester 28th-9mo-82
>   Afterwards at Peter Ramboe's house the Govern' bid me let him have 500a near his brother John Blunston's at Darby / Tho: Holme
> Memd
> That for & in Consideration of forty pounds New England Money, or value thereof I have consigned & do hereby consign to John Bowne of Ulissingen upon Long Island one Thousand acres of Land in the Province of Pennsylvania. wittness my hand at Philadelphia the 2d 9th Mo 1682
>   W: P.
>   vera Copia / Tho: Holme

The docket on the record indicates that Thomas Holme issued an order to Charles Ashcom to survey the first five hundred acres of Bowen's land just before leaving with Penn for the scheduled meeting with Baltimore, and for the remainder of the thousand-acre purchase nearly two years later to Israel Taylor in Bucks County:

> Governrs letter / about Jno Bownes land / 500a.
> Darby Ex Chester
> 14 10mo 82 to C. A.
>   Entered / Recorded
> 30 8mo 84 ordered the latter 500a.
>   to I. T. in Bucks.[13]

---

[13] ADS, Book D-62, DLR, PHMC, Harrisburg (Micro. 3: 662). *PWP* 2: 313–314. Although Bowen did not remove from New York to Pennsylvania, the map of 1687 shows a large and extremely well-located tract allocated to John Bowen (Bowne) in the angle of Neshaminy Creek and the Delaware. Probably the owner was a son of the grantee mentioned by WP and TH. Bowne's "brother," John Blunston, was an enterprising early arrival whose warrant for 250 acres in Chester County is dated 3 July 1682, and an order for "sundry tracts," 24 August 1682. The map of 1687 shows two tracts in his name fronting on the west side of Mill Creek in Darby Township. On 2 April 1683 he obtained a warrant for thirty acres of liberty land, a city lot, and on 24 July for a second city lot.

Fig. 16. Drawing of William Penn in Middle age by Francis Place. Used with permission of the Historical Society of Pennsylvania.

The nature of the public business on which the Proprietor wished to see his surveyor general and the president of the Free Society of Traders, who was also president *pro tem* of the council, is not recorded. In view of the court to be held at Upland/Chester on 6 December to consult with the Proprietor "for the common good of the inhabitants of that province," the assembly scheduled to meet on 4–7 December, Monday to Thursday, of the following week, and of the meeting with

Lord Baltimore which the returned messengers had arranged for 19 December, the conference no doubt was related to all three matters.

If Penn wished to see Thomas Holme at once, Thomas was no less eager to see the Proprietor. The grid for the city as a whole was not likely to be challenged, but protocol required that he present it for the governor's approval; nevertheless, with winter approaching and his possible absence in Maryland coming up, he ordered the first lines of the city to be staked out as promptly as possible, and the first streets along the Delaware front, where the squares were made difficult by the incursion of the dock and the dry gut at what is now Arch Street.

Dr. More's presence was important also at this stage of the work, since the Free Society would be the largest shareholder, with a corporate purchase of twenty thousand acres. It was thus entitled to first choice and the largest amount of land in both city lots and liberty land. Many of the members had now arrived and it was important that business get under way during this first flush of enthusiasm.

Thomas Holme and Nicholas More could scarcely have received Penn's letter and arrived at Upland before the twenty-ninth or thirtieth of November. The interval before the opening of the assembly was brief enough for the discussion of the agenda and the organization and laws that would be necessary for the province.

When the assembly convened on Monday, 4 December, with More presiding, the first business attended to was the setting up of committees. The representatives were, on the whole, distinguished among the early arrivals. Christopher Taylor, perhaps the most learned man in the province at this time, represented Bucks County. Nicholas More represented Philadelphia County, and John Simcock, deputy president, Chester County. William Clark, from Deal, was a well-established resident who had been a justice of the peace as early as 1680. Jones County was represented by Francis Whitwell. These five were authorized by the assembly as a *Committee for Elections and Privileges*. They were to meet at eight the next morning and sit until the assembly at ten.

A Committee for Justice and Grievances was next nominated and elected. The members were Griffith Jones, Luke Watson, William Sample, William Yardley, John Griggs, and Thomas Brassie. Brassie had brought with him a large shipment of merchandise and had lost no time in applying for his land, returns having been made on only a little less than a thousand acres between 8 October and 30 November. The only other business recorded for the first day was the granting of the request of Ralph Withers, deputy treasurer of the society and personal representative of James Claypoole, "on an extraordinary occasion" to be excused from attendance on the next day.

On Tuesday, "About the Time appointed, the House sat." The Committee for Elections and Privileges having nominated More for chairman, he was promptly confirmed in office. The first act of the assembly was to call to account the sheriff of New Castle County "for undue electing a Member to serve in the Assembly of that County." The speaker took the chair, freeing the chairman to explain that through some illegal procedure Abraham Mann had managed to be elected a member of the House. Mann was a chronic troublemaker recently under suspicion of sedition.[14] The explanation did not establish a friendly feeling between the two men. John Moll appears to have been efficient and responsible, obviously an organization man, already conspicuous as the one chosen to receive Penn into his southern territory. It was decided that he, rather than Mann, actually was elected, and the decision was confirmed by vote. The next step was the election of a Committee of Foresight for preparation of provincial bills. The members, Christopher Taylor, John Simcock, William Clark, Nicholas More, Griffith Jones, and Luke Watson, were chosen from existing committees.

With these preliminaries over, the assembly was ready to consider the laws upon which Penn had been working. Thomas Holme, William Clark, Thomas Winn, and Edward Southrin were deputed to go to the governor "humbly to desire him to honor the House with a Transmission of his Constitutions." Penn replied that the constitutions were not yet ready, but that as soon as they were ready he would send them to the assembly by one of his servants. As it was, the afternoon was consumed by the determination of disciplines and procedures necessary to the conduct of ensuing action. The time of adjournment is not mentioned, but it must have been late, closing with the mere statement that "The House adjorn'd till Nine a Clock the Next Morning." The next morning they reconvened "about Ten in the Morning."

Wednesday was a long and busy day. It opened with a consideration of a petition by the freemen of the Ten Lower Counties and of the province of Pennsylvania for union as one province "with the same Privileges of Law and Government." After two readings the act was approved with a unity that seems somewhat misleading in the light of

---

[14] For the setting up of committees and subsequent business of this assembly, see *Votes of the Assembly*, PA, 8, 1: 1–13. Notes on members not already mentioned are from "Twenty-three Ships." The account of Brassey's surveys is from *PA, OR*, 3, 2: 668. For something of Man's record see RCNC, 1676–1681, 5–8 April 1680, 47.

future developments. After a third reading it was presented by More and Christopher Taylor to the Proprietor, who confirmed it. A further petition was submitted by other nationals—Swedes, Finns, and Dutch living within the province—that they might be as free as other residents and that "their lands might be entailed upon them and their Heirs forever." The consideration of these two petitions was not mere routine. The variety of political, social, and religious backgrounds represented by the previously established population could not but lead to some disagreement in time to come.

Penn, meanwhile, had finished the constitutions. Now he presented them to the assembly with the printed laws, to which they were to be regarded as an appendix. One by one the "chapters" (individual articles) of the laws were read, sometimes debated, and acted upon. At the reading of the twenty-fourth of the printed articles, "That the First Assembly in the Province of Pennsylvania shall be desired to *Ratifie* the *Patent Granted* by the *Governour* to this Society [the Free Society of Traders]," a sudden foreboding chilled the air, despite the presence of the chief officers of the Society. The article was debated, then reserved for discussion with the Proprietor. Of many special privileges granted to the Society, that of electing three of its members to the provincial council was particularly objected to. On the whole, it was felt that it gave too much power to a privileged few and was prejudicial to individual purchasers of large tracts and, on religious as well as economic ground, to the inhabitants of the Lower Counties. This was an unexpected blow to the Free Society, mitigating as it did both its economic advantages and the political power it had counted on to enhance these. The House adjourned for recess until half past two in the afternoon but succeeded in reassembling only at about four. The reading of the printed and written laws continued, with more debate than had been anticipated.

As was to be expected, Penn's concern touched upon every aspect of life in his province. The first chapter of his constitutions concerned liberty of conscience. The laws then proceeded, after inquiring into the qualities of officials, to treat of offenses against God, sexual offenses, alcohol abuse (not only over-indulgence, but even the drinking of healths was forbidden), respect for property rights, interpersonal relations, care for the poor, commercial arrangements, imprisonment, and numerous other subjects. On the concluding day of the session, Thursday, 7 December, the House met at half past seven in the morning. The governor himself presided at the opening, and "expresses after an obliging and religious Manner to the House." Then after signing the bills of naturalization and union and conferring with the president on various concerns, he again urged "upon the House his religious Counsel." Adjournment was for twenty-four days—a term inconveniently brief for members who came from the southern counties. The session had been fruitful, and the weary participants were, for the most part, optimistic about the future.

If Thomas Holme shared this optimism, he was more reserved about immediate prospects. He had brought with him the initial draft of the city plan and wanted to get on with perfecting it and laying out as many lots as possible before the first winter of the newcomers in Pennsylvania set in. Before this could happen, there would be another confrontation with Lord Baltimore. Now he would be more in the background than before, because he would be with the Proprietor himself; but he did not relish the possibility of witnessing or perhaps participating in further observations which could only reenforce the disappointing results of preceding ones.[15]

The Baltimore meeting took place on 11–13 December at Thomas Tailler's (Taylor's) house in Anne Arundell County, Maryland, somewhere between Baltimore and Annapolis. It turned out to be a confrontation between two determined proprietors. Baltimore was incensed. Fifty years before Penn arrived his father had obtained from the crown a grant of any land not already settled by Christians, which lay between Watkins Point, south of the Potomac, about two minutes below the thirty-eighth parallel, to the fortieth parallel, which was considered to lie approximately one minute below Upland. This location, according to Baltimore, had been verified not only by his own surveyor, Augustine Hermann, but by William Penn's friend, William Haige.

Penn acknowledged the terms of Baltimore's grant, but he challenged the location of the fortieth parallel. The first observation had been taken with a small, hand-held nautical sextant which, he maintained, was not adequate for measuring the boundary of a province. When Haige's instrument and the large sextant that Markham had borrowed from Colonel Lewis Morris had produced the same results under the hand of surveyor Richard Noble, Penn asked for verification by taking observation from the capes. This proposal was countered by the statement:

> 'Tis well known, that can never be effected by reason the wayes from the Capes to Watkins Point are not passable, there being not only waters to

---

[15] Although the members of Penn's party on this expedition are not listed in extant records, the nature of Thomas's position as surveyor general and as an official of the Free Society of Traders presupposes that he would be included in the group.

pass over, but likewise much rotten grounds, as noe person can get there; and from Watkins Point (the Lord Baltimore's south bounds) there are severall large rivers to crosse over, besides that a due north line will crosse Chesapeake Bay towards the upper part thereof. . .[16]

The demand had to be withdrawn. Both men were obdurate. Actually, as has been stated, neither of them had unquestionable claim to the three-county territory. It had been settled by Swedish and Dutch Christians when the Calvert grant was given, and the Duke of York had only oral right to it from his brother, King Charles, until he was able to obtain the correct legal document the following March. For Penn the possession of New Castle was crucial, providing the natural outlet for Pennsylvania to the sea. In Baltimore's hands it would be a station for the collection of heavy tariffs on all goods shipped that way. Baltimore refused to consider Penn's suggested alternative that he purchase the lower portion of the Susquehanna, which would give him access to the head of Chesapeake Bay, and so to the ocean. Ultimately both claimants would return to England to argue the case before the Lords of Trade. With the approach of winter it had to be left in abeyance while attention was given to more immediate affairs.[17]

On their homeward journey Penn and the Friends who accompanied him visited Quaker settlements. They were escorted to the place of the first meeting by Baltimore and his council, and the next day went across the bay and a few miles southward to Choptank, where again they had the company of a distinguished escort. Here they were welcomed not only by the already well-established Friends' meeting, but also by James Harrison, Phineas Pemberton, and others who had been marooned there when their ship had discharged them on their way to Pennsylvania.

If the conference had not been productive of tangible results, its fringe benefits, at least, were gratifying, Political sympathy at Choptank accrued to Penn. More practical was the greatly increased knowledge of the topography of the upper Chesapeake Bay area. Particularly did Thomas Holme look appreciatively at the vast shining blue expanse of the Susquehanna. With Penn, he saw some part of it as a possible viable alternative to the Delaware outlet to the ocean, if by

---

[16] *MdA* 5: 379.
[17] HSP, Pa. Misc. Papers, *Penn and Baltimore*, 10. Documents pertaining to the controversy are reprinted from the British State Papers in *MdA*, vols. 5 and 17. For Penn's grant of Pennsylvania from Charles II see *PA*, 8, 1: xl. For the Duke of York and the New Castle grant see Hazard, *Annals*, 606. For Baltimore's claims see Charles II to Baltimore, *CSPC*, 1681–1696, 277, no. 659, Baltimore to William Blathwayt, 11 March 1682, 206, no. 437, and commissioners to Baltimore, 17 June 1682, 251, no. 569.

some means it could be wrested from Baltimore. He would not cease to think of its valley as highly desirable, even apart from its maritime potential.

Secular considerations aside, it would be unfair to discount the spiritual significance the visits to Quaker communities held for Penn, Thomas Holme, and many other members of their party. William Penn was revered and loved by Friends everywhere because of his eloquent witness to truth, and Thomas Holme was known to many for his active role in Quaker affairs in Ireland. The welcome and supportive warmth of the meetings and the time of silent "waiting upon the Lord" took the edge off the bitterness of the conflict just past and afforded a needed respite before taking up the strenuous work of the ensuing months.

The return from Maryland marked the end of a series of preliminaries. Now at last William Penn, William Markham, and Thomas Holme were in one place, within walking distance of the projected city, a plat of that city in their hands, the city squares outlined on paper, and, for the time being, conveniently located centers for Friends' meetings settled upon. Physical boundaries were set, except for the continued problem with Baltimore, and a frame of government adapted from that prepared by Penn in England was tentatively drawn. Thomas Holme could move as quickly as possible with orders for surveys, and, in consultation with the governor and the settlers concerned, with the allocation of lots on the city platform to be cleared for dwellings and business establishments as soon as their outlines were surveyed.

With the possible exception of Richard Noble, to whom was delegated the responsibility for the bounds of the liberty lands, Thomas Holme set every available surveyor in Philadelphia County to work on the city. In addition to the northern and southern bounds there were seven east-west streets to be staked out and twenty-three intersecting streets, of which those nearest the rivers, especially on the Delaware side, were imperatively needed. Then there were the lots in the squares within these streets to be measured and marked. A beginning had already been made, but it was only a beginning.

The little Blue Anchor tavern near the cove was already in business.[18] It was a small structure, sixteen feet square, built by William Dare, a ship's master from Virginia, after the site of the city had been chosen. Under different ownership and in various sites it served the

---

[18] Roach, "Planting," 42, and 43, n. 70, documents the history of the tavern, which reappears periodically in the story of these early years.

accumulating population sometimes not wisely but too well. Adjacent to it was Guest's house, said to be the first dwelling built on the new property. Nearby was or soon would be the small warehouse of the Free Society of Traders, at the Delaware end of the city-wide strip of land that constituted the first allotment to the society.

Although the "Selections from the list in the *Pennsylvania Archives* anterior of May 1, 1695," printed in Volume 2 of the third series, record very few new warrants for city lots given before February 1682/83, Roach had documented a sufficient number allocated and settlement begun to justify her estimate that the number of settlers whose lots were determined by the end of December approximated that represented by drawings on the *Portraiture*, although not all in the same locations. A few warrants for city lots had been issued before the map was drawn, presumably to fully paid purchasers who requested them; and a number of these could be honored now, as well as those given after the Proprietor arrived.

The fortunate warrantees, and some whose property allegedly was designated though so far without warrant, set about the strenuous task of clearing enough trees to furnish wood for building and room for at least temporary dwellings, and, under urgent reminders, cutting trees and brush and removing stumps from streets staked out as far as settlement was in progress.

Difficulties were compounded by labor shortage, since nearly everyone was busy with his own establishment. Thomas Holme had at least one indentured servant, Edward McVeagh. John Osborne and John Fletcher who came with him to Pennsylvania seem to have been obligated to at least some assistance, personal or professional. Osborne probably belonged to the family of the Cork surveyor of the same name. Probably McVeagh's first task was the building of a house for Thomas Holme and his family. Certainly Thomas Holme had little time for personal affairs.

Among the first to be seated were Christopher Taylor and Thomas Holme's son-in-law, Silas Crispin. Taylor had a large lot with a hundred and two feet on Front Street, south of the present Chestnut Street, the south half of which he soon sold to Thomas Hooten, and a lot on High Street extending fifty feet back on Fourth Street. Silas, to whom originally was assigned the lot that would have been his father's, adjoining Penn's liberty land, chose instead a forty-foot lot near the dock. Although James Claypoole and Samuel Carpenter, both of whom would be important persons in the province, had not arrived, the coming of both was assured and choice lots were assigned to them. Claypoole, who depended on Withers to see to the building of a house for him, was situated at the corner of Front and the street that would be named for him, the modern Walnut Street. A lot for Carpenter was reserved in the next square to the north. Thomas Holme himself was established on the corner lot at Front Street and the sixty-foot-wide street north of High Street that was originally named for him, now Arch Street. A house, perhaps his, on Front and Arch Streets is conspicuous on the *Portraiture*.

If thirty-odd purchasers had received their lots in Philadelphia by the beginning of January, this is by no means to say substantial dwellings were at once erected on pleasant tree-lined streets. Many streets existed only on the map. For the most part log houses more primitive than even the poorest immigrants had occupied before coming to Pennsylvania were put up as quickly as possible to furnish shelter for colder weather to come and for headquarters for business, on which some had already embarked.

Although the narratives of Watson are not always accurate as to dates and historical details, the reminiscences he gathered from eighteenth-century descendants of these early Pennsylvanians undoubtedly give, on the whole, a realistic account of the foundation. The terrain was more difficult than its relatively regular modern condition would suggest. There were differences in elevation—hills to be reduced, swamps to be drained, low places that were filled to avoid their being turned into puddles when rains came. Dock Creek, visible now only as a pleasant declivity lying diagonally behind Carpenters' Hall, was a considerable stream, marked by swamps and, north of High Street and west of Fourth, forming a good-sized pond frequented by ducks and geese. Another large duck pond that lay behind the site of the present Christ Church, was, according to tradition, the center of an Indian party in honor of William Penn.

Anecdotes of these pioneer days abound. One of the most charming records the experience of Rebecca Coleman, a small child whose family were among the first settlers, living in one of the caves. As Watson relates it,

> At the door of her cave, when one day sitting there eating her milk porridge, she was heard to say again and again, "Now thee shan't again!" "Keep to thy part!" &c. Upon her friends looking to her for the cause, they found she was permitting a snake to participate with her out of the vessel. . .[19]

---

[19] This and the anecdote which follows are related by Watson, 1: 53 and 48.

An equally engaging story involves a couple who, unused to manual labor though they were, were felling trees to build a log house and were not provided, as more experienced adventurers usually were, with game for food. When the husband suggested that his obviously tired helpmeet give up her end of the crosscut saw and go back to their tent to prepare dinner she acquiesced, praying for forgiveness of her despondency at not having enough food for a meal. When she turned to look for something she could prepare, she met her cat coming in with "a fine large rabbit which she thankfully received and dressed as an English hare." When her husband came in and heard the story, "they both wept with reverential joy." The providential gift was commemorated years later, when, having prospered and graduated not only from their tent but from the log house that succeeded it, they acquired a large silver sugar box, on which they had engraved a likeness of the cat catching and bringing in the rabbit. Converted into a soup tureen, the vessel became a family heirloom.

William Penn had urged that houses be spread along the river so that the city would appear as well populated as possible. Viewed from the Delaware this was sound strategy, but it was less agreeable for settlers whose neighbors would be invisible to them until not only their own property but streets and unclaimed lots were cleared. Before long, owners were dividing their lots, selling portions to later arrivals. On the whole, settlement proceeded remarkably smoothly, thanks not only to the mutual helpfulness of Friends, but also to the generosity of earlier settlers and of the Indians, who brought gifts of game and corn or sold them at low prices.

Thomas Holme's attention during the early weeks of the winter was divided among his tasks as surveyor general, active Friend, and father. No record of the marriage of Hester and Silas Crispin is extant, but traditionally it is said to have occurred during the winter of 1682–83. Probably Silas built his house as soon as he settled on the lot on which he proposed to live, and he and Hester were married as soon as it was ready. There is no indication, either, of the date of erection of Thomas Holme's house, across from which Robert Turner would build two years later what he claimed was the first brick house in the city. Roach in "Planting" gives what is probably as complete as possible an account of these early seatings.

Urgent as was the work on the city, warrants for liberty land and for larger tracts had to be honored promptly so that purchasers would at least be able to plan their dwellings and commence clearing their land for spring planting. Since the deputies were engaged in the actual measurement and laying out of land, Thomas Holme himself often showed purchasers available tracts, riding along narrow paths through the woods and beside creeks. Some property was being laid out in areas safely apart from still unsurveyed boundary lines. He must also have accompanied William Penn when, under the guidance of Thomas Fairman, he examined his demesne and selected choice tracts where he wished thousands of acres reserved as manors for himself and his children. The Proprietary's manor of Springettsberry was interposed between the northern edge of the city and the liberty land.

Fortunately, in these early months of settlement a relatively large number of requests were for land in Chester County, which was less heavily wooded and more populated than the upper reaches of the Delaware and the Schuylkill. What proved to be a less happy circumstance was that Charles Ashcom was the principal surveyor in the county, and it was to him that Thomas Holme appointed his elder son, Tryall, assistant.

With settlement now well under way a further major step in the life of the province was in order: the establishment of its spiritual center, the Monthly and Quarterly Meetings of the Society of Friends. The first meeting ocurred on 9 January 1682/83, at the house of Christopher Taylor.

The first business enacted was the establishment of a calendar. The first third-day of the month was chosen for the regular men's and women's meetings for Philadelphia city and county, with each third meeting constituting the Quarterly Meeting.

The next step was the selection of a site and the choice of style and materials for a meeting house in Philadelphia, and the provision and care of books necessary for the meeting. Responsibility for all of these was delegated to Thomas Holme, John Songhurst, Thomas Wynne, and Griffith Jones."[20] This would be a long and tedious process. It did not begin until summer, with Christopher Taylor furnishing hospitality until June. The delay probably was at least in part due to Thomas Holme, who, in addition to his duties as surveyor general, was endowed with other responsibilities that were time-consuming and sometimes vexatious.

On 8 January Penn appointed him a commissioner of estates and revenue, a position he would share with James Harrison, Robert Turner, Samuel Carpenter, and Penn's personal secretary, Philip Theodore Lehnmann.[21] Harrison was Penn's steward, Turner a fellow

---

[20] MBE, *Minutes of the Monthly and Quarterly Meetings of Philadelphia*, 1683–1705, Arch Street Meeting House Library, Philadelphia. *PWP* 2: 335.

[21] Micro. 4: 18.

member of the active body of Friends in Dublin in foundation days in Ireland, and Carpenter a well-to-do immigrant from his sugar plantation in Barbados. They were, in effect, to be guardians of Penn's personal financial returns from his province. With all this, Thomas Holme was to serve on the provincial council and, though he probably did not know it at the time, on other demanding commissions. All of these posts involved important activities that increasingly required the skill of a juggler.

As the Proprietor gained increasing familiarity with his province he ordered specific tracts for purchasers who sought special consideration. Everyone wanted frontage on a sizable stream and good arable land enclosed in regular bounds. Thomas Holme had tentatively plotted rectangular tracts that could be combined or divided, but the nature of the warrant sometimes defeated the plan. He received the warrants and gave orders for surveys to his various deputies, often conducting the purchaser's tour of inspection himself. If the proposed tract proved acceptable the survey would be made and returns filed in the surveyor general's office—at least, that was the prescribed procedure. If the tract was not acceptable to the purchaser, another would have to be found.

During exploring and marketing excursions Thomas Holme took careful note of the land traversed and position and quality of the tracts he ordered to be surveyed. His handling of questions and complaints that arose from time to time shows remarkable memory for details and the accuracy of such a working map as he was able to construct in the absence of field maps that deputies sometimes failed to turn in.

A particularly trying problem was the unexpectedly long time it took Richard Noble to survey the bounds of the liberty lands, which in turn delayed the assignment of lots on the Schuylkill side of the city. How far the delay was due to dilatoriness on Noble's part and how far to the awful obstruction of woods, underbrush, patches of swampy ground, and winter rains, it is hard to say. Certainly the task was difficult, and patience was not conspicuous among Penn's many virtues, nor, for that matter, one may assume, among those of Thomas Holme. As a surveyor Thomas Holme was prepared to make allowances for the time consumed; but he voiced annoyance at not being able to seat purchasers with warrants for city lots on the Schuylkill.

Much of the land along both rivers was still in the possession of Swedish and a few other earlier settlers. In their eagerness to be seated before the onset of winter some of the First Purchasers went into the country and negotiated with these earlier inhabitants for desirable accommodation. One of these, Thomas Paschall, who had arrived in

August on the *Society of Bristol*, obtained a warrant for 490 acres on which return was made on 13 September, and for two five-hundred-acre tracts on which returns were registered on 19 September. His warrant for a city lot is recorded as of 19 April 1683. In a letter to a friend dated the last of January 1682/83 he gives a comprehensive view of life in the hinterlands as it existed during the first winter of the province: "I have hired a House for my Family for the winter [he writes] and I have gotten a little House in my Land for my servants, and have cleared Land about six Acres; and this I can say, I never wished myself at Bristol again since my departure." He has traveled extensively about the area, and has found that "The Country is full of goods." Brass and pewter are available—this is of special interest to him, since he is a pewterer by trade—though there is a shortage of "iron-potts." The "brave pleasant River"

> is planted all along the Shoare, and in some Creeks . . . mostly by Sweads, Finns, and Dutch, and now at last, English throng in amongst them, and have filed all the Rivers and Creeks a great way in the Woods, and have settled about 160 Miles up the great River; some English that are above the falls have sowed this Year 30 or 40 bushels of Wheat and have great stocks of Cattel. . . .

Thomas Holme's map, finished three years later, shows Paschall's land jutting triangularly into the liberty land west of the Schuylkill on a lively tributary of Mill Creek, with Neels and Mouns Johnson, Peter Yocom, and, on the south, Robert Longshore as neighbors (fig. 17). The Swedes were masters at simple building. Paschall avers:

> They will cut down a Tree, and cut him off when down, sooner then two men can saw him, and rend him into planks or what they please; only with the Ax and Wooden wedges, they use no Iron; They are generally very ingenuous people, lives well . . . having great plenty of provisions, but then they weer but ordinarily Cloathed; but since the English came, they have gotten fine Cloaths, and are going proud.

Acquaintances of Paschall have discovered that farther inland there are areas of open country with very few trees, so that a purchaser can commence cultivation at once. His account of the proliferation of all sorts of grain and fruit and the abundance of fish, venison, wildfowl, and even bear meat, which he likens to beef, anticipates William Penn's later enthusiastic sales pitch to the London members of the Free Society of Traders. He mentions other denizens of the Pennsylvania countryside as well, not all of which the Proprietor notes:

Fig. 17. Detail of 1687 map with apportionments next to Liberty Lands. Used with permission of the Historical Society of Pennsylvania.

> Here are Beavers, Rackoons, Woolves, Bears, a sort of Lyons, Polecatts, Mushratts, Elks, Mincks, Squirrils of several sorts and other small creatures, but none of these hurt unless surprised: also Rattle Snakes and black Snakes, but the Rattle Snaks I have not seen. . . . [22]

Such was the land that Thomas and his deputies were engaged in laying out.

Not all of the newcomers were as resourceful as Paschall. Understandably, some were confused when confronted by winding streams and for the most part unpathed woods. Sometimes they accepted tracts that they later found unsatisfactory, or refused to believe that the surveyor general had given them fair choice. Others, pleased with a proposed tract, proceeded to improve it at once, even before it was surveyed. Judging from the warrants issued by the time Paschall wrote and the number of returns made, he was not exaggerating in his description of English settlement by the end of January. The names of many of the warrantees of late 1682/83 remain on the map of 1687. The surveys represent an enormous amount of work on the part of Thomas Holme and his deputies, with remarkably little later dissatisfaction.

At the end of Thomas Holme's first six months in Pennsylvania returns of the survey of over twelve thousand acres of Penn's province belonging to at least thirty-five or forty purchasers had been entered in the records by his son William. Later Thomas Fairman would unwittingly give witness to something of what this cost Thomas Holme in sheer physical exertion, when he complained to William Penn of lending horses to Thomas and sometimes even riding with him on long distances into the woods. Holme had met the Indians and had participated in the first provincial council. He had twice encountered the powerful adversary to the south, Lord Baltimore. He had been singled out for special responsibility in the establishment of the Philadelphia Meeting of the Society of Friends. And he had laid out a city.

For the next month surveyors and settlers would battle the February cold, rain, and snow, staking out streets and lots, making some progress against a great backlog of warrants for surveys, felling trees and clearing out brush and vines. As the weeks passed they were spurred on by intimations of spring.

---

[22] DR, City Hall, Philadelphia, Thomas Fairman, Release to William Penn, Proprietor of Pennsylvania, 10 December 1713. Attested and entered at Philadelphia in *Deed Book* D-13, in 1785. Cited by Westcott, *History of Philadelphia*.

Chapter 9

Foundation

With March 1683 commenced what, in terms of service to the province of Pennsylvania, might be considered the most important year of Thomas Holme's life in America. The raw plat of the city would be perfected and lots distributed and surveyed, and thousands of acres would be settled. Thomas would accompany Penn, or go as one of a small committee of emissaries, on missions to New Jersey and on further challenges to Lord Baltimore, and would participate in purchases of land from the Indians. Most important of all, he would be on small committees for preparation of laws of the province, and would play an important part in the formulation of an extensively revised Frame of Government. Because of the occasional extra demands on Thomas Holme's time Penn appointed Richard Noble as deputy surveyor general to act in Thomas's absence.

The first of Thomas's absences was occasioned by his trip with Penn on 1 March 1683 to the meeting of the Council of East New Jersey at Elizabethtown, on the invitation of Thomas Rudyard. The meeting seems to have had no substantial purpose except to give moral support to the beleaguered governor *pro tem*, but it gave Thomas increased insight into the problems of land distribution and settler-proprietary relations. It was followed shortly by another meeting with Baltimore at Colonel Taylor's plantation in Maryland on 6 March, again without results.[1]

---

[1] Thomas Rudyard to William Penn. Copy, FLL (Micro. 4:024); *PWP* 2: 39–41. HSP, *Misc. Papers, Penn and Baltimore*, 10.

Back in Philadelphia, Thomas Holme turned to the survey of city lots and problems of purchasers eager to clear and plant land, while Penn set about preparations for the provincial council. The major activity of the month would be the establishment of the government. On Saturday, 10 March, William Penn, the sixteen members of the council, and the assembly met together. They then summoned to join them sheriffs of the six counties, whose responsibility had been to call the election of delegates. Richard Noble, already with a full schedule of surveying to attend to, was sheriff of Bucks.[2]

It was decided that the membership of the government would consist of twelve men from each county, three of whom would be members of the council and nine of the assembly. The council included men prominent from the beginning of the province and others influential in their own communities: William Markham, Christopher Taylor, Thomas Holme, William Haige, John Moll, Lasse Cock, Ralph Withers, John Simcock, William Clark, John Hilliard, Francis Whitwell, Edmond Canholl [Cantwell], William Clayton, William Biles, James Harrison, and John Richardson. The returns of the sheriffs and the petitions of the freemen of the province were first read, then the Proprietor's Charter of Liberties. After some discussion concerning the number of members satisfactory for council and assembly the Proprietor expressed his willingness "to Settle such Foundations as might be for their happiness and the good of their Posterities, according to the power vested in him," although originally he had proposed a larger number.

The assembly withdrew for its own deliberation and the election of a Speaker. They chose for the office Dr. Thomas Wynne, one of the distinguished Welsh gentlemen whom Penn had first approached with his proposal for a Welsh settlement. On taking the chair Wynne reminded the members of the seriousness of their responsibilities and of their "Duties towards one another," and read the "Orders and Decorum of the House"—a document that was destined to be ignored on future occasions. Then they proceeded to a careful scrutiny of the charter.[3]

Points were proposed for debate but abandoned for more crucial discussion. Two points the assembly prepared to propose to the council: that they should be empowered to initiate bills for the action of the council, that they should have the privilege of conferring with the council. Submitted to the council, both of these proposals were

---

[2] *MPC* 1: 1.
[3] *MPC* 1: 2–3.

"passed in the negative." A bill from the governor and provincial council "touching their *Fidelity and Allegiance to the Governor*, requiring subscription of their Names, &c . . . at the present was suspended." Plainly, this would not be an assembly of yes-men.

The day ended with a satisfying sense of accomplishment for both assembly and council, and the new bicameral government adjourned until the following Monday.

Not in either governmental body was Dr. Nicholas More, president of the Free Society of Traders. At the meeting of 4 December he had represented Philadephia County, with Christopher Taylor for Bucks, John Simcock for Chester, William Clark for Deal, and Francis Whitwell for Jones, to constitute a Committee for Elections and Privileges. He was the only member of the committee not included in the council. Since the council objected to the special privileges Penn had intended for the Free Society they may have passed over its president in silent protest. It may be noted in passing that more than the quota of members of the Free Society specified in the original *Laws Agreed on in England* were members: Thomas Holme, John Simcock, William Haige, Lasse Cock, and Ralph Withers, deputy of the treasurer James Claypoole.

When the council convened on Monday, 12 March, it was to a storm of astonished outrage. Several council members reported that Dr. More had proclaimed "in a publick house" that the

> Govern[r], Prov[l] Councill & Assembly, as that they have this day broken the Charter, & therefore all that you do will come to Nothing, & and that hundreds in England will curse you for what you have done, & their children after them, and that you may hereafter be impeacht for Treason for what you do.[4]

More's outburst was more than an insult to the governor and to a council that, pleased with the outcome of the elections, had opened the season with dignified but vigorous consideration of questions basic to the government of the province. Whether the council recognized it as such or not, it was symptomatic of trouble to come, a small but ominous crack in the structure.

The governor and council summoned Dr. More to a hearing. When confronted with the reports of his misconduct he lamely defended himself, declaring that his comments had been misunderstood and misrepresented. Charitably, he was charged only with unreasonable conduct and admonished not to repeat the offense. This concluded

---

[4] *MPC* 1: 3.

the business of the day for the council, and they adjourned until the next day.

The council and assembly met regularly six days a week until 4 April, after which they met at intervals as business required. The meetings of the first four weeks were devoted largely to consideration of the Frame of Government and the specific Laws of the Province, with necessary interruptions for immediate concerns. Thomas Holme was present at all but one meeting, his absence on that occasion being due to a trip to the Schuylkill with Christopher Pennock, no doubt to show him the magnificent tract with a two-and-a-quarter mile river frontage on which Pennock's name appears on the 1687 map. Pennock's warrants for a city lot and four-hundred-acre and five-hundred-acre tracts are listed in the record of Old Rights as of 29 May, 19 June, and 10 December 1684, but he may well have reserved this tract at this visit.

On his return from Schuylkill Thomas Holme wrote about observations and matters discussed on the way:

Govern^{er}:
I went yesterday with Christo: Pennock to Skoolkill & Richard Noble hath not yet set out the front street there, & so is gone again to day, & Christopher being Concerned for his (now) own Lot & Limerick Lot, as I am for Wexford Lott, & Sa: Claridge in al 4 Lotts, if thou please to grant us Liberty to take the 4 together, where wee think meet (the Corner Lotts of the high street, the promiseing place of Advantage, we shall decline unless permitted by thee), wee are willing to set to work with all speed to build upon them, which may inCourrage others to do the Like, seeing us begin please to favor us with thy order here under this, that wee may signify it to Ireland, for the satisfaction of the Concernd
The 17 of 1 monthe 1683 / thy fr: to serve the
Tho: Holme

Penn's reply, dated 18 March, was prompt and succinct:

The side of the high street next my hill and the two Corners of the street answerable to thy hous in that street excepted chuse for the Irish Lotts[5]

Taking his seat in the council on Saturday, 17 March, the day after his trip with Pennock, Thomas Holme learned that in his absence he had been appointed to a committee to prepare bills concerning the burning of woods and marshes, the marking of chattel—an important

---

[5] *Dept. Sur. OB*, 1682–1693, Division of Archives and Manuscripts, Pennsylvania Historical Manuscripts Commission, 88. Cited by ACM, Box 28, CCHS.

procedure where livestock roamed at large through still unfenced territory—and the building of fences. These were among the varied duties that would have accrued to regular committees provided for in Article 13 of the Frame of Government.[6] It had been decided at the third meeting of the council, however, that "during the present infancy of things," they should be performed by the council in "such manner as numbers permit." While the Laws of the Province were being formed, the Act, or Bill of Settlement, later incorporated into the Frame of Government, was undergoing extensive amendment. Finally, after much debate, on 17 March the House reported their acceptance of the bill with its amendments, and Griffith Jones and Robert Wade were appointed to bring the fair copy to the governor and council.

Less than a week later, on 21 March, preparation of nineteen bills was assigned to three committees. With William Clayton, William Biles, and John Richardson, Thomas Holme was appointed to propose bills concerning:

To arrest Goods in case of Danger.
Limits of Courts in Criminal Causes.
Justices of the Peace to Marry People.
How farr Exet^{rs} and Adm^{rs} are obliged to proceed, & how to pay.
Publique houses to credit no unresident for above 20^s or else to lose it.
Not to remove his Neighbor's Landmark.
Punishm^t for those that shall presume to alter their
Neighbors Eare or Brand Mark.

The committees brought in their bills the next morning for consideration by the council, and on 23 March Thomas Holme carried bills to the assembly in the forenoon and, with William Clark, in the afternoon. In the interim the council heard the petition of John James, presumably the husband of Thomas Holme's niece Susanna, and other seamen of the *Friends' Adventure* to force the master to pay them the wages contracted for in England.[7] At the hearing ordered for the petitioners before the governor and council they were told to bring up the goods they had left at Upland, and then they should have their wages. It was decided that all except John James had done their duty.

Throughout the legal considerations the council and the assembly were in regular communication. Sometimes the entire assembly joined the council in combined session, and bills regularly were carried from the council and formally presented to the consideration of the assem-

---

[6] *MPC* 1: xxvi. These were Committees of Plantations, Justice and Safety, Trade and Treasury, Manners, Education, and Arts.
[7] *MPC*, 8.

bly. In afternoons the council commonly assembled at three or four o'clock and sat until six or later, so that additional duties such as preparation of bills had to be attended to at night or before opening of the morning session. Attendance at the council alone was enough to make the month's program strenuous, and evening work by candlelight did not make it easier. Whether Thomas Holme was able to attend at all to his surveyor's duties while the council was in session is questionable.

The Frame of Government in its first form was not altogether satisfactory to either body. On 27 March Thomas Holme and John Moll were ordered by the governor and council to go to the assembly for a conference on proposed amendments. In the afternoon session, they, John Simcock, and Christopher Taylor were appointed to consider the amendment to the charter and give a report on the following day. Finally, on 29 March, Thomas Holme, as councilman from Philadelphia, and John Moll of New Castle, Francis Whitwell of Kent, William Clark of Sussex, James Harrison of Bucks and William Clayton of Chester were appointed a formal Committee of the Council to draw up the charter with amendments, presumably for presentation when the council would "sitt upon the charter this afternoon att 6 of the clock." It was decided that "the general Surv^r and Purchasers" would meet the following evening in the council chamber "about the Fees of Surveying." This would be an extremely important meeting for Thomas Holme. Deputy surveyors were already withholding fees, and he had no way of extracting his share. Having invested most of his capital in Pennsylvania real estate and shares in the Free Society of Traders, he needed the fees to which he was legally entitled for day-to-day expenses.

At the council meeting on the thirtieth Penn demanded of the council whether the old charter with amendments would serve, or whether a new one should be drawn. It was "agreed that it should be drawn again and the admendment put in." The original committee was ordered to prepare it by eight o'clock the next morning. In view of the meeting concerning surveyor's fees to be held at six, Thomas Holme would have a taxing evening; but fatigue seemed unimportant on 31 March, when the Speaker and whole assembly joined the council for the reading of the charter. Penn proposed cutting the five hundred maximum number of members that Thomas Holme and his associates had specified to two hundred, but his suggestion was "passed in the negative." The bills were read and passed into laws unanimously. Finally, on 2 April, a triumphant new note rang out the conclusion of the long evolution of the charter when

The Speaker audibly read in the house, a Petition to the Governor from the Council and Assembly, That the Charter of Liberties of the Province of Pennsylvania, *might Date at Philadelphia, and not in London.* The above-said Petition had been signed by the Council, was now sign'd by the House.[8]

The Frame of Government at last completed, the tedious formulation of the Laws of the Province continued for another six weeks. Finally, on 23 May, "It was proposed to have attested Copy of the Laws Printed." The proposal was "carried in the Negative," but it was agreed that attested copies under the secretary's hand should be "transmitted to the President & Clark of each respective County" for the people to refer to for their information.[9]

In the course of the month two other events important to William Penn occurred. On 22 March the Duke of York finally received from his royal brother King Charles II a patent to "all that the town of Newcastle and port therein or thereunto belonging, situate, and lying & being between Maryland and New Jersey in America," and "all lands etc. within the circle of twelve miles about said town,"[10] and on the twenty-third Penn received from John Fenwick a grant of half of New Jersey.[11]

With April came a great surge of activity. Settlers who had arrived late in the fall saw the rich Pennsylvania landscape burst into flower. Forests and cleared land were suddenly as green as England and Ireland, and fragrant with the new growth of familiar and excitingly unfamiliar trees and shrubs and the ubiquitous tangle of vines. It was time to plant, and new warrants for more than twenty-five thousand acres poured into the surveyor's office.

The need for city lots was equally imperative, and warrants for forty or fifty of these had accumulated. Thomas Holme's small mercantile cargo went quickly. He was in a position to offer saddles and shovels to the newly arrived—supplies less decorative than the raw silk and glass bowls of shipments to New England, but more eagerly sought. He had no intention of adding further shopkeeping to his multiplying civic duties.

Lord Baltimore became increasingly angry and determined when he learned that the Duke of York's claim to the New Castle area had been authenticated by a bona fide grant. Not only was this a sealed

---

[8] *Votes*, 40. Italics the author's.
[9] *MPC*, 18.
[10] *CSPC, AWI*, 1681–1696, no. 1011, p.408. This is a document recording a grant that had been given orally some time before.
[11] *PWP* (Micro. 4: 142).

document, but it was at once surrendered for a larger one. The attorney general informed King Charles:

> The Duke of York surrenders patent to Newcastle & other lands you are hereby pleased to grant him that same town & all the river of Delaware & a tract of land on the west side thereof from Skoolkill Creek on the Delaware to Bomboy Hook, & back into the woods so far as the Minaquas country & from Bomboy Hook to Cape Henlopen, now called Cape James, & back into the woods 3 Indian days.[12]

At the same time there were rumblings in New Jersey as Pennsylvania increasingly took on the aspect of a rival.

At home William Penn was besieged by newcomers who sought preferential consideration in choice of land—requests that he received graciously and passed on to Thomas Holme. As further problems of establishing a new country arose, more legislation was required, and there was much traffic between council and the assembly, and much debating of bills. The pressure, fortunately, had been alleviated by the settlement in the preceding month of the Frame of Government, and the calendar of meetings was slightly relaxed.

With the increasing demand for land it was imperative that present holdings and records be regularized. William Penn's previous order to freeholders of Philadelphia County to "bring in court a full & exact account of all their lands. . ." had not been complied with: on 14 April Thomas Holme, Nicholas More, and Thomas Fairman, as justices of the peace for the city and county of Philadelphia, issued a further order, recapitulating the earlier one and adding:

> the thing being neglected hitherto Contrary to the Governours Command & the Charge Given in Court For the Same, This are therefore to require & give in Command to all the Constables in the Forenamed County to summon all the Freeholders of this County to bring in the same betwixt this & three Weeks inclusive to the Clerk of the County under the penaltyes of twenty shillings per head to be Forfeited For the Governours use & this shall be your Warrant
>
> N:More
Tho: Holme
Tho:Fairman

Signed & Sealed this 14th of / The Second Month 1683 / att Shakemakese

To the Sheriffs & Constables of the Citty & County of Philadelphia[13]

---

[12] PRO, SPC 50: no. 94. Copy signed by R. Sawyer.
[13] APS, *Penn Letters and Documents* 1: item 186. See also *Survey and Warrant Book*, PhA.

The enforcement of this order would require not only time and effort but diplomacy, a quality for which neither More nor Fairman was distinguished, and which, if he possessed it at all, was an acquired virtue in the surveyor general. Its accomplishment was a slow and tedious process, but the record was an essential preliminary to the enclosing of the liberty land available to first purchasers.

Finally, on 4 April, the council adjourned until 2 May. The governor, in keeping with the prescription in the Frame of Government that selected members of the council attend him, ordered Thomas Holme and Christopher Taylor (three-year men), Edmond Cantwell and Edward Southern (two-year men), and William Clayton and John Richardson (one-year men), to attend him. There is no indication of Penn's immediate need of their assistance, but the order may have been given in anticipation of Baltimore's projected visit, which would take place on 29 May.

The matter of purchases from the surrounding Indian tribes was also on the agenda. On 19 April Penn gave Thomas Holme a warrant for five hundred acres of land on Neshaminy Creek for Lawrence and Joseph Growden, on which Thomas noted: "26. 4mo [June] Ordered it there as soon as bought of the Indians."[14] On 24 April Thomas ordered Fairman to survey ten thousand acres in Philadelphia County for Penn himself, "where the Governor shall direct."[15]

The council meeting of 2 May was held at Lewes in Sussex County, with only the Proprietor, Markham, and five council members present. Thomas Holme was absent from this and the two meetings that followed it. The only business of the meeting seems to have been the governor's announcement that he had chosen Nicholas More to be secretary to the council; Markham and Simcock were sent to summon More for installation. Holding the meeting at Lewes at the mouth of Delaware Bay, sixty-odd miles from New Castle, may have been either a further statement of validity of ownership incident on the latest grant, or a diplomatic gesture toward the Lower Counties, not all of whose inhabitants were in favor of union with Pennsylvania. After the meeting the council adjourned until 23 May.

In the course of the Friends' May half-yearly meeting Thomas Holme was drawn into two unpleasant actions. With Griffith Jones he was appointed to speak to James Atkinson touching his arrival in the province, and as one of a committee to arbitrate a dispute between

---

[14] Dept. Sur., *OR*, 68, p. 157, DAM, PHMC. Cited also by ACM. The purchase from the Indians had been accomplished on 23 June.
[15] *OR*, D 86–196, no. 50.

Griffith Jones and John Songhurst. The Atkinson affair was still hanging fire when the Quarterly Meeting opened on 5 June. A certificate from Clanbrazill in county Antrim, Ireland, had been brought to the 3 April Quarterly Meeting. It said that Atkinson had come into the province contrary to the consent of the Friends of the meeting to which he belonged, very much in debt.[16]

As was customary with the Friends, he was informed of the accusation and given an opportunity to defend himself or set things right. This he seems to have accomplished to the satisfaction of the committee, for at the July meeting it was agreed that Thomas Holme, Thomas Wynne, and Griffith Jones should write to the Friends at Clanbrazill, assuring them of the regularity of James Atkinson's transfer from England and Ireland to Pennsylvania. It may be inferred that committees on which Thomas Holme served were prone to reach charitable conclusions about possible offenses. This had certainly been the case with Samuel Claridge's problems in Dublin and with Grace Edmundson's remark about her unfortunate suitor's death.

Thomas Holme's third assignment during this meeting was of more agreeable nature. He was appointed to meet with Christopher Taylor, Thomas Wynne, Thomas Ducket, Henry Lewes, and Benjamin Chambers to prepare a succinct but full description of the procedures of the men's and women's meetings in England.[17]

Thomas Holme was not present at the meetings of the council on 23 and 24 May. On the twenty-third the only business transacted was the decision not to print the laws. The governor also ordered the council to attend him during the stay of Lord Baltimore "in these parts." Only four members appeared for the meeting on the following day, and the council adjourned until 6 June.

It might be assumed that with the approval of the Frame of Government as it was submitted by Thomas Holme and his committee, there would be some slackening of pace, but this did not occur. By the end of May warrants had been presented for more than thirty thousand acres of land for more than sixty petitioners, and, more pressing, at least seventy-five warrants for city lots lay on his desk.

Until late in May no special activity by either Thomas Holme or William Penn is noted in public records. Albert Cook Myers states that sometime during the spring Penn went into the interior. Thomas Holme was to urge the importance of the Susquehanna on subsequent

---

[16] *Genealogical Society of Pennsylvania Magazine* 1 (December, 1898), 255; Minutes of the Philadephia meeting, Friends' Library, Arch Street Meeting Archives, Philadelphia.
[17] Arch Street Archives, 5 May 1683.

occasions, and when Penn and his council met with Baltimore on 29 May, the Proprietor again demonstrated his eagerness to acquire the river and a substantial corridor of land along its banks. He had appointed Richard Noble as deputy surveyor general in Thomas Holme's absence. It is very probable that Thomas Holme and William Penn, perhaps accompanied by Thomas Fairman, explored the Susquehanna area in preparation for the encounter with Baltimore.

The meeting took place at New Castle, the site chosen by Baltimore as lying within the territory he claimed as his own. Again Penn proposed purchasing the lower Susquehanna, and again Baltimore refused to sell it, although he would consider trading it for Kent and Sussex Counties. Penn would not surrender these. In August Penn sent Markham to London to plead his cause, armed with all the supporting documents he could assemble, including the signatures of Thomas Holme, William Clark, and Christopher Taylor, dated 22 August, as witnesses of the meeting with Lord Baltimore at the house of Colonel Taylor.[18] The following spring Baltimore went to England to urge his case before the Lords of Trade and Plantations, with Markham to oppose him before this powerful and not entirely friendly body.

Meanwhile, east of the Delaware other complications were brewing. The problems of New Jersey went back to the tangled roots of its foundation, in which William Penn had been involved for over half a decade. When, in 1664, England acquired New Netherland, Charles II ceded all of the territory from the Connecticut to the Delaware River to his younger brother, the Duke of York. On 23 June the Duke leased the land between the Hudson and the Delaware to two members of the Privy Council, John, Lord Berkeley, and Sir George Carteret, issuing a release on 24 June.

Assuming the land soon to be called *Nova Caesarea*, or New Jersey, to be within the jurisdiction of New York, two separate groups petitioned Governor Nicholls for tracts which he, equally innocently, granted. The first of these was what now comprises Cape May County in the south. The other grant was what would later be known as Elizabethtown, Shrewsbury, and Middletown neighborhoods, secured for the site of a previously planned settlement. Inevitably the fact that the grants obtained from Governor Nicholls lay within the territory ceded by the Duke of York to Lord Berkeley and Sir George Carteret gave rise to difficulties.

---

[18] HSP, DS, *Pa. Misc. Papers, Penn vs. Baltimore*, 10. For convoluted reports of Penn-Baltimore negotiations see *MdA*, vols. 5 and 17. For a succinct account of them see *PWP* 2: 381–383, headnote to D 115, and D 155, 484–499.

After a brief Dutch reconquest ended, the crown lawyers reconveyed the Duke's former title and power to Carteret in East Jersey. Berkeley, meanwhile, had sold his right to Quakers John Fenwick and Edward Byllynge.

The Duke received his new patent on 29 June 1664 and on 28–29 July confirmed Carteret in all rights in New Jersey between Barnegat Creek and Rancocas Kill—over half the province—but sent Sir Edmund Andros as governor of the area between the Connecticut and the Delaware. Carteret, on the other hand, installed his cousin Philip as governor of his portion of the province.

In the somewhat reduced remaining part of the territory, now distinguished as West Jersey, a power struggle had developed between Byllynge and Fenwick. They called upon William Penn to arbitrate their dispute, and he awarded nine-tenths of the territory to Byllynge and the remaining tenth to Fenwick. Byllynge, in financial trouble, assigned his shares in trust for his creditors to three Quakers: William Penn, Gawen Laurie, and Nicholas Lucas. Fenwick, also suffering financial reverses, sold parts of his tenth, and heavily mortgaged the rest to John Edridge and Edmund Warner, who bought Edridge's portion.

In 1675 Fenwick, with his family and sufficient immigrants for his purposes, arrived from England on the *Griffith* and founded Salem, the first settlememt in New Jersey founded directly from England, Elizabethtown having been settled largely by Quakers from Long Island, and Shrewsbury and Middletown chiefly from New England. The chief surveyor of Fenwick's property was Richard Noble, who within a decade would be Thomas Holme's deputy. Andros resented Fenwick's activities and in December 1676 had him arrested and jailed, but he released him a month later. Byllynge's trustees demanded a more equitable division of the entire territory.

Finally the Duke persuaded Sir George to surrender his grant of 1674, and on 1 July 1676 a "*quinquipartite* deed" was executed, defining the rights of all factions concerned. The dividing line was set from Little Egg Harbor to a point on the Delaware River at 40° 40′ north latitude, with the eastern portion awarded to Carteret and the western—about five-eighths of the total—to the Quakers. In February of 1682/83, following the death of Philip Carteret, East New Jersey was sold at auction to William Penn and eleven others, each of whom then sold half his purchase to a second purchaser, thus forming a coalition of twenty-four proprietors. The Duke confirmed the sale on 14 March, and Robert Barclay, a prominent Quaker proprietor, was chosen governor for life, with the privilege of appointing a deputy. For this post he chose Penn's attorney and agent, Thomas Rudyard.

The *Kent* had arrived in August of 1680 with 230 Quakers from London and Yorkshire. They founded what would become Burlington. Richard Noble joined them and laid out the town, which has been mentioned as one of the possible prototypes of Philadelphia. The Duke confirmed the territory to Byllynge, who commissioned another prominent Quaker, Samuel Jennings, as deputy, an office he held until 1682.

Fenwick, out of jail, persisted in his attempt to reestablish the government of Salem with himself "Lord and Chief Proprietor of West Jersey," but his move was contested by the officers of the Duke. In March of 1682/83 William Penn was again called upon to make peace. With Thomas Holme he went to New Jersey and, as he thought, settled the difficulty by buying Fenwick's remaining claims, and on 23 March 1682/83 Fenwick delivered the deed, witnessed by Philip Theodore Lehnmann, Thomas Holme, Samuel Hodge, and John Smith.[19]

This at least was one transfer of property to which the New Jersey settlers would not be averse. Fenwick, arrogant and autocratic, was exceedingly unpopular. Robert Wade, one of his purchasers, said as early as 1675: "Had John Fenwick done wisely, we had not been desperst."[20] Others were even more vocal in their dissatisfaction, until finally Penn's agent, James Nevill, offered the Proprietor practical advice: "I thinke it may be the best, to setle Jo^n Fenwick in the Province of Pensilvania, and remove him, so, that he have no interest or Clayme here; least being in possession he should adde to his parties wch he hath already made...."[21]

Confronted as he was by tensions between settlers and absentee proprietors, Quakers and other Protestants, power and property-hungry landholders, and not affluent but independent settlers, William Penn, who was a proprietor of both Jerseys, reacted promptly and furiously to rumors from abroad that threatened the prosperity and prestige of Pennsylvania. Letters from his wife, Gulielma, and James Claypoole, now preparing to emigrate, reported letters of Thomas Mathews of New Jersey, attorney of Scottish Quaker proprietor Robert Barclay, evidently intimating that hostilities between Baltimore

---

[19] *NJA*, 1, 1: 310. (Micro. 142).
[20] Letter to his wife, April 1676, ACM (HSP, reel 39).
[21] LS, *Records of the Provincial Council*, Misc. MSS, Bureau of Archives and History, DAM, PHMC (Micro. 4: 088). *PWP* 2: 357. For the reaction of Thomas Holme and other members of the government in Pennsylvania, see below.

and Penn verged on actual combat, and that Baltimore had, or soon would, cut Pennsylvania off completely from the Atlantic. The matter was debated at the council meeting on 6 June 1863. The minutes of the provincial council attribute the letters to East New Jersey, but since, as the editors of the *Papers of William Penn* point out, it was Robert Stacy of West New Jersey who consulted in the matter and it was to West New Jersey that investigators were sent, the attribution must have been intended for West New Jersey. At any rate, the consultant assured the council that if they would make a formal complaint it would be answered as satisfactorily as possible.

Penn promptly deputed Christopher Taylor, James Harrison, and Thomas Holme to go to the offending province and "communicate to the Gov' & Councill, their Certaine passages written to England, by some of their Province, as injurious to the Welfare and Prosperity of this." The council appears not to have met on the following day, which was Thursday, but Thomas Holme and Christopher Taylor were present on the eighth and ninth.

On Monday, 11 June, the minutes of the council record that "the members of the Councill being not returned which went to New Jarsey, the Govr was pleased to prolong the adjourm^t till the 20th of the 4th Mo., 83," although Christopher Taylor and Thomas Holme were marked as present. Their commission to treat with the governor and council of New Jersey is dated 11 June, as are Penn's letter to the governor and council of West New Jersey and his instructions to his commissioners. It is possible that a preliminary attempt at gaining reparation was made on the seventh, its failure provoking the documents of 11 June.

The commission is a formal document delegating complete powers to the commissioners "to treat, transact, and conclude with the Governor and Counsell" for the wrongs Penn and his province have received and "to settle a right understanding between me and them about the Trade and the Islands therein, and w^{t}soever you shall do herein, I do hereby ratifie and confirm and this shall be to you a sufficient credential."[22]

By the time the commission was written Thomas Wynne was added to the group. Armed with William Penn's letter, their commission, and a formidable and explicit set of directions, the commissioners crossed the Delaware to Burlington on the afternoon of 11 June. The next morning was frustrating. The governor of the colony had gone

---

[22] *PA*, 2, 1 (1852), 60–61. Df. in hand of PTL, ACM, NYPL, 301; HSP, Penn Papers, Misc. Letters 1: 9.

to the Falls on the tenth and had not yet returned. Preparing their presentation they were forced to write back to Penn "near noon":

> We are preparing our business, but find a want of J F [John Fenwick] letter; and other letters, that may either generally or rather pticulary change matter of fact; therefore we could wish, thou wouldst please to send us these letters with speed; which may help us to strengthen our charge: The rumor of our grievenses agt N. Jersey arrived here before us, and most we have yet spoken with, seem much concerned and very sensible of our great injuries, and say, they wish the p'ties may be found out and punished. . . . We have Tho: Mathews named but in one letter, and if there be any other letter that mentions him, it will do well (we think) to send it us.[23]

The letter was marked *Hast*, and endorsed "Tho: Holmes, Christ. Taylor, Tho. Wynne."

Penn's letter to the governor and council of West Jersey opens with expressions of love and peace, progresses to sorrow, and rises to a crescendo of angry accusations, ending with faith in the ultimate restoration of good relations and the signature of "your loving Neighbor & sincere friend."[24] In his instructions to his commissioners he is not conciliatory. He directs them to follow formal ambassadorial procedure in presenting the charges against Thomas Mathews, supported by letters, and then demanding "Satisfaction first in General by a certificate under their hands to give the lye to such rumors," followed by a proclamation forbidding "any such scandalous Reflections for the time to come." For Mathews severe punishment is suggested, ranging from a fine of £500 sterling to public disgrace by a paper posted on the courthouse at Burlington, to banishment from the colony for six months, to exclusion from office forever. Deviation from these choices, banishment excepted, was not allowed.

If these demands are not acceded to, the commissioners are "to make your protest against the said Governor and Councell, and their Refusal, and so with a meek, and quiet, yet grave behaiour, to return." Everything said or done relating to their mission is to be taken down in writing and the exact report delivered to Penn on their return.

Once the question of Mathews's libel is settled, the commissioners are to insist upon William Penn's title to the river, with the soil and islands thereof, but if the easterners deliver up the islands of Matinicum [Burlington] and Sepassing [Biddle's Island] the commissioners are to return half of Matinicum as a gesture of generosity and good will

---
[23] ACM 65, 172. Photostat of document in the collection of Gilbert Cope of West Chester.
[24] Df., ACM, NYPL (Micro. 4: 224); *PWP* 2: 391.

on Penn's part. The surrender of the river is to follow the customary ceremonial that was observed at New Castle.[25] Since the minutes of the deferred meeting of the council have no reference to the West Jersey affair, it may be assumed that the return of the commissioners was quiet, although we may be tempted to question their meekness.

Whatever the disposition of his messengers, Penn was not altogether satisfied with the outcome of their mission. On 20 June he again wrote to the governor and council of West Jersey. After courteous recognition of their "Justice & Kindness," he protests their response with regard to Mathews, Baltimore, and the islands. He suggests the form of reply he desires, and leaves the situation unresolved. On 18 July he issued a proclamation stating that the governor of New Jersey had requested him to warn citizens against purchasing land from Thomas Mathews.[26]

Actually Penn's right to the islands was questionable, and controversy concerning them would be of long duration. On 12 May 1681 Sir John Werden, secretary to the Duke of York, had written to Sir Edmund Andros, that the Lords of Trade and Plantations, he presumes, "have taken to uphold existing rights," and that the islands in the Delaware seem to be excluded from Penn's patent; and again, on 16 July 1681, he had written to Penn on the same topic. This time he stated that he had assumed that the Delaware was Penn's eastern boundary and that the islands were not, so far as he could see, included in the grant.[27]

The affair of New Jersey, it is true, has only peripheral relevance to Thomas Holme's professional obligations; but he was tangentially concerned with all that related to Penn's welfare. He may also have profited somewhat personally through his connections with them. His son Tryall had at least a minor role in a land transaction. At any rate as a charter three-year member of the council as well as surveyor general and justice of the peace, Thomas Holme could be called upon without impropriety to be consultant and messenger; and, circulating among all ranks of society he was able to observe, estimate, and to some extent influence the feelings and opinions of the population in general.

Penn's concern for both West and East New Jersey was well founded. Not everyone was on his side in the dispute with Lord Balti-

---

[25] *PA*, 1, 1, 1683: 58; Df., Chew Family Papers, HSP (Micro. 4: 218). *PWP* 2: 392-394.
[26] *CSP Colonial Entry Book* 70: 34, 35, printed in New York Documents 3: 286-287 and 290.
[27] C, *Penn MSS*, FLL (Micro. 4: 024); *PWP* 2: 340. The surveyor general here maligned by Rudyard is sometimes erroneously identified as Thomas Holme.

more. Some believed that their economic interests lay with Baltimore's control of both Chesapeake Bay and the lower Delaware, and they had sufficient influence to produce a threat to Penn's claims. East New Jersey as a neighbor to New York under the wary eye of the governor of that territory was a potential menace to Penn's ambitions regarding the Susquehanna, which was of vital interest to the fur trade. Penn was only one of twenty-four proprietors, most of whom resided in England. Many of them had small concern for the largely Quaker province of Pennsylvania across the Delaware from their very considerable property in New Jersey.

Penn wrote to the proprietors of East New Jersey on 11 July 1683 as one who, "being on the Spott," was in a position to make better judgments than transatlantic observers. Speaking as one of them he states that the people are not easily deflected from any point they aim at, but that they are less wise than is desirable in choosing their goals, and the present government is not altogether beneficial to either the people or the proprietors. He recommends that more of the proprietors or their representatives should take up residence in New Jersey to safeguard the rights of both groups. He had recommended the replacement of certain "Old Officers" who held their positions since 1671–1673, and of Robert Vicars, who had been provincial secretary during the preceding year. Currently his friend Thomas Rudyard was acting deputy governor, though he would be replaced by Gawen Laurie, one of the original proprietors, in 1684.

The letter was no doubt intended to reinforce Rudyard's wish expressed in his letter to Penn on 13 January 1682/83 for removal of certain of the old officers. Rudyard's difficulties sprang in part from the apparent senility of his fellow proprietor and surveyor general, Samuel Groome. Groome, according to Rudyard, doggedly followed the direction he allegedly received from England to reserve the good land for the use of the proprietors, selling the inferior tracts to settlers. Rudyard wished to make the best land available to purchasers. Groome, he averred, "is grown into an angry and pettish humor, & in a manner intractible." It was the invitation issued in this letter that prompted Penn's attendance at the meeting of the assembly of Elizabethtown on 1 March, 1683. Thomas Holme, with Penn during his visits to New Jersey in March, was an astute observer of the complications of divided ownership and adminstration. By July the situation in New Jersey was even worse. Groome's memory was failing, but he was obdurate in his hold on land distribution, refusing to appoint the badly needed deputies. Rudyard was worried about the planting of settlers.[28] Robert Barclay, writing in another context, voiced equal concern. It is said "that the Surveyor General has Orders to pick & cull the prime land of the Country for the Proprietors and place the Planters only in barrows and incommodious ground." He writes almost enviously of Pennsylvania, in terms that would have given solace and encouragement to both Penn and Thomas Holme, had they received the letter:

> I know nothing has more contributed to the quieting & satisfying of all people in Pennsylvania than an expeditious placing the Planters & Adventurers upon the land they must have, And I have been credibly informed that the readiness of the Surveyor General, and the assistance of the Deputies appointed, no one has been 10 days without Settlem^t after he has set foot on Shoure, which is a reputation to the Governm^t & that Countrey.[29]

In Pennsylvania, he states, they can settle two thousand or three thousand people in one year; in New Jersey, with difficulty if at all, a hundred. He may be recalling the promptness with which Thomas Holme had settled Rudyard along with Haige and others, in August 1682. In New Jersey poor Groome was having his own problems. Writing from New York on 11 August 1683 he mentions, among other problems, that William Penn has written him

> to lay out his 10000 A about Burny Gatte^{xr} [Barnegat] but I writt him (Marke that well) that I would not see how I could in my life time lay out 24 times 10000 A, because I at p^{r}sent see no way to have it except I take all swamps, mountains Xc. All wch cannot at p^{r}sent be purchased from the natives if had enough.[30]

Ironically, Mr. Groome's lifetime ended before October of that year.

Anxiety about William Penn's threatened territorial expansion was not merely a matter of local rivalry. Sir John Werden, who had at first appeared neutral in New Jersey matters, became increasingly partisan. He advised the Duke of York not to give Penn any further advantages with regard to boundaries, and warned Governor Dongan of New York against surrendering any territory or rights in the Susquehanna region. Dongan was untiring in negotiating trade arrangements and in bar-

---

[28] Thomas Rudyard to William Penn, 30 July 1683, Penn MSS 1: no. 12, FLL. A clue to Thomas Holme's apparent partiality to Rudyard may be detected here, in their objection to the reservation of the best land for the proprietors and the surveying of the less desirable land for purchasers.
[29] ACM, box 39.
[30] ACM, box 39. The number twenty-four refers to the total number of proprietors.

gaining for land with the Susquehanna Indians. In this he was encouraged by George Fox, who wrote to him, urging him to see that the *status quo* was preserved in this regard; and Barclay urged that the next governor of East New Jersey have power to enter ships and make the province a port, "else New York may contest with us, to enter all ships bound into the province at the port of New York." William Penn, he pointed out, required all ships bound thither to enter at New Castle.[31]

---

[31] NY Documents 3: 340; CEB, 70: 47.

Chapter 10

The Home Front

While problems were multiplying east of the Delaware, warrants for land were accumulating on Thomas Holme's desk, settlers were complaining of delays, and the land on which they were to be seated was still to be purchased from the Indians. Thus far only one tract of land had been bought: that negotiated for by William Markham on 15 July 1682, reaching from the Falls of the Delaware along the river to Neshaminy Creek and as far back as the Indian town, Playwicky, an area that included the Governor's future seat of Pennsbury. As noted above, his witness to the memorandum attached to the deed on 1 August 1682 is the earliest evidence of Silas Crispin's presence in Pennsylvania.[1] In addition to the fact that in 1675 the Indians had sold some land to the governor of New York, the apparent finality of this document was misleading.

Relations with the Indians were friendly but lacked the legal definition necessary to satisfy the natives and to provide security for the settlers. Penn's picture of the Indians in his letter to the secretary of state, the Earl of Sunderland, presents them much as they must have appeared to him and to some extent to Thomas Holme on ceremonial occasions in this third year of the Province. Penn wrote:

> They are Savage to us, in their Persons, & furniture; all that is rude; but they have great shape, Strength, agility; & in Councel (for they (tho in a

---
[1] *WP's Own Account* . . . , 79; *PWP* 2: 256.

kind of Community among themselves) observe property [propriety] & Governm^t) grave, speak seldom, interspaces of silence, Short, elegant, fervent; The old sitt in half moon upon the Ground, the middle in the same manner behind them. None Speak but the Aged, they haveing Consulted the rest before; thus in selling me thier land they ordered themselves . . . [He believes] that their obscurity consider'd, wanting tradition, example & instruction; they are an extraordinary peoples; had not the Dutch, Sweeds & Englesh learn'd them drunkenness. . . .[2]

Francis Pastorius's more graphic description of the native Americans of this time and place probably rounds out also the realistic Thomas Holme's perception of them:

They are, in general, strong, agille, and supple people, with blackish bodies; they went about naked at first and wore only a cloth about the loins. Now they are beginning to wear shirts. They have, usually, coalblack hair, shave the head, smear the same with grease, and allow a long lock to grow on the right side. They also besmear the children with grease, and let them creep about in the heat of the sun, so that they become the color of a nut, although they were at first white enough by nature.[3]

The weakness for rum on the part of some of the Indians was a source of temptation to unscrupulous traders seeking instant riches in the enormously profitable fur trade, and sometimes a provocation of disorders that Thomas Holme had to deal with.

On 23 June the most immediately needed of the desired transactions had been initiated with the purchase of the land between the Delaware and the Indian town of Playwicky and the Neshaminy to Pennypack (Dublin) Creek from Essepenaike, Tammany, and Swampees. A set of successive deeds and receipts, signed by various combinations of Indian and white witnesses, appears in the *Archives of Pennsylvania*. All of the documents involve "all my lands" between Pennypack (Dublin) and Neshaminy Creeks, "and all along Neshamine Creek," and two specify the land to extend as far back as a man can go in a two-days' journey on a horse. Lasse Cock, the usual interpreter, witnessed all the deeds; and Joseph Curtis's and Philip Theodore Lehnmann's names appear on two. Thomas Holme, Nicholas More, and Christopher Taylor witnessed the deed of Essepenaike, Swampees, Okettarickon, and Wessapoat—one of those that specified a two days' journey. Essepenaike was a principal in two of the sales and the

---

[2] ALS, Henry Bradley Martin Coll., New York City (Micro. 4: 338). *PWP* 2: 417.
[3] ACM, *Narratives*, 383.

famous Tammany in two. Tammany and Metamequan gave the most detailed receipt for goods paid by William Penn. They received:

5 p Stockings	5 Hatts	10 Tabacco Tongs
26 Barrs lead	25 lb Powder	5 Capps
10 Pair Sissers	10 Tabacco Boxes	1 peck Pipes
15 Combs	7 Half Gills	6 Coats, 2 Guns
38 yds Dufills	5 Hoes	6 Axes
8 shirts	14 Knives	2 Blanketts
2 Kettles	12 Awles	9 Gimbletts
4 handfull Bells	4 yds Stroud Water	100 Needles
20 Fishhooks	26 Handfuls of Wampum[4]	

Since both Neshaminy and Pennypack were valuable streams, Neshaminy extending some twenty miles into the interior, and Pennypack half that distance, it may be assumed that the various Indian signers of the deeds were owners of contiguous lands. Two or three miles beyond the source of Pennypack and over half the length of Neshaminy were involved in the purchase.[5]

The locale of the transactions north of Philadelphia is not mentioned, but because of the multiple concerns of the various signers they probably took place at one point, either Shackamaxon or, more probably, as the editors of the *Penn Papers* suggest, at Philadelphia. Two days later, in Chester County, Wingebone sold his land between the upper portion of Chester Creek and the Schuylkill to William Penn. Since John Moll had already transferred his land—a triangle between Christian and Red Clay Creeks within the twelve-mile circle at New Castle—with the exception of his personal plantation to the Proprietor in February, this sale concluded the acquisition of the west side of the Delaware from Upland/Chester to the Falls a little above the present Trenton, New Jersey, with territory extending various distances into the interior.

Three more purchases later in the year would make valuable additions to Chester County holdings. On 10 September Kekelappan sold his land on the Susquehanna, including the territory around Octoraro Creek, and on 18 October Machaloha sold to the governor the coveted tract along the lower Susquehanna to its mouth, including Jacob Young's trading post. These two purchases embraced in the neighborhood of two hundred square miles, with approximately twenty miles of frontage on the Susquehanna and, above all, an outlet on Chesa-

---

[4] *PA*, 1, 1: 262–265. This and other deeds are printed in *PWP*, vol. 2.
[5] *PWP* 2: 491.

peake Bay. So crucial was this purchase in the mind of Penn that he published a declaration that he had bought of Machaloha all of his land between the Delaware River, Chesapeake Bay, and the Susquehanna River. He warned all existing settlers to behave themselves, and all other persons not to settle there without his leave. He signed the document and sealed it with the seal of Pennsylvania. The final deed was that of Seketarius and his associates on 19 December for

> all our lands between Christiana and Upland Creek unto William Penn after the same manner as Kehlappan and others sell theirs . . . of which I have already received a very good gun, some powder, and laid [lead], 2 pair of stockings, one match coat, and ten bitts Spanish money.

The deed was witnessed by Thomas Holme, John Moone, and John Songhurst.[6]

On the face of it, these purchases appear to have been an outrageous conning of the Indians by the cunning white men, but the Indians themselves considered them an equitable exchange. The goods were valuable to them, and they trusted these white men who were friendlier than the northern tribes, and who respected them and appreciated their friendship. Moreover, it must be admitted that if inequities did occur, neither purchasers nor sellers were altogether innocent victims. Indians were known sometimes to sell each other's land; and the white purchasers saw to it that the deputies running lines as far as a man could walk or ride a horse within a specified time trained ahead of time in order to include the maximum amount of territory.

Anxious attendance on the affairs of New Jersey, the southern boundary, and the final acquisition of the land along the Delaware interfered with the laying out of city lots and the tentative assignment of liberty land and larger tracts. Roach estimates that by the end of April only about twenty-five lots had been surveyed on the Delaware side of the city, most of which were "on backward streets," "for men such as weavers, tailors, coopers, carpenters or joiners," the Front Street lots being held for or already assigned to large purchasers who would be principally merchants or planters.

Apparently during the greater part of May Thomas Holme and William Penn were absent and Richard Noble issued only a few orders for lots, the clearing of which commenced during that month.[7] During

---

[6] *SPC, AWI*, 1681–1696, 521, no. 135; *PWP*, 2: 492. This purchase is the first in which money was exchanged.

[7] Roach, "Planting," 105–107. For details of individual holdings, this article is indispensable.

the summer, with the Proprietor and the surveyor general both back in Philadelphia/Shackamaxon headquarters and the land coming through Indian purchases firmly in Penn's hands, surveyed tracts were cleared as rapidly as possible. Philadelphia commenced to take on the aspect of a town, and farmers proceeded with the cultivation of crops planted earlier in anticipation of the incontestable ownership of the land and the clearing of the remainder of their property. The Schuylkill side of the city was also being surveyed, with a number of lots reserved for settlers yet to arrive, giving definition to the city. It was with justifiable pride and optimism that Penn wrote to the Earl of Rochester on 14 June,

> We gett us Houses apace, & shall have two of the three Blessings of Canaan, Corn & Wine; and admirable place for Air & good living, . . . having about 80 houses in our Town, & three hundred & odd Farmers settled since last fall.[8]

Tactfully he brings to the Earl's attention the future value of exports—timber, iron, flax, hemp, and tobacco—to the crown with the hope that appreciation of these will be expressed in favorable regards on the other side of the ocean. He is even more particular in his letter to Sunderland on 28 July, quoted in part above. Although this account of his province was prompted as much by diplomacy as by friendship, it sparkles with the enthusiasm of the young proprietor—he was not yet forty—that conveyed itself in varying degrees to his immigrants. He becomes almost lyrical as he assures Sunderland that "The Country is in Soyle good, air sereen . . . & Sweet from the Cedar, Pine, & Sarsefrax, wth a wild Mertile that all send forth a most fragrant smell, wch every brees carrys wth it to the inhabitants where it goes."[9] He goes on to describe the game, fruit, and fish (there are oysters "monst'rous for size") to be had in abundance. He plans to give a "Collection of the most valuable of w^t this place affords for Arstrope [Althorp, the Earl's estate]."

Reading Penn's exultant catalogue of his accomplishments during his first ten months in Pennsylvania, the observer of the life of Thomas Holme recalls the long journeys into the woods complained of by Thomas Fairman, the non-commercial encounters with the Indians, the bickering over choice tracts and lines of surveys, the piecing together of the meager field maps he was able to extract from his deputies,

---

[8] Hazard, *Register* 1: 453; Proud, 1: 245–246; ACM, *Narratives*, 224.
[9] ALS. Collection of Henry Bradley Martin, New York City (Micro. 4: 338).

and the "attendance on the Governor" that constituted Thomas Holme's contribution to this good beginning. Nevertheless, the letters present a charming portrait of a land that seemed to Thomas Holme as well as to William Penn well worth the risks and hardships that made it habitable.

Although Thomas Holme foresaw the necessity of certain alterations in his city plan, it was basically accurate enough that now he committed to vellum for the English professional draftsman and printer *A Portraiture of the City of Philadelphia in Pennsylvania*. What is believed to be the original drawing, as mentioned above, survives in the State Archives at Harrisburg. The fair copy was engraved on copper plate that, with subsequent minor changes, is preserved today in the library of the Historical Society of Pennsylvania. It was published with Penn's letter to the Free Society of Traders, dated 16 August 1683 and Thomas Holme's *A Short Advertisement upon the Scituation and Extent of the City of Philadelphia And the Ensuing Plat-form thereof*.[10] It was a laborious piece of work, and both the Proprietor and the cartographer were proud of this tangible evidence that the capital city was actually rising between its two great rivers.

There was more to the *Portraiture* and to the settling of some three hundred farmers than met the eye. Sometimes the warrants included directives that could not well be fulfilled. In February, for instance, Penn had given Thomas Holme a warrant for ten acres to be surveyed to Thomas Durkin "on the other side of Skuylkill . . . in a place not already taken up." Thomas Holme, looking at the vast tract on the other side of Schuylkill, was somewhat irked by a directive that was both restrictive and vague. He returned the warrant to the surveyor and made note of it: "eodem a warrant issued to Richard Noble to set out land as above, but because it's not said how many foot by the creek, whether within or without the lands taken in for the city, surveyor to observe the Governour's direction therein."

Symptomatic both of spring and of the greater mobility of the settlers was the first order for survey of a road issued on 4 April by Holme on the authority of a warrant from Penn on 29 March, directing Charles Ashcom to survey and set out a thousand acres to John Hazelgrove and John Bezar near Marcus Hook to be divided equally between them with the understanding that the road from Marcus Hook to Con-

---

[10] For an account of the early history of the *Portraiture*, see Martin P. Snyder, *City of Independence* (New York: Praeger Publishers, 1975), 16–22. The alleged original vellum exists in a dilapidated condition in the State Library, Harrisburg. Because of its fragility it, like other early MSS, is no longer available to public inspection. The photostat reproduced here was made before this measure was taken.

cord could run through the tract where it would be "most convenient to travel and fit for horse and cart carriage . . . the original fieldwork and protracted figure to remain in my office."[11] Various sorts of complications with regard to surveys continued to arise throughout the summer, made more difficult by the absence from the office of Thomas Holme's youngest son, who had turned eighteen on 5 March. The last item *intra per Wm. Holme* seems to be that recorded on 26 May.[12] William must have been much in his father's thoughts during the ensuing Indian purchases, assignment and direction of surveys, council meetings, Friends' meetings, and continued altercations with Baltimore. Three days before the first Indian purchases in which Thomas Holme participated, Clifton Joyner appeared with a warrant which he had obtained from William Penn on 25 December. Thomas Holme noted that it was "Not called for till now," and ordered C[harles] A[shcom] to lay it out in Chester County.[13] On 11 July a problem arose with a relatively liberated female member of the community, Hannah Salters, when Allen Foster complained that she had taken up a warrant for the survey of land that she had bought of him but had not paid for. He enlisted William Penn's assistance in ordering Thomas Holme to stop the survey, since he would not sell the property now.[14] Another member of the Foster family occasioned confusion a little later when his rights were questioned. On 25 February 1683/84 John Holland alleged that William Foster had more land than he was entitled to and demanded a resurvey. Foster was defeated, and Holland held the property.[15]

Then there were the purchasers who would not accept the land proposed for them. On 19 May Thomas Holme added a postscript to the governor's warrant for 250 acres for Joseph Phipps: "The party desires the land at Pemmapacka, which I grant after former warrants are answered, but is not acceptable to him." Evidently Thomas Holme was able to find a location satisfactory to Joseph Phipps, for his map of 1687 allocates a 250-acre tract to Phipps. Although the land is not exactly on Pennypack Creek, a small tributary of Pennypack cuts diagonally across its northwest corner.

---

[11] *PA, OR*, D-82, p. 114. According to the *Old Rights* record, Hazelgrove had received a warrant for five hundred acres on 10 August 1682 and for a thousand acres on 29 May 1683. Returns on a tract of two hundred acres and fifty-six acres on 3 July 1684.

[12] *Book of Surveys and Returns* 6: 20, no. 267, DAM, PHMC, Harrisburg.

[13] *OR Book* D-77, 171. The name Joyner does not appear in *OR* records, but returns for a hundred acres surveyed to Thomas Clifton in Chester County were made on 20 June 1684. No doubt *Joyner* was the trade, not the surname, of Clifton.

[14] Dept. Sur. MS *OB*, 1682–93, 96, DAM, PHMC, cited by ACM, 64: 252. For the Holland-Foster resurvey, see *OR*, D-85, 6.

[15] LR, *OR*, D-81, 113.

Sometimes displaced earlier settlers posed a more serious problem. On 6 August Penn gave Thomas Holme an order to survey twelve acres of marsh for Peter Rambo on Peter Yocum's side [of the Schuylkill], measure the tract, and file returns. Thomas Holme delegated the surveying to Robert Longshore. The endorsement, dated 1 December, bears a marginal note by the surveyor general: "I and Richard Noble was there with the book but cannot get them to agree." The record contains a rough sketch of the map.[16] On the map of 1687 no names appear on the marsh near Yocum's property, but Peter Rambo's tract of arable land appears on the east side of Schuylkill, opposite Yocum's. The importance of surveying marsh land appears in Penn's order to Thomas Holme to survey all marshes and meadows on both sides of Neshaminy Creek so "that it may be fairly allocated to the inhabitants to use until they have acquired some English grass."[17]

On 1 August an order for two resurveys of the land of John Bouls [Bowles] either originally given without Thomas Holme's authorization or challenging his own surveys evoked a protest and petition to the Governor:

> [If] the survey of al lands in the Province by my pett [obl.: petition] this way proceed, then my Patent is so far vacated, i.e. the power & profit thereof, so that I hereby apply to thee in making my exception to the passing the pattent by my survey, but by & from thy Survey^r Gen^{ll}.[18]

Later Thomas Holme was forced into a controversy concerning the liberty land of Peter Neilson. If as requested, the land would "much hinder the laying out of squares of 80 acres to a 5000 acre purchaser."[19] It seems to have been an "irregular tract lying between two creeks." His correspondent countered that "the land was taken into the liberties of land not seated according to order & rule, & that the gen. please have the thing examined." The request seems to have concerned a tract at Shackamaxon. Thomas Holme rejoined that the applicant already had land at Shackamaxon. Rambo, Bowles, and Neilson were all naturalized pre-Penn Swedish settlers.[20] A note at the foot of Penn's 14 July warrant to Thomas Holme, for the survey of land to Robert Presmall in right of John Martin for 250 acres, hints at a possible housekeeping problem in the surveyor general's office, perhaps

---

[16] LR, *OR*, D-86, 112, no. 2123, William Brigdale.
[17] Dept. Sur. *OB* D-68, 7, DAM, PHMC, cited by ACM, 6.
[18] Dept. Sur. *OB B*, *OR*, 22–46, DAM, PHMC.
[19] *OR*, Book D-87, 26, DAM, PMHC.
[20] APS, Penn Letters and Ancient Documents, Naturalization of Swedes, Finns, Dutch, &c., 202 (Micro. 4: 006.) Cited in *PWP* 2: 490.

due to the absence of William Holme as assistant: "A warrant granted formerly but cannot be found now."[21]

Autumn brought long-awaited settlers of outstanding importance to the province. The first of these was Francis Daniel Pastorius, who arrived on 20 August.[22] Not only was Pastorius learned and pious; he was a well-informed, well-organized businessman and administrator. Before sailing for America he had bought fifteen thousand acres of land, and he brought at least a dozen families to settle on a single large tract and the three hundred acres of liberty land and three city lots to which he thought he was entitled. Unfortunately, the book of First Purchasers had been closed before he made his purchase, and it was only after some consideration of his need and the value of a company of sober and industrious professionals, artisans, and tradesmen to the province that the Proprietor made the necessary concessions and he was able to proceed with his plans.[23] It is small wonder that his initial impression of Philadelphia was less enthusiastic than that of William Penn and Thomas Holme. In 1718, recalling his arrival he wrote:

> Then Philadelphia consisted of three or four little cottages [He seems to have missed William Penn's eighty houses that do very well] . . . all woods, underwoods, timber and trees, among which I several times have lost myself in travelling no farther than from the waterside . . . to the house then alloted to a Dutch baker.[24]

Thomas Holme's *Portraiture* is embellished with drawings of some fifty houses, and Roach declares that "Penn could not have been far wrong when he wrote on July 28, that there were then 'built about 80 houses in town.'"[25] By the end of July seventy-nine surveyed lots, the same authority demonstrates, had been cut out of the forest. Certainly Pastorius's three large lots, reaching from Front to Fourth Streets, would enhance the prospect of the city. He at once made plans to locate four families on each lot, two side by side facing each street, with the understanding that they would cultivate the generous plots surrounding their houses. For immediate accommodation he purchased a cave for £5 from Thomas Miller "in the midst of the Front Street." In view of the fact that these caves were initially useful emer-

---

[21] Book of Surveys and Returns 6: 20, no. 267, DAM, PHC, Harrisburg.
[22] LR: *OR* D-81, 117.
[23] Photostat of DS, Learned Coll., HSP (Micro. 4: 565); *PWP* 2: 490.
[24] Francis Daniel Pastorius, MS account of his arrival in Philadelphia, quoted by Watson, *Annals* 1: 44.
[25] "Planting," 147.

gency dwellings and, later, occasions of stormy controversy, his description of them is of interest: "The caves . . . were only holes digged in the Ground, Covered with Earth, a matter of 5. or 6. feet deep, 10. or 12. wide and about 20. long; whereof neither the Sides nor the Floors have been plank'd."[26]

Another August 1683 arrival was Thomas Lloyd, who would immediately occupy a conspicuous place in government affairs. William Penn appointed him keeper of the great seal and master of the rolls at the final December meeting of the council, and in March he became a member of the council.[27]

Three First Purchasers who would be among the most important men in these early years of the province arrived in the space of a couple of weeks in early October. The first of these was Samuel Carpenter, who had first emigrated from England to Barbados, where he made a considerable fortune as a sugar planter. Now, at thirty-four, in the first week of October, he arrived at Philadelphia, where a choice lot had been reserved for him between Wynne and Pool streets. He brought with him a large number of servants and settlers to seat on the five thousand acres he had bought in England.

The next to arrive was James Claypoole, treasurer of the Free Society of Traders, with his family, servants, a company of Low Germans from Crefeld who would be assumed into Pastorius's German settlement, furniture, supplies of all sorts, and excited expectation of moving at once into the house that his indentured servant, Edward Cole, was to have ready for him. The house, he had written to John Goodson, in August, 1682, would do "if it be but a slight house like a barn, with one floor of two chambers and will hold us and our goods and keep us from the sun and weather. . . . " Although it was to be built "with the advice of William Penn, Dr. More, Thomas Holme, Ralph Withers," and Goodson himself, whom he no doubt expected to endow it with a certain amount of comfort and taste, he reported a little wryly on his arrival slightly more than a year later that his servant had indeed built him "a house like a barn, without a chimney, 40 foot long and 20 broad," but it had a good dry cellar and proved very satisfactory for lodging his family and storing his belongings. To this he added a twenty-foot square kitchen with a double chimney. Pastorius helped the Crefelders with their initial arrangements.[28]

Claypoole was delighted with the location of his lot. It was near the

---

[26] ACM, *Narratives*, 405.
[27] *MPC* 1: 166; *PWP* 2: 555.
[28] ACM, *Narratives*, 223.

Society's river-to-river territory and warehouse, and Carpenter was a near neighbor. There would be a fair market for his goods, and, with his supervision, his family could carry on the personal business, leaving him free to devote his time to the interests of the Society. For his services he would receive £100 a year (approximately the equivalent of $10,000 today).

Thomas Holme's earliest acquaintance among these three was the last to arrive, Robert Turner, who had shared imprisonments with him in Dublin for their Quaker faith, and with him had signed the indenture for land for the first Meeting House in that city. Robert had amassed considerable wealth in his Dublin drapery [fabric] business, augmented by proprietorship in both New Jerseys. He was a First Purchaser and a member of the Free Society of Traders. He was quickly assimilated into the offical life of Philadelphia, and within two weeks of arriving was on jury duty.[29]

The arrival of these prosperous and dynamic newcomers gave immediate stimulus to the Pennsylvania economy both on the spot and abroad, as reported back to England in their own and other letters. Their coming also compounded the responsibilities of the surveyor general. Their city lots were already staked out, and they were enterprising enough to have them cleared and improved in short order. The selection and surveying of liberty land and large tracts in the interior, on the other hand, would put a not inconsiderable load on Thomas Holme's small number of deputies. For the most part, although the property may have been selected promptly, most of the actual surveying of large tracts was not begun until late in the winter.[30]

If the multiplication of surveys caused personal problems for Thomas Holme, it was also a source of encouragement. Surveyors were well paid—the local fee was 5s for a hundred acres, approximately £2.5 probably about $250.00 in today's U.S. money. Impossible to make an accurate estimate for a five-hundred-acre tract. Thomas Holme was entitled to a third of this amount. His office of surveyor general was theoretically one of the most lucrative in the province.

The Proprietor and the surveyor general were already fairly well established. Penn's house at Front and High Streets, on the lot designated for his small daughter Laetitia, was finished; and Thomas Holme's house on Front Street at Holme (later Mulberry, and finally Arch) Street had probably been built as soon as this lot and the one at Sixth and High streets were laid out on 21 June.[31] As a First Purchaser

---

[29] ACM, *Arrivals*, 407.
[30] Letter of John Jones, 1725, ACM, *Narratives*, 454-n459.
[31] *Exemplification Book* 1: 32, 33, Office of the Recorder of Deeds, Philadelphia.

of five thousand acres, Thomas Holme enjoyed 102 feet of ground facing Front Street, with 426 feet lying west on Holme—ample ground for the orchard and garden that Penn visualized surrounding the dwellings in his "green country town," or, if occasion arose, to be divided and sold in lots for extra revenue.

The rural estates of both William Penn and Thomas Holme were also taking shape. Penn's mansion was being erected on his manor of Pennsbury near the great westward bend of the Delaware, on land twice purchased from the Indians. The Proprietor had reserved for himself ten thousand of every hundred thousand acres in the province, including manors for each of his children and for his sister Margaret Penn Lowther and her husband. On 24 April Penn presented a warrant for ten thousand acres for a manor for himself in Philadelphia [County], which included Pennsbury.[32] In September he proceeded with warrants for surveys for land for his eldest son, William Penn, Jr. He was to have liberty land appropriate to a ten-thousand-acre purchase, ten thousand acres in any part of the province, and five hundred acres in the most convenient place on Neshaminy Creek near the Indian town of Playwicky.[33] On 8 October he gave a warrant for himself at Schuylkill on both sides of Perkiomen Creek.[34] The 1687 map bears witness to the Proprietor's astuteness, displaying here a tract with a substantial river frontage and the largest portion of the creek, with many tributaries, bisecting the tract, which is called The Proprietary's Manor of Gilberts. On the map the eastern portion of the tract bears the name of Philip Ford, but since Ford did not emigrate it is thought that this remained for the use of William Penn. Below this is the Manor of Williamstadt of William Penn, Jr. By the time the map was drawn Penn would have added to his reserves in this area several more miles on the opposite side of the Schuylkill as William Lowther's Manor of Billton, Laetitia Penn's Manor of Mountjoy, and another tract for William Penn, Jr. Thirty thousand acres were included in these surveys.

Later Thomas Holme would have misgivings about such concentration of large quantities of the most valuable land, for the most part idle, in the names of small children, when bona fide settlers were restricted in the amount of contiguous property they might have

---

[32] The bounds of Philadelphia County were not fixed until, during the presidency of Thomas Holme, the council drew the line between Philadelphia and Chester Counties on 1 April 1685, and that between Philadelphia and Bucks Counties, a week later, after the return of Thomas Lloyd to his office on 8 April. *MPC* 1: 74, 78.

[33] The exact location of Playwicky has never been determined, but there is no record of land surveyed for William Penn, Jr., in the upper Neshaminy area.

[34] See map, p. 282: The Proprietary's Manor of Gilberts.

without guaranteed occupancy. Inevitably it would lead to dissatisfaction among purchasers. For the time being he was silent about the situation. At Pennsbury the governor's mansion was already an imposing edifice, although its master would continue to improve it even after his return to England.

Thomas had chosen for the site of his house a hilltop on his Well Spring Plantation overlooking Pennypack Creek to the south and a spring of clear water in the valley to the west. Tradition places the site of Thomas's house on or near the spot on which stood houses of descendants of his daughter Hester and Silas Crispin for several generations, the family occupants to be succeeded by the residents of St. Margaret's School for Girls. The spring near this large country house was known as Crystal Spring until it was finally filled in, in the mid-twentieth century.

Pleased though he was with the sites of his two houses, Thomas Holme nevertheless was anxious about the amount of land remaining in his thousand-acre purchase. He wanted to reserve land for his remaining unmarried daughter and, perhaps, to augment his income to replace unpaid surveyor fees. He petitioned Penn for an additional six hundred acres, to which Penn reluctantly agreed:

Tho: Holme
Esteemed Friend: Before thy last came I writ an answer to the first wch was that the State of Govern^r on his Public Business required also considerable to maintain it . . . yet because of thy Necessity alleged was wiling to consent thereto, that is to take up 600a.
Mine to thine and you.

Endorsed, "Governour's consent for 600a. to you 1/3 set back to sell."[35] There is no clue as to the meaning of the phrase "set back to sell," although it was probably Thomas Holme's reminder to himself that he could dispose of the quantity without encroaching on that which he had earmarked for other purposes. Below the endorsement he seems to have speculated on the extent of possible land sales: "12 6 80x33 gives a total of 2640; 70x33 gives a total of 2310. . . . 16 . . . 33. . . . " These appear to be proportions of lots in a town.

He proceeded immediately to the rapidly developing Chester County, obtaining 250 acres in Darby Township, reaching from Mokornipates Kill to Darby Creek, and in Newtown Township "30 acres in the townstead [apparently at the east end of the town itself] and

---

[35] *OR, Book* D-85, p. 86.

245 A. & A. & 30 A.," in the townstead, all except the undated single thirty-acre tract, on 29 December 1683.[36] Since this is the date of Penn's reply to his request, Thomas may have arranged for these surveys in advance. He sold these tracts sometime before he made the 1687 map. One wonders if his urgency in securing them was sparked by Charles Ashcom's receipt of a warrant for four hundred acres north of Crum Creek on 19 December.[37]

Except for assigned official business relating chiefly to New Jersey affairs, Thomas Holme was at all of the meetings of the provincial council that occurred from June to the end of December, 1683. A series of six meetings, from 24–29 October, and another on 27 December, was largely concerned with the trial of Charles Pickering for his enterprising counterfeiting business. With the assistance of a few associates he had coined and circulated "new bits" extensively before his activities came to the attention of the council. Although he defended himself on the ground that his coins were equal to or higher in value than those of legitimate circulation, it was "Ordered That the Sheriff go to Char: Pickering and receive as much good money, or Vallue thereof, as he hath reced of the People in bad money, and pay the same respectively to the People as he reced the other from them."[38]

Occasional notes by Thomas Holme on warrants give glimpses of the surroundings among which official business was transacted. On 24 July 1684 he annotated a warrant issued on 20 October 1683 for 350 acres to John Howell, "The Governour ordered this above interlineation in his parlour, before John Howell and Thomas Holme."[39]

In addition to warrants for over forty city lots during October and early November, to say nothing of those for liberty land and tracts in the interior, there were two purchases from the Indians on the coveted Susquehanna, and the on-going responsibility for the integrity of the land. The constant activity had at least the merit of distraction from personal anxiety. Hester and Silas Crispin were living in their house on Front Street, and Elinor remained a devoted housekeeper for her father and ailing brother in the house on Holme Street. Thomas himself was fifty-nine on 1 November—on the verge of *senectute*, old age, according to the medical authorities of the day. He had survived many personal sufferings and losses. Now, at the close of a year of extraordinary endeavor, he was to encounter another loss. William, the son

---

[36] Benjamin Smith, *Atlas of Delaware County*, Maps 6 and 12.
[37] *PA*, 2, 19: 297.
[38] *MPC* 1: 36.
[39] *OR*, D-65, 123.

who had been nearest to him in his provincial labors, died on 8 November. On the next day his father notified William Penn: "Govern^r: Please to excuse my further attendance on thee today, 3^a clock (an hour hence) this afternoon, being appointed for the buriall of my sons Corps." The stark announcement is followed by advice of importance to the Proprietor:

> These few things I offer to thy consideration,
>> The necessity of ascertaining the bounds of the Counties of Chester & this, as also betwixt this & Bucks, least hereafter I may err, in placeing peopl. I finde it may be requisite for thy affaires in the concernes of this City, (where many people may (probably) come, more than formerly expected) to reduce the breadth of the high street lotts, and also to reduce the second streets & s/ other backward streets from both river fronts, & yet leave sufficient room, to make way for new purchasers amongst them to some content, to prevent being all placed backward, of which many are unwilling; yet I intend not the altering or removall of any in these back streets, that have already built or in the least improved.
>
> The orders for cutting trees in the Swamps for building,
>> is not observed; but havock made on dry lands, which Jo: Songhurst & I cannot avoyd, for it may not be expected that we can go, & see our orders executed, therefore there is need for a certain man to be appointed for that service, & to be paid by those that have warrants to cut any trees, that he may see it done, in the Swampes, according to orders; and thy proclamation (finally) to forbid any to cut any trees, not onely out of Swampes, but also, not without that said certain person be present, may be serviceable, in the opinion, of Thine to serve thee
>
>> Thos Holme
>
> [Endorsed]
> For the Govern^r
>> to peruse
> P[hilip] L[ehnmann] give this to the Govern^r
>> after Dinner.
>>> TH[40]

The letter is carefully written, but interlined inserted words give evidence of some difficulty of expression. The tone is one of the formality of a minor civil servant. Whether it was to be delivered after dinner to avoid troubling the governor with a feeling of duty to attend the

---

[40] ALS. Penn MSS, FLL (Micro. 4: 606).

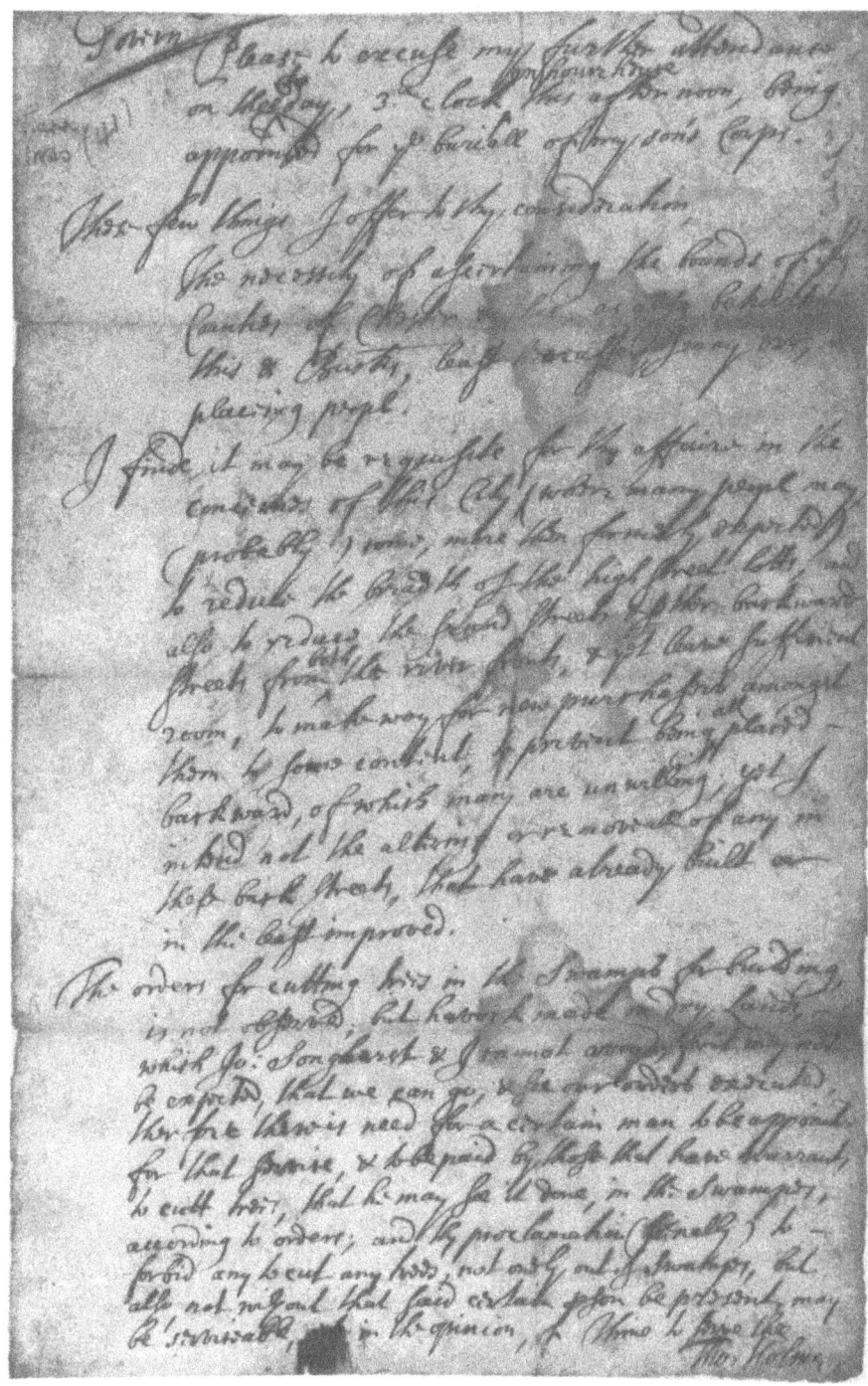

Fig. 18. Holme's letter to William Penn on the day of his son's burial. Used with permission of Friends House Library, London.

burial, or to take the edge off any annoyance he may have felt at Thomas Holme's absence, there is no clue.

William was the sixth of Thomas Holme's ten children to die, the first to be buried in this newly native earth. There is no record of his burial place, but very likely it was on the hilltop above what is now Holme Avenue where the Crispin family cemetery still preserves the remains of Thomas Holme himself and of descendants of Hester and Silas Crispin.

We do not know just what Thomas Holme's household arrangements were. Elinor appears to have remained his housekeeper, presumably in the Holme Street house in Philadelphia, which probably served also as his office, with one of his indentured servants, probably Edmund McVeagh, and his wife, caring for Well Spring. Hester was expecting a baby in the spring. Tryall was assisting Thomas's most troublesome deputy, Charles Ashcom, in Chester County. Penn considered Thomas Holme's advice and implemented it during the next couple of years.

Chapter 11

A Presence in the Delaware Valley

The year 1683 had been a time of building, a year of buying much of the province from the Indians, of the solidly documented granting of New Castle and the Lower Counties, of defining boundaries: of establishing a presence in the Delaware Valley, of setting not only the topographical frame of the province, but the Frame of Government that would distinguish it from all other provincial undertakings. The first half of 1684 would be devoted more particularly to the operation of this unique province.

The council, which had been largely concerned with the Pickering affair, had met on 7 November and would meet again on the twenty-first, after which it would adjourn until 26 December. A new problem surfaced at the meeting of 21 November, with the report of an unfree ship appearing under the name of *Mary of Southampton* but showing none of the validated documents requisite for legal trade with Pennsylvania. Investigation revealed that she was a Scottish ship, the *Alexander of Inverness*, and so forfeit to the crown.[1] This was the first of such imposters with which the council would have to deal. Within a year another allegedly English, but actually French, ship, the *Harp*, arrived. Thomas Holme's first encounter with the *Harp* had been a happier one, when he shipped goods on her from Ireland, but now President Lloyd, Thomas Holme, and the three other members of the

---

[1] *MCP* 1: 35, 69. The British Laws of Navigation forbade provincial trade with any but English ships.

council considering her case consigned her to the same fate as the *Alexander*.

Now, before the cold of January set in, Thomas Holme would be able to turn his attention to allocating and ordering surveys for city lots and land. The selected list of warrants in the printed *Pennsylvania Archives* includes over sixty for lots and approximately seventeen thousand acres, comprising about seventy-five tracts warranted during November and December. The average rural tract contained roughly 245 acres. The sometimes arduous rides that Thomas Holme usually took upon himself to show available land to purchasers were often welcome interludes of quiet enjoyment of earth and streams and trees and the rich grasses and briars and vines, often with fruit untouched by any harvesters but many birds and small animals.

On 19 December Thomas Holme accompanied William Penn to yet another Indian purchase. On this occasion Sectarius and his associates sold his lands "between Christiana and Upland Creeks unto William Penn after the same manner as Keklappan and others sell theirs." For this land they had "already received a very good gun, some powder, and laid, 2pr. of stockings, one match coat, and 10 bitts Spanish money." Thomas Holme, John Moore, and John Songhurst were witnesses of the transaction.[2]

Building on the newly staked-out city lots progressed rapidly in expectation of winter and of the opening of small businesses, frequently conducted in dwellings. On 26 December a project dear to the hearts of both Penn and Thomas Holme was inaugurated. Holme had served in Dublin on a committee to recruit a schoolmaster for the children of Friends. Now the governor and council decided to open a school "for the instruction & Sober Education of Youth in the towne of Philadelphia." They enlisted for the task Enock Flower, who

> embraced it upon these following Termes: to Learne to read English 4s. by the Quarter, to learne to read, Write and Cast account 8s. by the Quarter; for Boarding a Scholler, that is to say, dyet, washing, Lodging, & Scooling, Tenn pounds for one whole year.[3]

On this occasion Thomas Holme, William Clayton, William Haige, and Lasse Cock constituted the council. Christopher Taylor, to whom Thomas Holme had had recourse for advice concerning the Dublin school, was absent from this meeting, but he was present a month later on 17 January, when a further step in the educational life of the

---

[2] HSP, Cadwallader Coll., Thomas Cadwallader, Box 3 Deeds, Deed from Sectarius *et al.* to WP.
[3] *MCP* 1: 36, 38.

province was taken. This time it was "Proposed that care be taken about the Learning and Instruction of Youth, to Witt: a School of Art and Sciences."

With the resumption of regular meetings of the council a darker side of provincial life surfaced. One Anton. Weston was brought before the council to answer for his proposals. These seem to have been rebellious or seditious in nature—they are not clearly defined—but their consequences are shocking to the modern mind. On 16 January William Penn and the seven members of the council present, including Thomas Holme, sentenced Weston "for the great presumption and Contempt of this Goverment and authority . . . [to be] Whypt at the Market place on Market daye three times, Each time to have ten Lashes, at 12 of the Clock at noone, this being the first day." Apparently inspired by the Weston crime, the council before adjournment "Ordered that Wm. Clayton build a Cage against the next Councill day, 7 foot high, 7 foot long, & 5 foot broad."[4] This was to serve as brief accommodation for a petty criminal, much like a large hollow tree with a lattice door in use in one English village well into the twentieth century. Imprisonment would be right and proper, but public whipping at the public market for three successive days was a punishment reminiscent of the *Articles of War*.

Another extraordinary matter which must have troubled both Penn and Holme was the presentation before the council on 7 February 1683/84 of Margaret Matson and Yeshro Hendrickson "Examined and about to be proved Witches." The husbands of the two women, Neels Matson and Jacob Hendrickson, each posted fifty pounds for his wife's appearance before the same board (Thomas Holme, John Simcock, Lasse Cock, William Clayton, and the governor) at the meeting of 27 February. On this occasion the council personnel differed slightly. John Simcock was absent, but the number was augmented by James Harrison, William Biles, William Haige, and Christopher Taylor. At the afternoon session a petty jury of twelve members was impaneled and extensive testimony was heard, most of which dealt with spells cast on cattle and geese. Margaret underwent exhaustive examination, but Yeshro, or Getro, Hendrickson seems to have escaped on Jacob's recognizance of fifty pounds for her good behavior for six months. Margaret pleaded innocent of all charges. The jury "Brought her in guilty of having the Comon fame of a Witch, but not Guilty in manner and forme as Shee Stands Indicted." Thus were the accusers mollified and Penn's Holy Experiment spared the shame of a witch conviction. The accusations against the alleged witches all seem to have come

---

[4] *MCP* 1: 37.

from the Dutch community, though Charles Ashcom gave hearsay evidence, which Margaret denied "At her Soul, and Saith where is my daughter; let her come and say so."[5]

Most of the cases demanding the consideration of the council were less spectacular than these. There were alleged errors in accounts, appropriation of property that had been bought but not paid for, apparent irregularities of boundaries, intoxication. Hearings were time- and energy-consuming, and were not well attended. Apart from Penn, Holme was the only councillor with a perfect record. On the whole, affairs were progressing satisfactorily in the province, though rumblings were again coming from neighbors.

Occasional adjustments had to be made in designation of city lots. At the time of Holme's already noted trip with Pennock on 16 March 1682/83, Thomas had proposed to Penn that lots be allocated for purchasers from Dublin and county Cork (represented by Pennock), and from county Wexford, the site of Thomas Holme's Irish holdings (represented by himself). The Schuylkill side of the city presented more problems for the seating of purchasers than did the Delaware side, by reason of the marshy, irregular border of the city. Now, on 9 January 1683/84, Penn issued a proclamation for solving the difficulties as equitably as possible. For "the more Compact and Speedy Building and Comfortable Enjoyment of Neighborhood there" he ordered that the purchasers now already in the country might have their front lots together and those placed on the backward streets might move toward the Schuylkill by one street, from Third to Second, and so on.[6] Thomas Holme indicated the projected settling by numbering the lots and providing an identifying table as the lots were seated.

January was a relatively quiet month, with Thomas Holme and his deputies occupied largely with surveys, and purchasers clearing their holdings as weather permitted. There was cold enough to discourage some enterprises: witness a letter of William Clark from his home at New Castle to Penn at Philadelphia on 15 January 1683/84, stating that he

> did Intend According to thy order that my wife Should A picled sume oysters to A sent thee and in order to it I sent my servants to get sume; And it being the beginning of the hard weather they were force to Leave the Connoe and Com a way with out it after they had got them; but as sone as the weather is fitt for it; I doe Intend to take Care about it.[7]

---

[5] *MCP* 1: 38–40.
[6] DLR, DAM, PHMC (Micro. 4: 689). *PWP* 2: 515–516.
[7] ALS. Penn Papers, Add. Misc. Letters, l, HSP (Micro. 4: 716). William Clark to WP.

The witch trials were the only spectacular occurrences at the four provincial council meetings during February unless one includes the judgment on 20 February that Benjamin Acrod "killed himself with drink." This circumstance might have given the province a claim to his estate, which was not inconsiderable, but the governor renounced it and asked the council to appoint an administrator who would see to the payment of the debts of the deceased and the distribution of the remainder according to law. His decision was consistent with the action of the council the previous summer, when they voted that due provision be made for the sustenance of the people, "though our Provisions be but small." Patrick Robinson was trusted with the responsibility for Acrod's affairs. These would not be settled till after 28 July, when Thomas Holme and other councillors were appointed to inspect Acrod's accounts before they were settled.[8]

Meanwhile the laborious process of setting out and surveying land continued. Of major importance was the satisfaction of three large companies already mentioned: the Free Society of Traders, the German Company, and the Welsh.

The first of these, as we have seen, was already organized and presumably ready to function.[9] Down to the December 1682 assembly it had seemed off to a good start. The *Jeffrey*, the Society's ship, arriving almost simultaneously with the *Welcome*, had brought the president, Nicholas More, and his family, with a personal warrant for ten thousand acres of land. Also on board were the Society "chyrrugeon" (barber and surgeon), John Goodson; James Claypoole's advance representative and deputy treasurer, Ralph Withers, with instructions to build a house for Claypoole; and a large number of indentured servants to work on the Society's twenty thousand acres of land.

The core members of the Society, experienced businessmen that they were, had planned a comprehensive organization for agriculture, manufacture of linen and glass, whaling, and processing of oil and whalebone. There would also be shops to meet local needs, and above and including all, commerce with the West Indies and the Mother Country. The Society's warehouse would be conveniently located within the city, just above the dock. Although the twenty thousand acres purchased by the Society was to be paid for at the regular rate of £500 for five thousand acres, it would be subjected to only a shilling quitrent annually for the whole. Membership with right to vote was available to non-resident purchasers of a thousand acres, but office was restricted to purchasers of five thousand.

---

[8] *MCP* 1: 39, 65.
[9] *PWP* 2: 246–254 (Head note and Co. 66).

Penn seems to have seen the Manor of Frank, as the Society holding was called, as a single tract within which the Free Society would enjoy almost the autonomy of a province within a province. In addition to having its own courts, tax system, and property arrangements, it would choose three members of the provincial council. A fund was set aside to commence fur trade with the Indians, and three-fifths of any ore which might be found in the twenty thousand acres of Society land would be the property of the Society, the remaining two-fifths to be divided equally between the Proprietor and the crown. All whales and fish in any of the waterways within or adjoining the manor would be the property of the Society, for payment to Penn or his heirs of only one shilling annually. The Society was also empowered to conduct fairs and markets within the manor, and its books, warehouse, and houses were not to be inspected without its consent. In the eyes of the Society the charter was a very agreeable document, particularly because it did not restrict the use of individual purchases outside the shares subscribed by the organization. In addition to the privileges inherent in their involvement in the Society, members were selected for most of the choice offices. The position of the Society in the province had been further assured by its inclusion in the *Laws Agreed On In England*. The refusal of the assembly to accept the Society's establishment in the laws was a blow to the members and, as Nash suggests, may have played a part in their haste to improve their personal estates before busying themselves with the Society's affairs.

The setting out of the Society's land is not perfectly documented. The record of *Old Rights* printed in the *Pennsylvania Archives* lists a warrant for ten thousand acres dated 25 January 1682/83; an undated draft of the Society's land in Bucks, also undated and for unspecified quantity; and an undated draft of 310 acres in Bucks. How much of this land was included in the warrant for ten thousand acres is not indicated, but the tracts that remain reserved for the Society on the 1687 map would approximate a total of from sixteen thousand to twenty thousand acres. The warrant for the entire twenty thousand acres was not entered until 17 November 1684, which may have shortly preceded the undated drafts.

Four undated drafts of city lots of the Society are listed, and one for 25 July 1684. This is not to say that city property was not chosen for the Society as soon as the *Portraiture* was completed, or at least as soon as Penn returned from Baltimore and set himself to the assignment of lots. The warehouse near the dock certainly was erected soon after if not before the arrival of the *Jeffrey* with its cargo of merchandise from England. Not only the ground on which it stood but a strip of land nearly a square wide, extending from the top of the hill to the Schuylkill, was granted to the Society by the Proprietor in compensation, Roach suggests, for failure of the assembly to ratify the charter of the Society as proposed in article 24 of the *Laws Agreed On In England*. Nicholas More, as president of the Society and purchaser of ten thousand acres of land in addition to his subscription of £300, received a compensating grant of the balance of those squares from the beginning of the Society's land through the fourth square—about eight acres of city land.[10]

Like all other purchasers, the Society was entitled to a hundred acres of liberty land for each five thousand acres purchased. The large tracts mentioned above appear on the 1687 map in two widely separated areas, one in Bucks County on the south side of upper Neshaminy Creek, the other about the center of Chester County, where it protrudes into the Welsh Tract. A third tract with a two-mile frontage on Frankford Creek constituted the liberty land allotment of the Society. A warehouse sufficient for the goods brought over for the Society had been built promptly, but with the president intent upon settling his own manor, Thomas Holme occupied with boundary problems, maps, surveys, and seating of newcomers on his own land, and other Society members likewise employed with their own affairs, not much progress was made in the corporate interests during the first winter. Beginnings were made in the spring, but it would be nearly a year before the larger projects were well under way. For all his divided interests, Claypoole's business acumen and aggressiveness had been needed from the start.

Unlike the Germans and the Welsh, the Englishmen who comprised the Society had no taste for corporate living arrangements. They were, rather, independent investors in real property and in jointly owned and administered manufacturing and marketing enterprises. In his letter of 11 August 1683 to the members of the Free Society of Traders in England, William Penn had enthusiastically described the situation of the Society in Philadelphia and vicinity at that time:

> I will venture to say, Your Provincial Settlements both within and without the Town for Scituation and Soil, are without Exception; Your City-Lot is an whole Street, and one side of a Street, from River to River, containing near one hundred Acers not easily valued, which is besides your four hundred Acers in the City Liberties, part of your twenty thousands Acers

---

[10] Possibly the larger and uppermost of the two buildings to the south of the dock on the *Portraiture* is intended to suggest the location of the Society's warehouse.

in the Countery. Your Tannery hath such plenty of Bark, the Saw-Mill for Timber, the place of the Glass-house so conveniently posted for Water-carriage, the City-lot for a Dock, and the Whalery for a sound and fruitful Bank, and the Town Lewis by it to help your People that by Gods blessing the Affairs of the Society will naturally grow in their Reputation and Profit.[11]

Pastorius, in his not strictly chronological account of the early history of his colony, states that "another English Company has built the new city of Frankfort, at a distance [from the German settlement] of an hour and a half," where "they have set on foot some mills, glass-works, and brickkilns."[12] These enterprises were situated in the bend of Frankford Creek. The sawmill may have been purchased from earlier settlers. Other Society land included a choice L-shaped tract on upper Neshaminy Creek with an additional fine tributary, and a further large tract between the Schuylkill and the Brandywine. When this tract was surveyed at Thomas Holme's order, his chief Chester County surveyor, Charles Ashcom, laid it out in such a way that it almost bisected the large Welsh Tract, infuriating the Welsh purchasers. The advantages granted to the Free Society appeared outrageously disproportionate to some of the other purchasers, who still were entitled to take up much of the land which they had purchased.

Some of the most able individual leaders of the society approached life in Pennsylvania with divided hearts. Mention has already been made of the presidents's Manor of Moreland. Return of six city lots to Nicholas More had been made on 1 April 1683, and one of liberty land would be registered on 4 June 1684. The latter may have been for the two hundred acres for which he received a warrant on 5 May 1683. On 25 May 1684 he received a warrant for additional city lots. He seems not to have been energetically concerned with the establishment of corporate business. His relationship with other members of the Society was not altogether happy. His disposition was none of the best, and he lacked the binding force of common religious faith and responsibility shared by the others.

Treasurer James Claypoole, carrying on his own business affairs as well as he could in his new environment, was nevertheless, at least at the outset, loyal to his responsibilities as one of the top officials of the Society. He seems to have been particularly interested in whaling, which was potentially an extremely lucrative pursuit, although it involved considerable overhead expense. Writing to his brother Edward

---

[11] Draft, WP to FST, 16 August 1683, Penn Papers, HSP (Micro. 4: 438). *PWP* 3: 442–457.
[12] ACM, *Narratives*, 241, 380.

on 2 December 1683, he asks him to "Advise what commodity whale oil may be with you, for we have 24 men fishing in the Bay that are like to make a good voyage." Late in March of 1684 he visited the whale fisheries and on 4 April he wrote particulars to Edward Hastwell:

> I have been three weeks from home, about 150 miles, of where they take whales. They had killed about 12 in all and lost 3 of them . . . They . . . must be paid the market price for 2/3 of the oil and bone, besides some other charges we are at, so that we are like to get no great matter by it this time. . . . they were not provided with the necessities in time, else they might have made 100 L each man, here being great plenty of whales and very easy to take them.

Phineas Pemberton reports a non-commercial sighting on 19 October 1687: "A mighty whale came by my house down the river he gave one great snort above the house one near ag^t the house one below the house." It escaped those who chased it. Phineas does not tell how the chase was prosecuted.[13]

By the end of May 1684, Claypoole's zeal for the Society had evaporated. He wrote again to Hastwell, "For my part, I am so weary of the Society's business that I will get clear as soon as I can, and then I shall be capable to serve myself and others."

Claypoole was nothing if not capable of serving himself. He carried on his customary voluminous correspondence with business associates, usually mingled with religious exhortations or edifying sentiments. Like all merchants on the western side of the Atlantic, he was sometimes frustrated by the slowness of communications and the inconvenience of paying and collecting bills. On some occasions Thomas Holme was able to help him out with bills for small sums, as when he gave him a bill on John Tottenham, probably for part of the payment for land in Wexford. As for real estate, Claypoole's first warrants, dated 8 November, were for his city lots and liberty land, followed on 25 April 1684 by a warrant for 500 acres in Philadelphia County, with a draft of the tracts apparently on the same date. On 12 May and 31 October he obtained warrants for tracts of 1,000 acres each in Bucks County, and on 12 December a return for 1,050 acres in Chester County was registered, with a warrant for 1,000 acres following in February 1684/85. He had also the satisfaction of seeing his sons advancing, James as bookkeeper for the Society, and John writing for the register. He was pleased at the proximity on Front Street of

---

[13] *CLB*, 225, 239–240.

Samuel Carpenter, who, he rightly prophesied, would become very prosperous.[14]

Carpenter, occupied with establishing himself in town, deferred seeking warrants for country property until spring. On 13 March he obtained a warrant for five hundred acres, and on 12 June and 4 August warrants for 4,420 each, all in Bucks County. He lost no time in the settling and cultivating of his land, thus financing commercial enterprises at home and trade overseas.

John Simcock, deputy president of the Society, was, like Thomas Holme, a member of the Committee of Twelve destined to live permanently in Pennsylvania. Like Thomas Holme, he would be active in government proceedings from the first. He obtained a warrant for his city lot on 1 September 1683, and warrant and order for liberty land on 13 September. On 22 September return was made on the survey of his 1,100-acre tract in Chester County, and he received warrants for himself and others for "sundry tracts," one thousand acres and five hundred acres, and return of a survey of 1,100 acres, all in Chester County. The location of his large holdings in Ridley Township is charted in Smith's *Atlas*.

The German settlement actually consisted of two groups brought together, apparently with some reluctance, by Francis Daniel Pastorius, the liberally educated and well-traveled son of a prominent judge and burgomaster of Windsheim, Germany. In his mid-twenties he had joined the Pietist movement in Frankfurt. More mystical and less rigidly theological in outlook than the Lutheran communion from which it was derived, the group was naturally disposed to respond to Penn's exhortations when he visited them in 1677 and, in 1681, to his invitation to participate in his "holy experiment" in America. A number sufficent to establish a colony decided to emigrate under the leadership of Pastorius. At the same time a second group, Low Germans from Crefeld, had assembled with Jacob Telner as coordinator, assisted in its arrangements by Penn's agent in Rotterdam, Benjamin Furly. These groups, only later amalgamated into a German colony, arrived in the autumn of 1683, the High Germans with Pastorius, and the Crefelders with Claypoole.

Pastorius had received a grant for six thousand acres on 12 October 1683, and one for two hundred acres of liberty land on 14 December; and he would receive warrants for two more liberty land tracts and an unspecified number of acres "to make up the deficit to the German Company" on 16 July, with another warrant for city lots on 16 Septem-

---

[14] *CLB*, 231, 230, 234.

ber.[15] He had been very demanding, but Penn respected his learning, administrative ability, and piety. Pastorius was justifiably pleased with his situation and proud of the speed with which the German colony developed into a progressive, well-ordered community. On 7 March 1684 he wrote to his associates in Germany, describing the fifteen thousand acres "in one tract, and bordering on navigable water . . . [and] three hundred acres in the liberties of the city, for building houses thereon."[16] He was cheerfully presumptuous in claiming one-hundred-acre allotments of liberty land proportionate to his original purchase. In the first place, the ten thousand acres of liberty land proving insufficient for such portions, Penn had reduced the one-hundred-acre allowance to eighty acres; in the second, Pastorius was not a First Purchaser, since the book of sales had been closed before he bought his land. Thomas Holme noted on the warrant for liberty land to Pastorius on 16 July 1684, "Governour: I know not of any land in the liberties on this acct, being not of the first 100 purchasers. Thomas Holme."[17]

At the end of November Pastorius wrote of his "newly founded city, 'Germanopolis,'" which he described more at length, with an error in date, in his later history of the German foundation: "On October 24 [1683] I, Francis Daniel Pastorius . . . laid out another new city of the name of Germanton, or Germanopolis, at a distance of an hour's walk from Philadelphia. . . . " The soil was fertile, water was abundant, there was good pasture, and there were many valuable trees. There were only a dozen families in the first settlement, most of them mechanics and weavers, in anticipation of the need for linen cloth. Pastorius planned the town himself, "the main street . . . sixty feet wide, and the side streets forty," and he allotted as much as three acres for each house and garden, "but for my own dwelling twice as much."[18] He informs his friends that he has acquired for his high German Company fifteen thousand acres in one piece, with the understanding that within a year "they shall actually place thirty households thereon; . . . that we High Germans may maintain a separate little province, and thus feel more secure from all oppression."

Like the Germans, the Welsh settlers sought to form a self-con-

---

[15] *PA, OR.*
[16] The passages cited here are culled from the various documents quoted or abstracted in ACM, *Narratives*, 375-448. The dates of Pastorius's warrants are given in *PA* 1, vol. 2: *OR*, 662-670. See map, p. 185.
[17] W. W. Thomson, *West Chester County and Its History* (Chicago and New York, 1898), 162; ACM, *Narratives*, 451; *PWP* 2: 527-528.
[18] *PA, OR* D-81, 264. PHMC. Penn finally gave way to Pastorius's demands and approved the hundred-acre allotments.

tained community in which they could follow their own traditions, speak their own language, have their own courts and meeting houses, and be economically independent, limiting their external financial obligations to the basic commitment to the Proprietor in purchase and rents. Thomas Holme's involvement with the Welsh was largely in overseeing the surveying and maintaining a suitable tract for the settlement, but it would be among his most difficult.

The Welsh were to have a longer wait than the Germans for their establishment, although negotiations had seemed promising enough in the beginning. Late in 1681 Penn had held a conference with a group of influential Welsh professional and businessmen, some of whom would later be prominent in his province. Among them were Dr. Griffith Owen, Dr. Edward Jones, Dr. Thomas Wynne, John ap Thomas, Charles Lloyd, John ap John, Richard Davies, and Edward Pritchard. He proposed the establishment of a Welsh barony in Pennsylvania consisting of forty thousand acres, large tracts of which would be financed by the purchases of well-to-do leaders, while the remainder would be settled by less affluent but earnest buyers of small estates.

The proposition was attractive in that Wales had been a fruitful field for Quaker proselytizing ministers, most prominent of whom had been Thomas Holme of Kendal (1627–1666), sometimes confused with Thomas of Monk Coniston and Ireland.[19] Many were poor, but there was a sufficiently large number of comfortably well-off inhabitants to justify the Proprietor's expectations, particularly because his plan seemed to guarantee very considerable autonomy and the preservation of native culture.

John ap Thomas and Edward Jones were the first to form a company. They enlisted seventeen families, and Edward Jones and four of the families—a total of forty persons—arrived at Pennsylvania on the small *Lyon of Liverpool* ten days after the *Amity*. There was no forty-thousand-acre tract awaiting them, but the 1687 map shows a very well-placed tract of about four thousand acres with a two-mile frontage on the west side of Schuylkill for "Edward Jones & Compa^y, being 17 Families," allowing about 240 acres each, with an adjoining tract of a thousand acres bearing the names of Charles and Thomas Lloyd, John ap John, Richard Davis, and John Bevan. This total of five thousand acres was surveyed on 16 and 17 September 1682. Ad-

---

[19] T. Mardy Rees, *The Quakers in Wales and Their Emigration to North America*. According to Rees, Wynne owned the first brick house in Philadelphia, returned to England with WP in 1684, and came back to Pennsylvania and settled in Lewes.

A Presence in the Delaware Valley

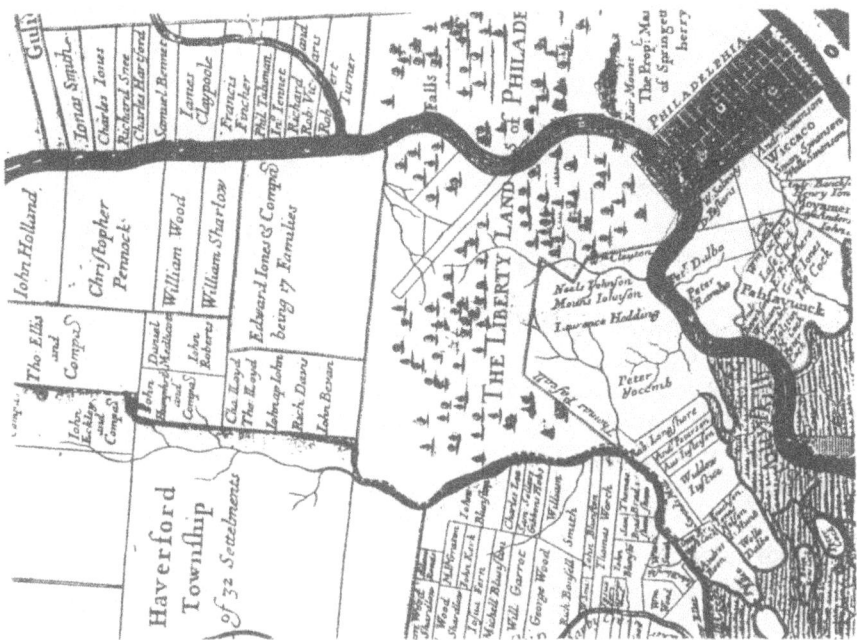

Fig. 19b. Further detail of 1687 map showing first group of Welsh settlers. Used with permission of the Historical Society of Pennsylvania.

Fig. 19a. Map showing German Settlement.

joining the second of these, along the north side of Darby Creek, Haverford and Radnor Townships were designed for a total of seventy-two Welsh settlements. It was not until 13 March 1683/84 that the Welsh Company received a warrant for forty thousand acres, and not until 4 April that Thomas Holme added below the warrant "ordered David Powell to execute this warrant." The survey would not be made for another three years. Perhaps one reason for the delay was Penn's directive to his surveyor general:

> I do hereby Charge thee, & strictly require thee to lay out the said Tract of Land in as uniform a manner as conveniently may be upon the West side of Skulkill River, running Three Miles upon the same, & two Miles backward, & then extend the parallel Line with the River Six Miles & to run westwardly so far as [the] said Quantity of Land be completly surveyed unto them.

The fact that, although the governor knew exactly what he wanted, he did not always know just how the land lay, was sometimes a cause of embarrassment to Thomas Holme. In this case he found it necessary to notify Penn that this "cannot be without prejudice to the liberties."[20] The validity of the statement is easily verified by a look at the map of 1687. For several miles the lower portion of the Schuylkill was bordered by marshy land not suited to settlement, with only a couple of miles intervening between the marshes and the liberty lands. The territory of the Welsh settlers lay above liberty lands. The large tract intended for the barony appears on the 1687 map as a misshapen area lying west of Haverford Township and irregularly southward. The result was less than satisfactory. Five years later Thomas Holme and the Welsh would still be involved in the struggle for a Welsh barony.

The hoped-for barony did not materialize. There were not enough immigrants to settle the unrealistically large tract, and its eastern border was intruded upon by the Society's land mentioned above and by individual surveys made by Charles Ashcom in defiance of orders. Some Welsh settlers preferred property in other locations and did not settle on the common tract. During Blackwell's governorship (12 July 1688–12 August 1689) the land was divided for political reasons, Radnor and Haverford Townships being included in Chester County, allegedly to prevent election of a disproportionate number of Welsh members from Philadelphia County to the assembly and council.

---

[20] DSPA, BLR, *OR*, D-88, 69, PHMC (Micro. 4: 773). *PWP* 2: 527. Thomas's reply to Penn is assumed to belong to this situation, although it is here referred to an order by WP dated 7 June 1683.

Finally, by the end of the first decade the original plan for a cultural enclave had to be abandoned. The Welsh settlers spoke English. Patronymics were relinquished, and names took English forms. The experience was bitter, but it resulted in the enrichment of the province at large rather than in the confinement of the very considerable gifts of individuals within the relatively narrow bounds of a purely ethnic community.

While these attempts at settling three homogeneous societies were going on with varying degrees of success, the staking out of city lots, marking the boundaries of the liberty lands, and surveying such tracts as could be laid out before the boundary was indicated continued as rapidly as weather, thick undergrowth, and necessarily irregular boundaries permitted. The fourteenth of February brought a sheaf of eleven warrants comprising 4,750 acres, with liberty land proportionate to purchases. This was followed on 21 February by a warrant to lay out three townships on the east side of Schuylkill, joining the German township, and of a town above Farmer's land. Thomas Holme gave the order for survey to Thomas Fairman, with an additional order that they were not to "incroach" on another warrant in his hands for a township at Umbelicamence. If Fairman had not already received instructions from Penn concerning these, he was to ask about them. Thomas Holme believed that the governor

> intends that these three townships run back from the Skuylkill one behind another so that the German township must of necessity be first run out, and if there be no people ready to go along with thee that are to be confirmed in some of these townships, especially the first, then thou must hire men to carry the chain and mark the bounds, for it must be done forthwith.[21]

Plainly, the German township had not yet been surveyed, although its site had been indicated.

A glance at the 1686/87 map reveals that there was not room for three townships between the Schuylkill and the German township. The compromise seems to have been the strip of land between the German township and the river, with the Farmer tract and Plymouth Township successively "behind" it, i.e., reaching toward the interior. The only suggestion of a town above the Jasper Farmer tract is a narrow strip of land between Farmer's tract and Plymouth Township marked *Townstead* on the 1687 map.

---

[21] Dept. Sur., OLR, *Proprietary Papers*, PHMC, cited by ACM, Box 24.

On 12 June Penn issued a warrant to Thomas Holme to "plant back of the City Square forthwith with renters, notwithstanding other warrants dated two months before this not yet executed and let their fronts be equally 50 foot." No doubt it was the governor's hope that Friends would wish to live in the vicinity of the Meeting House, which Thomas had originally conceived to be, with other important public buildings, seated on this square.[22]

At the meeting at Christopher Taylor's house a year and a half before, Thomas Holme, John Songhurst, Thomas Wynne, and Griffith Jones or any three of them were delegated for "the care and management" of choosing "a fit Place to build a Meting house in this City, as also the Manner & Form of Building it."[23] The result was the first Meeting House in Philadelphia, the "Boarded Meeting House" on the west side of Front Street, near the present Sansom Street. Whether it was for this or for a more substantial building erected later is not specified, but on 3 July 1683 the committee requested the governor to discuss the location of the Meeting House with them. It was decided that £60 should be raised for the building, the rest of the expense to be satisfied in goods. At the meeting of 6 November Thomas Holme and others volunteered to supply fourteen-foot forms (benches) for the Meeting House. The question of the situation of the building was still unsolved when Thomas Holme and the other members of the committee again approached the governor concerning the matter. Now, on 6 May 1684, they again went to him concerning the best location for a permanent Meeting House. Penn chose the Center Square site as being most convenient to Friends on both river fronts and contributed a generous shipment of stone, lumber, and shingles for it.[24]

He was not to see the building, but a letter from his secretary, Phillip Lehnmann, describes its progress and the first meeting held on the site.

While settlement in Bucks, Philadelphia, and Chester counties progressed more or less smoothly, there were the annoyances of dissatisfied settlers who refused to accept their originally selected tracts. When more satisfactory land was located the adjustment was made readily enough, particularly when there was good reason for the request, as in the case of Richard Russell. Thomas Holme's original

---

[22] BLR, *OR* D-78: 138. Transcription in ACM 26: 229-n232.
[23] See above, Chap 8, n. 20.
[24] Rachel Buck Coll., GSP 1: 2015; Edwin B. Bronner, "The Center Square Meeting House and Other Meetings of Early Philadelphia," *Bulletin of the Friends' Historical Association*, 44, no. 2: 67–73.

note in the *Old Rights* record states that Russell's lot was set out above Francis Fincher's but "he after surveyed refused it & pd not the survey." The entry is crossed out and marked "regardless," to be followed on the next page by further narrative and explanation. On 11 April it is noted that "Richard Russell's City Lot & spot to be directed by the Governor second street back from Schuylkill." Return was made on 31 May. Thomas Holme adds, "I showed him Kendentamassen & he says there is not a place to put a slip for a ship for one of the stops, but at the upper cove he thinks it may do, and prays him there." Thomas endorsed the record, "A place for ship granted," and it was entered in Fol. 9, No. 2120. At the end of another warrant of 12 June 1684 Thomas Holme added, "Christopher Pennock having refused the 500 A next above Silas Crispin's land, I granted it to William Stanley & ordered D F to set it out there to same the 500 A."[25]

At times Penn's changes of policy caused embarrassment to the surveyor general. Some purchasers challenged Penn's reduction (from one hundred acres to eighty acres) of the liberty land allotted to a First Purchaser of five thousand acres. One such purchaser was Denis Rocheford. Thomas Holme appealed to Penn: Rocheford's warrant called for the originally specified hundred acres, but "Thou hast ordered me to allow no more but 80 A to any whosoever; please to afford me that positive pleasure for that he is very unwilling to accept of less than 100 A." On the back of the note "W P" acceded to the request: "Let him have the 1,00 A." The warrant had been issued on 20 December 1683. The same record of *Old Rights* contains another informal note by Thomas Holme, this one addressed to Robert Longshore, directing him to draw a return for Denis Rocheford of three thousand acres surveyed by T[homas] F[airman]—a simple enough order, except that Thomas Holme added, "I am paid for the survey." He continues, "Now begin the return to Capt. Markham. . . . a patent I couldn't find at any time." This entry is dated 8 January 1685. It appears that Thomas Holme—or could it have been someone else?—was practicing writing his name. Under the order appears: "Tho, Tho, Tho: Holme. Th." Thomas Holme was not accustomed to receive or to record payment for survey in orders, but he may have done so in this case to prevent Robert Longshore from exacting the fee from Fairman, since payment normally was required at the making of the return. That a man who had been signing documents for the Society of Friends in Ireland and the Province of Pennsylvania for

---

[25] *PA, OR*, Book D-78: 83, Bureau of Internal Affairs, DAM. PHMC.

thirty years should be practicing his signature is curious, to say the least.

If the official labor of the surveyor general was arduous, it nevertheless sometimes redounded to his own advantage. Of the eleven thousand acres he now owned, at least between twelve hundred and fifteen hundred in addition to his Well Spring Plantation were laid out to him and available for sale. One of these, comprising a little more than six hundred acres lying in the bend of Poquessing Creek, he would later sell to Nicholas Rideout.[26] Now he took advantage of the opportunity to straighten the lines of the northwest corner of the tract by selling an inconvenient triangle. He directed Thomas Fairman to

> Survey and lay out to the bearer, Edward Godwin, 100 A, at that end which is between John Carters and Giles Knight on the northern part or end thereof so as the residue may be entire toward the creek, and the said 100 A may be compact, and a pretty straight line between the 100 A and the rest, and make me a return thereof. . . .

The entry is dated 3 March 1684, and closes with the admonition to "prepare, and hasten return."[27]

If Thomas Holme was solicitous for the symmetry of boundaries, the Proprietor was no less watchful, at least where his own limits were concerned. Irregularities perpetrated by the deputy or deputies who surveyed tracts for purchasers along the Delaware adjoining the Manor of Pennsbury brought down on Thomas Holme an angry order from Penn:

> Whereas I understand that the Lands of Sepassing that have cost me more than I sell the same Quan. for to any Purchaser at this day, are run into my back crooked and disorderly Lines, to the spoil of the said Land for convenient Settlement & contrary to Justice & Equity these are therefore to authorize thee, & strictly charge thee forthwth to turn the lines of those lands beginning at George Browns & folow on to John Wood's. that so that Land may have a contingent of ends wth the Lands adjacent & make returns thereof into my office at Philadelphia, the 9th of the 3^d m^o. [May] 1684. Wm Penn for Thomas Holme Surveyor General.[28]

Busy though he was with his survey concerns and Quaker affairs, Thomas Holme was aware of, but except as a provincial councillor

---

[26] *PhA. Deed Book* E-1.5. The deed is dated 4 May 1685. Between this date and Thomas's completion of the 1687 map, Rideout sold the land to eight other purchasers, reserving for himself a triangular tract with a fine frontage of approximately three miles on Poquessing Creek.
[27] Howell-Harnstead Coll., Hbg., C. 25: Bound volume. *Old Surveys, Original Grants, etc.*
[28] DS, PTL, DLR, *OR* D-83: 291; ACM 26, no. 182.

not immediately involved in, two areas of major importance to the governor. Baltimore's harassment accelerated, and Governor Dongan of New York wrote the governor of Pennsylvania to alert him to his Lordship's designs on the Susquehanna, at the same time making it clear that, although they should cooperate in thwarting any plans that Baltimore might have for expansion in that direction, he himself was already in agreement with the Indians for a monopoly of the fur trade. Penn sent Thomas Lloyd and William Welch, a provincial councillor from New Castle, to New York to confer with Dongan concerning the mutual problems of the two governors.[29] Dongan assured them of his friendly cooperation in matters that equally involved himself and Penn, but noted that he had already arranged with the Iroquois for the fur trade.

On 25 May Samuel Land wrote from New Castle to inform Penn of Baltimore's departure for England, and of the nine deputies, including his volatile and aggressive cousin, George Talbot, left to carry on his affairs in his absence. Markham had written to Penn on 27 March to report Baltimore's arrival in London, and to enclose copies of his Lordship's instructions to his agents, but the letter did not reach Philadelphia until 28 August, by which time Penn himself was on his way to London.[30] The spring of 1684 was marked by Penn's preparations for the journey, which to him now seemed imperative if his province was to survive in anything like the form in which he perceived it.

At the first meeting of the provincial council in 1683/84, held on 20 March, after hearing a "Complaint being made . . . of a Notorious Robbery comitted on the goods of Hannah Saulter," it was "Ordered that the first thing to be done to-morrow be the Running over the Old Laws." This was postponed from the designated day, a Friday, until the following Monday, 24 March. On that day the laws were duly read and discussed, and "A Committee was appointed to Inspect the Margenall notes upon the Old Laws, Viz. Tho: Holmes, Wm Welch, Tho: Lloyd." The committee was directed to make their report the next morning.

The laws were to be drawn out with reasons and preamble, and then the bills made at Upland/Chester examined. The committee, no doubt in consideration of the intrusion of purely local and temporary

---

[29] For reports on Baltimore's activities, see letters of John Richardson (ALS, Penn Papers, AML 1 HSP [Micro. 4: 752]), and William Welch (ALS, Peter Force Papers, Series 9, LC [Micro. 4: 757]). For Dongan's response to the mission of Lloyd and Welch, see ALS, Dreer Coll. HSP (Micro. 4: 671). All three of these letters are printed in *PWP* 2: 521–523.
[30] Chew Family Papers, HSP (Micro. 4: 865). To the Honorable William Penn Esquire. Docketed: Sheriff Samuel Land the 25th 3d mo 1684 concerning Baltimore and Talbott. *PWP* 2: 557. See also *PWP* 2: 546–548, printed from ALS, Penn-Forbes Coll., HSP (Micro. 7: 701).

cases on the permanent body of law, proposed the constitution of another council for state matters. The merits of the suggestion were recognized and aroused considerable debate, but finally it was defeated. During the ensuing weeks the council meetings were concerned chiefly with scrutiny of the laws, sometimes with spirited debate, culminating in approval, amendment, or abolition.

Establishments like the London Coffee House were features of eighteenth-century Philadelphia; during these early years of the province taverns were the centers of conversation and conviviality. Abuse of refreshments was not unusual, with the result that the laws of 1683/84 were preoccupied with liquor. The Proprietor pleased the Indians but put the legislators somewhat on the defensive by telling the former that they might have rum, provided they would accept the same punishment for its abuse that was visited upon the English, and that the law against selling it to them would be repealed. Experience had shown the settlers that the Indians in general were less able to handle rum than they themselves were, although abuse among the white population occurred. The law was modified rather than repealed. A further problem was the manner and severity of punishment for drunkenness, and there was repeated discussion of the extent to which business deals made under the influence of liquor were to be considered binding. Controls on liquor sales and the suppressing of ordinaries excited extensive discussion. Samuel Carpenter proposed a tax on liquor. The measure was passed on 28 March. The monies thus derived would be used to defray the costs of government, and would be designated as public aid.[31] Although beer was the common beverage of the day, the quality thereof varied to the extent that it was found advisable to impose regulations on the brewers.

Some of the laws that had appeared necessary at the opening of the province could be dispensed with, now that agriculture and trade were fairly well established. Such a law was that against the slaughtering of cows and ewe lambs, since herds had already increased appreciably. On the other hand, it was still necessary to require that animals that roamed across unfenced lands be marked. Penalties were set for removing such markings and for taking possession of vagrant animals. Animals confiscated by officials were to be delivered to the Proprietor. Theft of trees was a serious and frequent offense, and one that was

---

[31] Not only did Carpenter propose a tax upon liquor, he allotted what he considered to be the suitable tax to each class of beverage: "*Vizt.* upon Brandy 12d. the Gall; Beer, Ale, Mum, Spanish Wine, 5d p. Gall; Medera, Each Pipe 50s; French Wine 4lL. p. Tunn." Penn put the question in a simpler form, that "all Rum, Brandy, Wines, & all sorts of strong Liquors & Spirits under the same head, Imported, shall pay 12p. p Gall."

difficult to monitor. Thomas Holme was particularly distressed by marauders trespassing on the governor's property.

There was a sense of urgency now about the deliberations of the council. Only two new bills were read on 31 March: the bill of custom and a bill concerning the joining of the governments of Pennsylvania and New Jersey in warrants for the apprehension of criminals. Both of these were appointed to be read for the second time the following morning. Thomas Holme had further reason to be excited. He was present and active on the council on 31 March, but he could not help being aware that, a few squares away, his daughter Hester Crispin was giving birth to his first American grandchild, who would be named for her grandmother Sarah Croft Holme. On 1 April it was

> Ordered that the seeing to the Bills fairly to be transcribed and Examined by the Originalls, be referred to Tho: Lloyd, Wm. Welch, Tho: Holmes, and Wm. Clark. The same Committee to draw up Orders for this board for preparing, proposing, & Resolving, against their next meeting.

Perhaps to insure full attendance of the members from the Lower Counties as well as to integrate militants of the area who leaned toward Baltimore in the contest between the two Proprietors, it was decided that the next meeting of the assembly should be held at New Castle.

The council held four more meetings in Philadelphia during April 1684, chiefly to consider what course to take with regard to the continued disturbances of Baltimore's faction in the Lower Counties. On 3 April William Clayton, William Wood, Christopher Taylor, Thomas Holme, and Thomas Lloyd were ordered to stay with and attend the governor. Evidently the council felt that they should have some special recognition, and it was voted *Nemine Contradicente* (unanimously) "that the Gov. shall appoint some distinction for the Councillors." After much discussion of disturbing news and rumors from the Lower Counties the session adjourned until 10 May, when it would reconvene in New Castle.

On 10 May the assembly and council met in joint session at New Castle for a half-hour address by Penn that had almost the tone of a farewell:

> [The Governor] having assum'd his Seat of Authority, makes his Address to the General Assembly in the Way of Christian Council and Exhortation, advising the Members of Assembly, to look unto "God, in all their Proceedings, and to act in every Thing, not with any unadvised Rashness, but with serious Consideration."

His address concluded, the governor withdrew, accompanied by the whole audience, after which the assembly again convened and the council continued with the governor. Meeting again, the sheriffs announced the results of elections, and the governor reported on his conversation with the Indians regarding the purchase of rum. The assembly also attended this session and presented as its speaker Nicholas More. In the afternoon the council heard the report of the mission of Lloyd and William Welch to New York, and a copy of the charter was delivered to the assembly.

Until 29 May, when it returned to Philadelphia, the council continued to meet at New Castle, within easy access of the assembly, which studied the bills and accepted them, proposed amendments, or suggested that they be allowed "to fall of themselves," as in the case of selling rum to the Indians. Sometimes the strain of meetings and the necessity of mutual acceptance of bills and orders taxed the patience of the councillors, as when they responded to the messenger who came from the assembly in the forenoon of 15 May to inquire if they were ready to hear their proposals that they "had been ready ever since Eight in the morning." Generally speaking, however, they strove to maintain an atmosphere of peace. The typical conclusion of personal altercations was that, after judgment had been passed, the parties involved should shake hands and give bonds for good behavior, and records of the difficulty should be destroyed—an admirable solution, but one that stirs the curiosity of the reader.

At the meeting of 13 May groups of six councillors were appointed to attend the governor. Thomas Holme, with William Welch, James Harrison, William Wood, William Clark, and William Sothersby, was appointed to attend him the second month after the rising of the assembly, which would be July. On 22 May Thomas Holme, with William Welch and Thomas Lloyd, was appointed "to inspect the Journall of the Last Sessions of the Provll Councill & Genall Assembly. . . . also to inspect both former & Latter Laws."

Meanwhile, reports of the misbehavior of Baltimore's representatives in the Lower Counties continued to come in. On 3 April "It is left to the Govr in a Small Councill [? those ordered to attend the governor] to send Agents to York to acquaint the Govr of York of the abuse of Ld Baltimore's Agents." On 7 April "The Question was put whether any One should be sent to the Lord Baltimore, to acquaint him of the Coll. Talbot's Unmill. Actions, also of Marfey's, in the Lower Countyes. . ."[32]

---

[32] MPC 1: 49. See also 1: 50.

On 3 June Thomas Holme, William Welch, and Thomas Lloyd were appointed to "Looke into the Actions of the Lord Baltemore, and to draw up a Declaration to hinder his illegal proceedings." Presumably their report was the basis for a declaration by the governor "By and with the Advice" of the council on 12 and 18 June, when, the minutes of the council relate, "The Govr again read the Declaration Concerning the Difference between the Lord Baltemore & himself, desireing the Councills approbation; who approved of it, but desired that some things for the present might be left out."

Interspersed with council meetings were the ever-present land affairs. On 12 March Thomas Holme added to Charles Ashcom's draft of Thomas Pascall's five hundred acres:

> Ch. Ashcom. Hasten to me the returnes of all the land surveyed by thee, wherein insert the first dates of the warr^{ts} & from whom the warr^{ts} are. & let the figures or map be drawn according to the [obl.] perch in an inch, with a scale in or by figures, & compass distinct, & the field work exactly of every station, & the number of perchs in every station, together with the day of the moneth & year of the survey thereof. Philadelphia 12° 1mo 1684. Tho. Holme Survey^r Gen^{ll} Let the boundings of each man's land be expressed very exactly, because it must be so mentioned in the patent. Tho. Holme.[33]

Earlier Thomas Holme had been confronted with an unwieldy assortment of warrants. He had warrants for "300a. a peece for Wm Lowther and Phil: Ford 10000a. more for this overplus, but the land will not hold so much." The governor had allowed Joseph Growden 252 acres in the same area. After considerable computation and maneuvering of boundaries he was able to fit Growden's manor in, but on 12 April Thomas Fairman noted: "Resurveyed by virtue of a warr^t from Tho: Holmes . . ." Both Ashcom and Growden would be thorns in Thomas Holme's flesh for some time to come.[34]

At the end of May Thomas Holme had another problem with conflicting surveys, this time caused by the intrusion of a warrant for Thomas Bowman where land had already been laid out for Thomas Rudyard, a problem already recorded. Penn placed the matter in the hands of a committee, which reported its findings on 2 August.[35] On 13 March Penn issued the warrant for the long-anticipated forty-

---

[33] ADS, directive of TH to CA added to Ashcom's draft of Thomas Paschall's five-hundred-acre tract. PA, *Dept. Sur. Book*, B-22: 183, DAM, PHMC.
[34] For the culmination of Thomas's long conflict with Ashcom, see below
[35] See above, 119–120.

thousand-acre Welsh Tract, but it was not until 3 June that Thomas ordered David Powell, a Welsh surveyor, to make the survey.[36] That it lay in what generally seemed to be Charles Ashcom's territory may explain some of the later difficulties.

Thomas Holme's delay may have been due his appointment, on the day after he received the warrant, to a committee to draw up a report on the actions of Lord Baltimore. On the afternoon of 3 June he was one of four witnesses of the deed of Maughoughsin to William Penn of all his land on Pahkehoma Creek (Perkiomen, a tributary of the Schuylkill about twenty miles west of Philadelphia), for which the Indian received two matchcoats, four pairs of stockings, and four bottles of cider. Three days later Richard Mettamicont sold lands on both sides of Pennypack Creek to Penn. This time Tryall Holme and Philip Theodore Lehnmann witnessed the transaction. It is the first time that Tryall's signature appears on a document in his father's home territory. The land purchased included the large tract bearing the name of Elinor Holme and that of Thomas Holme's Well Spring plantation as seen on the 1687 map.[37]

One more important governmental duty would be assigned to Thomas Holme during these last weeks of the Proprietor's first stay in his province. On 26 July he, Thomas Lloyd, and William Haige were appointed to draw up a charter for Philadelphia "to be made a Burrough." It was "Left to the Governor's Discretion to have the Laws and Charter printed at London"—an act to which Penn's discretion did not dispose him for some time. The commission very probably was prompted by a phrase in the remonstrance addressed to Penn earlier in the month by substantial citizens of Philadelphia to the effect that "to this day they are onely a Nominall Citie, having no Charter to Incorporate them, Or grant of the least privileges of a Corporation."[38]

The remonstrance was a tabulated summary of the grievances and anxieties of First Purchasers settled on the Delaware Front, to which they wished Penn to respond before leaving for England. Although most of them were experienced and highly successful businessmen, they had presumed too much on the undocumented privileges of the purchaser of five thousand acres. Whereas they had expected their lands to lie in compact units, they found that they were limited to five hundred acres in one tract, and that they must secure warrants for each desired portion of their purchased land and seat it within a year or lose it. They objected to the reduction of the proportion of liberty

---

[36] DS, BLR, DAM, PHMC; *PWP* 2: 526–527 (Micro. 4: 773).
[37] *PA*, 1, 6, 1684: 88, 92; Smith, *Laws* 2: 111. N.B. Boileau, *Book of Indian Deeds and Charters*, 62.
[38] ALS. Proud Papers, Box 2, no. 1, HSP (Micro. 4: 925); *PWP* 2: 569–578.

land originally promised by the Proprietor, and to the reduction of the size of city lots. They had assumed that ownership of a front lot carried with it the right to construct storage facilities in the bank before the lot, but they had been informed otherwise. Persons who were not First Purchasers and had even purchased as little as five hundred acres were being accorded the same privileges as themselves. Whereas they had assumed that they would have possession of the produce of their land, including hunting and fishing rights and any minerals that might be found in it, they now learned that the Proprietor reserved mineral rights to himself. Furthermore, they had understood that their land had been unqualifiedly purchased from the Indians, assuring them of possession and of the safety of themselves and their dependents. They hoped that all these matters would be adjusted before Penn's departure.

The Proprietor's explanations were not altogether satisfactory to them, and they show up badly beside the clear and concise statements of attorney Thomas Rudyard. The challengers had to be satisfied with the few concessions the governor could or would make. The whole affair left both sides less trusting and united than they had been two years before, and Thomas Holme was left a buffer between the governor to whom he strove to be loyal, and the settlers, who sometimes had justice on their side.

One enterprising purchaser at least had already expanded his activities in the bank area. With the advent of spring Samuel Carpenter had petitioned Penn for permission to build a wharf before his Front Street property. It would undoubtedly be a valuable addition to the city, and, the permission granted, would be begun at once. Another expansion outside his immediate property, though not impinging on the waterfront, was the rope walk constructed by Barnabe Wilcox.[39]

Perhaps to avoid last-minute importunities and farewells, William Penn boarded the *Endeavor* a few days before his actual departure. On board he wrote a final set of documents. The first of these concerned the government of the province during his absence. Thomas Lloyd was to be president of the provincial council, which was to have executive power, together with the making of new laws as it saw fit, subject to the Proprietor's approval.[40] In Lloyd's absence the council was "to nominate from time , as you see just cause, one from among

---

[39] SP, Proud Papers, Box 2, no. 1; Ad. Philadelphia Land Grants, Penn Papers, HSP (Micro. 4: 801); *PWP* 2: 541-n543.
[40] As the editors of the *Penn Papers* point out (2: 584, n. 2), this power of veto was not accorded him by the charter. The commission is a DS, Penn Papers, HSP, printed in *PWP* 2: 583-584, and Soderland, 388-389 (Micro. 4: 016).

you to be your President; To act & do all things that to that place belongeth, by the Commission I granted to the sayd Tho: Lloyd as President of the Provincial Council. . . ."

A second document executed at this time was a hastily composed will, in which the Proprietor distributed to his family, servants, and charity approximately three hundred thousand acres of land in addition to that already laid out to them—a legacy that must have made Thomas Holme wince. Thomas Holme, Thomas Lloyd, James Harrison, and William Clark witnessed the will.[41] On the next day Penn appointed Lloyd, Harrison, and John Simcock guardians of his son Springett. Lloyd, James Claypoole, and Robert Turner were to locate and sell land. This assignment would cause some complications because the commissioners had rather vague ideas of the land available.

Thomas Holme, Robert Turner, Samuel Carpenter, James Harrison, and Philip Theodore Lehnmann received perhaps the most difficult commission. Penn appointed them commissioners of estate and revenue. Their duties as tabulated by the Proprietor were:

1. To meet on 1 October 1684 and inspect the Secretary's and Surveyor General's offices to compile a rent roll.
2. To call in receivers and audit their accounts.
3. To meet every quarter to make an exact account of the names of all persons who have received warrants that are executed, as submitted on the first day of every month by the secretary and the surveyor general.
4. To require all renters to pay their arrears of rent before the first day of March, 1685.
5. To try to get the rent in cash, not corn [grain], in order to prevent charge.
6. To try to collect second quitrents as cheaply as possible—by sheriffs or other collectors or taking pay from traders, allowing them a modest profit, when rent could not be paid in cash.
7. To replace any careless receivers.
8. To audit the accounts of the receivers and of James Harrison at least twice a year.
9. To give a report of finances to William Penn, annually on 1 March.
10. To make sure that the accounts were fair and duly stated to the Proprietor.[42]

---

[41] AD, Pierpont Morgan Library, New York. Pages crossed out, signature torn off. ACM, vol. 26; *PWP*, 585–587 (Micro. 4: 022).
[42] *PA*, 3, 1; HSP, Peters MSS.

Clearly, the office of commissioner of estate and revenues of an absentee landlord was no mere sinecure.

Governmental appointments ended with the naming of Nicholas More, William Welch, Robert Turner, William Wood, and John Eckley as judges of the provincial court. There remained for Penn to write directions to his gardener, Ralph Smith; and a letter to his wife, Gulielma, expressing his love for her and for their children, and giving instructions for their care and education. He mentions as "friends of his family and interest" T. Lloyd, T. Holme, J. Harrison, C. Taylor, J. Simcock, J. Claypoole, R. Turner, S. Carpenter, with others.[43] Finally, perhaps even as the editors of the *Penn Papers* suggest, after the *Endeavor* was already on her way down the river, William Penn wrote his *Farewell to Pennsylvania*, the mood and style of which recall the gentle city of *Revelations* that he must have had in mind when he named his capital city three years before.[44]

Exactly when the *Endeavor* sailed down the Delaware is not recorded, but it docked at Lewes for what would be William Penn's last meeting with the provincial council before the turn of the century. There a disagreement between Watson and Bellamy over apparently overlapping boundaries was settled amicably, and the council adjourned until 18 August. Farewells said, Penn again boarded his ship, and his erstwhile companions went back to New Castle. There the council sat on 18, 19, and 20 August, perhaps at the house of William Welch, where it had met on at least one earlier occasion. At any rate, he was present at the meeting of 18 August. It would be his last attendance. After the reading of the various commissions the council adjourned until 7 September, when it would reconvene in Philadelphia.

It was the end of an era. Heretofore if there were differences regarding property or other problems, the governor had been readily accessible for consultation. Although intimate association for two years in a pioneer community had, in the natural course of events, brought to light some of his limitations, William Penn was still the moral and spiritual mentor of most of the population. He was the head of the power structure. Now communication with him would require about three months at the least. Within these bounds he was leaving behind a company of friends whose loyalty and judgment he trusted with an all-too-vulnerable faith that had had perhaps been a little shaken by

---

[43] ALS. PML (Micro. 4: 028). *PWP* 2: 587–588.
[44] ALS, Penn Papers, HSP (Micro. 4: 043). *PWP* 2: 589–590.

the remonstrance. Perhaps if the signatures of the authors of the document were available they would help to explain attitudes the Proprietor held later. At any rate, Penn left behind him as the ministers of his authority eleven of his most proven colonists, among whom he had distributed the responsibilities for which each seemed most fitted.

Thomas Holme considered the future with a mixture of resolution and apprehension. He was the oldest man in the company, approaching his sixtieth birthday. James Harrison, at fifty-six, was next. The median age was forty-six. The Proprietor himself was twenty years his junior. Thomas Holme knew these men in a way that Penn could not have known them—their varying degrees of confidence in him, the extent of their dedication to the province, their virtues, their personal ambitions and rivalries. In some ways he had worked more closely with the governor than had many of the others. As a survivor of the hardships of war and the persecutions visited on himself and his co-religionists for nearly thirty years, he still subscribed to the austerity of the early years of the Society of Friends. He would do everything in his power to protect and further the governor's interests and to help mold this vast territory into a homogeneous unit. After this, he would try to maintain at least a subsistence income for himself and to settle land enough to leave a respectable legacy for his children and their offspring.

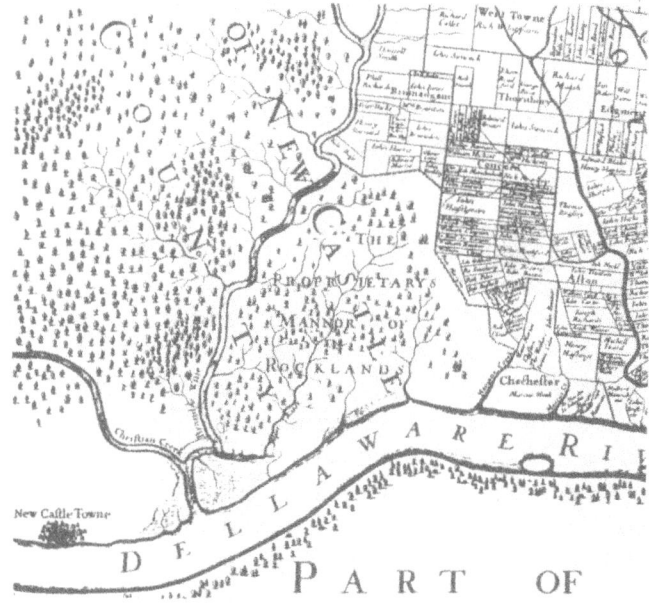

Fig. 20. New Castle area.

Chapter 12

Watershed

As the *Endeavor* disappeared down the Delaware a new era in the history of Penn's province commenced. Now at the head of the provincial council, Thomas Lloyd at first enjoyed his position. With him presiding, the council remained at New Castle for a couple of weeks, during which the governor's latest commissions were reread. The council then recessed until 10 September, when it would reconvene in Philadelphia.

When the council met again on the appointed day, the first order of business was to send a writ to New Castle to order the selection of a new member to replace William Welch, deceased. Welch would be a severe loss to the council. He had been a faithful member, a buffer between the basic province and the often wavering or even hostile inhabitants of the Three Lower Counties. He and Thomas Holme had shared special assignments, and, like Thomas Holme, he had known the Proprietor for a dozen years or more. He and the recently deceased Francis Whitwell would be missed both for their personal characters and for their support of the governor in New Castle and Kent Counties.

In the afternoon it was decided to extend Thomas Holme's surveyor generalship to New Castle County, with Thomas Pierson as his deputy. Hoping to forestall any difficulties such as he had had with some of the deputies, he wrote to Pearson a detailed account of what would be expected of him. First, he was to present himself to the local authorities and give them his credentials as the deputy appointed to carry out the surveys directed to him by Thomas Holme in terms of his commission from the Proprietor. Thomas Holme's directions to him recall those of Sir William Petty to the Down surveyors. In all his works he was to take care

> to jot down in the margin all memorable matters as rivers, lakes, meadows, bog, rocks, mountains, mines, quarries... more than ordinary sorts of wood, leaving not out any quantity of land or waste or unprofitable, as per special order from the Proprietary Government.

In all his protractions of quantities of land he was to lay down the draft or figure on the paper on which he marked the scales of distances. Failing these records, he would be responsible for the cost of resurvey. Thomas empowered him to demand and receive the survey money allowed by the governor for all the land he surveyed. The document ends formally, "Given under my hand and seal at Philadelphia, 24-7-1684." There follows a postscript: "And further, if any of you have a warrant for land not yet given in, from the office there, thou are to take this warrant without further order from me and execute them carefully and bring them to me. Thomas Holme." The order bears the only perfect wax seal of the Holme arms known to have survived among Thomas Holme's papers.[1]

The council met regularly during the remainder of September, with Thomas Holme present as usual and Lloyd presiding. Most of the time of the first meetings was occupied with the filling of vacancies and settling of administrative procedures. On 12 September came a report that an unauthorized ship—"a ship with unfree bottom"—had arrived at New Castle. A committee was named to investigate its presence and report back to Lloyd, or, in his absence, to Thomas Holme. Thomas Holme's appointment was prophetic of various auxiliary services he would be drafted to perform, but this one was not required. Lloyd was present at the meetings at which the fate of the ship (confiscation and sale) was decided. When this affair was settled the council adjourned until 24 October.

Thomas took advantage of a relatively quiet interval to settle land on his one remaining son. On 30 September James Claypoole and Robert Turner for Thomas Holme issued a grant at the request of

---

[1] ADS, HSP, Taylor Papers, vol. 16, no. 3303. Instructions to Thomas Pierson, deputy surveyor for the county of New Castle. That Pierson's appointment may not have been altogether unexpected may be inferred from earlier correspondence between the two surveyors. Pierson seems to have petitioned Thomas for deputyship of a county before this opportunity arose.

Tryall Holme for a thousand acres in right of his father, part of it to be in the county of Philadelphia, and on 2 October the order for survey was issued. It was endorsed by John Hughes, "Entered, recorded, returned, no. 1042." On 19 December 1684 a warrant for five hundred acres of land in upper Dublin Township in Philadelphia County was issued by the commissioners, and at the order of Captain Holme, surveyor general, was ordered to be laid out by Thomas Fairman. A map of the tract shows it to be "400 perches on the SW and NE sides, and 167 perches on the NW and SW sides, on the Susquehanna Road, "William and George Palmer's land lying to the SW, the Susquehanna Road between them. Take a rising slant to the east. . . ."[2] The 1687 map records a five-hundred-acre tract of choice land bisected by the northwestern course of Dublin (Pennypack) Creek, with lively tributaries to north and south, adjoining the Manor of Moreland on the northwest. It lay in the column of tracts that contained part of his Well Spring Plantation, on which Thomas Holme had built his house, as well as tracts belonging to, among others, Samuel Claridge, Robert Turner, and Tryall's brother-in-law, Silas Crispin. Tryall Holme was twenty-one now, the only one of Thomas's sons to have reached his twentieth year, and, it was to be hoped, ready to take an adult's place in the province. The survey was ordered with high hopes.

All this is not to say that between the middle of September and the first week of October activity in Philadelphia was minimal. On 23 September Philip Theodore Lehnmann reported to William Penn in a long letter the large Yearly Meeting of Friends held at the hastily constructed wooden Meeting House at Center Square, and the seizing of the French ship in the harbor. He remarked in passing that Ralph Fretwell's business was "not going well."[3]

All that can be said of Lehnmann's casual comment about Fretwell's business is that it was true. The business had already reached a pitch of acute discomfort for the commissioners of property, other purchasers and settlers, and, most of all, for Thomas Holme.

The problem had its origin in a burst of entrepreneurial zeal that had prompted Penn to write to a wealthy, aggressive Barbadoan sugar planter, Ralph Fretwell, suggesting that he establish a settlement of his fellow islanders on the Susquehanna. When the hoped-for acquisition of the Susquehanna did not materialize he wrote again, suggesting a foundation west of the Schuylkill.

---

[2] Hbg., *OR*, D-85, 4, 14, 16. The tract remained unseated at the time of Holme's death in April 1695.
[3] ALS, ACM, CCHS; *PWP* 2: 599–600 (Micro. 4: 034).

Although there is no indication that Fretwell was a personal acquaintance of the Proprietor, he was prominent enough to be known to him by reputation, witness Penn's letter to George Fox, written on 4 March 1676: "I have given order about the books for R. Fretwell. But some that saw the letter wonder'd first that thou shouldst be . . . so kind to him that is, say they, an odd spirited & imperious man."[4]

Despite his apparent lack of social attractiveness, Fretwell must have seemed a desirable settler in the province. He was wealthy and prominent and a faithful Friend, having been deprived of his seat on the bench of the court of common pleas on his convincement to the Society of Friends, and suffered other heavy penalties for his steadfastness.[5] It was only natural that the possibility of establishing a settlement on land that was not depleted by previous plantings, surrounded by Friends, in a society that promised opportunity for his commercial expertise and, perhaps, political ambition, should appeal strongly to him. To Penn's invitation he responded all too quickly, setting out at once to secure the land, without sufficient knowledge of the situation.

Just when he arrived in Pennsylvania is not recorded, but, judging from Penn's letter dated 3 April 1684 to "Dr: R: Fretwell," and his presence in Pennsylvania during the summer, he must have sailed or been preparing to sail before that date. At any rate, he did arrive, expecting to be accommodated at once with twelve miles square of good land on which to establish a colony of fellow Barbadoans. He was disappointed, and he did not take disappointment easily.

Whether William Penn acceded to Fretwell's expectations with faith in his surveyor general's ability to create ten or twelve mile squares of land in already well-populated country (the size of the proposed tract differs from document to document), or was thinking in terms of six to twelve square miles, or, being human, reflected gratefully that he would be on the high seas before the day of reckoning came, is immaterial. On 16 August, two days before he left for England, Penn issued a warrant for Ralph Fretwell for the required land in either of two areas. If in Chester County, the tract was to be not under ten or over twelve miles square. Specifications for a tract in Philadelphia County were more detailed. It would be on the "hither End of the long Island Barbados & to run upward on each side of Skulkill Six miles on the Waterside, not to go [less] backward than

---

[4] ALS, Luke Howard Coll., FLL (Micro. 2: 421); *PWP* 1: 359, 361.
[5] ALS, John Rylands Library, Manchester, Lancashire. (Micro. 4: 915); *PWP* 2: 546–547.

Seven Miles [not to exceed Twelve] on each Side where not already taken up according to the Method of Townships." The warrant was dated at Lewes, 16 August 1684.[6]

The warrant notwithstanding, the selection of the tract was repeatedly delayed. Other purchasers claimed priorities, and the deputy surveyor of Chester County showed no eagerness to comply with directions. As delays continued, Fretwell's frustration increased. Finally, on 8 October, he poured out his grievance in a letter to the Proprietor. Naturally the surveyor bore the brunt of his wrath:

> I fear I may say thy D^{ty} Surveyor wants abilities or honesty for the true interest of the country, for people to Act above board a little more of the accord: to the may be said unto them but to act underhand against what they pretend to is truely to be loathed and denied. . . .[7]

Whether he here intends Deputy Surveyor Charles Ashcom, to whom the order was given, or Surveyor General Thomas Holme is debatable. Fretwell seems to have found a sympathetic ear in John Simcock, to whom he refers Penn for substantiation of his allegations. He further suggests adding James Harrison and Simcock to the commission for granting lands in the president's absence in New York, "at times considerable." The current remaining commissioners, he believes, may hesitate to issue grants in his absence.

On 18 October Charles Ashcom returned a survey of two hundred acres of land for Ralph Fretwell on the east side of Naaman's Creek, beginning at the mouth of the creek.[8] This was a very desirable tract in Chester County which later appears to have been included in Penn's Manor of Rockland; but it was a far cry from the ten or twelve mile squares—64,000 or 92,160 acres—he wanted.

By 24 October Fretwell's attempted negotiations had gone on long enough that, with William Clayton acting president *pro tem*, the council turned the problem over to Thomas Holme. For him the difficulty was compounded by the fact that the proposed tract lay in Ashcom's bailiwick. The minutes of the provincial council for that date reveal Thomas's anger at his deputy and the difficulty, if not the impossibility, of satisfying Fretwell:

---

[6] Eighteenth-century copy, 2p. To the copy the copyist added a careful description of revisions in the text: "The Word (less) in the 8th Line hereof being written on a Razure And the Words [not to exceed twelve] being interlined in the Original. 7th July 1742. William Parsons Survey^r Gen^{rl}—The original . . . is not subscribed by, nor directed to, any Person."

[7] ACM, Box 2: no. 7, CCHS (Micro. 5: 005).

[8] Dept. Sur., B-22: 171, DAM, PHMC; HSP, copy (Micro. 5: 017).

Ralph Fretwell Complains to the Councill that he cannot have his Land Laid Out by reason of the Contention of the Survey^r.

Tho: Holmes being sent to by the Clarke of the Councill, to know his reason of not Issuing out his Warrant to Survey the Said Ralph Fretwell's land, his answer was, he would not Issue out his Warrant to Charles Ashcom, but he would Issue out his Warrant according to his Commission.

The council ordered Thomas Holme "to put the said Warr^t in Execution, Viz^t to direct Charles Ashcome, Survey^r of the County of Chester, to lay out the Same." Again Thomas Holme refused to issue the order. Again the council issued it:

These are therefore to will and require Thee fourthwth to Survey or cause to be surveyed, unto Ralph ffretwell, the said Tract of Land, beginning halfe a mile above Concord, and soe through New Towne, Saveing Every man's right to their already Surveyed to them in the said Towne Ship, and Soe up N.N.W. till you come to the full Extent on that side, and soe onwards untill the said warrant be Accomplished, by a Square of tenn or twelve miles, or any Quantity that may be Conteined in the same, according to the Treu Intent of the Gov^{rs} Warrant.

Thomas Holme once more refused to issue the order. In the first place, it is doubtful that, even this early in the development of the province, tracts of such size in popular Chester County could be found without including or at least encroaching upon already surveyed land. In the second, Ashcom was not only dilatory in making surveys, but he was slovenly about lines and did not turn in his field maps. Furthermore, he put all of the surveyor's fees into his own pocket, denying Thomas Holme the one-third share to which he was entitled by the terms of his commission. James Harrison and John Simcock were "Ordered to Discourse Tho. Holmes Concerning Ralph Fretwell."[9] Unfortunately we do not have a record of the "discourse," but when Nicholas More wrote his catalogue of bad news to William Penn on 1 December he did not omit Fretwell's place in the lands and heart of Pennsylvanians: "Ra: Frewell is become Burthensome to the Spirits of Most peoples . . . most that Wish you and the Province well, Wish him in Barbados agine, he is become abusiff both to Councell and officers, onely to C.[hristopher] T.[aylor]. . . ."[10]

It was improbable that Fretwell's demands could be met, even with the best will on the part of the surveyors. The warrant called for a

---

[9] MCP, 1838, 1: 71.
[10] ALS, ACM, CCHS. *PWP* 2:608, 609, n.

tract twelve miles square, which would contain 92,160 acres, or one ten miles square, containing sixty-four thousand acres. The warrant specified that it was to be at least nine miles long on one side. To make the equivalent content of the warrant the other sides would have to extend either slightly over eleven or full sixteen miles into the interior. Considering the fact that many thousands of acres of Chester County were already settled, the possibility of locating the required amount of land in one piece was remote. Moreover, Thomas Holme must have been skeptical about the size of the warrant. A twelve-mile square of land would be more than twice the size of that allotted to the Welsh Tract. Fretwell was not registering his demand for a company, but for a large development under his own name alone. The whole matter went against both Holme's inclinations and his judgment. Tracts of ten or twelve square miles containing 6,400 or 7,680 acres would have seemed more likely and would have been easier to locate.[11] This seems to have been the ultimate decision.

By 9 December Fretwell's business seemed at last to be getting under way. He had a warrant for six square miles in Chester County,[12] for which he gave bond to pay to Phillip Ford for the use of William Penn £300 in 1685, with an additional £300 to be paid in six months on demand to James Harrison, Samuel Carpenter, or any of the commissioners of the governor's revenue for an additional six square miles of land "above the above mentioned,"[13] and a warrant from William Penn for "the Long Island on the Skullkill called Barbadoes."[14] On 9 December Thomas Lloyd and James Claypoole gave Thomas Holme formal, if not totally intelligible, orders that the northerly line of Ralph Fretwell's tract of land above [New] Town should be "southerly bounds as far as it Reaches to Answer the Contents of the Warrant Granted by the Governor to the Friends of Wales, and so to Extend their Tract to make up the Complement."

Any hope generated by these developments was short-lived. Less than a week later, on 13 and 15 December, Fretwell was pouring out his grievances in letters to the Proprietor. He had written to Penn in October, he states, but "after Tinicum" he had acquired some new light on his position and, not having had an opportunity to send the earlier letter, had written again on 30 November. Philip [Theodore Lehnmann] was nought, he declared, and "Thomas Holmes thou

---

[11] This supposition is based upon the apparently free area on the 1687 map showing a section marked Eastland some distance west of New Town.
[12] Dept. Sur., Book D-65: 22, DAM, PHMC, Hbg.
[13] Copy, HSP (Micro. 5: 034).
[14] Dept. Sur., Book D-65: 203, DAM, PHMC.

Knowest: and Tho L:[loyd] is one wth him as to my Concerne." Lloyd, he continued, had declared on 5 November before John Gosling that he could have no land for his friends but that he could have a manor for himself, and so he was put off from thinking of land on the former spot. At the beginning of December Christopher Taylor, "thy true friend," came to town and "layd matters Close home to them" and some others who upheld his claims. At the meeting in the council room the next day he set forth all his rights and succeeded in having as much land run out as could be done in two days. Then John Simcock arrived with a letter from Thomas Holme stating that Lloyd had written "that itt must not be to answer and accommodate the same [until] Warrants for other purchasers had been satisfied." William Wood with a new warrant had run out two thousand acres and had a warrant for thirteen hundred more out of Fretwell's supposed tract. James Claypoole wrote to the Chester County surveyor (Ashcom); he could do that because the Barbados tract was not included in William Penn's grant. He did not reveal that he himself would require over a thousand acres a couple of weeks later.[15] Ashcom said that so many warrants had come in that all the townships were given out and none was now available for Fretwell.

Claypoole seems to have dealt directly with Ashcom, a breach of protocol agreeable to the deputy surveyor, though not designed to nourish the Holme-Claypoole friendship that had begun so cordially in the early days of the Free Society. The widening of the breach between Thomas Holme and his deputy was financially as well as professionally deleterious. The aggregate of some twenty-four thousand acres to be surveyed represented approximately £80 in fees, one-third of which was rightfully due to the surveyor general. At the time, it may be recalled, Claypoole's son John had been destined to be an assistant to Thomas Holme and had started out as an associate of Ashcom in Chester County. The ordering of surveys as much as the execution of them involved more than met the eye. The large tracts of Judge William Wood and William Shardlow (probably the "company" of the survey) and the smaller one of James Claypoole appear on the 1687 map adjacent to the tract of the Free Society of Traders, along with the lesser plots of a number of the other warrantees of the fall of 1684. It is not surprising that Fretwell felt that he had been cheated in the distribution of warranted land.

Despite all his difficulties, Fretwell persisted throughout the winter and spring of 1685. In a series of letters from 10 February 1684/85 to

---

[15] Deed Bk. E-1, DAM, PHMC, Hbg. (Micro. 5: 254).

23 May he documented his attempts to gain a foothold in the province. Samuel Carpenter in his letter to Penn on 25 December 1684 had given a progress report on Fretwell's affairs to that date:

> Ralph Fretwell is still here and I Suppose will Stay untill Spring. he went downe yesterday to See his land run out. which is 6 mile Square in Chester County. he looks upon himself unkindly dealth wth by Tho: L:, the Surveyor gen^{ll} and some others as haveing Endeavoured to keepe him out of the Province by not accommodating him wth Land according to thy Warr^t. There hath been a great deal of Time & words Spent about it . . . Ralph was preswaided to take 6 mile Square in Lieu of the 12 Mile Square. The paym^t of it the President (to remove Occasions) left to the commissioners of Thy Revenue and (wee) will doe as well wth him as wee can. Thou knowes he is a Tuff man to Deal withall, but I don't doubt his Punctuall Compliance.[16]

Not only was Thomas Holme accountable for having the land surveyed, but, as a commissioner of estate and revenues, he would share responsibility for seeing that it was paid for.

However irksome Fretwell's persistence was to commissioners, council, surveyors, and president *pro tem*—President Lloyd stayed in New York away from it all, so that Thomas Holme had to play a triple role—it must be admitted that Fretwell had cause for complaint. He continued to voice his grievances to Penn, writing on 10 February that Charles Ashcom had been a "naughty packe, especially where Thomas Holme was most down or inclinable." He was, moveover, a "sturur up of the people in manifest contempt to the commissoners." Penn's "men and mannors" have almost made ineffectual his long voyage. His characterizations of the concerned persons are apparently fairly accurate. Christopher Taylor is Penn's true friend; John Simcock not much an enemy to Fretwell's cause; "plain James Harrison has somewhat leaned and credited other more than expected of late plain and sensible . . . William Wood thy seeming friend unmannerly in seeking larger morsels for himself." He was thoroughly miserable. Even "The wethr is coald and many Journeys I have undergone of late in and to Chester County as if new Begon on the left Fott."[17]

On 9 March the commissioners gave to Thomas Holme another

---

[16] ALS, ACM, Box 2: no. 6, CCHS. Docketed: Sam. Carpenter 25 December 1684. ab^t. Fretwell. *PWP* 2: 611 (Micro. 5: 052).

[17] ALS. ACM, Box 2: no. 11, CCHS. HSP (Micro. 5: 089). This and the letters that follow are from this collection and are recorded in the ACM microfilm, Reel 57, at HSP. *Packe* is defined in the *OUD* as "a term aplied to a person of worthless character, almost always with naughty," and *naughty*, as of 1699, as "morally bad, wicked."

warrant to survey land for Fretwell in Chester County, with specific descriptions of the outline of the tract. The warrant calls for a tract six miles square. Whether the commissioners were not aware that they had authorized a survey of thirty-six square miles (23,040 acres), or had no intention of permitting a survey of any size being executed and so were not much concerned about the specifications, is hard to say.

The matter was still hanging fire when on 20 May Thomas Holme wrote, telling Fretwell that he had searched his office and had found a warrant from the commissioners "Posterior to the warrant which I this day recieved from ye." This was for a tract six miles square, which seemed to him too distant to execute. He should try to obtain further orders from the commissioners. Thomas Holme could not answer the first warrant from William Penn to Fretwell because the later warrant from the commissioners remained in force until otherwise altered and ordered by them, "Which is the rule by which I must walk."[18]

By mid-March Penn had received reports of the warrant for a six-mile square tract. On 16 March 1684/85 he voiced his disapproval in a letter to Lloyd: "I had rather give him five thousand acres than allow w^t is allowed of six miles square." The warranting of such a great quantity of land in one piece was to take the sale of so much land completely out of the Proprietor's hands, and he was in need of money.[19] He appears to have forgotten the literal terms of the warrant he himself issued before sailing for England.

On 23 May Fretwell commenced a final recapitulation of his troubles, most of which he had reported in earlier accounts. Thomas Holme, he averred, had been delaying and evasive and finally had gone out of town without warning and remained there. When Thomas Holme had sent for Charles Ashcom, Ashcom had not come, but had stated to others that Fretwell could not have the land. Afterwards he came to town, refused absolutely to survey the land, and then placed it with a friend. Fretwell issued a caveat to prevent any part of the land warranted to him from being surveyed to anyone else, but the caveat was disregarded. Lloyd had come down from New York in April, only to concur in the denials of the surveyors and commissioners.

Finally, frustrated and bitter, Fretwell gave up. He asked to have his warrant deposited conditionally, and absolved himself of any obligations toward the province. He hoped for some remuneration for his expenses and ill-fated venture. In a letter to Penn on 29 May, Philip

---

[18] Dept. Sur. Book D-66: 230, DAM, PHMC, Hbg.
[19] ACM, Box 27, no. 154: 9. Printed in part in Proud, *HP* 1: 290.

Theodore Lehnmann reported on the end of a year of expectations and strife:

> R Fretwell left yesterday [28 May] for Barbados. He left two caveats, one against the disposal of the overplus of Woolly Rawson's 200 acres he had . . . the other for land grant to him at Skuylkill which I suppose is most layd out (though the Indians say it is not bought of them) by reason that he firmly purposed to settle in the County of Chester, wch not by fault of Charles Askom, who hath placed others in the sic Miles Tract granted to Ralph Fretwell by the Councill is relinquisht.[20]

In a letter to James Harrison written before he received Fretwell's final communication, William Penn was kinder and perhaps more just in his estimate of Fretwell than others had been. He wrote, "R. Fretwell's business has been a great grief to me. I love the man, he has something lovely in him, & some uneasy, and some too reaching; use him well; but wrong not me nor the people."[21]

The trials of Fretwell reveal much of the temper, ambition, and *modus operandi* of the society he attempted to enter, which was the milieu of Thomas Holme. They also seemed to have caused some fissure in the political landscape.

Fretwell had by no means monopolized Thomas Holme's attention. His hands were full not only of the official duties of a surveyor general—the fall and winter had brought to his desk a total of more than a hundred and fifty warrants for survey—but of other official and *ad hoc* responsibilities. Penn had stipulated that at least three commissioners of proprietary estates and revenue, of which Thomas Holme was a member, should meet on 1 October and inspect the secretary's and surveyor's offices in order to make a true rent roll and call the receivers before them to audit their accounts. Since Thomas's office was to be examined, he was doubly concerned in this. In his letter quoted above, Samuel Carpenter reported that

> President Lloyd went to N Yorke the 11th Instant wth an intent to take his wife . . . I thinke this is the third Journey thither Since thy departure. Thomas Holme is President in his absence. I suppose he will Stay there untill the Frosty Season be over & I feare the Riches & Splendor of that place will Somewhat lessen his affections to this, but I hope better.

Actually, after the meetings of 24 and 25 October, when the council adjourned until the "30 of the 1st month [30 March 1684/85]," proba-

---

[20] ALS. PTL to WP, ACM, CCHS (Micro. 5: 175).
[21] ALS, 11 July 1685. ACM, Box 27. CCHS.

bly, as Carpenter suggested, to admit of the Lloyds' spending the winter in more comfortable quarters in New York, Thomas Holme was acting president of twenty-eight of the fifty-one meetings before his term as a "three-year man" expired in March, 1686/87, and was charged with all the interim duties of the president during Lloyd's absence when the council was not in session.

One of the happier events of the winter for Thomas Holme was the wedding of Samuel Carpenter and Hannah Hardimann on 12 December. Carpenter in his letter of 31 December tells William Penn of his marriage with carefully restrained satisfaction: "I have been getting a wife which was accomplished the 12th Instant to the General Satisfaction of Friends, & to my owne Satisfaction beyond Expression. and I must Say that I am much Engaged to thee on that acc^o For thy Encouragem^t & furtherance therin."

A particularly significant but less happy duty dealt immediately with the Proprietor's claim of the territories belonging to his province. In his efforts to nullify Baltimore's claim to the Lower Counties he had invoked the authority of the original Calvert grant "for a certain country . . . not then cultivated and planted though in some parts thereof inhabited by certain barbarous people, having not knowledge of Almighty God. . . ."[22]

In order to prove that the land had been occupied by Christians before Baltimore's grant was issued, Penn had had affidavits of descendants of the early Dutch and Swedish inhabitants collected to establish their previous settlement. When preparing to leave for England to present his claim at court, Penn entrusted the assembling and packing of these documents to Lehnmann, his private secretary. On reaching England he discovered that they had been left behind. On 7 October he wrote desperately to Lloyd to recover them or, if that was impossible, to secure others: "Wherefore instantly away to New York, & gett affidavits of the 3 that N Byars says can speak to that matter . . . all depends on this."[23] To his steward, James Harrison, he wrote on the same day in even stronger terms:

> Phil. Lemain has most carelessly left behind, the york papers that T. Lloyd brought & should have come as the ground and very strength of my coming, so that I am now here wth my finger in my mouth. he could not have done me a worse injury nor balt. a greater service.

---

[22] Hazard, *Annals*, 29; MdA, Calvert Papers, no. 80. *PWP* 2: 603.

[23] ALS. The Henry E. Huntington Library, San Marino, Ca. (Micro. 5: 0390). *PWP* 2: 603–604.

Lehnmann was to send the papers by the "first ship that comes out of Maryland or Virginia; . . . & endorse the letter to me, for his Royal highness service spead spead [*sic*] & care," and "Tho: Lloyd [was to] step to york and gett fresh affidavits of the 3 men that can swear the Dutch possession of River & bay before Baltimore's Patent, in the Govern^{rs} presence & under the seal of the Province."[24]

Penn's letters seem not to have reached Philadelphia when Nicholas More wrote to him on 1 December, expressing hope that he had had a safe voyage; and there is no record of a ship arriving from England before Lloyd and his family left for New York on 11 December. Harrison was at Pennsbury, and Thomas Holme in Philadelphia, functioning in Lloyd's place as far as possible. The first mention in Philadelphia of the missing documents is in his urgent letter to Harrison written on 5 February 1684/85. He echoes the concern of the governor:

> Loving Friend James Harrison: I have several letters from the Governor, and thy company is desired here with all speed. The Governor wants some materiall papers, and his affairs is like to suffer from want thereof. We have searched all the papers in the closet here and cannot find the papers that are wanting. I desire thee to look among the Governour's papers at your house for any papers that relate to the Dutch being possessed of this country. There came some writings from the records of New York under N. Bayard's cover and if no such papers can be found then we only have the Scriptorium to search, so bring the key with thee . . . I need not say more, but expect thee here tomorrow. . . . from thy friend, Tho: Holme.
> Addressed: for James Harrison at Pennsbury. These hast for the Governor's service. Per G. Emlin on purpose sent.[25]

It appears that Harrison did not so much as answer Thomas Holme's letter. Not succeeding in locating the missing papers, Thomas Holme sent Lehnmann to New Castle as a last resort, with orders that if he found the papers there he was to "go away with them to Mary Land." On 1 July Penn still had not received them. He wrote to Thomas Lloyd that "My affidavits are not come yet to my great trouble."

There was also other trouble for Thomas Holme to worry about. The Indians were growing restive, social problems were emerging, warrants for survey were accumulating, the Free Society of Traders was threatened by internal dissension and neglect, the rapid expansion

---

[24] ALS. HSP, Penn Papers, Domestic and Miscellaneous Letters (Micro. 5: 008).
[25] ALS. HSP, Etting Papers, Pemberton, 1: 8. Extract in *PMHB* 63 (1939), 255. Emlin was the head of the recently established postal system.

of the city was eroding the clean lines of the Platform, and Thomas Holme was unable to rouse other members of the government to share responsibility. Nicholas More, who as a provincial judge was officially concerned, at least notified the governor of one of the problems. In his letter of 1 December cited above he wrote:

> The Indians are Mutch displeased at our English settling upon Their Land, and seeme to Threaten us, saying that William Penn hath deceived them not payeing for what he bought of them. And Ninichican is Mutch out of patience, sayeing that William Penn shall be his brother no More, and that he shall pay him more then was agreed before because he has not paid him.

Ninichican had additional reason for hostility. His dignity had suffered a public blow when "one day being in Towne drunken a black of John Jones stole his Crowne and rune away with part of it, having sould some in Towne." Since the magistrates had done little about the insult, More ordered the purchasers, a Dutch baker and his wife, to be indicted at the provincial court on 17 December, hoping to pacify him.[26] Before closing, he returned to the Indian problem.

> I would desyre you to Consider some Expedient to satisfye the Indians speedily, the Sineker have rebucked them for what they have sold Cheape to you. I supose that the souner you Satisfy them the better it will be for you and the province in generall. and you may assur yourself that no purchase will be made untill you come yourself (if then.)

More was wrong on this point. It was Thomas Holme and Samuel Carpenter who would pay the Indians, and it was Thomas Holme who would mollify them and make a new and shrewd purchase the next summer. During the winter it was Tammany, "king" of the Bucks County area that included Pennsbury, who seemed most threatening. In a second letter on the subject addressed to James Harrison and two fellow magistrates, William Biles and Gilbert Wheeler, on 8 February, Thomas Holme details the situation and, in his capacity of president *pro tem* on the governor's behalf urges them to take action:

> Friends: I formerly writ to you about Tameney, who played the rogue in hindering our people to plant and seat upon their lands by war^t. He threatens to fire their houses. I have looked in the Governour's papers and do find that he had sold the Governour all his land between Pemapacca and

---

[26] The name of the king appears in records of land transactions as Nanacussey and Nannecheschan. Variations in spelling of this and other Indian proper names are due to the interpretation of sounds by the recorder of the purchase.

Neshenimeh Creek. I expected you would have sent for and spoke with him about his abuse which must not be longer borne. I once more on the Governour's behalf do desire you to speak to Tameny and to let me have his full answer, that I may know what to do in this matter. He hath so discouraged our people that we can not get them to go into Bucks County to settle. so by all means let me hear from you shortly . . . Your Friend, Thomas Holme. . . . The Governour desires to have his love remembered to the Magistrates and people, and in your public meetings and courts let it be mentioned.[27]

Ten days later Thomas Holme was again trying to get some action in the Tammany situation from the magistrates of Bucks County:

Friend J. H.: I formerly wrote to thee to communicate to the rest of the Magistrates about a child at one Robert Marsh's house in Southampton Township, which place you allege to be in your county, but have not heard from you about it. Also I wrote to William Biles and others there about that base villain Tamena, how he had abused our people who had warrants to take up lands in your county . . . which made them come away complaining and we can not persuade them to go again, and they said they were afraid, and some went over to Jersey.

Thomas Holme was frustrated almost beyond endurance. For the first time he launched into personal complaint:

I am sorry that public matters are so sleighted and neglected to the prejudice of the Governour and the Government. I am fain to lie here and spend my time and have not all this hard frosty time been so much as at my plantation, but engaged in public matters. I cannot bear it thus, and several accidental charges I am at. If all of you slip yourselves out of the trouble I may do so too, and then farewell Government. . . . Pray let me have answer speedily about Tamena and the child. Farewell. From your Friend, Thomas Holme. Philadelphia, 18-12-84 [18 February 1684/85].[28]

Thomas Holme did not go out at once to his Well Spring Plantation. For the most part he stayed on in his house at the northwest corner of Front and Arch Streets, trying to cope not only with Fretwell's importunities, but with the governor's interests, the emerging probability of needed changes in the original plan of the city, the sometimes arbitrary demands of purchasers. A letter somewhat doubtfully attributed to Fretwell but more in line with Thomas's responsibilities outlines a number of the problems that beset him as surveyor general,

---

[27] ALS. HSP, Etting Papers, Pemberton, 1: 7. TH to James Harrison, William Biles, Gilbert Wheeler, or any of them. These at the Falls of the Delaware.
[28] ALS. HSP. Etting Papers, Pemberton 1: 8.

active member of the Society of Friends, president *pro tem* of the provincial council, and member of the Committee of Twelve of the Free Society. It merits attention for both information and atmosphere:

As for the Town, he has tried to keep the meeting in the center wholly. He knows whenever the meeting is divided and the new Meeting House not built it will be hard to carry out religious and public interests of those of the First, High, and Second Streets. As a compromise, it is proposed that accommodation be provided near High Street about Third for convenience in inclement weather and for those who are not able to go to the center location. He wishes that Penn had taken his advice to encourage tradesmen in and around the center with larger portions and long-time loan of lands etc. For instance, William Wood would not build on his city lots until he had his country tract (two thousand acres out of that designated for Fretwell) free. He introduces a word of caution characteristic of Thomas Holme's occasional avuncular advice to the Governor: "Thou knowest not men soe well as thou may or how little credit thou wilt gain by the Society . . . those that pretended to have mended the matter are found otherwise let them write what they will. . . ." It would be better for Penn to withdraw from the Free Society and let the members go their own way, to re-form later if they see fit when they know the country better. It is now obvious that brick and stone buildings can be erected as easily and cheaply as wood. He has tried to keep the meeting at the Meeting House, but wishes it had been placed as printed. He has left a letter about that with John Goodson for William Penn.

It is true that some passages of the letter favor Fretwell's authorship, but if so he was attempting to dictate in matters in which his circumstances hardly entitled him to a decisive voice. The transcript of the docket shows doubts of attribution on the part of the unnamed archivist.[29] It reads:

	53. F.	
	R ffretwell	Robt Turner
[l. conc]erning][	[conc.] his	2T. Holmes
	Case	
[conc.]erning]]	of Land. & [conc.?]	
	surveying it by T.H.	
	10^m 1684	

---

[29] There is nothing except his solicitude for the province to link the letter particularly to Robert Turner. Since he had brought a brickmaker with him, he did not need to purchase bricks from the Society, although he may have considered the Society as a possible employer of his protégé.

Could this have been the long letter of April acknowledged by William Penn in his letter of August to Thomas Holme?

The Friends' Yearly Meeting held in the hastily constructed Center Square building in the autumn had been attended by a thousand members of the Society. The need of a larger, permanent edifice was obvious, as was the desirability of a more conveniently located Meeting House. The "boarded Meeting House" on Front Street near the present Sansom Street had never been regarded as more than a stopgap. Both a new Front Street building and the new Center Square Meeting House were to be begun during 1685. The provision of a suitable building had in part been one of Thomas Holme's responsibilities from the first.

Thomas Holme continued to share in the special assignments of the Society, including the ministry to the personal needs of the meeting. At the Quarterly Meeting of 6 January 1684/85 he was assigned with John Cook and William Austin to write to England for a certificate of clearance from the woman with whom John Austin had been involved in England and for the permission of his parents to marry Christian England. At the Monthly Meeting of 9 February he was appointed with John Moore and James Claypoole to take care of the business concerning the relief of the widow Warner, according to the advice of Thomas Lloyd and the women.[30]

Along with the nagging problem of surveys, including Fretwell's, lost documents, the threats of the Indians, and the indifference of men who should have shared responsibilities for the day-to-day conduct of the province, the winter was frustrating and unproductive. The mud of fall had become hard ruts, and streams were frozen. Most of the houses had only scanty provision for warmth, and diet lacked the variety afforded in clement weather by streams, woods, and fields. The ordinaries that had multiplied during the slightly more than two-year life of the town were all-too-convenient gathering places for lonely and frequently dissatisfied residents. Too many, Thomas Holme included, overindulged their thirst.

It must have been during January or February 1684/85 that Thomas Holme succumbed to the extent of giving scandal to some and opportunity for censure to others. On 19 May 1685 William Penn wrote to Thomas Lloyd, asking him to speak privately to Thomas Holme about his drinking. Zachary Whitpain had written to his father in England stating that Thomas had not acted promptly on warrants for surveys without first receiving the equivalent of £12 in gifts of wine and enter-

---

[30] *Abstracts of the Falls Meeting*, GSP, 308, vo. 1, 1682–1707: 26, 29.

tainment.³¹ On 5 July he wrote more fully regarding the same accusations, both originating with Zachary:

> Complaint is made agst T. Holms and P. Lemain, that they move slowly on their offices without bottles of wine & treats, especially Thomas; ten or twelve pounds at least, being given in account to R. Whitpain & company for entertainments to Thomas wch grieves me to hear, knowing his infirmity. And if true so hateful and abominable that I may on proof thereof dissolve his patent, wherefore in the fear of the Lord & in the gravity of truth, examine the matter, & call Zachary Whitpain about the business; for such things are to be punished in one of them.
>
> He is a man I love, & wish well & I believe loves me & my interest, but his infirmitys & follys have cost me dear, in trouble of Spirit, and my reputation. Tho as to this I judge not till all is heard.³²

Whether the fact that complaints had come also "Agst the Court of Philadelphia & perticularly agst John More and P. Robinson for Reviling R. Whitpain and Company," and that More and Robinson appeared on the same side as Thomas Holme in other disputes had anything to do with the reports is a matter of conjecture. Certainly there was a problem concerning Whitpain's property, and Penn was anxious about it. In the same letter the Proprietor had written, "Repair R. Whitpain and Company—it makes a fear full cry here," discouraging others from emigrating. "Also," he wrote, "I allow R. Whitpains 1500 Acres he bought, or R. Marshall for him and co., goe for part of his greater quantity." However this may be, obviously Thomas Holme was not without fault, and this was by no means a first offense.³³ Obviously, too, in spite of this very serious problem, he managed to accomplish more than would seem possible if he were an unregenerate alcoholic.

Hot-headed, schooled in his youth in the tough life of the Cromwellian army, a veteran of the Irish campaign and the struggle of the early Friends in the harsh environment of Ireland, sorely tried in the province to which he had come with great prestige and high hopes less than three years before, the oldest official in the province, already old by seventeenth-century standards, bereft of a son on whom he had relied for assistance and companionship, he needed the confidence and compassion of the governor. He was vindicated in his trust. On 8 August William Penn acknowledged Thomas's long letter of April,

---

[31] ALS. Dreer (Micro. 5: 158).
[32] ALS. HSP, Penn Papers, Dom., 79–81, HSP (Micro. 5: 219).
[33] ALS. WP to Thomas Rudyard, 26 June 1684. HSP (Micro. 4: 913).

expressing appreciation of "thy care and particularity in state of affairs," and giving directions for further undertakings.[34]

As the weather relaxed a little at the end of January and, by the latter part of February, started to bear a slight promise of spring, Thomas Holme grew more restive with the confinement of town and the lack of cooperation of his associates, and more eager to get out to his Well Spring Plantation, where his servants would soon be engaged in spring planting. Hester and Silas Crispin were doing well as an independent family. His daughter Elinor was a faithful housekeeper, but he would be pleased when she too had a home of her own. Meanwhile, there were the Indians and, at the end of March, the first month of the new year according to the calendar of the time, the convening of the provincial council. The council would meet, sometimes at irregular intervals, until the beginning of the next February, when it would adjourn until 30 March 1686.

Thomas Holme presided at the first six meetings of the new session. The business reflected the resurgence of activity with spring. The sheriffs were called upon to return the names of officials elected for their counties, and stiff fines were levied on those who defaulted. On Christopher Pennock's petition, Philip England was ordered to expedite the provision of a sufficient ferry to carry horses and cattle across the Schuylkill and to make both sides of the river clear and passable for horses and men.

A year and a half before, Thomas Holme had urged upon Penn the need for demarcating the bounds of counties.[35] Now settlement had progressed to the point that the need for explicit boundaries between Philadelphia and Bucks on the north and Chester on the south was imperative. On 1 April it was determined that

> It being moved in Council to have the Line of Separation known & distinguish[t] between the Countyes of Philadelphia and Bucks . . . the County of Bucks to begin at Poquesson Creek, and so to take in the Easterly side thereof, togather with the Town-ships of Southampton & Warminster, and thence backwards.
>
> And several Members of Councill acquainted this board that they heard the Gov[r] Positively grant & say, that the aforementioned Line should be the Devision between the two said Countyes, and being put to the Question, whether that should Stand as the division of the Countyes aforesaid, it was carried in the Affirmative, *Nemine Contradicente.*

---

[34] AL. Ford Coll., NYPL; photograph and transcription, ACM, 27 (Micro. of ACM, copy at HSP).
[35] See above [MS p. 210]. *MPC*, 1: 78.

Orders were then sent to the sheriffs of the two counties to define the limits of their jurisdiction.

Following a similar procedure the southern bound of Philadelphia County was delineated. The line was to commence at the mouth of Bough Creek,

> being the uper End of Tenecum Island, and soe up that Creek, deviding the said Island from the Land of Andros Boone & Comp^y; from thence along the Severall Courses of the said Creek to a W:S:W Line, which Line devided the Liberty Lands of Philadelphia from Several Tracts of Land belonging to the Welch & Other Inhabitance; and from thence E:N:E by the Land of John Ekley, 880 perches more or Less; from Thence Continuing the said Course to the Scoolkill River afterwards to be the Natural bounds.

John Simcock and William Wood were witnesses to the governor's statement that the bounds of Chester and Philadelphia Counties "should begin at the Mill Creek and Sloping too the Welch Township, and thence to Skoolkill &c." The boundaries were accepted without demur.

The remaining meetings of the week were devoted chiefly to the annual scrutiny of laws. An interesting amendment of Law 47 was that the word *person* should be substituted for *man*. On Monday, 6 April, a "foreamble" for the order of the council for the boundaries of the counties was adopted, stating the reasons for making the divisions and ordering commissions for justices of the peace for Bucks and Chester counties. On 7 April Thomas Lloyd reappeared in the chair, and on 8 April the need for establishing boundaries was again introduced and again established as had been specified the week before for the Bucks-Philadelphia line, with the insertion of the names of Joseph Growden and Company and Nicholas More and some further detail.[36] Lloyd made no acknowledgment of the previous action.

It was proposed that the laws and the prepared bills be in force as they were for the current year, but the proposal was defeated, and accordingly the annual scrutiny of bills got under way, with the addition of new bills, the need for which had become evident during the past year. Lloyd occupied the chair on 7, 8, and 9 April, but Thomas Holme was regularly in attendance. Bills potentially made official the apprehension of runaway servants, the collection of goods in kind as payment, the standard of quality of leather tanning, the inspection of

---

[36] *MPC* 1: 96–97.

fences. Thomas Holme again presided at the council meetings of 25 and 28 April. Maritime problems at both meetings evidenced the acceleration of ship arrivals now that winter was over. The first of these was the not uncommon suit of seamen for their wages. The second was modern in manner if not exactly in subject. The master of the *Wren*

> set forth that John Harrison, seamen, George Ambler, and Tho. Pringle, Servants belonging to the said Ship were at the Prov[ll] Court held at New Castle, Ordered and Sensured to pay ten pounds seaven Shillings for a hogg, Valued at One pounds three Shillings, besides two of them to be Whipt. . . .

Master Deering petitioned the board to have the sentence suspended. The board continued the case for further consideration. The case would go on for a long time, becoming more complicated with each hearing. Finally the council adjourned until 15 May.

Lloyd conducted the next two meetings of the council for the formal announcement of the death of King Charles II and the accession of his brother, the Duke of York, as King James II. The news of the accession of James was received with cautious expectations. He was a personal friend of William Penn, but he was a Catholic—anathema to the Quakers even more than were the Anglicans.

Meanwhile the business of the province must go on. Richard Inglo, clerk of the council, appointed Thomas Holme, John Simcock, William Wood, John Cann, Phineas Pemberton, and William Frampton to receive proposals from the assembly. The committee, with Thomas Holme as chairman, met on 13 and 14 May, delivering three bills on each day to messengers from the assembly. These were duly returned with some quibbling about style and proposed amendments. Further evidence concerning the overcharge for the hog was brought in and placed on file. Pemberton reported that the Indians were killing the settlers' hogs near the Falls. Obviously, something must be done about this. Letters from the lord mayor of London arrived, attesting to the widow Acrod's having been married to Benjamin Acrod, and appointing Nicholas More her attorney. He called upon Patrick Robinson for an account of the estate. There had been no break in activities for Thomas Holme, who was in attendance when the council reconvened on 15 May, with Lloyd again presiding.

Chapter 13

Politics

The assembly was embarking on a turbulent period. It had convened on 11 May and would remain in session for a brief but strenuous nine days. John White of New Castle was unanimously elected speaker, and John Southern of Philadelphia County, clerk. John Bridges of Kent County and Abraham Mann of New Castle were chosen to present the speaker to the council and president. Mann had achieved reinstatement after the invalidation of his election to the first assembly in December, 1682.[1]

From the beginning the 1685 assembly was fraught with difficulties. On 13 May the council called for a meeting of both houses that they might reach a better understanding of one another. The assembly sent the message that the attendance of the whole assembly was desired. The assembly felt that the council was overbearing in its handling of legislation, and the council were not backward in exercising their authority. John Bridges made uncomplimentary comments about the House, of which he was a member. When asked to recant he averred that he would rather die, whereupon he was expelled. Reconsidering, he was reinstated the next morning.

Nicholas More, who was the Speaker of the House during the previous session, and had been appointed a provincial judge by Penn on 16 August, took exception to the fines stipulated in the bill relating

---

[1] *PA*, 8, 1: 1. The official title of this series is *Votes and Proceedings of the House of Representatives of the Province of Pennsylvania*, but it is commonly referred to as *The Duke of York's Laws* or *Votes of the Assembly*. Hereinafter it will be cited as *Votes*.

to justices, the bill providing for payment in kind, and the bill permitting trial of cases before justices "without the charge of provincial judges." All of these bills held personal interest for More both as a judge and as a well-to-do landowner who was creditor for more debts than he cared to have paid in "fresh pork, Tobacco, or Corn, &c."

Exasperation at More's objections and remembrance of Mann's humiliation before the assembly two years before, when More was chairman of the Committee of Privileges and Elections, may have had something to do with what followed, but when at last on 15 May "the Council declared themselves well satisfied with the proceedings upon the proposed Bills; and that the said Bills should be returned and a fair copy made," the assembly turned its attention to a list of ten grievances asserted "by a member of the House" against More, chiefly in his conduct as judge.

What was perhaps the most damaging grievance against More was not enunciated: that he did not suffer fools gladly. This was not the first time that More's impetuous speech had got him into trouble, nor would it be the last. Later he would say of Thomas Fairman, "I esteem him to be an ignorant ffoole If not a Malicious knave"[2]—a comment that must have given some vicarious satisfaction to Thomas Holme. Now, it must be admitted, there were some serious charges against More, along with some that appear merely frivolous. After the compiled accusations had been read,

> it was voted by the House that the Speaker, Abraham Mann, John Blunston, Thomas Usher, William Barry and Samuel Gray, should prosecute the said Nicholas More, before the Council, in the Way of Impeachment; and that in order thereunto, the whole House should . . . request the President and Council, to remove the said Nicholas More out of his great Offices . . . which is thought fit by the House to be the first Thing to be insisted on in this proceeding.

Of the six elected to prosecute More, four were from the Lower Counties, two from the border county of Chester, and none from Philadelphia or Bucks. At the meeting of the council on 15 May two members of the House appeared, requesting a conference. They formally presented

> The Assembly's Declaration against Nic. Moore, . . . to the President and Prov[ll] Council . . . by the Speaker [Abraham Mann] & Members of the

---

[2] See above, p. [148].

Assembly: For the Speedy redress of divers Evils & Mischiefs wch this Province and Territories labour under, & for the preventing the farther growth and Increase of the same, & to the honour and Safety of the Governm^t of this Province & Territories, and by good & Welfare of the People thereof. . . .

Having heard the accusations, the council appointed Thomas Holme, John Simcock, William Darvall, and Phineas Pemberton to notify More and to request him to come to the council chamber at seven in the morning. It was not an easy assignment for Thomas Holme. He and More had been summoned by William Penn to confer with him on the eve of the first meetings of assembly and council, and had served the province in one or another capacity ever since.

On Saturday, 16 May, the assembly opened with another charge against More: Abraham Mann declared that More had broken the "Order and Privilege of the House" by calling him a "Person of seditious Spirit." The House voted to call More in to face this charge, and if he did not submit, to eject him "as an unprofitable Member of the House."

Next, the members unwittingly introduced a stirring diversion by summoning Patrick Robinson, clerk of the provincial circular courts, to bring into the assembly the records of the courts. Patrick declined to produce them. It was then unaminously voted to put Patrick into the sheriff's custody. The sheriff duly performed this duty, and More was summoned. More refused to come. Since he had been voted out of the assembly, he would not return without being voted back in. Patrick Robinson was voted "a public enemy to the Province of Pennsylvania, and Territories thereof, and a Violator of the Privileges of the Freemen in Assembly met." Patrick had compounded his offence by declaring that the assembly had drawn up the impeachment of More "Hob Nob at a Venture." Meeting some of the members in the street he threatened them with retribution.

On the afternoon of the sixteenth Mann complained that a prisoner (presumably Patrick) "was sheltered in the Gov^{rs} house." Upon questioning, Mann admitted that Patrick had been arrested only on the authority of the assembly—a step of questionable legality; nevertheless, the council unanimously declared Robinson's remarks concerning the impeachment of More "indecent, unalowable, & to be disowned," though they took no further action against him until they "weightily Considered and answered" the assembly's petition against him. It was not until 2 June that the council answered that

> The Petition of the Assembly against Patrick Robinson being debated of in Councill . . . Wee doe Conclude that he cannot be Regularly removed from his Clarke's places or Office till he is legally Convicted of ill fame, and those Crimes & Misdemean^{rs} alleged against him, which was presented to this board by John White, Speaker, in behalfe of the Assembly, and after such Conviction, it is resolved that he shall be readily Dismist from any Public Office of Trust in this Government.

Abraham Mann and the assembly then requested of the council another reading of the charges against More, "wch was accordingly done; wch Was without Direction to the Councill, nor Subscribed by the Speaker or any of the Assembly, nor noe place mentioned therein"—clearly a breach of the courtesy customarily observed in council. On 19 May the council considered the charges against More. Undeniably the House had grounds for complaint against his high-handed administration of his office. He had not given sufficient notice of the time of the court, he had reversed decisions of county courts and dismissed jury decisions that he thought were based on other than proper evaluation of evidence. He had advised three members of the House to protest the last three bills under consideration. A final damaging accusation was that of

> severall Contemptuous & Derogatory Expressions Spoken by Judg Moore of the Prov^{ll} Council and of the present State of Governm^t by Calling the Memb. thereof fooles and Loggerheads, and that it would never be good Times as Long as the Quakers had the Administration.

Despite the insult, the council deferred further action in the case and proceeded to the recording of the fifteen proposed laws, twelve of which were passed and three defeated. The assembly, satisfied with its accomplishments, resolved "That Abraham Mann, and John Blunston, shall be the Prosecutors of Nicholas More, upon his Impeachment," ordered the journal of the sessions to be deposited with Joseph Growden and a copy thereof given to Barnaby Wilcox, over the hand of Speaker John White wrote an account of their entire proceedings against More and Robinson to William Penn, and adjourned until 10 May 1686.

After a voyage of thirteen weeks William Markham and his bride arrived from England on 21 May.[3] At a council meeting a week later Lloyd read the Proprietor's letter appointing Markham secretary of

---

[3] ALS. Blathwayt Papers, Colonial Williamsburg, Inc. Precis in *CSPC*, 1666–1688, No. 69.

the province and the Proprietor, and ordering him with the officials of the county to proclaim at New Castle the succession to the throne of James II.

His two new commissions notwithstanding, Penn still had some misgivings about his cousin. In a private letter to James Harrison, after stating that Markham was to have the use of his house and a contribution to the larder of a barrel of meat and ten bushels of corn, he added, "He had promest a new conduct. Watch over him, & give him advice. I think he is in a good frame, & has since his marriage been more diligent to serve me."[4] He reiterated his concern two months later, again to Harrison. "I desire y^{ee} have an eye over W^m. Markham that [he] do not dishonour me nor himself by idleness and profligacy. He promest me very fair."[5]

Although nepotism undoubtedly accounted in large part for his commissions, Markham, whatever his weaknesses, was a loyal supporter of his distinguished cousin's interests and a promising intermediary between two increasingly conspicuous rival factions in government: the Protestant sects, including Anglicans (due to his own Protestant affiliation); and the Society of Friends, now generally called Quakers (because of his relationship to the revered Proprietor). His arrival was comforting to Thomas Holme. They had worked amicably together, and they shared genuine concern for the interests of William Penn.

Lloyd again presided at the meeting of 2 June, at which William Haige's petition for a special court at New Castle was granted. Notice was sent to More that he should desist from further acting in any of his judicial capacities until the articles of impeachment "Exhibited against him by the Assembly be Tryed, or Satisfaction be made to this board." As noted above, it was decided that Patrick Robinson could not be removed from office until he was legally convicted of the crimes alleged against him by the assembly.

With the exception of the meetings of 25 and 28 May, Lloyd had presided over the council since 7 May. Now he disappeared from the scene and Thomas Holme was acting president until Lloyd would reappear on 14 September. Lloyd appears to have presided over the most substantive considerations and relegated local concerns to Thomas Holme's jurisdiction. There were a dozen meetings during the summer: four in June, six in July, and two in August. They were sparsely attended, sometimes with only one member beside Markham present when the business at hand did not require the vote of a quorum.

---

[4] ALS. HSP, Penn Papers, Dom. and Misc. Letters (Micro. 5: 143).
[5] ALS, WP to JH 11, 30 July 1685. ACM 27, no. 283 HSP (Micro. 5: 210).

It had been a full spring. Thomas Holme had been present at every meeting of the council, and during the two-day interim of 13 and 14 May he had been chairman of a committee that attended to much business that ordinarily would have been the work of the council as a whole. From 21 to 27 July he transacted interim business at Well Spring, briefly escaping the stifling heat of the Philadelphia summer. Fretwell was gone, but there were still warrants to be filled, the Indians were still threatening, litigation was increasing, disaffection among some elements of the Lower Counties was increasing, and the Free Society of Traders was obviously in trouble. With other concerned citizens, Thomas Holme spent too much time in ordinaries, perhaps trying to bolster his spirits with alcohol, which seems to have compromised his reputation more than his activity.

A major disappointment to the Proprietor and to many of his Purchasers was the gradual breaking down of the Free Society of Traders. Claypoole, the treasurer, was the first to reassess his position and decide that he would profit more as an independent merchant than as a member of the Society. He had resigned the office of treasurer that he had campaigned for at the outset, and Penn in his letter of 7 October 1684 had directed James Harrison to "take and cancel the 1000 pounds I gave the Society for J. Claypoole when treasurer, etc. The old president [Nicholas More] delivered it up to him."[6] Nicholas More had completely dissociated himself from it, as John Goodson reported to Penn in his letter of 6 March 1684/85: "The Society has bought Dr. More's stock so that he is completely gone off."[7] In his letter of 25 December cited above, Samuel Carpenter had given Penn a depressing account of its condition:

> I desire thee to be cautious, for nothing but shame & Confusion will attend them, the way they Endv^r to uphold them selves pulls them downe as wth both hands and all things they undertake or doe goe as formerly their ship Lyes by and their glass-house comes to nothing, & their debts lyes out notwithstanding all their Counsells [Courts] & Comitties & grandure therin, & people unpaid to their Perpetual Shame & dishon^r of the Province. I am heartily Sorry thou and soe many good Friends should be concerned.[8]

Carpenter himself, sorely in need of money, had sued the Society for debts it owed him, the payment of which further embarrassed it.

---

[6] ACM, *Narratives*, 211, 229.
[7] ALS. ACM, CCHS. MSP (Micro. 5: 109).
[8] ALS. ACM, CCHS (Micro. 5: 052).

Shareholders in England were suspicious and angry when returns on their investments failed to appear, albeit some of them had failed to pay for the share for which they had contracted. On 15 June eighteen members of the Society in London petitioned William Penn for an accounting on their investment.[9] On 13 July Penn wrote to Thomas Lloyd, John Simcock, Christopher Taylor, James Harrison, and Robert Turner that the situation in England was serious because of the failure of the expected king's revenue.[10]

Carpenter's reflections on the original members of the Free Society were symptomatic of the drawing apart of two factions of Friends: the earliest purchasers and others who were intensely loyal to Penn not only as Proprietor but as a profoundly spiritual guide, and others who, faithful Friends though they were, nevertheless took a more material view of their worldly affairs; and, on the other side, the Anglicans and other non-Quakers, for whom purchasing shares in the Society and land in Pennsylvania was a more pragmatic venture.

Development of the embryonic commercial ventures of the Society was hampered not only by differences among personnel but also by lack of funds for initial installations, salaries for workers, and, perhaps, of knowledge and managerial competence. There was plenty of raw material and there would have been adequate demand for products of the tannery, glass factory, and whaling industry if the plants had been fully functional and costs could have been kept within the means of the purchasers. In the first little house Pastorius had built in 1683 he was forced to use oiled paper in lieu of glass in the windows.[11]

Demand for brick burgeoned as soon as settlers fixed upon their chosen sites for dwellings and places of business. Robert Turner erected what he alleged was the first brick house in Philadelphia. Although he was a member of the original Committee of Twelve, there is no indication that his brick came from the yard presumably in operation by the Society. It may have been entirely the product of the labor of the brickmaker he had brought with him from England, and his assistants. Various entrepreneurs unhampered by the red tape of a not very homogeneous organization were quick to establish enterprises

---

[9] *Friends Address to Governor Penn* . . . 15 June 1685. HSP, Penn Papers, Petitions, 1681–1764 (Micro. 5: 183). *PWP* 3: 58–59.

[10] ALS. HSP. Penn Papers, Domestic and Miscellaneous Letters (Micro. 5: 219). *PWP* 3: 58–59. The entire entry comprises letters of WP to TL and others, dated May-15 August 1685. For a comprehensive treatment of the economic, religious, and political ramifications of the Society's problems, see Gary Nash, "The Free Society of Traders and the Early Politics of Pennsylvania," *PMHB* 89: 2, 147–173.

[11] Pastorius, *Circumstantial Geographical Description of Pennsylvania*, in ACM, *Narratives*, printed in part in Soderland, 353–360.

with which they already had some experience. Writing to William Penn on 3 August 1685, Turner declared,

> Brick building is said to be as cheap [as wood]: Bricks are exceeding good, and better than when I built [he had laid the foundation of his own brick house before Penn left for England]: More Makers fallen in, and Bricks cheaper, they were before at 16s. English per 1000, and now many brave brick houses are going up.

Turner's brick house was at the southwest corner of Front and Mulberry, across the street from the house of Thomas Holme.[12] He lists a large number of brick houses in progress with a variety of architecture, some of it apparently very comfortable and attractive. Among those preparing to commence brick making in the near future was Pastorius. Two additional pieces of information in Turner's strongly upbeat description of the growing town were particularly significant for Thomas Holme:

> Lots are much desir'd in the Town, great buying of one another. We are now laying the foundation of a large plain Brick house, for a Meeting House, in the Center, (sixty foot long, and about forty foot broad) and hope to have it soon up, many hearts and hands at Work that will do it. A large Meeting House, 50 foot long, and 38 foot broad, is also going up, on the front of the River, for an evening Meeting, the work going on apace.

He adds that many "Towns People [are] setling their Liberty Lands." He is optimistic about the future of the Society, which he hopes will "rub off the Reproaches some have cast upon them." He makes no mention of the intended whaling activities of the Society, although he understands that "Three Companies for Whale Catching are designed to fish in the River's Mouth, this season."[13]

The defection of More and Claypoole from the Committee of Twelve and the failure of two members to come in the first place reduced the number of guardians of the Society to eight: Turner, William Haige, Ralph Withers (deputy treasurer), Griffith Jones, William Shardlow, William Wood, John Simcock (deputy president) and Thomas Holme. As Nash points out, most of these were concerned chiefly in their personal fortunes. Of how the various enterprises fared there is no coherent record.

---

[12] *Planting, PMHB,* 39.
[13] ACM, *Narratives,* 268–272. Penn included this letter in his *Further Account of the Province of Pennsylvania.*

In April Thomas Holme wrote a long letter to the Proprietor. This missive has not been found, but from Penn's reply we can gather something of its contents.[14] Thomas Holme, it must be remembered, could not receive Penn's answer until, at the earliest, late September, and more probably the end of October if the vessel in which it was dispatched came by way of Barbados. In the meantime Thomas Holme could only continue to do the best he could, making necessary decisions according to his own best judgments, with small support and sometimes opposition or what looks like careful counter-maneuvering on the part of wealthier or more politically influential purchasers. Relations with Thomas Lloyd, who enjoyed the complete and affectionate confidence of the governor, were not altogether affable. Despite his frequent long visits to New York, Lloyd was watchful for his authority and prestige. It was to be expected that he should preside to present communications from William Penn to the province, such as the announcement of the death of King Charles II and the succession of James II, with the order for proclamation of the succession. Lesser affairs, sometimes troublesome, were left to the president *pro tem*. From the end of May until the end of the year—February 1685/86—except for the month of September, Thomas Holme occupied this post. Perhaps it was to affirm the legality of his position that at the meeting of the council on 11 July "The Gov^{rs} Commission to Impower the Councill to Chuse President out of themselves, in the absence of Thom. Lloyd was Read: Ordered to be recorded." The choice fell upon Thomas Holme. Much had already transpired during the council of 1685, and he had a full summer's work to do outside the governmental responsibilites the choice put upon him, but the document carried with it the security of having been the choice, and perhaps some small remuneration came with the position.

Along with his governmental responsibilities, Holme had two perennial concerns: land matters and Indian affairs. Within these bounds were three major areas of activity. The first was the assessment of land available for warrants to new purchasers and for surveys to early purchasers who, already settled on their original property, now applied for warrants for land remaining in their purchases. No one was to have more than a thousand acres in one piece unless he was prepared to seat a household thereon within three years. Penn himself had already reserved for himself and his family large estates of the best land in various areas of the three upper counties. In August he directed, "Let

---

[14] ALS. Penn to TH. Ford MSS, NYPL. Copy in ACM, CCHS, vol. 28 (Micro. 5: 254–256).

care be ta[ken] that all vacant land be survey'd as deep into the Country as can be, in 1000 acr. tracts in the three lower countys, that I may have bounds by survey to claim by, though it be done in a privater manner than ordinary."[15] He ordered another large reservation along the Schuylkill.

Thomas Holme as far as possible presurveyed or at least laid out on his working map tracts in sizes not frequently in demand by settlers, usually in two-hundred-acre lots that could readily be expanded by fifty or a hundred acres or more. Neat columns of such tracts, by 1686 filled with the names of settlers, are conspicuous on the map of *The Improved Part of the Province of Pennsylvania* published in 1687. A further problem lay in following the governor's direction to exercise special care to give an exacting or especially important newcomer just what he wanted, insofar as it was available from land not already taken up. Attempts to carry out his order ruffled the feathers of already settled or settling purchasers, who resented what they considered favoritism on the part of the Proprietor or, more conveniently and prudently, the surveyor general. One such directive came from Penn, probably on the ship on which Markham arrived, just as Fretwell was preparing to depart:

> Pray be carefull of thy carriage to one Gray a Rom. Cath. Gent. that comes over now [Penn wrote to Thomas Lloyd]. He is subtile & prying & touchy, a temper not unlike somebody there, but not such [deletion] a bottom in other things. he is a Scholler & avers [averse] to the Calvinists, lett Dr. More be cautioned of him. he comes in a port. Be sure to please him in his land & for distance he must take where it is clear of others pretentions.[16]

If anything was required to increase Thomas Holme's weakness, the settling of Gray would be adequate to the occasion.

Fortunately, Gray did not arrive until June. Having acquired proprietorship in West New Jersey in addition to his purchase of five thousand acres of Pennsylvania land before leaving England, he went first to New Jersey. By June he had examined the possibilities of Pennsylvania and had chosen the site of his first establishment in the province.[17] This he proceeded to commence on a thousand acres he purchased from Joseph Growden, who had a large tract in his own right

---

[15] See above, n. 10; *PWP* 3: 47.

[16] ALS. Penn Mutual Life Insurance Company, Philadelphia (Micro. 5: 120). *PWP* 3: 31.

[17] See account of later litigation based on transactions with Joseph Growden in 1685, related by Henry H. Bisbee in "John Tatham, Alias Gray," *PMHB* 83 (1959): 153–264. Unless otherwise stated this meticulously researched and documented article is the source of information concerning Gray cited herein.

augmented by an equally large tract in partnership with his father, Lawrence, as Joseph Growden and Company, extending form Neshaminy to Poquessing Creek, with a fine frontage on the Delaware. It was here that Gray set up his first Pennsylvania dwelling, Tatem House. He made the deal for a thousand acres directly with Growden and enlisted Thomas Fairman to make the survey. Although his procedure was not in accordance with custom nor, for that matter, with William Penn's expectation, he seems to have enjoyed his property in peace until some months later, when Growden discovered how the lines had been run. Thomas Holme had had no part in the transaction, though eventually it was to become one more complication in his mapping of the province.

Also recommended to the special solicitude of officialdom were Major Jasper Farmer and his family. At the end of his letter of 6 August to "My excellent Frds. Tho Lloyd, James Claypoole, Robt. Turner, Wm. Frampton, Thos Holmes & Sam. Carpenter" William Penn requests,

> With the salutation of my kind love, these are to desire you, to show and express the utmost friendship and courtesy of a wilderness to Major farmer, Jasper (whom you know) and their co. . . . If any houses or accommodations I have can convenience them, let them have it, and if it will not do, I know you will not let them want, til they are in . . . condition in Farmerstown.[18]

The Farmers were a generally respected family. Thomas received at least one more letter on their behalf from a mutual friend. Writing from Limerick to "Dear Brother Penock," on 2 September, Richard Pearce notes that Thomas Webb has married Jasper Farmer's daughter and that the couple and the family are going over. Webb, his "intimate acquaintance," thinks he has more than enough servants to help set up his establishment in America. Major Farmer has offered to service the lots of Pearce and his associates and put families on them if they will allow him a thousand acres. Pearce is writing to Thomas Holme to welcome him, giving this and other letters to Farmer to deliver.[19] In a letter to William Frampton, Charles Jones, Jr., writes from Bristol on 25 September to enlist Farmer's aid in his own land problem. He asks Frampton to call on Philip Lehnmann for an account of a servant he has sent over "and dispose him for my best advantage . . . Jasper Farmer to whom I write will give him assistance and soe will my Friend

---

[18] ALS. HSP, Dreer, fol. 12 (Micro. 5: 249).
[19] ALS. HSP, Am 2532.

Thomas Holmes, to whom pray remember me."[20] Major Farmer and his son Jasper died on shipboard, but their families were well provided for. Two years before embarking for Pennsylvania Major Farmer and company had purchased five thousand acres, which on the 1687 map appears laid out intact, adjoining on the east Gulielma Penn's Manor of Springfield.[21] It was under the stewardship of John Scull, probably a brother-in-law of Mrs. Farmer.[22] Thomas Holme and Robert Turner were overseers of the major's will.[23] The warrant for the Schuylkill tract indicates that it was for Jasper, Jr., and was laid out in January of 1683/84. Considering the desirability of the company's property, with its fine frontage on the Schuylkill, it seems likely that it was laid out well before the family arrived.

The governor also asked that special care be taken of the interests of Joshua Cart, to whom he was indebted, and his wife. He directed that Thomas Holme look at once to the building of the house—presumably for the Carts—for which he had been given money, and that if the sum was not enough it should be augmented from the public fund, which, it may be recalled, was the tax on ordinaries that had been designated for the support of the government. Cart seems to have expressed immediate interest in outlying territory, but Thomas Holme seized the opportunity to sell him eighty acres of liberty land and two city lots which he had purchased from Nicholas Walne in February 1682/83.[24]

There was at the same time a ferment of sales among those already settled, bartering for more desirable or convenient locations, or seeking additional conveniently located acres for business purposes. Robert Turner reported one such program in his letter to Penn on 31 October, in which he states that Thomas Lloyd has bought five hundred acres of Christopher Taylor, has the offer of Francis Richardson's land adjoining Taylor's, and has bought Griffith Jones's next to that.[25] The three tracts were bounded on the east by the Delaware and on the west by land belonging to Thomas Holme. Since the names of Taylor, Richardson, and Jones appear on adjoining tracts on the 1687 map and on the version tentatively dated 1690, it appears that the deal did not go through.

---

[20] ALS, Charles Jones to William Frampton, 25 September 1685, HSP, Am 2532.

[21] *PA*, 3, 2: 2 records warrants for two five-thousand-acre tracts, one for Jasper Farmer and Company, 31 January 1683, and a second on 12 September 1689 for, obviously, a younger member of the same family.

[22] ALS. HSP, Penn Papers, Dom. and Misc. Letters (Micro. 5: 219).

[23] *PGSP*, 1: 54 (25 September 1851).

[24] PhA, *Index of Deeds, Grantors Books*, 1683–1751, Book E-1, vol. 5: 467, and *Grantees Books*, Book E-1, vol. 5: 469.

[25] ACM, Box 2: 161. CCHS (Micro. 5: 321–324).

In the same letter Turner thanks Penn for permission to take up some land for meadow and for the opportunity to buy off the quitrent of the land bought of the Fullers. This latter boon was also a source of income for Penn in a time of serious shortage. By 1684 the Fullers had, among them, amassed over two thousand acres of land, on which the purchase price of the annual quitrent at the rate at which Thomas had purchased his would amount to a little over £7 (approximately the equivalent of $700 today), and would slightly increase Turner's income. Robert planned to use his new land to support "a horse or two, a few sheep, and some cowes" for his servants to take care of during lulls in his business in Philadelphia.

If there had been no special recommendations, the volume of new but routine regular warrants would have been enough to keep the surveyors busy. A total of over 160 had come in over the year, for an aggregate of more than 240,000 acres, exclusive of liberty land and city lots. By far the greatest number of warrants was for land in Chester County, where over forty warrants of from fifty-acre to four-hundred-acre tracts required twenty-five thousand of the 142,000 acres warranted for the county. Philadelphia County was second in demand, with warrants for nearly seventy-seven thousand acres, some in small tracts. Finally, 22,500 acres were to be surveyed in Bucks County for thirty-eight warrantees.[26]

A number of factors accounted for the increased number of warrants during the year following Penn's departure. Ships arrived in the fall, having taken advantage of the favorable summer weather, bringing weary but eager new settlers. Some of the small tracts may have been headrights. Others may have been for indentured servants whose time of service had expired. A final group was that of First Purchasers of thousands of acres confronted with the fact that if they wanted the land they had purchased, they had best claim it now and manage to settle a household on each thousand acres or have it repossessed, now that the three-year limit specified by the Proprietor in the *Concessions and Agreements made in England* had elapsed. Thus we find James Claypoole securing warrants for a thousand acres each in Bucks, Philadelphia, and Chester Counties. And Thomas Holme could not forget that he was among these purchasers. Moreover, he appears to have needed money.

The past two years should have been lucrative for him, but Charles Ashcom, deputy in the most rapidly developing county, refused out-

---

[26] These numbers are only approximate, having been taken from the list of "Selections from the list in *Pa. Ar.*" in the printed *PA*, ser. 3, 2: 662–670.

right to surrender Thomas Holme's third of the survey fees, and some of the other deputies were equally uncooperative. Fairman, it seems, at least on choice occasions, as in the case of Gray/Tatham, had taken warrants direct from purchasers, thus bypassing the surveyor general's office altogether. The ploy was illegal, but it succeeded. A further offence, not monetary but even more serious, was their failure to turn in their field maps. These were needed for the surveyor general's guidance in locating property, and for the master map he was preparing for the Proprietor. Penn fumed and blamed Thomas for negligence, and Thomas pleaded in vain for the maps.

In the spring of 1685, with Fretwell about to give up his struggle for a settlement in the province, Thomas Holme reviewed his own situation as landholder. He was possessed of some four thousand acres of surveyed land: Well Spring and Shaftesberry Plantations, five hundred of the thousand acres obtained by his son Tryall in right of his father, a tract on Dublin Creek adjoining Well Spring, the irregular tract above the row of Delaware tracts ordered surveyed when he arrived in the province, two tracts of liberty land, and four city lots. He had done some buying and selling during these early years. Now he was considering some further changes in his situation. He had surveys recorded—a procedure frequently neglected in order to avoid payment of the required fee, but necessary when property changed hands. Thus, the six-hundred-acre survey of Shaftesberry was recorded on 8 July; on the next day Thomas sold it to Nicholas Rideout for £60—the customary rate of £10 a hundred acres. This was an irregular but valuable property, a triangle with an enviable frontage on Poquessing Creek. On 28 August he recorded the survey of Well Spring done the previous year, and on 2 September mortgaged it and the lands contiguous to it to Andrew Robinson for £270. On 4 November he recorded the survey of eighty acres of liberty land on Cohocksinc Creek, and two days later sold it to Nicholas More for £40.[27]

There is one curious feature of these real estate dealings. Even allowing for the failure to collect his fees, why was Thomas so in need of money that he would risk losing his Well Spring Plantation? And how could he be certain of paying off the mortgage in a year if he had not saved that much money in three years? Could he have fallen into the temptation to use the money given him to build a house that was not immediately needed for purposes of his own, and did he now face the fact that he must build the house without delay? This had been

---

[27] PhA. *Philadelphia Deed Book, Grantors*, E-1, 70, 102, and 134.

the case with at least one other man in a like situation. John Songhurst had diverted money sent him to build a house for Charles Hartford, along with the labor of two carpenters, to his own use.[28]

Meanwhile there were the Indians. The euphoric mutual admiration that had appeared to exist between them and the founders of the province had somewhat eroded. They still lived at the western edges of the inhabited territory, trading with the white interlopers while eyeing them with too-often justified suspicion and hostility. Moreover, they had discovered that these English enjoyed among themselves a wonderful mind-altering potion called rum, which they refused to share with their erstwhile native friends.

Rumors of their dissatisfaction reached William Penn, and he tried to mollify them with gifts. On 16 March in a letter to Thomas Lloyd he states that he has sent them some caps "as per letter to T. Holmes, J. Claypoole, . . . R. Turner & Sam. Carpenter," and hopes that "care is taken to buy of the Indians, a days journy above Consciahockin. I have given earnest for to Sickotickon, as my store book shoes [shows]."[29] In his letter of 18 May to the Commissioners he lists these gifts:

> I have sent eleven caps. one with my Arms, for sicotickan, Another that has a tossel, for Messepenaick. three other shag ones without tossels for Neshecasho, westicke & -T-a-m & shikane. the other six, to Tamene, Jonotta, sacoquean, kalup, seccetareus & christian, or sombody below. . . . pray Remember that there are goods at new york, w^t cost me dear, of all sorts, fitt for Indians. pray pay the Indians out of them.[30]

At the end of July Thomas Holme succeeded in concluding the urgently needed purchase of the very large tract that extended from Upland (Chester) Creek fifteen miles or so south of Philadelphia to Pemapacke (Dublin, now Pennypack) Creek eight or ten miles north of the town, and as far back into the interior as a man could go in two days. His letter to his "very loving ffriends Shakhoppa, Secamiang, Malebore, Tangoras—Indian Kings; and to Maskecasho, Wawarrin, Tenoughan, Tarrecka, Nesonhaikin—Indian sakamackers, and the rest concerned" shows his careful attention to protocol and at the same time demonstrates his ability to drive a hard bargain:

---

[28] ALS. WP to TL *et al.*, 18 May 1685. HSP, Penn Papers, Dom. and Misc. Letters (Micro. 5: 219).
[29] ALS. Penn Mutual Life Insurance Company, Philadelphia (Micro. 5: 120). *PWP* 3: 33.
[30] ALS. HSP, Dreer Coll. (Micro. 5: 155). Evidently Penn demoted Tammany after first including him on the third level of recipients of gifts.

> Whereas I have purchased and bought of you, the Indian Kings and sakamackers, for the use of Governor William Penn, all your land from Pemapecka creek to Upland creek, and so backward to Chesapeake bay and Susquehanna, two days' journey; that is to say, as far as a man can go in two days, as under the hands and seals of you the said kings may appear.

He tells them that he hereby appoints his friend, Benjamin Chambers, with a convenient number of men to assist him, to mark out a westerly line from Philadelphia to Susquehanna in preparation for the two days' journey. He continues:

> and I do hereby desire and require, in the name of our said Governor Penn, that none of you the said kings, sakamackers, or any other Indians whatsoever, that have formerly been concerned in the said tracts of land, do presume to offer any interruption or hindrance in the making out the said line, but rather I expect your furtherance and assistance, if occasion be herein; and that you will be kind and loving to my said friend, Benjamin Chambers, and his company for which I shall, on the governor's behalf, be kind and loving to you hereafter, as occasion may require. Witness my hand and a seal, this 7th day of the 5th mo., called July, being the fourth year of the reign of our great king of England, and eighth of our proprietary, William Penn's Government.
>
> Tho. Holme

The deed to this territory is rich in detail not only of the extent of the land, but in the extent and kind of goods which the Indians considered adequate compensation for it and which according to his own estimate had cost William Penn dearly:

> We, Shakhoppah, Secane, Malebore, Tangoras, Indian sakamackers, and right owners of ye lands lying between Macopanackean, alias Upland, now called Chester river or creek, and the river or creek of Pemapecka, now called Dublin creek, beginning at a hill called Conshonhockin, on the river Manaiunck, or Schoolkill, from thence extending a parallel line to the said Macopanackan, (alias Chester creek,) by a south-westernly course, and from the said Conshohockin hill to the aforesaid Pemapecka, (alias Dublin creek,) by the said parallel line north-westernly, and so up along the said Pemapecka as far as the creek extends, and so from thence north-westernly back unto the woods, to make up two full days' journey, as far as a man can go in two days from the said station of the said parallel line at the said Macopanackan, alias Chester creek—*For and in consideration* of 200 fathoms of wampum, 30 fathoms of duffels, 30 guns, 60 fathoms of strawd waters, 30 kettles, 30 shirts, 20 gun belts, 12 pairs shoes, 30 pairs stockings, 30 pairs scissors, 30 combs, 30 axes, 30 knives, 21 tobacco tongs, 30 bars

of lead, 20 lbs. powder, 30 awls, 30 glasses, 30 tobacco boxes, 30 papers of beads, 44 lbs. red lead, 30 pairs of hawks' bells, 6 drawing knives, 6 caps, 12 hoes,—To us in hand well and truly paid by William Penn, proprietary and governor of Pennsylvania and territories—Do by these presents *grant, bargain, sell, &c.*, all right, title and interest *that we or any others shall or may claim* in the same—hereby renouncing and disclaiming forever any claim or pretence to the premises, *for us, our heirs and successors, and all other Indians whatsoever*—In witness whereof we set our hands and seals, &c., this 30th day of the 5th mo., called July, and in the year 1685. (Signed)
Shakahappoh.   Secane.
   Malebore.   Tangoras

Sealed and delivered to Thomas Holme, president of the provincial council, in the presence of us—

Great men of the Indians.

Tareckhoua	Lasse Cock
Penoughant	Mouns Cock
Wesakant	Swan Swanson
Kacocahahous	Ism. Frampton
Nehallas	Saml. Carpenter
Toutamen	Will Asley
Tepasekenin	Arthur Cook
	Tryall Holme[31]

While the purchase was in the making, Thomas Holme was also presiding at meetings of the council, where cases belonging as much to the provincial court as to the council consumed time and patience, notably that of the captain of the ship *Wren* of London introduced two years before, and the suit of Samuel Carpenter against the Free Society of Traders and James Claypoole, former treasurer. The heat of July in Philadelphia did nothing to mitigate the heat of the arguments. It was with relief that he was able to adjourn the meeting of the eleventh until the twenty-eighth, and go out to the peace of Well Spring.

His seclusion was short lived. On 21 July a party of Indians complained to the secretary William Markham against the servants of the Jasper Farmer family "making the Indians drunk, then lying with their Wives, and of their beating both men and their wives." The secretary told them to come to the next meeting of the council, when the servants would be summoned, and the matter would be taken up. The Indians, unwilling to neglect hunting for so long a time, insisted

---

[31] "A true copy of the original by Jacob Taylor," Watson, *Annals* 2-X, 175–176. The copy of the deed which follows is from the same source, 176–177, quoted by Watson from the book of *Charters and Indian Deeds* in the secretary of state's office, p. 62. The accompanying draft shows the extent of the purchase—a large territory for a man to cover in two days!

that the hearing be on the twenty-fourth. Markham accordingly directed the sheriff to summon the servants for that day and sent a letter to Thomas Holme at Well Spring. The Indians confused the days and did not appear until the twenty-fifth—it has been suggested that they had again been seduced and addled by rum—and the sheriff's deputy sent to summon the accused lost his way in the wood. The Indians then consented to come on the twenty-eighth.

John Scull appeared with the miscreants at the appointed time, but the Indians "being drunk in the woods, & the servants declaring they were affraid to goe home before the Business was Ended, the Council ordered they should Stay in Towne till the next day, when the Indians were to be in Towne to Receive pay for the Land bought of them." As the date of the deed above quoted indicates, the kings and sachems at least were present on the thirtieth. There is no record of the outcome of the grievance.

The council met in long and contentious sessions on 28 and 29 July and in a brief morning session on 6 August, then adjourned until future notice. Old cases had been continued and new problems had arisen that would demand Thomas Holme's attention. A brief session was called for 19 August to hear the petition of Richard Blakleach of New England regarding a debt of £41 owed him by Benjamin Chambers. Thomas Holme again presided, this time with only three other members present: Christopher Taylor, William Frampton, and William Markham. They directed the justices of the county to make a commission for a hearing of the case on 24 August and again adjourned until further notice. The further notice called the council for the nomination of judges on 14 September, with Thomas Lloyd presiding. James Harrison, James Claypoole, and Arthur Cook were appointed. All declined to accept the office.

Lloyd returned to conduct the series of strenuous meetings of the council during September. A wide variety of cases was presented: settlement of estates, an accusation of adultery, debts. Thomas Holme would be concerned in two areas. Irritation with Ashcom mounted. The complaint of James Sanderlin and Neals Lawson regarding his refusal to resurvey their land, introduced on 29 July, was read again on 16 September, and judgment was against Ashcom. The Welsh complained that Ashcom had disregarded their rights by "his undue Execution, of several Later Warrants," which "prevented [them] from the quiet Enjoyment of the tract that was legally laid out for them." Furthermore, in two instances he had surveyed land for Charles Pickering outside the specifications of warrants. The surveys were therefore declared invalid. As a result of these irregularities, Ashcom was ordered to

> prepare and bring in to the Council a Draught by a scale of a 160 perches in an Inch, for all the Lands Surveyed and laid out by him Westwardly of the N.N.W. line, runn by Ralph ffretwell and himselfe, and to attend the Councill & Comm^{rs} with it the next Third day by 9th hour in the forenoone, for the Speedy Composing the Chester Friends and others, and the Welch friends, & in the meantime to Survey no more Land until further Ord^r.

Ashcom did appear at the next meeting with the required draft, which was then compared to the draft of the original survey made by David Powell. It was ordered that the differences be adjusted by the next meeting. The map of 1687 shows the same irregular surveys into the tract: "Captain Thomas Holme, Surveyor General, gave the Commissioners a statement under his hand that he gave no order for the laying out of any land within the Welsh tract."[32] He voiced his exasperation by presenting to the council a catalogue of his deputy's wrong doings:

> acquainting the Councill that notwithstanding the Gov^{rs} Express Orders to Charles Ashcome upon his going for England, under his hand, and by his Letter since, of his Complying with the Gov^{rs} Determination of the Differences between them, & that Charles Ashcome was to Continue in his place, under Tho. Holmes, for so he was and so he must be, (were the Gov^{rs} words), in Case he will behave himselfe, and did make Exact Returns [records of surveys], & pay to the Survey^r Genall [his] share of ffees.

The council put the terms to Ashcom, but he refused to comply with them, whereupon "they have agreed to Continue their Order to forbid Charles Ashcome to Survey any more land in the County of Chester, till he submitt to the Gov^{rs} Instructions, or be Impowered by the Councill and Comiss^{rs} to proceed further." Their decision left loopholes for questionable handling of both warrants and surveys in the future.

Other business had been dealt with in the course of the summer—the appropriation and slaughter of a hog by the servants of the captain of the *Wrenn*, first introduced the previous year, in which the captain considered the charge to be excessive; a couple of murders of women, numerous neighborly altercations, the unlawful marriage of Richard Noble in June.[33]

---

[32] *Old Surveys and Registers of Land Warrants*, Book no. 14, DAM, PHMC. *Memoirs of the HSP*, vol. 3, part 2.
[33] W. W. Thompson, *Chester County and Its History* (Union History Co., 1898).

On 22 September Captain Cock (Lasse Cock, the interpreter) notified the council that the Indians were now ready to sell the large tract of land from Upland to Duck Creek, a stream in Maryland well below the extent of the 1687 map. It was probably about this time that Thomas Holme received Penn's April letter, in which he states that at a conference in the council room he has received permission from the Sacotikan to plant on the east side of Schuylkill to Pehkama, and has given them many matchcoats, stockings, and some guns in earnest. He goes on to advise Thomas Holme on how to treat the Indians:

> if therefore they are rude and unruly you must make them Keep their word by Just courses. If they see you use them Severely when Rogueish, & Kindly when just, they will demean themselves accordingly; the vast number of Matchcoats & other things, as Shirts Stockings &c: that I have given Sicotickan & his famely over & above; shd compell them to a better & easier compliance. for Tamine, he sould all, & if the Indians will not punish him, we will & must for they must never see you afraid of executing the Justice they ought to do.[34]

Although it was true that Thomas Holme should never show fear in executing justice, it was easier to aspire to such courage at a distance of more than three thousand miles than on the margins of a territory still claimed by its original owners, especially when they were given to occasional bouts of exuberant intoxication and threatening demands for what appeared in their eyes to be justice. Nevertheless, the suggestion that they now sell all the land to which they had laid claim between Duck and Perkiomen Creeks was an opportunity to be seized with alacrity.

Thomas Holme was absent from the council meetings of 25 September and the forenoon of the twenty-sixth, presumably to make preparations for the impending purchase, but he reappeared on the afternoon of the twenty-sixth and was present on the twenty-eighth, when the session was adjourned until further order, and Lloyd went back to New York. The next day met with the Indians to commence negotiations for the last great transaction of his career. He, John Simcock, and William Markham, or any two of them, had been delegated to meet at the place designated, the widow Scalcop's, "with full power to treat and Compleat the purchase wth them, and to Call to their assistance what members of the Council can Conveniently be there." The purchase proceeded as had the previous one, opening with a

---

[34] AL, incomplete. ACM, CCHS, 27: 346–350; photograph and transcription of the original in the Ford Coll., NYPL; Micro. of ACM Coll. in HSP.

statement of procedures and conditions of sale and a promise that the measurement of the territory backward from the Delaware as far as a man could go on a horse in two days, would proceed without harassment, then giving the measurement of the land, and, finally, the deed itself. A retrospective record of it in the State Library reads:

> New Castle. Marepacmeh, Parckhan, Sickaim. Pettquessip-Powis, Essepenaick, Pepkhoy, Keklapan, Cecomus, Machaloha, Methoncka, Wissa Powey, owners of lands from Inintuf or Duck Creek up to Upland/Chester Creek & backwards as far as a man can ride in two days with a horse to William Penn. Signed, sealed, and delivered to Captain Thomas Holme, Surveyor General, for William Penn, in the presence of Pieter Almeck, Lasse Cock, Philip Theodore Lehnmann, Jame Atkinson, Christopher Grae, mark of John Walker, Edward Feras, John Mantye, marks of Pammasquaran, Owekham, Oweg[her], Sikphunun, Pataska, Mackhfnipe.[35]

In a letter dated 12 November 1685 Thomas Holme reported the transaction to the Proprietor: "Enclosed is the Copy of the Indian Purchase from Upland to Duck Creek & so backward, & hope 'twill be to thy Contnt; the former Purchase was also sent thee." He had been disappointed in his attempt to acquire for Penn the land above Pennsbury Manor, but was optimistic about the results of the completed transactions:

> . . . betwixt Neshamineh & Delaware backward of the Purchase made per C[aptain] Markham, is not done, some of the chief Kings refuseth, to sell, so that lyes not done. These two purchases of New Castle County, Chester County, and most of this County is done, for 2 Days Journey which hath quieted both Indians & our own People.[36]

It is to be hoped that Penn was pleased, although assuredly he must have been disappointed at the failure to acquire the upper Neshaminy land.

In Philadelphia matters continued as they had before the purchase. The council resumed meetings on 5 November, with Thomas Holme presiding. A new case involved that of a ship's master who had brought servants from England. They were expected to serve in Pennsylvania, but he was determined to bring them to Virginia. It was discovered that their indentures were "to serve James Skinner from the Day of the Date untill their first arrival in Virginia, or any other part of Amer-

---

[35] Penn Papers, Indian Affairs, 4: 21, 26, HSP.
[36] Fragment, apparently of a retained copy, TH to WP, Peters MSS, vol. 5 (Micro. 5: 334). See also Thompson, above cited.

ica, and after, for and during the Terme of four years." The interruption of their voyage highlighted the shortage of labor in the province, particularly the shortage of workers who could be installed on large tracts. Lloyd reappeared for three meetings, then again left for New York, with Thomas Holme again acting president, this time until the expiration of his term as charter three-year-man on the council.

Complaints came from Chester County that the Indians were stealing and killing hogs in New Town and in the Welsh Tract. The Indian kings were summoned to answer the complaint, but apparently did not come. Charles Ashcom was likewise summoned to answer the complaint of Joshua Hastings, but "it was Concluded no proper place to End their Differences it being a matter of Law." The commission of Penn's cousin, James Bradshaw, as chief surveyor and register of New Castle County, which was ordered during Lloyd's visit in September, "was signed by the Presid^t. Capt. Tho. Holmes, with the consent of the Councill."

There had been attempts by proclamations and orders to clear the caves along the bank of the Delaware of squatters and stored material. Now William Frampton petitioned for the removal of the caves before his door, since he was going to build a wharf.

The absence of the president did not prevent the multiplication of problems belonging to his office. Thomas Holme again officiated. On 9 January 1685/86 all those who had been selling hard liquor by retail were ordered to bring in their licenses to be either withdrawn or renewed. Thomas Holme was among the number. Finally, after sessions occupied for the most part with public concerns such as the appointment of various officers, on 3 February 1685/86, Thomas Holme as president met with three members of the council, William Frampton, William Southersby, and William Markham, adjourned the council until further order, and for the last time stepped down from the chair. The council would not meet again until 30 March 1686.

Chapter 14

Serendipity

When Thomas Holme laid down the gavel on that first Wednesday morning in February of 1685/86, he may have felt somehow demoted. Actually he would be working as hard as ever. The chief difference in his life would be that he would not attend council meetings, and he would never again have a vote in council, or stand before his peers as president. His professional duties as surveyor general with the inevitable role of buffer between William Penn and the people and among the settlers themselves would go on. He would continue as justice of the peace and from time to time he would be called upon with others to judge in local disputes. And the Indians. There were always the Indians to be placated, cajoled, bargained with. Since his profession was the laying out of land, he was naturally the obvious choice for all of these marginal affairs. When any untoward experiences involving them occurred it was Thomas Holme and Secretary Markham who would be sent for.

A personal on-going real estate concern was his sale of the portion of his Front Street lot on which the Meeting House stood to the Society of Friends. John Goodson and others were appointed to secure title to the land, to find a means of paying for it, and, finally, to make a house-to-house collection. Thomas Holme, in need of money and not disposed to donate a valuable piece of property for the use of a not impecunious society, would not relinquish the title until he received cash in hand. Finally, on 25 January 1686/87 the committee would report that they had almost finished their commission. At the next monthly meeting "Friends desired [them] to go to Thomas Holme to get title to the meeting house ground and have the ground fenced in."[1] At the outset the transaction may have suffered from a recurrence of Thomas's old failing,

> Evan Prothero saying in the open Court that Peter Dalbo did report that some of our ministers were at his father in law Peter Rambo's drunk, and particularly named C[hristopher] T[aylor] and T[homas] H[olme]. The meeting desired for the clearing of the truth the said C. T. and T. H. with Henry Lewis, John Songhurst and John Goodson to enquire into the said Scandal.[2]

Songhurst and Goodson had had a somewhat adversarial attitude toward Thomas Holme in the Fretwell matter and were not likely to be benevolently inclined toward him in this.

Judging from the selective list in the *Pennsylvania Archives*, relatively few warrants for surveys were issued during 1686. Some who had acquired land in the country now claimed or purchased city lots and liberty land; others, already situated in town, sought tracts for investments or personal estates. One such transaction, almost atypical in its regularity, was the warrant issued to Thomas Holme by James Claypoole and Robert Turner, commissioners of property, for rent of five hundred acres of land in Philadelphia County, "and being recommended by Captain Thomas Holme, and likewise assured us that he expects three family's out of Ireland to seat the same." On 12 April Thomas Holme ordered M. B. to lay it out.[3]

By far the largest undertaking was that of the grandiose scheme under the patronage of Sir Mathias Vincent, Dr. Daniel Coxe, Major Robert Thompson, and others, who proposed to establish a colony on Lake Erie, which they conceived to be within the northern limits of Pennsylvania. On 21 April William Penn wrote to Thomas Lloyd that they "have engaged for 18000 Acres, and are sending 60 families.[4] On 17 June Penn granted to the group as "The New Mediterranean Sea Company" in addition to large individual grants, ninety-five thousand

---

[1] *Records of the Philadelphia Monthly Meeting, 1686-1687*, 5 April, 3 May, 2 and 27 August 1686; 25 January, 25 February 1686/87. HSP, Rachel Buck Coll., GSP, vol. no. 308, 2: 53.

[2] *RPMM*, 4 May 1686 (above collection).

[3] *Index of Deeds and Surveys*, PA, 1682-1759. Philadelphia City Hall Annex, Exemplification Records, LS 841.

[4] ALS. Penn Papers, Dom. and Misc. Letters, HSP (Micro. 5: 416). See also Albright G. Zimmerman, "Daniel Coxe and the New Mediterranean Sea Company," *PMHB* 76: 86-96; 7: 317-318; 34: 75; 53: 330-331; 75: 141-144; 80-158, cited in *PWP*, 3: 86, n. 5. It must be remembered that a communication from WP dated 21 April could not at best reach Philadelphia until about the end of May.

acres bordering on or near the Great Lakes.[5] The tract appears on the 1687 map on the south side of the Schuylkill above the Welsh Tract, with the names of Vincent, Coxe, Adrian Vrouzen, and Benjamin Furley. Naturally Penn was solicitous for the satisfaction of prospective settlers of such great substance. Unfortunately the promise was not fulfilled.

Another less pretentious company for which the Proprietor was particularly concerned was that of Katherine Mildmay, daughter of Colonel Henry Mildmay, and eight associates. Penn's warrant to Thomas Holme in her behalf is dated 15 April 1686, and is specific in its requirements. The land is to be "as near as may[be]" to the lands of Thomas Hudson, in Bucks County, one end on the Delaware River, and so that a quarter of the [Savanna] that Penn had ordered to be reserved would be included in the township. The warrant for Thomas Hudson's thousand-acre tract on the Delaware was issued on 12 October 1683, with an additional five thousand acres warranted on 6 February 1684/1685.[6] On the 1687 map Col. Mildmay's (presumably Katherine's) land adjoins a large tract of Society land on the northeast, and Thomas Hudson's five-thousand-acre tract on the SE/SW. It is bisected by Neshaminy Creek and watered with many tributaries, though it is far from the Delaware. Since all of the land near Hudson's thousand acres on the Delaware had been taken up well before the warrant was issued to Katherine Mildmay, the best that Thomas Holme could do was to place her company on an excellent tract on the Neshaminy that at least satisfied the requirement of being near Hudson's property.

An unwelcome intrusion into Thomas Holme's routine activities at this time was a lawsuit by Joshua Cart. What charges Cart brought against Thomas does not appear in Secretary Patrick Robinson's *Records of the Philadelphia Court*. They may have had something to do with the house that Thomas had been ordered to build or with Penn's debt, which he may have directed Thomas to pay out of revenues collected in Pennsylvania, which, of course, were not forthcoming. Possibly Robinson, who seems to have been on the same side as Thomas Holme in local difficulties, was protecting the reputation of the surveyor general when he recorded only that the suit of Jos. Cart against Thomas Holme was continued. No continuation appears in the fragment of the records that remains.[7]

---

[5] DS. Bedfordshire Record Office, Bedford, Wynne Papers (Micro. 5: 460).

[6] DS. Bureau of Land Records, Department of Community Affairs, Book D-69: 108, DAM, PHMC. Copy, ACM, vol. 24, CCHS; ACM Micro., HSP.

[7] AD. Fragment, *Records of the Earliest Court of Philadelphia*, 4, 5, 6 August 1686. After he returned to England Cart sued WP for the sum owed him: *PWP* 3: 54, n. 65.

John Gray, the Roman Catholic gentleman for whom Penn had requested special courtesy a year before, was having increasing problems with his purchase from Joseph Growden. William Markham wrote a detailed account of the proceedings to William Penn.

Gray maintained that the overplus of Dunk William's land included the site of a barn he was building. He therefore asked the commissioners to grant it to him. Accepting his explanation, the commissioners acceded to his request, and he presented his warrant for resurvey and land to Thomas Fairman. Growden contested the deal, and Fairman returned the warrant to Gray, "advising him what to do with it."

Gray, who, William Penn had discovered, was a renegade Benedictine monk from St. James Priory in London, had married an unidentified woman and set out for a new life in the still new world of Penn's province. He was not about to be deterred by ethical considerations. Markham's narrative continues:

> So Gray got [Israel] Taylor to Execute it tho not Directed to him and found 500 acres overpluss and all without the thousand acres he had bought of Joseph Growden. This occasioned the first letter to James Claypoole and soon followed by an other directed to the Commissioners R[obert] T[urner] and J[ames] C[laypoole]. The first I was desired to answer, but Joseph Growden haveing it to send I understand he never sent it.

Markham, bent on giving a full, objective, and restrained account of the business, gives all necessary details. Phineas Pemberton, in his letter to Penn on 27 January 1686/1687, gives a pungent account of the encounter of Gray and Growden before the council. After stating that Wright is considered "a cheat and a runagade" and has not been here in several years, he reveals Wright was chosen with others to arbitrate the differences between John Gray and Joseph Growden,

> but it was the most railing revileing business that ever I saw. I never since I came into the province Saw such unmanliness & unmannerliness betwixt the worst in the province as that day past between them. We only Sat to see them befoole them selves and returned home.[8]

Israel Taylor, obviously, and perhaps Fairman, were out of order in accepting a survey not authorized by the surveyor general. Their collusion with Gray in his irregular procedure was reprehensible on several counts. It appropriated to the perpetrators the authority of a government official and defrauded Thomas Holme of his rightful fees,

---

[8] ALS. Phineas Pemberton to WP, 27 January 1686–87. HSP (Micro. 5: 648).

it gave them the opportunity to prosecute boundary irregularities for which he would be blamed, and it enabled them to ignore the requirement of turning in field maps. This last occasioned such inconvenience to both Thomas Holme and William Penn that it caused misunderstanding on Penn's part and frustration to the point of fury on Holme's.

Suddenly a new opportunity for riches entered Gray's field of vision. Again it is Markham who, in the letter cited above, reports the complications that followed. In his commentary on a letter of Gray to Thomas Holme, a copy of which he is enclosing with his own letter to William Penn, Markham writes that when Charles Pickering found a mine and brought some of the mineral to town for evaluation, excitement ensued. Robert Hall of Bucks County came to Markham for a warrant to take up tracts of various purchasers. Turned down by Markham, he went to Gray, who had warrants for execution, which he agreed to exchange for knowledge of the land. Markham seems to relish his task of reporting:

> First haveing by some means wheedled the Indians to Discover the place to him Gray takes Thomas Fairman with him who Lays this Land out for him tho it was Twenty miles from any inhabitants and many miles from any land that was laid out and not near the County he used to Survey for. Capt. Holme would not admitt of this irregular survey, first because it was on that side of the Scoolkill he was not to Survey on and Secondly it was not contiguous to Land Laid out.

Thomas Holme had his own solution to the problem. Having a backlog of surveys to lay out he

> takes his Deputy and Laies out Land Contiguous one to the other untill he Comes to this tract of Land, and then Lays out 4000 acres for Charles Pickering (takeing in the 1000 acres Fairman had Surveyed for Gray) by vertue of four warrants, one was for 1000 an other for 500 . . . an other for a thousand . . . all granted before my time was in right of Bowman who had sold his whole purchase to one Samuel Richardson a Bricklayer of Jamaica of whom Pickerin had bought 1500 acres. This 4000 acres are Laid out in one tract and a Returne made of it to my office and a Pattent Drawn.

Markham was "at a non plus what to doe with it." He would not validate the warrants until he heard from Penn. Both Thomas Holme and Pickering said they had written an account of the affair to the Proprietor. Pickering was already building a very good house on the property and Gray a little one, the two the length of Penn's garden apart. Pickering evidently implied in his letter to Penn that Markham had consented to the surveys, which Markham denies. As for what Captain Holme has done in Penn's interest, Markham knows not. According to the *Concessions or Conditions*, the mines would be the property of the landowner:

> William Penn, does accord and declare, all Rivers, Rivulets, Woods, and Underwoods, Waters, Watercourses, Quarries, Mines and Minerals (except mines Royal [i.e., gold and silver],) shall be freely and fully enjoyed and wholly by the purchasers into whose lot they fall.[9]

It is quite possible that Thomas Holme did have great quantities of land to lay out. Enclosing copies of warrants he had issued, Markham said that he thought it would be better that Thomas himself send copies of those that had been laid out. He estimated that perhaps only half had been surveyed. As for the survey to Pickering, Thomas Holme states in his letter to Penn that the survey is regular, but the patent will not be given without Penn's approval. This was not forthcoming. The survey appears on the British Library map, allegedly the original sent to William Penn. It appears as Markham describes it, but it was expunged by the time the approved copies were printed.

In the same much-quoted letter Markham gives us a gently humorous account of Thomas Holme's encounter with Gray, and the only glimpse we have of his personal appearance. He writes,

> When I had Read the Letter and Capt. Holme was come to me for it againe told me Gray was in towne. Then said I pray lett us go speake with him. I Could by no means perswade him to goe with me but as wee were taulking together, Gray looks out of the window at an ordinary in the towne (which is Arthur Cooks brick house Kept by Thomas Hollyman), and beckoned us to come up.

Thomas Holme, who had fought in two wars and faced probably all of the tribes of Indians in the Delaware Valley, reneged at the prospect of encountering Gray; so Markham went by himself. Gray "civilly saluted" him. The narrative continues:

> There was with him his Inseperable Compannion John Songhurst and Benjamin Whitehead. I Replyed Mr Gray I am Sorry I had not met you before I had Read the Letter you sent Capt. Holme wherein you abused

---

[9] *MPC* 1, 300: ix.

me that instead of greeting you with friendshipp, I must Demand Satisfaction of you. He was exceedingly Dash'd. Much more passed which to Repeat would seem ostentatious but were Reconsiled before wee parted. Capt. Holme was then in the House [and] sent for me from Grays Company. . . .

Markham urged Thomas to make peace with Gray, who interrupted the conference. Markham continued in his role of would-be peacemaker:

Now said I Capt. Holme you have as faire and oppertunity as I had. If you have wronged Mr. Gray make him satisfaction. If he has you, make him make it. Mr. Gray began with him pretty sharply. I have seen Capt. Holme shake his Cane and stroak his beard sometimes in anger but now he was soe sheepish that for shame I left them.[10]

Unfortunately no letters of Thomas Holme concerning this encounter have been found. Fortunately Markham was faithful in reporting all that came within his observation. There would be repercussions with regard to both Pickering and Gray, but for the time being Thomas Holme felt that he had at least solved the Pickering side of it.

Now the Indians again required attention. Markham, with a combination of sensitivity and humor, recounts an adventure shared by him and Thomas Holme, "Least by any Mistake or Disaffected people a Rumer Should Come to England of a family in Pennsylvania Destroyed by the Indians." Early in the morning of 31 July 1686, "Zachariah Whitpaine came to Towne and gave out that Nicholas Skull with all his family was kil'd that night by the Indians." Markham continues,

I went to Zachariah to know the Certainty of it, who Related to me thus that there was a Cantico nere his house, that he himselfe had been among the Indians the Day before at their Cantico, that after he had been in Bed which he guest might be about Eleven in the night, Nicholas Sculls boy Came Running to his house Crying his master and mistress and all the rest of the House were Kill[ed], and swoare many oaths that he saw his master Killed . . . and that the Indians were Coming with firebrands to sett Zachariahs House on fyre . . . Zachariah looked out and as he said saw them Coming with fyre-brands (I believe they were fire flys).

---

[10] In a volume of the ACM papers, CCHS, which unfortunately disappeared before a copy was made, there is a letter of Gray containing what may presumably be taken as a description of Holme, though Gray denies knowing his identity. As far as memory over many years can be trusted, Gray describes a "tall, bearded, swarthy man entering the room," perhaps on the occasion here related by Markham.

Zachariah "left his house Immediately" and brought the news to Philadelphia. Lloyd was there and lent Zachariah his horse and sent him back to get the whole story. Meanwhile one of Thomas's surveyors, who had lodged at Zachariah's, arrived with his story. The wild-eyed boy from Scull's had come with his warning, and Whitpain had got up and called his servants. The surveyor heard the Indians making a noise, but he did not get up until daybreak. Not finding anyone in the house, he went outside and called, "and then out of the Bushes about the Runn near the house the overseer and his wife came." The surveyor then went to Scull's house, where everything appeared as usual. They had had some disturbance. Scull had refused to sell the Indians any more rum,

> so that in the night they broak into his house through the Windoor and he opposeing them they had a Cuff or two and pulled one the other by the hair. But the Indians overCuming [him] gott from him by force some Rum.

Scull had been warned by some Indians the day before that there was a plot to break in and take away his rum, so he had expected the raid. The surveyor then returned to reassure the Whitpaine household.

Learning that there was to be another cantico at the same place in a few days, the council ordered Thomas Holme to take Lasse Cock, Zachariah, and anyone else he chose to inquire into the affair. This experience, too, is included in Markham's letter—as one would expect, Thomas Holme had chosen Markham as one of the group—but a more interesting account is that in the fragment that has been called "Markham's Diary":

> in the morn[ing we came] fro[m Z]ach. Whitpaines towards the Indians Cantico, the C[ompany] was. [Captn (?)], Tho [Ho]lme, myself, Patrick Robinson, [Z]ach. Whitpaine, a Car[illegible] Zachs, Swan Swanson, Mons Cock, Capt. Holme's Man, and [we visited] many Indian Plantations, about 3 or 4, in the afternoon, we c[ame to Swam]peses Plantation, where the Cantico was [it had been relocated to this location, about thirty-five miles from Philadelphia]; we said little to them that night, expecting in the morning the Indians, concerned in the breaking into Nich° Scull's House. This n[ight] we laye in the Swanpese's W[igwa]m. but the young Indians, could no[t] for bear drinking.

Thomas Holme and his associates waited until morning, expecting the responsible members of the tribe to remain sober for the discussion of the raid, but by morning most of the Indians were incapacitated. Under the circumstances it was impossible to settle the question of guilt and punishment in the Scull affair; so the project was abandoned. In spite of the disappointment the journey proved not to be fruitless:

> Finding Swampese, and the Indian Kings, sober, that were the Proprietors of the Land, that was to be bought, in Bucks County, Capt. Holme desired to treat with them, about it, which was done: Pat. Robinson took it, in writing; as soon as we had done treating with the Kings, they fell to drinking with the rest.

These had threatened to kill Israel Taylor if he surveyed any more land before it had been bought. On the way home Thomas Holme and his party met the Indian that had broken into Scull's house, with his suekema, at a wigwam and made an appointment with him to be in Philadelphia the next Second Day. They reached Whitpain's house about noon, and Thomas Holme sent a warrant to Scull to appear for the hearing. Markham concludes, "About 7 in the evening, we got Home." Home looked very good to them after a round trip of seventy miles on horseback by unimproved trails, a night at the limited facilities of a remote farmhouse, and another in Chief Swampese's windowless wigwam with drunken young Indians carousing around it.

Among these local distractions letters from the governor laid a strictly confidential charge in the hands of James Harrison, Robert Turner, and Thomas Holme. In early 1686 he wrote to the three, sending the letter and £40 for a lady in England, purchaser of 5,300 acres. They were to see to the building of a small, rather elegant house in a relatively secluded situation on a three-hundred-acre tract near Arthur Cook's house, and to have it ready by 10 October. He gave full particulars as to location and structure, which were repeated and somewhat elaborated in a letter of 24 April to James Harrison.[11]

On the 1687 map a vacant tract slightly less than a mile square (640 acres) joins Arthur Cook's land on the south west. Half this tract would be the equivalent of the three hundred acres of the projected domestic estate of the lady from England. The *Records of Quarter Sessions and Common Pleas of Bucks County, Pennsylvania*, contain the record of a transaction that may be related to Penn's request. If it is, Thomas Holme must have known of the projected coming of the lady before the letters now extant. On 9 December, the record shows, a "bill of sale of 100 Ackers of Land lying near the lands of Arthur Cook of this County [Bucks] by David Powell Constitute Attorney by grifith Jones unto Thomas Holme for the use of Thomas Lloyd." This could have

---

[11] ALS. Penn Papers, Dom., Misc. Letters, HSP (Micro. 5: 430). *PWP* 3: 89.

been an inconspicuous way of reserving the correct location for the residence.[12]

The plans of the lady fluctuated. On 8 October Penn wrote to Harrison, "you may continue with that house by Arthur Cookes."[13] On 22 March Thomas Holme wrote to James Harrison, "I understand thou art about building for the Lady, I recommend the bearer,"[14] but on 21 January William Penn had written to James in a letter that had not yet arrived in March, "for that house for the Lady & her children, lett it alone until further order."[15]

Penn had issued another confidential mission to the president. Since the scrutiny of the laws of the province by the Lords of Trade and Plantations was approaching and he had misgivings about their acceptance in their present form, he directed Lloyd that

> at the very next session after the receipt of this [evidently, judging by replies, in November] a Bill be prepared to vacate all the Laws as they now stand, & prepare another with such abrogations, alterations & additions of laws as shall palliate the thing, that shall be read next to the other, so that the distance will be but probationary, & [will] take a new alteration, from experience, & thus have a speedy resurrection, a thing we have already done in the Province. . . .

After a long rationalization of such a procedure, the Proprietor added,

> I desire thee, on receipt hereof, to summon a few of the most discreet & reputable together, & impart so farr of thes things as may be convenient, especially to R. Turner, Cosen Markham, T. Holmes, J. Sim J. Blunston, [J. Clayp. J.eccle Tho ellis] especially as to my not coming . . . for that of the laws, to as few as thou wilt at first.[16]

Evidently Thomas Holme was still considered one of "the most discreet & reputable" officials. To what extent he participated in this project we have no way of knowing. He had been one of the committee who produced the Second Frame of Government in 1683. In a letter to James Harrison on 8 October, Penn reveals both his concern for justice and his unflattering view of surveying. Learning that a former servant of his had been elected sheriff, he directed the govern-

---

[12] *Records of the Quarter Sessions and Common Pleas of Bucks County, Pennsylvania, 1684-1700* (The Colonial Society of Pennsylvania, 1943): 33.
[13] ALS. HSP (Micro. 5: 595).
[14] ACM 63, A: Parke-Smith MSS.
[15] ALS. Penn Papers, Dom. and Misc. Letters, HSP (Micro. 5: 655). *PWP* 3: 137.
[16] ALS. *Penn Papers*, HSP. Printed and edited by Frederick Tolles. "William Penn on Public and Private Affairs, 1686," *PMHB* 80: 236-247. *PWP* 3: 118.

ment to find some other job for him. "He is said to pack the jury, Lett him learn survey or do anything else."[17] The perpetual trouble with dishonest surveyors evidently had little impact on him.

The estate of Benjamin Acrod was still not settled, and Penn responded to his widow's request for his intercession. Thomas Holme was one of those originally appointed to look after her welfare, and was included in Penn's appeal of 22 April 1686, addressed to Thomas Lloyd, Thomas Holme, and Robert Turner:

> This letter, solicited by the widow of Benjamin Acrod to recommend her case to you in reference to her claim & right in what he left. I do not know how it stands, but I desire you to do the just thing on all hands, his friends are displeased in what he did in marrying her, but that will not dissolve the obligation nor turn the law aside from giving her that which is due in that relation.[18]

Despite his usual Spartan refusal to let personal matters interfere with public concerns (recall his letter to the Proprietor on the day of his son's funeral), Thomas Holme must have been happily distracted by the birth of his third American grandchild, Mary Crispin, in October. There were three Crispin granddaughters now: Sarah, two and a half; Rebecca, not quite a year and a half, and now Mary. Working in his house on Mulberry Street where he had constant access to his records, he was near enough to the house on Front Street south of Walnut to see them often, but far enough not to be unduly disturbed.

---

[17] ALS. WP to JH, 8 October 1686. HSP (Micro. 5: 595).
[18] ALS. WP to TL, TH, RT. HSP, Gratz Coll., Governors of Pennsylvania.

Chapter 15

The Cartographer

Beleaguered by a multitude of concerns, William Penn was becoming desperate for a map. Buyers wanted to have some say in the location of their lands, and the Proprietor wanted to be able to adjust their choices to his own preferences. At best this was a difficult arrangement. Thomas Holme was constantly being criticized in laying out land. When a warrant was presented he or one of his deputies showed the available land, keeping in mind William Penn's directives with regard to its suitability to the purchaser, only to receive at a later date an order from Penn written from six weeks to two months before, directing him to give the land to someone else.

Obviously a map was urgently needed, but the surveyor general could not make it with any claim to accuracy without the deputies' field maps. He had appealed to the governor and to the council to exert their authority to extract the maps and his share of the fees from the deputies, particularly from Ashcom, but in neither case did his plea bring effective action.

His working map lay spread over his table in the house on Mulberry Street, a web of lines tracing the courses of two great rivers and their major tributaries, with many lesser but important streams. Significant features that had been discovered were added at intervals—high elevations, large rocks, great trees. Plantations that had been laid out and their requisite field maps and notes returned to his office were definitely recorded; many others, for which he had received no such documentation, were tentatively laid down. There were in various areas anticipatory tracts of estimated acreage that would facilitate future surveys, but the lands for which he had no bounds except those he had indicated in his orders to the delinquent surveyors were like a personal reproach.

On 20 October Thomas Holme sued Israel Taylor at the quarter sessions of Bucks County on behalf of the governor. Hearings continued through the reading of Thomas Holme's commission dated 8 February 1681/82, which proved the right of survey money to him, and the reading of Taylor's commission dated 10 September 1683, which proved that he ought to be accountable to the plaintiff [Thomas] for his surveys. The court gave the judgment that Israel Taylor should bring in his accounts and that he should pay the money due Thomas Holme as surveyor general. Taylor promised to perfect his surveys and make returns of them in three months time, and to make returns of Wright's Town in two weeks, and to give an account in ten days of all of the land that he had surveyed or had begun to survey since he came to office, and the time of the surveys.[1] Unfortunately the decree did not include sufficient sanctions to guarantee its being carried out.

If the session with Taylor was less than satisfactory, it was at least more focused than the perennial struggle with Ashcom. The council was not supportive. On 17 November 1685 the petition of Joshua Hastings against Ashcom was read the second time. This time Ashcom complied with the summons, but the council evidently decided it had had enough of Ashcom. "It was Concluded no proper place to End their Difficulties it being a matter of Law." Ashcom's transgressions were not limited to surveys. On 21 September 1686,

> The humble lamentation of Jann Van Cullen was Read [in Council]. setting forth the abuses of Charles Ashcom. Order that his Cattle be Returned, and that the Difference between him and Charles Ashcom be Valued by 4 men, and if they cannot agree that be left to be Desided by the Govr.

On 16 November 1686, goaded by the governor and his own sense of what was rightfully due both the governor and himself, Thomas Holme presented a petition before the council "Complayning against Charles Ashcom, one of his Deputy Survey^{rs}, for want of a mapp of his work don in Chester County." The only action the council took on the petition was to hear it read again in the afternoon. The petition may have been prompted by a second after-thought in Penn's letter

---

[1] Bucks County, Pennsylvania, *Minute Book, Common Pleas and Quarter Sessions Court, 1684–1730.* Taylor was subsequently indicted on a variety of charges.

to Thomas Lloyd, dated 21 September, which must have reached Philadelphia in November. The governor again chides Thomas Holme:

> I forgott one thing: pray put a stop to that Irregular way of disposing of land in the Lower Counties; there will come a day of Judgement about Surveys when I return; for I fear great wrong to me in that regard. tell tho: holmes we want a map to that degree that I am ashamed here; bid him send w^t he has by the first; he promest it two years since (& I upon his word:) all cry out, where is y^r map, w^t no map of the settlements! I entreat thee leave him not before this be done, tis of mighty moment.

In response to this message Thomas Holme concluded his letter to the governor of 25 November 1686:

> I cannot get a Mapp of the Pro[vince] yet, for C[harles] A[shcom] will neither give me his draughts and regular returnes, nor account of the survey money, [and] outdares all authority; the great controversy between the Welsh and others in Chester County, hangs still, it hath been above a year depending before Council and Commissioners but like other things, nothing done. I have complained to the Pres. and Council but to no purpose, I hear C[harles] A[shcom] intends to go away shortly out of these parts and sell all, and then thou wilt loose considerably for I have thy word for what is due to me. I write mostly by guess and not by sight, my sight goes away apace; I am as I write
>
> Thy true and faithfull friend
Thomas Holm^{e2}

Thomas Holme's suggestion that he expects Penn to make good Ashcom's default of fees can only have been a means of reminding the governor that he too was suffering from Ashcom's delinquency. He was well aware of the Proprietor's financial difficulties. Facing this stalemate, there was nothing for him to do but spread out on his desk his master outline of the improved part of the province, with its carefully charted streams and marshes and surveyed tracts of occupied and unoccupied land as far as possible without the retained field maps, and, in the shortened days of winter and with his failing eyesight, set about making the greatest of early American maps.[3]

---

[2] ALS. Chew Family Papers, Cliveden Manuscripts, HSP. Ed. Gary B. Nash, "The First Decade in Pennsylvania: Letters of William Markham and Thomas Holme to William Penn," *PMHB* 90: 348–392. *PWP* 3: 130–132.

[3] The editors of *PWP* (3: 643) have found that the map "covers an area of approximately 55 miles in length and 33 miles in width, plotted to the scale of 1 mile to the inch," and locates the holdings of some 670 settlers.

For the sake of accuracy and with suspicions stirred by increasing interest in overplus he examined the most controversial surveys that had been made during the past four years, particularly those of Fairman for the Growdens and Gray. For the time being verification of suspicions would have to wait, but he recorded them in his memory and set down the current holdings as he was sure of them. Even at that, although he had hoped to finish the map by the first of the new year (March 1686/87) it was well into the Pennsylvania spring before he could get it out to the governor. His reference to it in his letter to the governor on 24 May 1687 suggests that it at least was on its way to him. By this time he had received a letter from William Penn by way of Blackfan, with other letters dated 28 January 1686/87. Thomas Holme's letter from the governor has not been found, but from his reply written on 24 May we may judge of its contents.

For the most part, the letter recapitulates Markham's and his own accounts of the Pickering affair and the already rehearsed incursions of "that vile C.A." on the Welsh Tract. He admits that on occasion, pressed by exacting purchasers, he has failed to reserve the five hundred acres in every township that Penn required, but promises to do so in the future, regardless of objections. He reports on the plus land situation:

> As for plus lands by the river, I allowed one since thy departure; there are severall plus lands back, by the false surveys, especially in this and Chester Countyes; and I have begun resurveys, and was present my self, and found 3 or 400 acres plus, in 1500 acres by Thomas Fairmans surveys, who hath been naught, as I shall more at large acquaint thee; and I fear I shall be forced to resurvey much lands, and hope the plus will be such, as will allow the surveyors to be paid, and bring considerable advantage to thee, for I finde in 4 or 5 miles back from the river that I can sell the plus land at £20 per 100 acre, and where small quantities are found to have plus, judge it much better for thee to sell of this. Please to let me know thy minde, I can sell it for more than thou canst thy selfe.[4]

In the absence of proof we may make the gratifying assumption that the letter and the map itself were rushed at once to a waiting ship and sent off to England, to arrive, if the passage was direct and the weather favorable, in five or six weeks, but more likely after a side trip to Barbados, where a layover for exchange of cargo would, with the additional distance, extend the voyage to some time in August. Upon

---

[4] See above, n. 2.

reaching Penn the map would go to F. Lamb to be prepared for the printer. It was offered for sale sometime in 1687 as:

> A Map of
> The Province of Pennsilvania
> Containing the three Countyes of
> Chester, Philadelphia, & Bucks.
> as far as yet Surveyed and Laid out, the Divisions
> distinctions made by the different Coullers, respects
>
> the Setlements by way of Townships.
> By Tho: Holme Survey^r Gen^{ll}.
> Sold by Rob: Greene at the Rose & Crowne in Budg row
> And by John Thornton at the Platt in the Minories. London.[5]

The first map shows the controversial Pickering land above the Welsh Tract, across the Schuylkill from the Proprietor's Manor of Gilberts, and a vacant square adjoining Arthur Cook's plantation near Neshaminy Creek. The large property of the Growdens is cut into only by the irregular tracts of Claus Johnson and Francis Walker, with its long front on Neshaminy. Below it, in neighboring widths, are the long, narrow tracts of Walter Forrest, Joseph Growden, Nathaniel Allen, Dunk Williams, Nathaniel Hardin, and John Bowen fronting on the Delaware, and two irregular tracts, one of Samuel Allen touching Neshaminy, the other blank. Tryall Holme's tract is in the tier of surveys west of his father's, and a large tract on Dublin (Pennypack) Creek adjoining Thomas's Well Spring Plantation bears Elinor's name. Whatever his dissatisfaction with its unavoidable shortcomings and his misgivings with regard to Penn's reception of it, Thomas Holme must have looked with pride at a work which, with all its imperfections, was nonetheless a masterpiece. It is to be hoped that he laid down his quill and, for the time being, put away his rulers, compasses, and squares, and relaxed enough to celebrate Elinor's marriage to Joseph Moss at the Abington Monthly Meeting at the house of Richard Worrel on 30 May.[6]

---

[5] This map is held by the authorities of the Map Division of the British Library to be the original given to William Penn. The few variations in the copies at the HSP and the LC would seem to make these of a slightly later version, perhaps made later in the same year, after Penn's letter to James Harrison, or even after Thomas Holme's visit to WP late in the next year. The most conspicuous differences in the two large maps are the omission of Pickering's name on the tract on the Schuylkill above the Welsh Tract and the large irregular survey of John Gray/Tatham cutting into the Growden property on Neshaminy, with the location of Tatham house on the second map. A smaller version frequently circulated contains more changes in the names of landholders, indicating the increase in real estate transactions. It is estimated to represent the province at about 1690.

[6] Minutes of the Abington Monthly Meeting (transcription from the original presented to the GSP by Joseph E. Gillingham), GSP COLL. HSP, p.11.

Fig. 21. Original version of 1687 map. Note L. and J. Growden property with the intrusion of Johnson and Walker. Used with permission of the Historical Society of Pennsylvania.

The Cartographer

Fig. 22. Revised version of 1687 map with Gray portion. Used with permission of the Historical Society of Pennsylvania.

On 28 January and in February 1686/87 William Penn wrote a number of letters, all of them with the usual protestations of affection, followed by directives, complaints, recriminations, and devices for reserving more land to himself while at the same time satisfying the purchasers. With the most direct routes possible they could not have reached Philadelphia before the middle or end of March if sent by the middle of February. If, as frequently happened, they came by way of Barbados, they would at best arrive in May. If they arrived before Thomas Holme wrote to Penn on 24 May, he was obviously not apprised of parts pertaining to his office, such as the reprimand for granting irregular tracts to Pickering and Gray (which he had not done), and his appointment, with the commissioners and Markham, for the account of Samuel Carpenter's inventory of rents.[7] He was further

---

[7] ALS. Penn Papers, Dom. and Misc. Letters, HSP (Micro. 5: 665).

directed that there were to be no warrants for resurvey of land within five miles of the Delaware or any other navigable river, "that all overplus lands upon resurvey granted by the former Com^{rs} not already granted finall or not patented" be returned to his own use and disposal; that in every township one share and all Indian fields be reserved for himself; that no land containing mines was to be given out without William Penn's explicit orders; and that Thomas Holme stop the irregular grant made to Charles Pickering and John Gray alias Tatham.[8]

While these letters were on their way across the Atlantic Thomas Holme was putting the final lines on the map that may well have gone to England on the return voyage of the ship that brought the governor's letters. The map on its way, Thomas Holme turned to resurveys and to the land movements that always increased with spring.

The year 1686 had not been easy for Thomas Holme. His longtime friend Christopher Taylor had died on 26 June. Markham was incensed because William Penn had passed him by to grant to another the clerkship of the provincial court, to which he felt, with some justice, he was entitled. He had offered to resign his secretaryship on the ground that he "might as well sit still and do nothing and get no pay as to work and get no pay."[9] Thomas Lloyd and Nicholas More were still verbally at one another's throats. Lloyd's arrogance reached a climax when he had an armchair brought into the chamber for his seat. Markham reminded Penn in his letter of 22 August that Lloyd's term as councillor was about to expire; it was taken for granted that his presidency would, too. If Penn wished him to continue in it he would have to send a new commission. Lloyd's manifest feelings of superiority had alienated many in the province, but the governor continued to regard him with confidence and admiration; nevertheless, on 27 December Penn reluctantly acceded to Lloyd's request for release from the office. Benjamin Chambers's suit against the Free Society of Traders continued. Patrick Robinson had been put under house arrest because of his too outspoken championship of More and his outrageous behavior in court, provoked to some extent by Lloyd's extravagant attitude. Although Thomas Holme was not officially involved in these matters, the general atmosphere of contention among his associates was disturbing.[10]

---

[8] CC by WM, WP to commissioners of property, Bureau of Land Records, DAM, PHMC.
[9] ALS. WM to WP, 22 August 1686. Cliveden MSS, Chew Family Papers, HSP. Nash, cited above, n. 19; *PWP* 3: 99–109 (Micro. 5: 609).
[10] ALS. Penn Letters and Ancient Documents, APS, WP to commissioners of state; MHSP 4 (1840), 186; Proud, *History* 1: 333; *PWP* 3: 99–100 (Micro. 5: 884).

Mortality was high in the years 1686 and 1687. As already noted, Christopher Taylor had died in June of 1686. It was to him that Thomas Holme had written for advice concerning the establishment of a school for Friends' children in Ireland. Nicholas More died between the autumn of 1686 and late May of 1687. Thomas and he had been associated in varying degrees with the affairs of the province from the beginning and, despite the occasional irascibility of both, they seem to have been on the same side in provincial procedures, and there is no record of friction between them.

James Claypoole and Thomas Holme had become acquainted and apparently enjoyed an amicable relationship during the early days of the Free Society of Traders at its foundation in Bristol, Claypoole as treasurer and Thomas as a member of the Committee of Twelve. Claypoole had even sent his son John to Pennsylvania as assistant to Thomas Holme. Their friendship seems not to have endured, although there is no record of hostility between them. Claypoole became ill during the winter of 1686 and made his will on 5 February 1686/87, but recovered sufficiently to live until the following October.

William Frampton, who had served on the council, died in the fall of 1687. He seems to have been indebted to Thomas Holme for £7 although the executors of his estate find the question of payment complicated by subsequent real estate transactions.[11]

Joseph Moss, the son-in-law to whom Thomas Holme had relinquished his daughter Elinor only five months before, wrote his will on 3 September 1687, and it was proved on 9 November. Moss's bequests to Elinor were all-inclusive: "I give and bequeath to my beloved wife Elinor Moss all my Estate Goods, Chattles, Merchandises Debts portions or any other thing or things which of right is or may be due or apertaine unto me . . . whether in Europe or America."[12]

Two marginal factors of this will are of particular interest. First, one of the witnesses was Thomas Holme's brother Michael, of whom we have had no notice since his letter to Ormonde on 11 November 1662, quoted above. The signatures of the two documents are definitely by the same hand, although they are more than two decades apart. There is no record of Michael's having owned or rented property of any sort in Pennsylvania. Was he the Michael Holme who, as ship's master of the *Amity* (sometimes called the *Unity*), a smaller ship than that under Richard Diamond's custody, plied what seems to have been a lively

---

[11] ALS. Charles Jones to Andrew Robinson, 29 August 1687. HSP, Am. 2532: 40.
[12] PhA, Will Book A, no. 35: 71. Copy, GSP Coll., HSP.

trade between England and Danzig during the first half of the decade? The name will appear again with a slightly conspiratorial flavor.[13] Had Michael come to Philadelphia to pay a friendly visit to his brother, or to seek benefits from him or through his association with William Penn, the friend of the king? Was he the father of Susannah James of Philadelphia, the Mester Hulme of Bristol whose daughter Susannah was baptized there in 1657? Was he the brother who was the subject of John Tottenham's letter to Thomas the following year? Intriguing questions, the probably affirmative answers to which may have perished in the fire that consumed many of the Irish archives.

A second notable mystery is the absence of Tryall Holme's signature as witness of Joseph Moss's will. It would be expected that if he were near he would have witnessed his sister's wedding and would have been with his father and sister on the occasion of the will. The last notice we have of his presence is his signature as witness of the Indian deed of 30 July 1685. The record of the survey of his thousand acres was duly turned in to the secretary's office on 15 April 1686, and an undated receipt would be discovered sometime later. It has been assumed that he was lost at sea, but there is no extant record of his departure and no mention of his death in any correspondence nor in his father's official account of the family in the Wexford Friends' record. There are, of course, other possibilities: a rift between father and son, or removal to New Jersey, in which case he may have been the brother-in-law of his cousin Silas to whom William Penn refers in one of his letters.[14] In view of the fact that he had witnessed his father's deed of his Shaftesberry Plantation to Nicholas Rideout dated 9 May 1685 and recorded 9 July, and that the deed was lost by shipwreck on the way to the purchaser in England, the assumption that he died at sea seems plausible. A faint hope that this last of his sons might somehow have escaped could explain his absence from the family record and from his father's will.[15]

Of the seven deaths of acquaintances and fellow workers in a little more than a year, perhaps that of James Harrison in October, 1687, was most shocking to Thomas Holme. As Penn's steward and as the surveyor who was expected to look after Penn's interests in any matters relating to land, the two often shared communications from the Proprietor. With the exception of Christopher Taylor, Harrison was nearest to Thomas Holme in age—four years his junior—which made

---

[13] Port Books, E. 190. 109/1, PRO.
[14] Minutes of the Falls Monthly Meeting, GSP, HSP.
[15] Rideout states in a note dated 19 February 1695 that the deed was lost by shipwreck: Deed Book E-1, 5: 70, Office of the Recorder of Deeds, Philadelphia.

some bond between them in a society whose median age was ten years below Thomas Holme's.

On 26 December 1687 Philip Theodore Lehnmann made his will, and was so ill that he, a master penman, was forced to sign it with his mark. It was proved five days later. He and Thomas Holme had been associated from the first in the affairs of William Penn. Lehnmann as the Proprietor's personal secretary had been left behind to continue in that capacity when Penn returned to England in August 1684. He had justifiably incurred Penn's wrath by overlooking the Dutch affidavits when packing Penn's belongings for the return to England, and he shared with Thomas Holme accusations of slowness in laying out land and in the drinking of "libations." A bachelor with no relatives in the province, he was generous in his legacies to Thomas Holme and his family, devising

> To Silas Crispin 250 A of untaken up land within the province of Pennsylvania, and also the balance of an account if any. To Ellinor Moss 250 A to be taken up as aforesaid. To Captain Thomas Holme all my Liberty Land belonging to the Town of Philadelphia with my plantation called Green Spring Lying and being in the County of Sussex[16]. . . . with which the balance of accompt betwen us if any appear . . . to Susannah James wife of John James 300 A of land to be taken up in Pennsylvania . . . to William Penn, Charles Pickering [land in Kent] and my great horse called Brandy and my Chamblitt cloake and also a good feather bedd and bolster etc. green rug, 3 green curtains.[17]

It is possible that the deaths in 1687 were due to the effects of "a great mortality [that] occurred at the Falls of Delaware, (in 1687) occasioned by 'the great land flood and rupture.'"[18] Certainly these men would be greatly missed by the Philadelphia community, Taylor as scholar and Quaker minister, Frampton and Claypoole as business men, More as judge, and Harrison as custodian of Pennsbury.

The seasonal lull in warrants for surveys worked to Thomas Holme's advantage during the winter, though the review of the total distribution of lands made him acutely aware of a situation that was causing serious dissatisfaction among landholders and would-be purchasers,

---

[16] Sussex is the southernmost of the three Lower Counties, which constitute the present state of Delaware. No further mention of this property has been found. Lehnmann's legacy may have been included implicitly in Thomas's Holme's will.

[17] The records of Claypoole's, Moss's, and Lehnmann's wills are in Philadelphia Will Book A, 34, 35, and 37. Susannah James may have been the daughter of Mester Holmes christened on 1 August 1657 (see above, Chapter 4, note 8). It appears that parts of the legacies to Silas Crispin and Thomas Holme were in payment of debts, probably with surplus as gift.

[18] MSS of Phineas Pemberton, cited by Watson, *Annals* 2: 210.

and that he, more than anyone else, was in a position to mention to the Proprietor. A case in point was the "great meadow so called above the falls," into which Penn himself was making incursions for purchases that ate into the thousand-acre reservation he had ordered Thomas Holme to hold for himself in every county.

Large proprietary tracts incited murmurs among purchasers. At the risk of arousing the wrath of the governor, Thomas Holme from time to time offered advice on this and other topics. One such admonition appears in the peculiar combination of two fragments. At some point in the assembling of Penn's papers two separate undated documents tentatively ascribed to 1690, but more probably belonging to 1688 or earlier, were placed together. The first, addressed by William Penn to Thomas Holme, is torn off at mid-point. Attached to it is part of a document obviously by Thomas Holme to William Penn, advising him of the manner of both reserving and disposing of land of mixed value within his large manors, apparently specifically his Manor of Gilberts on the upper Schuylkill and the Manor of Rocklands fronting on the Delaware and bounded on the southwest by at least eight miles of Brandywine Creek. He writes:

> I have thorrowly viewed both these manners and know I propose with in Compass and have Considered & Consulted thy Intrist in that behalfe Methinks it Seems an Empty Injoyment to have all that Land lye meenly for the name, And Slipp a market I thinke to gett a good heith. . . .

He suggests further that eighteen miles be added to the back of the survey of New Castle on the branches of Elke River:

> Selling for a Consideration & reserving Such a Rent and So through out the Said County Some Thousands of pounds may be raised theire and thy Reavenew ffixt When thy 1/10 part w^{yh} Purchaso^{rs} is taken up and art pleased to accept of 500 ^{a} in a Township, that Never the less may not the Proprieto^r use his Naibours method to Sell w^t Land he Can while the market lasts But If the Proprieto^r depend to See Land before he Sells it business of that kinde will not be done to purpose.

The combined fragments are docketed, "Proprietors Instructions/ to the foormer Comissione^{rs}/ 0 4."[19] Although the addressee of the first portion is uncertain, the docket seems more applicable to the commissioners than to the surveyor general, though the use of the singular pronoun indicates otherwise. There is no doubt that the second frag-

---

[19] Fragment (Micro. 6: 405).

ment is in the style of Thomas Holme. It reveals also an eye adept at speculative wisdom. It may well be one of Thomas Holme's notes of suggestions for Penn's incorporation in a letter to the commissioners.

If these are late documents they may date from the new and expanded commission given by Penn to Thomas Holme on his last departure from England, but the surveyor general had been volunteering advice to the governor from the early years of the province when he felt that conditions required it. He had suggested the appointment of a woodman to prevent the indiscriminate cutting of trees, protection of marked trees, and procedures for carrying out orders in these regards. All of these Penn ordered in letters and proclamations.

Thomas Holme even went so far as to send Penn a model letter which he could copy and send to the commissioners of property to control the irregular procedures in Chester County, particularly with regard to the Welsh Tract. Beginning with the customary formal heading and history of the grant to the Welsh and his present information that great controversies have arisen between the Welsh and other persons, occasioned by Charles Ashcom's having surveyed several thousand acres within the tract to other purchasers, he orders that the integrity of the original surveys must be preserved and those wrongly seated there be removed to available satisfactory land elsewhere, in Chester County or any other locality. The order is addressed to "Thomas Lloyd, James Claypool and Robt. Turner my Com^{rs} for granting Patent Lands and lotts in Pennsylvania &c or any two of them." After a slash mark Thomas Holme explains, "Governor, I write not this to dictate a Copy for thee, but to mention the substantiall & necessary matter, leaving it to thy wisdom to word & order it."[20] If the letter was sent, the advice it contained was not heeded, and the Welsh Tract never recovered from Ashcom's incursions.

Whether because of Thomas Holme's advice or his own apprehension, the governor did at last reiterate his former rules concerning the cutting of timber and the seating of surveyed but unseated lands, both topics of concern to Thomas Holme. On 26 January 1686/87 (about 9 March-1 May or later) he issued a proclamation concerning the cutting of timber and clearing of lots in and around Philadelphia. He appointed a woodman for granting trees in the public domain, to be paid 6 d. a tree. The commissioners were to see to it that this arrangement was observed. He pointed out that one bad consequence of irregular cutting is growth of underwood, which does "not only hinder the Towne Stock of the benefit they might else have & render

---

[20] MBP, *PA* 2, 19, vol. 1: 5, 12–13.

the Town more a Wilderness, but if not cleared & prevented may become a common Nuisance being a covert for Vermin & too often for loose & evil Persons." The Proprietor then proceeds to the matter of seating the land so that every five-thousand-acre township will have at least ten families, "to the end that the Province might not be like a Wilderness as some others yet do by vast vacant tracts of Land, but be regularly improved for the benefit of Society in help, trade, education, Government, Roads, travill, entertainment, &c." He then instructs the commissioners to note tracts of land that, although taken up, are not seated "and are most likely to give cause of exception & Discouragement to those that are able & ready to seate the same" and dispose of them if they are not seated within six months, if the regular time for seating has expired. Conscious, perhaps, that consistency as well as popular opinion required that he do something about his own large empty tracts of land, he then made a limited gesture toward putting them to use. Again the Archives of the Province preserve his solution to the problem.

If his relatives, being infants, have ten thousand acres in one place, one thousand may be given to ten poor families to settle; if there are five thousand, the five hundred acres may be given to five families to settle. He protects his interests in the matter: "If any seat their Land let Care be taken that they have not the best places, & that for Nearness of the Land and goodness they pay some acknowledgemt after 3 Yrs, that is mor than Ordinary . . . if you can get them for less land 'twere better." He orders them to choose the most convenient place, the branch on the west side of the Schuylkill that was navigable by canoe, about thirty miles from town [in the?] ten thousand acres for his daughter Gulielma Maria Penn the younger—

> the same which goes towards Susquehanna, by which they rode when R. Fretwell went to view that r. & seat it in the same manner, 50 A inheritance & 100 on lease for 11 years for each family or rather than not encourage the poor give them 1/2 for an acknowledgment & 1/2 on lease of 150 A but so as their settlements be regular and after the exacted methods of townships. . . .

For Penn's brother (brother-in-law) Lowther's children the surveyors were to "advance backwards & add 2000 A more, making 4 mannors at 3000 A each for his 4 children . . . & on each 4 families." This process must be carried on with the utmost care, with inspection of all former grants and surveys, that no irregularities may pass without scrutiny & censure, for I am informed that in some Places Lands have been squandered away to nobody knows who for fees, & y't Warrants go to Markett, which is a most disorderly & condemnable thing. Whatever is Irregular vacate; for I shall be very strict.[21]

Taught by experience and perhaps with a bit of prophetic vision of more trials to come, at the beginning of what by the modern calendar would be the new year, "Capt. Thomas Holme Surveyor General, gave the Commissioners a Certificate under his hand, That he gave no order for the laying out any Land within the Welsh Tract."[22]

The first complaint was against the Welsh surveyor, David Powell, by John Day, who "complains vs David Powell for surveying or laying out to another land first laid out to him." He was told to put his complaint in writing and that Powell would answer it before the commissioners at their next meeting. Where Day's original claim was situated is not mentioned, but his tract is recorded as on Frankford Creek in Philadelphia County, between the tracts of Mitchell and Brown, on both versions of the map. Since David Powell's regular area of survey was Chester County, particularly that part of it designated the Welsh tract, it may be that Day's original tract was located in that area and that the accommodation for him above Philadelphia was arranged.[23]

On 13 May, David Powell with six companions, on behalf of the Welsh Friends, heard the reading of the council minute that ordered the surveyor general to make returns on the land that Charles Ashcom had surveyed in the Welsh Tract for T. Barker & Company, four thousand acres. "They deny that any of them had consented to the survey and wish it not to be confirmed." Finally, on 5 July, the bounds of the Welsh Tract were specifically entered in the minutes and it was declared that "any land within this tract other than that concerning the Purchasers of North and South Wales & adjacent Counties as Herefordshire, Shropshire, [was] illegal, irregular, except what was laid out of this [that was] laid out."

Numerous individual problems demanded Thomas Holme's professional attention, some of them having to do with procedures of questionable legality. It was learned that a small purchaser living between the north end of Philadelphia and the Proprietor's mill "having a tract held by him as 100 acres is disposing or has disposed of several small

---

[21] MBP, Book E-2: 56, 58.
[22] MBP, E: 60.
[23] MBP, p. 8.

parcels before the over plus . . . is taken out thereof." The commissioners had learned that there was a considerable amount of overplus, which would place a fairly large amount of land at his disposal for small sales. It was ordered that a warrant be given to Thomas Holme to resurvey the tract of land "in order to accommodate the Governor's Mill with the Over-plus."

Thomas Fairman took Thomas Holme to court early in the year, his accusation not recorded, and himself was charged with negligence that proved expensive to a purchaser. Walter King had a warrant for seven hundred acres of land on which he had established his dwelling, but unfortunately Fairman had proceeded to lay out other tracts nearby before finishing King's, so that finally King was short two hundred acres. He asked for a resurvey and a grant of such overplus as might be found to make up the deficit.

By the summer of 1686 the problem of the caves along the Delaware bank had become crucial. Originally they were permitted as temporary refuges from the elements until houses could be built. Citizens had complained about them almost from the first, and Penn had from time to time ordered them cleared. Not only had many of them fallen into disreputable use, but in some cases they were actually crumbling away the bank itself and endangering buildings on Front Street. Now, some time after the Ides of March, arrived a proclamation dated 24 January 1686/87. Taking into account these abuses and the fact that some were passing on their bank caves to others as though they were regularly obtained private property, Penn wrote:

> I do hereby desire and Strictly order and warne all the Inhabitants of the said caves to depart the same within two Months after the Publication hereof, And requiring my Loving friends & Commission^{rs} William Markham, Thomas Ellis, & John Goodson, or any two of them to see that the same be accordingly Effected. . . .

Some buildings, especially Benjamin Chambers's, had cost more than legitimately erected houses and had been built without official clearance. In such cases the order might be modified. The owner would be required to pay £100 for security for good behavior in them and for preservation of the bank, and rent at a half the real yearly value to be paid the Proprietor as long as he permitted them to live there, provided the building of the cave was "not worth less than £30" and "the owner is of sober condition."[24]

---

[24] Copy, Division of Land Records, DAM, PHMC (Micro. 5: 639).

One might expect such an edict to inspire a rush for lots back of the already fairly well settled Front Street, but such was not the case. Most of the cave dwellers already had land elsewhere. One, Henry Furnis, a woodworker of considerable skill, demurred on the ground that he and his wife were getting on in years, and finding another place to live would be difficult. Moreover, they had both business and family reasons for wishing to stay comfortably above the river. They needed to be able to transport wood by boat, and their married offspring used boats to come to see them. Eventually they were granted use of a piece of the Proprietor's land at the north end of town beside Coaquannock Creek, where Henry could land his timber until further notice.

Several inhabitants of caves refused to sign the obligation to leave by 19 September, keep order in the mean time, and repair damage to the bank. Otter, Allen, and Guest signed, but Chambers did not come. They signed as renters to pay half the yearly value, keep good order, depart on command, and repair the bank. Thomas Coburn was summoned, but he did not come. After what had amounted to mutiny on the part of some occupants, the remaining caves were eventually emptied or legitimized. It would be another year before an appreciable number of warrants for bank lots would reach the surveyor general's desk.

Two warrants for lots at this time are of special interest: one a city lot for Richard Corsley, which must have been requested by Thomas Holme, on 12 June 1687; and one for a bank lot for the enterprising Robert Turner, on 4 September.

Now that population had spread farther inward and more small purchasers and renters were being seated, more cleared, well-defined roads were in demand. At the 18 August Falls Meeting it was decreed that

> Whereas there was a late order for a main Road from the centre of Philadelphia by the shortest way to the Falls, it is requested that Robert Turner and William Man, with the assistance of the Surveyor General and his deputy to make use of the most speedy and successful method for the running the same.[25]

No such method seems to have been found, since the same source records that on 28 February 1688/89 the surveyor general was ordered to appear before the council to show cause why the road was not laid

---

[25] Records of the Falls Meeting, Bu-2F-2. GSP, HSP.

from the Falls to Philadelphia. Since Thomas Holme had not at that time returned from England he could not well appear; why Robert Turner and William Mann were not summoned to account for the delay is not explained.

On 28 October Thomas Holme finally finished a business transaction that had been a source of inconvenience for some time, when at the Monthly Meeting on the Front of Delaware he signed a deed of sale to John Goodson, Benjamin Chambers, Joshua Cart, and John Songhurst for the ground on which the Meeting House stood. The meeting decided that it would be wise to have the conveyance made to some others, and named Robert Turner, Thomas Budd, Samuel Richardson, Alexander Beardsley, and Anthony Morris, and requested John Eckley to "draw up the same and present it to the Friends for their advice and accomplishment thereby and give an account of it to the Friends before Joshua Cart moves out of the country."[26]

On 14 December 1687 (20 January-March 1687/88) the governor sent instructions that would have solved at least one map problem for Thomas Holme had he known of them at the time at which they were written. Addressing Markham, Thomas Ellis, and John Goodson, commissioners of property, he directed:

> Whereas John Gray alias Tatham, desired a warrant to resurvey for lands formerly granted to Francis Walker, Dunck Williams, & was at the charge of performing the same, & that the sd T. or Gray, has bought of many here the said overplus, having referred to myself all such quantities & if disposed of, then to those that have been at the charges of resurvey, these are to desire you to & strictly order, you forthwith to put the sd G/T into quiet possession of the same . . . I have communicated to him divers things for you and my Commissioners of State. . . . lett him be civilly & kindly used upon all occasions, for he has shown himself a friend unto the Province.[27]

Earlier in the year Penn had learned that Gray/Tatham's former congregation, the Benedictines of St. James, had reported his dereliction to the king, and had also notified Penn. The king had directed that he be returned to England. The governor had responded by alerting Gray in a letter enclosed with one to Thomas Lloyd, and had told Lloyd, "If he speaks to thee of it, or should talk of moving lett him know this, & that I shall do him w^t good offices he can Expect of me

---

[26] As above, 2: 124.
[27] ALS. Dreer, 23, HSP.

in reason."[28] A highly laudatory petition in defense of Gray seems to have secured his protection from the king and from a monastery that probably was well rid of him.[29]

Understandably, Growden was crushed. In a long letter to William Penn written on 16 March 1687/88, he gives a detailed account of his original purchase of his property on Neshaminy Creek and of the understanding he had of his sale of a thousand acres of it to Gray/Tatham, but Tatham's transaction was a *fait accompli*, and he was left with a fraction of his original plantation with Gray's thousand acres "fronting on the creek, two perches broad . . . and runs back into my manor tract in the form of a squaring axe, the pole and eye being next the creek. . . ."[30] and a liberal amount of overplus. The second version of the map shows that the survey that Penn approved could scarcely have been more irregular. If Thomas was upstaged by his subordinate and deprived of his fees he at least had the satisfaction that the most geographically irregular survey in the province had been approved by the governor himself.

On 23 March 1688 Thomas Holme received the inevitable post-cartographic letter from Penn. The letter has not been found, but again Thomas Holme's systematic reply reveals much about the content.[31] Although he treats of other matters first, the map must have been uppermost in his mind. It is enmeshed in a tangle of surveys. His explanations concerning them can best be understood by reference to the map as Penn by this time had received it. He writes:

> As for the mapp, it was done as well as it could be then, thou pressed so hard for it; and I am like to have litle for mee and Robert Longshore, nothing but a few mapps, which will not vend here.
>
> As for Lands at Nesheminek intended for thou and relations, didst thou but know what hard speaches I have met with from many about Lands, (thy selfe not escaping their Lashes) thou couldst not blame mee while one cryed out must Lands be kept wast etc., and we now came in cannot have lands to setle upon, others that they bought Lands long ago, and now come to live on them, and cannot have them etc. I could say a great deal, but it would not please thee, nor more than their cryes (without cause) against me.
>
> I long since gave thee account about Pickrings lands and he wrote to

---

[28] ALS. Penn Papers, HSP (Micro. 5: 511). Printed and edited by Frederick Tolles, "William Penn on Public and Private Affairs, 1686," *PMHB* 80: 236–47; *PWP* 3: 116–123.
[29] ALS. WP to TL, Penn Papers, HSP (Micro. 5: 511). Printed in *PWP* 3: 116–120.
[30] Joseph Growden to WP (Micro. 5: 951). ACM, Vol. 148: Addenda, 16 March 1687/88.
[31] TH to WP, Cliveden Manuscripts, Chew Family Papers, HSP (Micro. 5: 967). Nash, *PMHB* 90: 501–506; *PWP* 2: 177–181.

thee. The Lands were laid out, before I heard any thing from thee, neither is there so much in it, as it may seem. I have spoke with others that say they know such mines or better, but will not discover it to any but to thy selfe.

Thou art pleased to write, that thou hast no lands on the East side of Skulkill, which is a mistake, for besides the manour of Springfield [Gulielma Maria Penn's] which reaches (part of it as thou ordered it to the river) and though Thomas Fairman hath dealt falsely with thee therin and Major Farmer placed contrary to thy order by too much breadth on that river, and so left thy Manour but about 3000 acres instead of 5000 acres, yet I purpose to remedy that, and leave thy due, and yet Farmers have theirs also. Had that been right done by T[homas] F[airman] there would have been a good space behind that and by Plymouth Township; but their building so high up by the river prevents it there and makes that loss. The next above plymouth, is but 1000 acres, layd out to the two Chambers, and then begins next the B[arbados] Island, and the breadth Eastward takes in about 3000 acres, next above that is a great Tract of Land betwixt that and Perkomia where I inserted Phillip Fords name, who had no Lands, of all his 10,000 acres. But I know not yet the quantity of that Tract whether 5 or 6000 acres or more or less, and wrote to thee to let me know what quantity should be allowed him there, but had no answer, so that there may be about 5000 acres on the E. side of Skulkill there for one of thy children, besides all the Lands on the W. side of Skulkill from against Farmers to Lowthers lands. Only the Sweeds, think to keep their land there, which I warned them of, and told them thou sent me positive order to the contrary, i.e. that no old setler should have any lands there. And as for Perkomia, it was thy order to have a manour there. Tis true the Lands are bad backward for I have been there, but the 2 Rivers and large meadowes some on this side. Perkomia which I intend to be part of the Manour, will supply the deficit of the bad lands; I intend thee about 4 miles upon Skulkill for the front of the manour.[32]

Of purchasers whose names appear on the south side of Schuylkill on the 1687 map, E. Jones and Company, the first of the Welsh contingent to arrive, had received their tract in 1683. William Shardlow and John Pennington and Company received warrants and probably surveys the same year. It is quite possible that, as Markham implied, the tracts of William Wood, Christopher Pennock, and John Holland were now laid out in haste to accommodate Pickering, as well as the manor of William Penn, Jr., Laetitia Penn, and William Penn's brother-in-law William Lowther, which had been reserved but not necessarily surveyed. At any rate, the four-thousand-acre tract of

---

[32] The Manor of Gilberts.

Charles Pickering is conspicuous on the oldest version of the 1687 map. Interspersed among direct references to the map are explanations of omissions due to the governor's oversights, and advice not only on map-related matters but on governmental and economic affairs as well. As for Penn's additional interests, the surveyor general wrote:

> I wonder thou . . . not all this while ordered a manour for thy selfe in Chester County and that must be placed to thy own omission; though I purpose to have a Tract lookt at for thee that way as well as can be.[33]
>
> I also purpose a Tract of 1000 acres above the Falls for thy dispose,[34] next adjacent to the great Meadow and about 4 miles fronting the River, for above that is rocky by the river for a great space and within that Tract Gilbert Wheeler got Israel Taylor to place some warrants which I forbade when I heard of it, and shall not allow him any return for it.

Now a problem had arisen with regard to the Mildmay tract, which the surveyor general had situated as well as possible, considering the land available and the requested proximity to Hudson's property:

> Thomas Hudsons Agent here will not take up the 5000 acres for K. Mildmay & Company, pretending the Lands not good. Thou hast mistaken granting away the meadow, which lyes above 10 miles from Hudsons 5000 acres but I refuse to answer the Agent about what was secured from thee about that meadow, til I send thee a full account of that thing.

Thomas Holme then proceeds with advice and information, including information on the situation on the Susquehanna, in which he had been interested from the first:

> I formerly wrote to thee about Samuel Carpenter and recommended him, as one I know a true friend to thy interest. It may do well to Comissionate him as one with Col. Markham for he is more capable than the other 2., and I must needs enforme thee, that few [are] like him for thee and thy interest, and many may pretend much, but when thou comes, thou will finde otherwise.[35]
>
> I wrote to thee 2 or 3 times about Susquehannah, how many offered to go and live there and that the Government of [New] York, impedes thy dealing with the Indians, and unless thou obtaines a positive Comand from the King to that Governor actively to assist in it, thou will finde it difficult

---

[33] The Manor of Rocklands.
[34] The Falls of the Delaware; the Manor of Highlands.
[35] In January 1686/87 Penn had appointed Markham, Thomas Ellis, and John Goodson as commissioners of land. WP to JH, ALS. Penn Papers, *Dom. and Misc.*, HSP (Micro. 5: 655). *PWP* 3: 139.

to deal with the Indians concerned there but I heard nothing from thee about it, and if thou now bought it might tend to thy advantag, for Lands being taken up so farr back here, peopl are not willing to go further; but if now Susquehanah were begun to inhabite, people would be more willing to setle back that way, in hopes to conjoyne.

Responding later to Penn's rebuke for unanswered warrants, Thomas Holme avers

> that no man, after producing a warrant from thee or thy commissioners ever stayed an houre for want of any order or warrant from me to the respective Deputy Surveyor to execute the same, and if after that, they have neglected to pursue their own business, the fault is in them.... I know sometimes that peopl have long kept their warrants, before shewed me, and also they have taken mine to the Surveyors, have kept them long before they followed their matters or sought the Surveyors to lay out their Lands. I also know that after they have had mine to the Surveyors, that finding they could not have Lands near enough to their mindes, have caused to medle more a long time, and after that some have been faine to tak it where it could be had.

Thomas Holme suffered not only from the allegations of neglect that had been made against him to the governor, but also from a feeling of creeping insecurity in his office and the estimation of one he believed in as a friend; moreover, they were an attack on the integrity of the system. He asks the names of his accusers for

> this cannot proceed from the persens themselves concerned, for it is so false, and known to be so that they cannot be the informers themselves, but though this seemes to reflect on me, I know whom they wound through my sides, and the reflection is aimed at another more than me.[36]

Thomas Holme's personal hurt emerges, sometimes between the lines, sometimes explicitly, throughout the letter. He had written requesting payment for the Indians. Now he has heard that it has come to Markham, but "what or how much [he knows] not." Yet, although this had not yet occurred, it will be he and Samuel Carpenter who will be ordered to meet with the Indians to deliver the payment. He receives no reply from the governor to requests for advice in public matters or to personal appeals. He reviews the financial dishonesty and professional fraudulence of his deputies, which make his position, which the governor considers "the best in the Province," a mere sine-

---

[36] ALS. Cliveden MSS, Chew Family Papers, HSP (Micro. 6: 013). Nash, *PMHB* 90: 496–501; *PWP* 3: 185–192.

cure. His sight is extremely bad: "I write this most by guess, cannot read it, when writ, to mend words or letters so must be excused. I wrote to thee to consult some oculists for help for my sight. I have no [sore eyes, r-h-e- or deflution]." Surveys are a perpetual source of anxiety. When at last the Indians are paid "there will be charge to get the respective lines forward and backward." There is no money in the treasury with which to pay the surveyors, "nor ever was, nor like to be as I wrote thee; nay now some say, its against their conscience to pay country taxes." When he learned of Fairman's false surveys he wrote for a warrant to make a resurvey anywhere in the province at no charge to the governor,

> and though there be severall false surveys, yet in the end, it will tend to thy advantage, for the plus will yield much in many places . . . and not taking away in the plus, any of their improvements will setle their minds, who are now in fear hearing how wrong their lands are laid out, and their Patents false.

He reminds the governor that

> I also wrote to thee of the necessity of a Court, i.e., in the name or nature of an Excheqer with power, whereby thee may be righted and order all things relating to the proprietaryship for as the case now stands, thou canst not have quick remedy for or about thy interst and matters relating to Lands, Rents, etc. nor I and others that hold our places immediately from thee.

The hardest of all his difficulties to bear is the anonymous attacks of those around him:

> I perceive I am not free from secret enemies who Indian like stand behind a tree to shoot at one . . . I am sure its farr from a Christian spirit, or practise of friends, to back bite and skandall one, and never tell them of their faults; if any had seen me amiss, and told me of it, and I not answered expectation I might have been dealt with according to the order of truth, and charity words. I cannot but acquaint thee that I expect thou wilt be so just and kinde to me, to let me know the informers, though I engage to thee not to disclose it to them, without thy consent, and let me not be thus muethered and woulded by pretended friends, that may speake faire to my face, for I am not conscious to deserve it at any ones hands.

Feeling deeply the injustices inflicted upon him and the accompanying insinuations against the governor, he offers to sell back his office to the Proprietor for whatever he will give him, or with Penn's permission, to dispose of it to someone else. He will not follow the examples of his accusers, "to be an informer, els I might soon fill thy eares, with the infermities of others both in the like and other things, but its below me as a man much more as a Christian."

Thomas Holme's offer to resign a post that was more burdensome than profitable was not accepted. He continued with the routine of ordering surveys and adjusting the city plan as required by increasing demand from less affluent citizens for residences and business places. These adjustments had first to be approved by the governor, with the inevitable delays. In April he and Samuel Carpenter went to Pennsbury to pay the large sum of wampum and goods, probably that detailed in the contract reproduced above. Whether the goods had been deposited at Pennsbury or had to be transported there from New York or Philadelphia, the mission was tedious, but as the then president who had engineered the sale, Thomas Holme was known to the Indians and could conduct business with them with a suitable combination of firmness and friendliness. Payment was still due "the Indians of Christina," whom Nash tentatively identifies as "the Brandywine Lenape Indians from whom the land between Chester and Duck Creeks had been purchased on 25 September 1685."

Having finally extracted from Fairman and John Gray/Tatham the papers requisite to the recording of the Growden-Gray transaction, Thomas Holme revised the map to show the axe-shaped manor of Gray rising sharply to the center of Growden's land, and the location of Tatham House. Elinor Holme's name remained on the tract facing her father's Well Spring Plantation across Dublin Creek.

Thomas Holme's troubles about the map were not over. On 11 May Markham and John Goodson, as commissioners of property, served him a peremptory order:

> Whereas by the advice of the Proprietor we are given to understand that his daughter Laetitia's land along the riverside is encroached upon or devoured quite by William Lowther's, the which the Proprietor commands shall be rectified & not touch his land as was sent over by the map [not] to be endured, the which thou art hereby ordered to rectify . . . & forasmuch as the Proprietor is given to understand between Dr. Cox's and Samuel Buckley's land, & all the land contiguous which was laid out for Charles Pickering, in whose right soever the rewards were granted was a very irregular survey & obliterated or not to be allowed of, whereupon he doth will & require thee forthwith to survey . . . the sd Samuel Buckley's & Charles Pickering's land together with the aforesd 1800 unto the Proprietor's manor of Perkeoma of all which premises thou art hereby required to make a speedy execution & return the same to the Secretary's office.[37]

---

[37] Pennsylvania Land Records, *OR*, Book D-86, 234.

Thomas Holme duly expunged the name of Charles Pickering from the map, leaving his entire estate apparently annexed to the Proprietary's Manor of Gilberts across the river. Samuel Buckley's survey remains on the second map exactly as it was on the first, as do the surveys of William Lowther's Manor of Billton, Laetitia Penn's Manor of Mount-Joy, and the smaller estate of William Penn Junior. If William Lowther's Manor of Billton encroached on Laetitia Penn's manor, it was noted on William Penn's personal sketch in London, but not on Thomas's working map.

On 1 July Thomas Holme tried yet again to collect field maps and fees from Charles Ashcom, this time through his attorneys, since the deputy had departed. The attempt was no more fruitful than the earlier ones. Like them, it was continued to a later session.

With the bounds of the last Indian purchase provided for, Thomas Holme felt that the time had come when he could go no further without a conference with the governor and an on-the-spot revision of the map according to his orders. Furthermore, personal problems demanded his attention. To the surprise of his colleagues he embarked for England on 26 July 1688.

With him Thomas Holme brought a long letter from William Markham reporting on the state of affairs in the province.[38] Reading it, one can well believe that Thomas Holme was glad to set out across the Atlantic, even on a not exactly easy mission.

Benjamin Chambers still insisted that, having bought the front lot before his bank proportionable to twenty-five hundred acres, he should have title to the bank as well. The Quaker council would not prosecute him. Thomas was bringing some paper that would "much forward him [Markham]," presumably in Penn's understanding. He had done what he could about strays, but Penn's own attorney was against him. There was talk about moving the government to England. Markham seemed to favor the idea, but others were against it. They had a meeting on 20 July to discuss some business before Thomas Holme was to leave. Thomas Fairman moved for his brother's return of the six hundred or seven hundred acres on Neshaminy Creek that Thomas had marked on the map to be in dispute between Fairman and Growden, but Thomas Holme left it with his confreres to judge, and they decided that because of the controversy it should be left to the governor to decide. They will learn the decision "when the map comes," and do what they think best. The governor's directions

---

[38] Markham to WP, 26 July 1688, Retained copy. Cliveden MSS, Chew Family Papers, HSP. *PWP* 3: 195–203 (Micro. 6: 051).

concerning the map seem to have been a major reason for Thomas Holme's voyage.

With Markham's letter and his own planned presentation mutually supporting one another, Thomas Holme took the letter, sealed on 26 July 1688, and set off for England. He would never again be quite an integral part of the province.

Fig. 23. Pickering holdings near Penn's Manor of Gilberts.

Chapter 16

The Wayfarer

When or where Thomas Holme disembarked is not recorded. It is tempting to assume that the voyage was swift enough to bring him to Limerick in time to testify about the rights of the Duke of York, now King James II, in that city, at the end of August or early September.[1] The name Thomas Holme appears on the list of testators, and anything that might forward the cause of the besieged monarch would have been a favor to William Penn; but it is more likely that the Thomas Holme in question belonged to the Yorkshire family who were in the service of the Hattons.[2] The same is true of the Christopher Holme who was titulado in Limerick in 1659 and who died on 10 December 1688. The Christopher who was most probably Thomas Holme's brother remained in Lancashire and was one of two Christopher Holmes buried at Hawkshead, in 1667 and 1681.[3]

Certainly Thomas Holme had ample incentives to see the Proprietor as soon as possible. He arrived not yet knowing that William Penn had appointed John Blackwell as governor of Pennsylvania, and that the English had invited William of Orange, husband of the king's daughter Mary, to come and save them from a monarch who had encroached upon their civil rights by declaring liberty of conscience to members of all religions, even including papists.

Thomas Holme hastened to establish himself at Nathaniel Millnor's

---

[1] PRO, CSPD, vol. 8, part 4, 1688, p. 2032.
[2] Census of Ireland, 1659: 263; Limerick Wills, B-1A, 59, 3.
[3] *PRH*.

in Smithy Lane and arrange an appointment with William Penn.[4] The Proprietor was equally eager for the opportunity to revise the map, receive Markham's letter and other papers that the secretary and Thomas Holme thought he should see, and to discuss the complexities of the situation in the province. The meeting must have been successful, for as early as 14 October William Penn issued a new commission

> to my trusty and well-beloved Friend Thomas Holme, Philadelphia . . . know thou and all persons concerned that I hereby authorize, constitute, and establish thee in the office, trust, and employment of Surveyor General for the Province of Pennsylvania & annexed counties of New Castle, Kent & Sussex, & the is [islands] & tes [territories] thereunto belonging, for and during thy natural life. . . .[5]

No other papers of the fall of 1688 relating to Thomas Holme's stay in London are extant. He had been ordered by Andrew Robeson to pay their mutual friend in Bristol, Charles Jones, Jr., £50 "for effect is lying in my hands being I can get no returnes that I dare trust expecially to pay out . . . ready money upon uncertainish bills." He adds the obvious comment, "This is a ticklish Country in reference to these matters." Evidently Thomas Holme did not have an extra £50 (estimated by a modern historian at the equivalent of $5,000 in modern American purchasing power) with which to oblige Andrew, or was, perhaps cautiously, unwilling to do so. In August of 1700 Jones wrote to James Logan that

> in August 1688 hee [Andrew Robeson] sent me a long letter copy thereof comes inclosed in said letter advisee had ordered old Thoms Holmes to pay £50 but hee poore man neither did nor could spare any mony Besides that letter had never but 2 letters more from said Robeson.[6]

On 13 and 14 November Thomas Holme wrote two separate letters to John Tottenham, his steward in Ireland. The letters are not extant, but Tottenham's reply, written two weeks later, gives an idea of their contents as well as particulars of Thomas Holme's concerns in Ireland. Thomas's letter had brought the first news from England that the area had had for five weeks. The report that William of Orange had landed at Torbay was unsettling. Many still living in Ireland remembered the

---

[4] ALS. John Tottenham to Thomas Holme, 2 December 1688. HSP, Miscellaneous Papers, Am. 3841.
[5] ACM 30, no. 53, from Harrisburg, Dept. of Survey MSS, 322.
[6] HSP, Misc. Papers Am. 2532, p. 23, 2.

horror of the conquest of 1649–1651 and the disturbances that had continued, and they were apprehensive of another war.

Tottenham reports on the state of Thomas Holme's affairs. Although, like most of the Cromwellians, he had lost much at the Restoration and had sold part of the land that he was able to keep, notably that at Taghmon and the small tract sold to Tottenham himself, he still had enough to provide a convenient income. Tottenham had ordered Michael Smith to forward Thomas Holme a bill for £20, and Michael says that he had ordered Nathaniel Millinor to pay it. He has also sent to R. Butler for cash or a bill for Thomas Holme, but no one is willing to part with cash now. He wants to draw up Thomas Holme's accounts and join him shortly, but would prefer to have him in Ireland as his guest so that they can discuss various business matters about which it would take too long to write.

Finally Tottenham comes to what is plainly a painful matter to treat: "I find thy Brother a great plague to thee and I can truly say as I never aided, assisted, or advised him to go to thee," but would, if he had known it, have tried to prevent him. The reference, it would seem, is to Michael's appearance in Philadelphia. Tottenham has had some unpleasant experiences with him on the occasion of several visits. The brother's wife and children are well, and Tottenham has given her what Thomas Holme ordered him and more. She really needed it, "but he knew not of it, for if he had she tould me as she was afraid he would kill her." Tottenham had given the brother some money, and when he refused to give him cash he "gave me bad words." Tottenham has written to Col. Richard [Clifton?] about it, telling him as well as he could about the situation. If he could get the money from him he would send Thomas Holme his bond, but he thinks his brother never had any intention of paying his debts. He will give Thomas Holme a further account in his next letter. He concludes, "I can truly say I have a great desire to see thee as any, for I am faithfully thy cordial friend, John Tottenham."

So we have here an almost certain explanation of Michael's appearance at the demise of Joseph Moss, of Thomas Holme's desperate need of money, of the identity of the mysterious evil sibling Tottenham describes, and the reappearance of the brother who had long before sought an order on his brother on his behalf from the lord lieutenant of Ireland. It is possible that the second English household on Thomas Holme's land at Bregurteen was that of Michael's wife and children. What, if anything, Thomas was able to do about Michael is not currently of record, but the State Papers offer a possible clue. On record for 23 July 1690 is a treasury order to the customs commissioner to observe an order of the queen and council dated 21 July 1690, for ships to proceed when their complement of men is complete, regardless of embargo. One of the ships is the *Eastland Merchant*, fifteen men, Michael Holmes master.[7]

How much longer Thomas Holme remained in London we do not know, but he must have left not later than mid-February, when the crown was offered to William and Mary, and more probably some time in January, for Markham and the other commissioners gave him a warrant for survey on 3 April. He cannot then have been in England as late as 27 February 1688/89, when a warrant was issued against William Penn on suspicion of high treason.[8] Having been solicitous for his brother's family in Ireland and having property concerns about which Tottenham wished to consult him he must certainly have visited Wexford before returning to Pennsylvania. Certainly, too, he must have answered Penn's questions and made note of his directions and perhaps of information that might not be prudently entrusted to writing.

On 10 December the queen and the young prince were sent to France, and William Penn, because of his known long association with King James, was arrested on suspicion, but was able to post bail and avoid prison. On the next day James fled and riots broke out in London. James was brought back to the city on 17 December and retired to Rochester. William of Orange entered London on 19 December, and James escaped to France three days later. On 13 February Parliament offered the crown to William and Mary. Although the coronation would not occur until 11 April, Penn's situation was perilous, and the conflict of old loyalties, disappointment and anxiety over the state of the province, lack of money, and a deep feeling of responsibility for the Friends who looked to him for leadership placed him under a heavy burden that was not alleviated by the complaints that flowed in from Pennsylvania.

Sometime during this turbulent winter Thomas Holme went back to Philadelphia, to accumulating warrants for survey and to growing rivalries and complaints. He brought with him the second version of the map and a new commission as surveyor general of the entire province, with added responsibilities and governmental safeguards for his procedures and rights.

Government in Pennsylvania during his absence had been chaotic. By the end of the winter session of 1687/88 William Penn had finally,

---

[7] Census of Ireland, 1659.
[8] *CSPD*, 1689: 163.

much against his wishes, accepted Thomas Lloyd's resignation as president of the council. On 9 February, with Lloyd presiding for the last time, the council heard "The Governor's Commission under the broad Seal unto Thomas Lloyd, Robert Turner, Arthur Cook, John Symcock & John Eckley, Impowring them, or any 3 of them, to be his Deputy or Lieutenant." This awkward device of a five-part deputy governor did not work out. The council's substitute of a chosen three, was maintained until Penn's new appointee, Captain John Blackwell, took the chair as governor on 18 December 1688. The total business of the day was the reading of two orders, one dated 20 January 1687/88, "For the more Effectual Reducing & Suppressing of pirates and Privateers in America," and the other, dated 12 June, for the celebration of the birth of a prince.

Blackwell had at once attempted to systematize political and economic procedures in the province, but from the beginning official Pennsylvania was against him. Thomas Holme had once advised Penn to appoint a governor whose function would be separate from that of the Proprietor. In theory the proposal had seemed promising. The governor would thus be present, in a position to know all sides of matters relating to his office without relying for information on letters impeded by long delays in transportation. The Proprietor would still be landlord and the final court of appeals. The experiment had been an unhappy one from the first. No doubt the ship that took Thomas Holme to England carried complaints about the five-man government to William Penn. Now Thomas came home from abroad just in time to witness the second experiment's debacle.

A former Cromwellian officer, Blackwell had retained his old stance of dominance and, under threat of war, he was not in sympathy with the pacifism of the Quakers. Penn was bombarded with mutual complaints from the council and the governor. The people's dislike of Blackwell at least had the merit of being one point of general agreement. Finally, on 11 April 1689, Penn appointed Thomas Lloyd as lieutenant governor.[9]

Thomas Holme's feelings were ambivalent. He could not but be frustrated at not being in a position to offer advice and to participate in decisions. At the same time he was relieved at having nothing to do with the conflicts of goverment. The duties and responsibilites stipulated in his new commission, with specific instructions in an undated document that appears to have accompanied or followed shortly upon the new commission, included what amounted to the establish-

---

[9] AD. Commission to TL as Lt. Governor. HSP (Micro. 6: 293–294).

ment of one large portion of the archives of the province, in addition to the on-going duties of his office. The annexed counties of New Castle, Sussex, and Kent were named in the new commission. Omissions by previous surveyors were ordered to be made good. After reiteration of the terms of the original commission, the Proprietor decrees the formal institution of a public record office:

> Thou shalt order and direct to the end that any warrants under me or authorized under me for the setting out and serveying of any lots of land and the execution of the same will for time past as well as time to come may be brought in, left, and lodged in thy office, as well for the equal safety and benefit of those who are concerned in the said counties as those in said province . . . and further to answer the purpose and needs of so public an office as to have all the concerns of that nature reduced into a narrow compass, as belonging to the property of one people and proprietor, that there may be but one public record office in the place aforesaid, in testimony whereof, and of the power given and granted to thee, and thy office, I have caused these my letters to be made patent, witness myself, under the great seal, this 14 day of the month called October, in the fourth year of the reign of King James the Second, and the ninth year of my government, and the year of our Lord one thousand six hundred eighty-eight. William Penn.
> Thomas Lloyd: affix the Great Seal hereunto. William Penn.[10]

As was to be expected now that the caves were finally disposed of, warrants came in for bank lots, chiefly from merchants who planned to build wharves and storage facilities. There were a dozen warrants for bank lots from January to April of 1689, and nine or ten more in the course of the year, two of them for Robert Turner and Samuel Carpenter. A few more than a dozen city lots were warranted, a few liberty land tracts, and in the neighborhood of twenty other parcels of land. The greater number of the surveys were warranted for the first half of the year, when purchasers were eager to commence clearing land, building, and establishing or expanding businesses. These were routine requirements carried out for the most part without problems. The Proprietor was still much concerned about freed indentured servants. On 14 April he wrote to the commissioners of propriety:

> I am much troubled there is no entertaynm^t for servants out of their time, as ought to be; by which means they are forced to Jersey & elsewhere. We have lost some hundreds of inhabitants by those insufferable tracts of land

---

[10] Dept. Sur., 8: 322. Patent Book A, 1321–1322 (Micro. 6: 111).

that are un-seated which drive new comers so uncomfortably back, that they declyne the Province for it. Do, I pray, what you can herein, till a tract can be set apart for servants out of their time, that may be called Freman-town, or Freetown.[11]

William Penn's own large tracts of desirable land still remained vacant.

Actually, since indentured servants had not arrived simultaneously their terms of service did not expire simultaneously, and they did not necessarily wish to be seated in a single area set apart for those who had come as servants. Accommodations for one group who did wish such a tract were arranged by resurveying the Jasper Farmer land and granting the overplus to the freemen.[12] Only a dozen or so tracts small enough to be the customary allotment for such servants are included in the select list of surveys in the printed archives. Thomas Holme does seem to have made provision on his own land for at least two. Edmund McVeagh had settled on his fifty acres with an additional purchase of fifty acres in the township of Hilltown, a small settlement within Thomas Holme's Well Spring Plantation. John Hill, a previous purchaser who may not have been indentured, was his neighbor.[13] John Fletcher and John Osborne had not yet served out their indentures to Thomas Holme.

More complicated were the instructions designed in great part to make way for expected settlers in the long-awaited Susquehanna project. The governor instructed Thomas:

> In laying out the front lots between the Penny Pot-House so-called and the bridge at the north end of the town on Delaware, in my new commission now sent to be distributed among the purchasers, that had their front lots at Schulkyl, be very careful to pleasure such as builded and improved and taken up their lots there.

If owners of High Street lots would exchange them for lots on Second or Third Street or the backs of Front Street lots, and owners of front

---

[11] Copy by John Blackwell. HSP, Penn Papers, Governor Blackwell's MSS (Micro. 6: 299). *PWP* 3: 240.

[12] *PA* 2, 19, MBP: 125.

[13] On 16 March Thomas had sold McVeagh a hundred acres, 6.5, and John Hill the same amount of land for 12.10 and on 26 July, the eve of his departure for England, he gave a letter of attorney to Robert Longshore authorizing him to verify his sales of these and like quantities to Phillip and Richard Hill and to Isaac Page, all of Hilltown, and to Robert Prismall in Dublin Township (PhA, Philadelphia Deed Book, Grantors, E-2: fol. 56, 58, and 60). This last document was recorded on 2 November 1688. Having purchased the quitrent of his original five thousand acres from William Penn, Thomas Holme was now able to require the regular payment to himself, thus affording him a convenient annual addition to his income.

lots on the Schuylkill would exchange or disclaim their waste lots for waste lots on Delaware, Penn wrote,

> It may open a way for me to pleasure the Susquehanna Company, who may, perhaps, find it requisite to take up small lots at Schulkyll, to build and live upon, either for a certain time till they have settled in Susquehanna, or longer, which will not only be convenient to them, but also profitable for me. Rather than fail, if thou canst not get a pretty deal of the lots of Schulkyl, . . . then buy the lots of them if a small matter of money will do.[14]

Thomas Holme had been interested in the Susquehanna from the first sight of the broad, bright river flowing through land that at this point was level or gently rolling and relatively clear. He had engineered the purchase from the Indians and defined the bounds that would make a settlement possible. He looked with suspicion on the dealings of the governor of New York with the Iroquois, and he was convinced that a settlement in the valley embraced in the treaty with the Indians would be advantageous for William Penn and his province with regard to both agriculture and the fur trade. He was able to arrange some of the transfers of property that Penn requested.[15]

By winter Thomas Holme had decided to augment his own Front Steet lots with the adjacent bank lots. He authorized his attorneys, Patrick Robinson and Robert Longshore, to purchase for him the banks before the twenty-foot Front Street lot he had bought of Richard Corsley and the 102-foot Front and Mulberry lot whereon he had built his house when he acquired it as First Purchaser at the first apportionment of lots. They had duly obtained warrants for the lots of 19 and 27 January 1689/90. The deed to the lot attached to the 102 foot lot reveals ambitious designs. It was to join on each side of Delaware Front Street and run out into the river, to the extent of 250 feet, bound on the north with a vacant lot, south to Mulberry Street, west to Delaware Front Street, in order to erect a wharf. The lot had been laid out two days before the warrant was issued. Thomas Holme was to pay for fifty-one years from date every First-Day of First Month two English silver shillings. At the end of that time the yearly value would be assessed by appointed persons and a third of that value would be paid annually forever by the heirs of Thomas Holme to persons appointed for that purpose.

---

[14] ACM, Add., vol. 148, no. 20, Div., PR. MSS in vault, DAM, PHMC. Endorsed, "Proprietor's instructions to the foremost commissioners," but addressed only to Thomas Holme: "Instructions to Thomas Holme, Surveyor and Chief Agent."
[15] ACM 30, no. 53, citing PA MSS of Dept. Sur., DAM, PHMC: 322.

These quays or wharves would be lawful quays or wharves forever for landings and shipping all goods and merchandise giving contract for reasonable satisfaction for their use. Thomas Holme was to leave a cartway thirty feet along the bank, and if he had cellar stairs to any house on this lot he was to make them on his own ground and not let them encroach on the cartway. Moreover, he was to lay out his proportion and part so that in the center between Mulberry and Sassafras Streets a public thoroughfare ten feet wide could be made down from the east side of Delaware Front Street. Contingencies were provided for. If the buildings etc. were destroyed by inundation, a proportionate amount of rent would be rebated.[16] It would be an expensive development, perhaps for some time more remunerative to the town than to the developer; but it would have value as a speculative investment and as a pattern for future developments.

The year 1690 witnessed a burst of real estate activity in Philadelphia, not only in the purchase of lots by newcomers to the town, but in the trade of bank lots for lots farther into the interior and for additional lots by already established citizens. The latter sought not only lots but even entire squares to be planted for orchards or cleared for pasture. Precautions were to be used in the development of bank property. There was to be a thirty-foot street "clear of all porches, celler Stayres, payles, &c, to be a Common Publick Street forever." There must be a pair of accessible stairs between streets at or near the center, beginning at the east side of the sixty-foot street and extending through the thirty-foot street and down to at least the low-water mark of the Delaware. As far as any building was done, the central stairs should be built and kept in repair by the "Bankers" dwelling between the two streets, and there must be at least ten feet between each two streets, for public central stairs. Old patents for the bank were to be brought in and a rough draft made for the perusal of the commissioners. No one ought to build or lay the foundation of any house to be built on the bank without the direction of the surveyor general or one of the commissioners.[17] The prescriptions might well serve any further waterfront properties to use and protect the banks.

As early as February a half dozen Delaware bank lots were warranted for Schuylkill residents Christopher Pennock, Milissent Hodgkins, William Baldwin, Thomas Ducket, William Sotheby, and Mary

---

[16] Deed Book 1: 237, Index of Deeds, Book 1: 442, nos. 1051 and 1053, Office of the Recorder of Deeds, Philadelphia.
[17] MBP, *PA* 19: 30.

Sibthorp between Sassafras and Vine Streets; and Charles Pickering, seeking adjustment of some confusion of bank bounds, was given a thirty-foot lot among the Schuylkill Friends. On 7 June John James agreed to exchange his order for the laying out of a bank lot fronting the Proprietor's land for a lot on Mulberry Street, to be used as an orchard. Dennis Rockford asked for a ten-foot addition to his twenty-foot lot because "the 20-foot lot was laid out where there was a great breach made." His request was granted.

It appears that the early records were not impeccable. Henry Lakin, who had lived for some time on a lot laid out to purchaser Charles Lee, with an adjoining vacant lot, asked to rent the lot. Thomas Holme's deputy reported that those lots had been laid out first to Lee, but that afterwards the Proprietor had ordered that each should be divided because they were too large; so the resulting vacant lot was granted to Rockford. William Carter secured a grant of an entire square (fifteen lots) of Philadelphia for a horse pasture for twenty-one years, "he to clear it & sow grass & at end of 21 years leave it as it is & pay 10/ in good merchandable wheat as it shall be sold for silver in Philadelphia, the first year excepted. . . ." James West bought the Penny Pot House and requested the forty feet of bank adjoining the sixty feet already in his possession "for a conveniency to build ships & vessels." William Salway asked a grant of part of a cripple or swamp before his own land at or near Tawakawny (Tacony) for setting up a fulling mill. All of these requests were granted, with many others. Thomas Holme's deputy, Robert Longshore, made the necessary scrutiny of possible previous titles and specifying of bounds, in consultation with his nearly blind superior.

In the midst of this activity Thomas Holme again tried to settle his score with his recalcitrant erstwhile deputy surveyor of Chester County. Ashcom had departed for England, but attorneys in Chester were authorized to look after his business affairs. Thomas Holme brought action against him in the Chester County Court on 3 June by his attorneys Charles Pickering and Patrick Robinson, with John White and Caleb Pusey attorneys for Charles Ashcom, defendant. The plaintiff declared for 205.10.5, and acknowleged the receipt of £40 thereof. The defendant denied any indebtedness. Thomas Holme was shocked when a receipt "for £4 English mony Borrowed of Charles Ashcom under the hand of tryall holmes sonn to the s^d Tho: holmes" was read. The trial continued with the reading of an order from Governor Penn to resurvey the land of the old inhabitants of the Chester side of the Schuylkill and make returns to the secretary's office. The jury, all, of course, Chester County beneficiaries of Ashcom's methods, unanimously declared for him, the costs and 10s. damage to be borne by the plaintiff.

Thomas Holme at once appealed the judgment. When the trial proceeded on 3 September the defendant by his attorneys withdrew. Finally Caleb Pusey "Past a deed to Robert Longshore Attorney for Thomas Holme ffor Two hundred and Eighty Acres of Land with All its Appurtenants thereunto belonging Lying in the Township of Rydlye Bearing Date the 20th of April 1693."[18] The tract appears as part of a tract of 330 acres surveyed to Charles Ashcom 10 December 1684, with 280 acres to Thomas Holme, 20 April 1693, which he sold to John Cook on 25 March 1694 for £115.[19]

By September 1690, Thomas Holme was ready to retire. Almost blind, old by the usual life-span of his time, he had struggled with the complexities of the making of a province and had contributed all that he was able to give. The map had sorely taxed eyes and hands. He had been forced to delegate many business transactions to his attorneys, dictating his wishes to them but unable to see well enough to manage documents. Silas and Hester Crispin were doing well, with a houseful of five children. The eldest, William, was not as hardy as the little daughters, but his parents were optimistic for him. His daughter Elinor was well provided for and would remain at Well Spring. No doubt she would remarry. He was no longer needed in Pennsylvania. He would return to England.

On 13 October he gave letters of attorney to four friends, Silas Crispin, Robert Longshore, Jonas Wilkinson, and Patrick Robinson. He was not ready to go on the *Philadelphia Merchant* when she sailed in late September, but a less prestigious ship, the *Riggin*, of which his niece Susanna's husband, John James, was master, was waiting to be declared seaworthy for her return voyage to England. Politics and economics were perhaps as much responsible for the delay as concern about her condition. There seems to have been a problem about her official clearance at New Castle.[20] At any rate, she did depart, and probably with Thomas Holme aboard. More urgent concerns seem to have eliminated her problem, since it is not mentioned again in the *Minutes of the Provincial Council*. She probably sailed direct to England with her cargo of tobacco. If so, Thomas Holme may have arrived about the time of William Penn's release from prison by order of the Court of the King's Bench.[21] We have no account of their meeting,

---

[18] *Records of Chester County Court of Common Pleas*, 215–217; 317.
[19] *PA* 2, 19: 297. Smith, *Atlas of Delaware County*, 14, Map 6.
[20] *MPC*, 1: 303.
[21] ALS, WP to RT, 29 November 1690. APS, 1: 35, item 70.

but we may be sure that it took place. The governor could communicate orally more of his situation during this Glorious Revolution than he could prudently put in writing, and Thomas, whose letters were not likely to be intercepted as were Penn's, could convey messages to the province. Thomas Holme could also provide details of conditions in Pennsylvania.

Thomas Holme's affairs in Ireland demanded attention as well. His papers have not been found, but we know that the situation was serious. There is no further mention of Michael Holme, but the care of his family must have devolved upon his brother. There may also have been errands for William Penn concerning his property there.[22]

Back in England, Thomas Holme must have paid at least one visit to his daughter Sarah Holcomb, although there is no note concerning her or her family bearing on his visit.[23] If he had any employment in London there is no record of it. He may have been of assistance to Penn as messenger and intermediary with the province, largely because Penn was under surveillance by the new government and Thomas Holme could move about freely. He may have continued his Quaker ministry, although it seems to have declined or been discontinued before he left Philadelphia. The publication of the Susquehanna pamphlet in the fall must have given him satisfaction, but we do not know that he had a part in it beyond supplying the diagram of the Indian purchase that made the project possible. On 13 January 1690/91 George Fox died. William Penn delivered a moving homily at his funeral,[24] and Thomas Holme must surely have been present and must have recalled escorting him across the Irish Sea after his visit to the Irish Friends.

William Penn must have shared with Thomas Holme the news from Pennsylvania, bad though it usually was. Markham seemed to be crumbling under the pain and crippling effect of advanced arthritis, hard work, frustration, and lack of encouragement or appreciation. A letter from the provincial council to William Penn dated 11 April 1691 states that Markham has become "a chief upholder of loose clubs and late hours."[25] Growden wrote another long complaint about Gray/

---

[22] In his letter "per Thomas Holme" of 4 February 1692/93, Penn refers his friends to Thomas Holme for witness to the wastage of his Irish estate, which suggests that Thomas Holme may have been an emissary of Penn with regard to Macroom and Shangarry, as well as an anxious landholder on his own behalf. (ALS, Dreer, Letters and Papers of William Penn, HSP [Micro. 6: 725]).

[23] The fact that Thomas Holme was remembered by Sarah's family is evidenced in a not very pleasant way in the application of his grandson, Richard Holcomb, for a share in Thomas's estate.

[24] HSP (Micro. 6: 534).

[25] LS. HSP, Penn Papers, Autograph Petitions, 1681–1764 (Micro. 6: 564). *PWP* 3: 302–305.

Tatum's incursions on his land, which Penn tried to justify. The Welsh also wrote, seeking warrants beyond the original tract because of Ashcom's encroachments on it, but were refused, the surveyor general *pro tem* saying that no land could be surveyed for them beyond the original bound until all the land within was taken up. The commissioners refused to confirm their bounds, and they lacked room for newcomers.[26]

Thomas Holme must have been both glad to be away from these harassments and uneasy about having left them. Penn, it appears, thought that he might still be of some service in the troubled province. Finally, early in 1692/93, Thomas Holme gave up and went back to Philadelphia. He had lost his property in Ireland through political and personal misfortunes. His attorneys had sold property for him in Pennsylvania, but if they sent him money no receipt for it has been found. He did not even have enough to pay his passage back to America and had to accept a gift of £5.[27]

On 4 February 1692/93 William Penn gave Thomas Holme a letter to Robert Turner which was not received until 1 September.[28] In it the Proprietor asked that one hundred of the most affluent persons in the province each lend him, interest free, £100 for four years. Thomas Holme would explain his need if requested. Those approached were outraged. Ten thousand pounds was a very large sum of money, approximately $1,000,000 in terms of today's value. Not many could afford to contribute £100, and if they could they were unwilling to part with it.[29] It is doubtful that any of them knew that Penn had during times of need mortgaged the province to Philip Ford, parcel by parcel, and was desperate for money to redeem it. Relatively speaking, the Proprietor was as poor as his messenger. Thomas Holme could only put the letter in the hand of the addressee and witness its failure.

Warrants for surveys came in steadily, but in smaller numbers than before and for smaller tracts. The proceeds from land sold for him by his attorneys helped financially, as did a few additional appointments. He was executor of Samuel Moon's will.[30] Penn appointed him to the board of commissioners of propriety.[31] He received a legacy of £5.[32] He kept his house and office in Philadelphia, spending at least some of his time at Well Spring. Elinor took care of household matters.

---

[26] ALS. HSP, Penn Papers, Autograph Petitions, 1681- 1764 (Micro. 6: 590).
[27] ACM.
[28] MHL, September 1694.
[29] ALS. Dreer, Letters and Papers of William Penn. HSP (Micro. 6: 725).
[30] *PA* 2, 19: 421–422. 14 November 1694.
[31] 21 June 1694. ACM 88 (1691–1699).
[32] Will of Thomas Hooten of Philadelphia, 5 November 1693.

When Thomas Lloyd died in September Robert Turner suggested to William Penn that Thomas Holme would be a good choice to replace him, and pointed out that Thomas's income was limited by the many duties that the Proprietor had asked him to perform, so that the surveying was not regularly remunerative.[33] Thomas Holme attended the meetings of the commissioners of propriety, but his contributions were limited for the most part to the contents of a phenomenal memory. This was particularly true after the death in the fall of 1694 of Robert Longshore, a valued deputy and one of the friends he had appointed as attorney to conduct his business when he departed for England.

During the winter Thomas Holme took stock of his possessions. He lived simply, but comfortably; and there was enough money, or enough valuable real estate to be converted into sufficient funds, for legacies for his daughters and their children, and for token gifts to friends. On 10 February 1694/5, "aged full seventy years, considering the certainty of death but the uncertainty of the time when," he judged it now expedient "to set things in order" and dispose of his "small estate." He carefully estimated the value of his still considerable real estate, empowering his executor to sell certain tracts as might be necessary to fulfill monetary bequests and pay just debts, and divided household effects between his daughters Elinor and Hester. The fact that the document was witnessed by Edmund McVeagh, and Samuel Jones and George Eaton, apparently husbandmen at the plantation, indicates that it was written at Well Spring.

Thomas Holme lived long enough to enjoy the coming of another Pennsylvania spring, and died during the first week of April. He was buried in the small cemetery that he had had enclosed on a hilltop of Well Spring Plantation. In keeping with his Quaker preferences, no monument was erected; but a boulder was placed above his grave, so that it was remembered until, nearly two centuries later, the stone was replaced by a small granite obelisk.

---

[33] Retained copy. Stauffer Papers, Governors Papers, HSP (Micro. 6: 911).

Epilogue

There is a certain poignancy about the end. Thomas Holme was nearly blind and, for a man of his generation, very old. News of his death had not reached William Penn when on 20 June he wrote to Thomas Holme and Robert Turner. No letter to or from William Penn concerning Thomas Holme's death has been found.

It is remarked by writers about Thomas Holme that he died indebted to Thomas Fairman. This is a moot point. Thomas Fairman accepted warrants for land and surveyed tracts without the prescribed orders from the surveyor general, and when he did act upon orders frequently pocketed all of the fees, of which one-third were due to Thomas Holme. Each considered the other a debtor.

William Penn bitterly accused Thomas Holme posthumously of having cheated him, but no evidence of such action has been found. It is possible that from the first Penn expected Thomas Holme to confiscate and return to him the land that was taken up but not seated within the required three years. Whether this should have been done by the surveyor general or the commissioners of land is debatable. Another possibility is that Penn expected all overplus land discovered by resurveys to be conveyed to himself, as he stipulated late in Thomas Holme's career, whereas it seems to have been sold, at least in some cases, by the owner of the land in which it was found. Thomas Holme ordered no resurveys without the Proprietor's orders after the directive was given.

Thomas Holme's will was proved on 8 April 1695. His legacies were modest. The sale of real estate would be sufficient to pay any debts. His son-in-law and executor Silas Crispin did not sell Tryall Holme's five hundred acres, which had been surveyed but not seated, for more than thirty years.

When more than a century and a half after his death Thomas Holme's bequest of land for a school was honored, a small monument was erected over his grave. One of his descendants, M. Jackson Crispin, in his history of the Crispin Cemetery[1] describes the final commemoration of his ancestor.

Thomas Holme was buried in the family cemetery that he himself had had laid out beside the Susquehanna Road, which he had designed to run from the Delaware to the Susquehanna. His grave, in keeping with his Quaker principles, was marked only by a large field stone. It was decided to verify the site of his burial by deepening the excavation for the foundation of the monument. At a depth of a little over four feet was a hollow space three or four inches deep, and there lay "an almost perfect skeleton of a man at least six feet in length . . . the skull and head bones with jaws . . . perfect." The remains were reinterred "in a suitable box" in the stone foundation of the obelisk, on which was carved a memorial of the accomplishment for which posterity would most remember him, the "Portraiture" of his city.

---

[1] *PM* 16: 23–30. 1892

Works Consulted

Abbott, Wilbur Cortez. *The Writings and Speeches of Oliver Cromwell.* 4 vols. Cambridge, Mass., 1937–1947.

Ashley, Maurice. *Great Britain to 1688.* Ann Arbor: University of Michigan Press, 1961.

Balderston, Marion. "William Penn's Twenty-three Ships." *PGM* 23 (1963).

Berens, Lewis H. *The Digger Movement in the Days of the Commonwealth as Revealed in the Writings of Gerard Winstanley.* London: Holland Press and Merlin Press, 1906, 1961.

Besse, Joseph. *Collection of the Sufferings of the People Called Quakers, from . . .1660 to . . .1689.* 2 vols. Printed and Sold by Luke Hinde, at the Bible in George-Yard, Lombard Street, 1753.

Birch, Thomas, ed. *A Collection of the State Papers of John Thurloe.* 1742.

Boileau, N. B. *Book of Indian Deeds and Returns.* MSS vi. Pennsylvania Historical and Museum Commission.

Bowman, William Dodgson, and N. D. Harding. *Bristol and America: A Record of the First Settlers in the Colonies of North America, 1654–1685.* . . . London, 1928.

Brailsford, H. N. *The Levellers and the English Revolution.* Edited by Christopher Hill. London: The Cresset Press, 1961.

Braithwaite, William. *The Beginnings of Quakerism.* 2d ed. Revised by Henry J. Cadbury. Cambridge University Press, 1955.

Bristol and Gloucester Archeological Society Publications, no. 34.

Bronner, Edwin B. "The Center Square Meeting House and the Other Meetings of Early Philadelphia." *The Bulletin of the Friends' Historical Association* 44, no. 2.

—————. *William Penn's "Holy Experiment," the Founding of Pennsylvania, 1681–1701.* Temple University Press. Distributed by Columbia University Press, 1962.

Buck, Rachel. Collection. Genealogical Society of Pennsylvania. HSP.

Buck, William J. "History of Bucks County, Pennsylvania." *The Bucks County Intelligencer.* Doylestown, 1854–1855.

Budd, Thomas. *Good Order Established in Pennsylvania and New Jersey in America*. Edited by Edward Armstrong. New York, 1865.
Buranelli, Vincent. *The King and the Quaker: A Study of William Penn and James II*. University of Pennsylvania Press, 1962.
Burke, Arthur Meredith. *Key to the Ancient Parish Records of England and Wales*. N.p., n.d.
Burne, Alfred H., and Peter Young. *The Great Civil War*. London, 1959.
Butler, James, Earl of Ormonde. *Letters, MSS.*, 34 vols. National Library of Ireland, Dublin.
Cadwallader Collection. Collections of the Genealogical Society of Pennsylvania, HSP.
Calvert Papers, *Maryland Archives*, vols. 5, 17.
Campbell, Mildred. *The English Yeoman Under Elizabeth and the Early Stuarts*. Yale University Press, 1942.
Chew Family Papers. HSP.
Church, Randolph, et al. *The British Public Record Office*. Special Reports 25, 26, 27, and 28 of the Virginia Colonial Records Project. The Virginia State Library, Richmond, 1960.
Claypoole, James. *Letter Book of James Claypoole, London and Philadelphia, 1681–1684*. Edited by Marion Balderston. Huntington Library, San Marino, California, 1967.
Colonial Society of Pennsylvania. *Record of the Courts of Chester County, Pennsylvania, 1681–1697*. Philadelphia, 1910.
——————. *Records of the Court of New Castle, 1676–1681*.
——————. *Records of the Court of New Castle on Delaware*. Vol. 2, 1681–1689. 1935.
Conway, Alan. *The Welsh in America*. University of Minnesota Press, c. 1961.
Corcoran, Mary Irma. "The Family of Thomas Holme." *The Pennsylvania Genealogical Magazine* 26 (1969): 3–14.
Cowper, H. S. *Hawkshead*. N.p., n.d.
——————. *The Oldest Register of the Parish of Hawkshead in Lancashire, 1658–1704*. Edited with introductory chapters and 4 illustrations. London, Bemrose & Sons, 1897.
Cromwell, Oliver. *The Letters and Speeches of Oliver Cromwell . . . with Elucidations by Thomas Carlyle*. Edited by S. C. Lomas, intr. by C. H. Firth. London: Methuen, 1904.
Dalton, Charles. *Irish Army Lists, 1661–1685*. London, 1907.
Davies, Geoffrey. "The Parliamentary Army Under the Earl of Essex," *The English Historical Review* 49 (1934): 32–54.
Department of Survey, Order Books, 1682–1693. Pennsylvania Historical and Museum Commission. Harrisburg.
Dictionary of American Biography. Edited by Allen Johnson and Dumas Malone. New York and London, 1928–1938.
Dictionary of National Biography. Edited by Leslie Stephen and Sidney Lee. New York and London, 1885–1900.

Dunlop, Robert. *Ireland Under the Commonwealth*. Manchester Victoria University Publications, nos. 17 and 18. Being a selection of documents relating to the government of Ireland from 1651–1659. 1913.

Dunn, Mary Maples. *William Penn: Politics and Conscience*. Princeton University Press, 1967.

Dunn, Mary Maples, and Richard S. Dunn. *The World of William Penn*. Philadelphia: University of Pennsylvania Press, 1986.

Edmundson, William. Journal. 1715. BL.

Egerton MSS, 1762. BL.

Etting Papers. HSP.

Exemplification Book 1, Office of the Recorder of Deeds. Philadelphia.

Farrar. William, and J. Brownhill, eds. *Victoria History of the County of Lancaster*. London, 1914.

Firth, C. H., ed. *The Clarke Papers*. 4 vols. 1891–1901.

Firth, Charles. *Cromwell's Army*. Intr. by P. H. Hardacre. London: Methuen, 1962.

Fitzmaurice, E. G. A. *Life of Sir William Petty*. NLI.

Force, Peter. *Papers*. HSP.

Foster, Joseph. *Grantees of Arms Named in the Doquets & Patents to the End of the Seventeenth Century*. Edited by W. Harry Rylands. London: 1915.

Fox, George. *The Journal of George Fox*. Edited by Norman Penny, Intr. by T. Edmund Harvey. New York: Octagon Books, 1973.

Force, Peter. Papers, HSP.

France, Reginald Sharpe. *Guide to the Lancashire Record Office*. Library of the County of Lancaster, Preston, England.

Garrison, Hazel Sheeld. "Cartography of Pennsylvania Before 1800." *PMHB* 59 (1935): 255–283.

Garvan, Anthony M. B. *The Historian and the City*. Edited by Oscar Handlin and John Burchard. Cambridge, Mass., 1963.

Gilbert, John T. *A Contemporary History of Affairs in Ireland, 1641–1652*. For the Irish Archeological once Celtic Society: Dublin, 1875.

Gloucestershire Records, Established and Civil. Tewkesbury Abbey. Vols. 1, 2, and 6. Shire Hall, Gloucester, England.

Goodbody, Olive C. *Guide to the Irish Quaker Records, 1654-1860*. Dublin: Stationery Office, 1967.

Gough, John. *A History of the People Called Quakers. From Their First Rise to the Present Time*. 4 vols. Dublin, 1789.

Gratz MSS. HSP.

Great Britain. *Calendar of State Papers, Colonial, America and West Indies, 1574–1660; Calendar of State Papers, Domestic, 1603–1704, 1649–1650, 1656–1657; Addenda, 1660-1685*. London, PRO.

Habington, Thomas. "Statutes for Hawkshead Grammar School." *Antiquities of the Cathedral Church of Worcester .†. .* London, 1717–1723.

Hazard, Samuel. *Annals of Pennsylvania from the Discovery of the Delaware, 1609–1682*. Philadelphia, 1850.

Hazard, Willis P. *Annals of Philadelphia and Pennsylvania in the Olden Time*. . . . Philadelphia, 1879.

Hoag, John S. *Fundamentals of Land Measurement*. Chicago Title Insurance Company. Chicago, 1971.

Holme, Thomas, and Abraham Fuller. *A brief relation of some part of the Sufferings of the True Christians, the People of God (in Scorn called Quakers) in Ireland for the last Eleaven Years, viz from 1660, until 1671*.

―――――. *A Compendious View of some extraordinary Sufferings of the people called Quakers . . .†in the Kingdom of Ireland, from the year 1655 to the End of the Reign of King George the First . . .†in three parts*. 1731. (Part 1 is a reprint of the above volume.)

Hore MSS. Wexfordiana. St. Peter's College, Wexford, Ireland.

Hough Papers. HSP.

Howard, Luke. Collection, Library of the Society of Friends. London.

Howell-Harnstead Collection. Historical and Museum Commission. Harrisburg.

Indexes of Deeds and Surveys, Pennsylvania, 1682–1759. Department of Records, City Archives. Philadelphia.

Inrollment of the Decrees of Innocents: Restorees, Charles II. Inquisitionum in Officio Rotulorum cancellariae Hiberniae asservatarum Reportorium 1 (1826) 10, Car. 2, Wexford, 15 January, thirtieth year (1678). Manuscript copies, PRO, Dublin.

Irish Manuscripts Commission. Robert C. Simington, ed. *The Civil Survey, 1654–1656*. Vol. 4, *County of Limerick*, 1938; Vol. 9, *County of Wexford*, 1953. Dublin: The Stationery Office.

Jerusalem Bible, Reader's Edition. Edited by Alexander Jones. Garden City: 1968.

Journal of the Royal Irish Society of Antiquaries, Papers and Proceedings 36, part 2. 1906.

Lansdowne MSS. BL.

Latimer, John. *The Annals of Bristol in the Seventeenth Century*. Bristol, 1900.

Levy, Barry John. "'Tender Plants': Quaker Farmers and Children in the Delaware Valley, 1681–1735." *Journal of Family History* 3 (1978).

Lewis, Samuel. *Topographical Dictionary of England*. 7th ed. 1849. Vol. 1.

Leybourn, William. *The Compleat Surveyor: Containing the whole Art of Surveying Land* . . . London, Printed by E. Flesher for George Sawbridge at the Sign of the Bible upon Ludgate-hill. 1674.

Lingelbach, William E. "William Penn and City Planning." *PMHB* 68 (1944).

London Port Books. London, PRO.

Ludlow, Edmund. *Memoirs*. Edited by C. H. Firth. Oxford, 1894.

Map Collection, Group A. Pennsylvania Historical and Museum Commission. Harrisburg.

Mercurius Politicus.

Minute book: Common Pleas and Quarter Sessions Court of Bucks County, 1684–1730. Bucks County Archives.

Minutes of the Provincial Council of Pennsylvania. . . . Edited by Samuel Hazard. Vol. 1. Harrisburg, 1838.

Miscellaneous Papers of Philadelphia County, 1671–1738. HSP.

Myers, Albert Cook. Collection of Penn Papers. CCHS.

——————. *Narratives of Early Pennsylvania, West New Jersey, and Delaware, 1630–1707.* New York, 1912.

——————. *Quaker Arrivals at Philadelphia, 1682–1750.* Philadelphia, 1902.

Nash, Gary. "The Free Society of Traders and Early Politics in Pennsylvania." *PMHB* 89 (1965): 147–173.

——————. *Quakers and Politics, 1681–1726.* Princeton, 1968.

Nightingale, B. *Early Stages of the Quaker Movement in Lancashire.* London: Congregational Union of England and Wales, Inc., 1921.

O'Callaghan, E. B., ed. *The Documentary History of New York.* Albany, 1849.

The Oldest Record of the Proceedings of a Court in Pennsylvania now known. 1685–1686. HSP.

The Papers of William Penn. Mary Maples Dunn and Richard S. Dunn, gen. eds. 5 vols. 1981–1987. Vol. 2: 1680–1684, edited by Ned C. Landman et al.; Vol. 3: 1685–1700, edited by Marianne S. Wokeck et al. University of Pennsylvania Press, 1987.

Parrish Collection: Robert Proud. HSP.

Patent Book A-1. Department of Community Affairs, Bureau of Land Records, Harrisburg.

Peare, Catherine Owens. *William Penn, a Biography.* Philadelphia: Lippincott, 1957.

Penn, Granville. *Memorials of the Professional Life and Times of Sir William Penn.* 1833.

Penn, Thomas. List of Grants, Deeds, Papers &c in my possession. Penn-Forbes Collection, vol. 1. HSP.

Penn, William. *His Own Account of the Lenni Lenapi Indians.* Revised edition, Albert Cook Myers. Somerset, New Jersey: The Middle Atlantic Press.

Penn, William. The Irish Journal. MS, HSP. Printed in *PWP* 1.

Penn MSS: Private Correspondence, HSP.

Penn Papers. Additional Miscellaneous Letters, HSP.

Penn-Ford Accounts. HSP.

Penn-Physick Papers. HSP.

Pennsylvania Archives. 2d ser., edited by William Henry Egle. Vol. 19, *Minutes of the Board of Property of Pennsylvania.*

——————. 3d ser., Vol. 2, edited by Egle. *Old Rights.* 662–670.

——————. 8th ser., edited by Gertrude MacKinney, under the direction of James N. Rule. Vol.1, *Votes of the Assembly.* Pennsylvania Miscellaneous Papers, Penn and Baltimore. Maryland Archives. HSP.

Pennypacker, Samuel W. "The Settlement of Germantown, and the Causes which Led to It." *PMHB* 4 (1880): 1–41.

Peters, Hugh. *The Full and Last Relation of all Things concerning Basing House.* . . . 1645.

Petty, William. *The History of the Survey of Ireland, commonly called the Down Survey, A. D. 1655–56*. Edited by Thomas Askew Larcom. Dublin: Irish Archeological Society, 1851, reprinted by Augustus M. Kelley, Publishers, 1967.

———. *Sir William Petty's Account Book*. MSS. Library, Trinity College, Dublin.

Philadelphia Archives, Deed Books. City of Philadelphia, Department of Records.

Pomfret, John E. *The Province of East New Jersey, 1609–1702*. Princeton, 1962.

———. *The Province of West New Jersey, 1609–1672*. Princeton, 1956.

Prendergast, John P. *The Cromwellian Settlement*. 2d ed. Dublin, 1875.

Proud, Robert. *History of Pennsylvania*, vol. 1. Philadelphia, 1797–1798.

Quakers: See Society of Friends.

[Ram, Robert.] *The Souldiers Catechism*. 1644.

Records of the Court at New Castle, 1676–1681 and *Records of the Court of New Castle on Delaware, vol. II, 1681–1699*. Colonial Society of Pennsylvania, 1904, 1935.

Records of the Courts of Chester County, Pennsylvania, 1681-1697. Colonial Society of Pennsylvania, 1910.

Records of the Courts of Philadelphia County. HSP.

Records of the Provincial Council. Miscellaneous MSS, Bureau of Archives and History, DAM, PHMC.

Rees, T. Mardy. *The Quakers in Wales and their Emigration to North America*. Historical Society of Carmarthen, 1925.

The Registers of the Parish Church of Poulton-le-Fylde. Lancashire Parish Register Society: Wigan, 1907.

Registers of the Parish of Coniston, Lancashire/Conistone Church. Transcribed by Hector Maclean . . . and Henry Brierly. . . . Wigan: Printed by Strowger & Son at the Clarence Press, 1907.

Registers of Tewkesbury Abbey. See Gloucestershire Records.

Reps, John W. *The Making of Urban America: A History of City Planning in the United States*. Princeton, 1965.

Richeson, Allie Wilson. *English Land Measuring to 1800; Instruments and Practice*. Cambridge, Mass.: and London: Society for the History of Technology and the M.I.T. Press, 1966.

Riddell, William Renwick. "Libel on the Assembly: a Pre-revolutionary Episode." *PMHB* 52 (1928): 268.

Roach, Hannah Benner. "The Planting of Philadelphia: a Seventeenth-Century Real Estate Development." *PMHB* 92 (1968).

Rogers, Sophie Seldon. Collection. GSP, HSP.

Sanford, Edmund. *A Cursory Relation of all the Antiquities and Familyes in Cumberland*. Edited for the Cumberland and Westmorland Antiquarian and Archeological Society by the Worshipful Chancellor Ferguson. Tract Series 4. Kendal, 1890.

Scharf, J. Thomas. *History of Maryland from the Earliest Period to the Present Day*. 3 vols. Baltimore, 1879.

Scroope's and Ireton's Regiments. *Unanimous Declaration of Colonel Scroope's and Commissionary General Ireton's Regiments.* 1649. BL.

Seymour, St. John D. *The Puritans in Ireland, 1647–1661.* Oxford: Clarendon Press, 1921.

Sharpe, R. R., for the Corporation of London. *Calendar of Letter-Books.* 1899. BL.

Sharpe, R. S., ed. *Calendar of Wills, 1258–1688.* BL, 1889—.

Smith, Benjamin H. *Atlas of Delaware County, Pennsylvania.* Philadelphia, 1880.

———. (Attributed to), Patents of Townships in Delaware County, Pennsylvania. MSS, 32 pages.

Snyder, Martin P. *City of Independence.* New York: Praeger Publishers, 1975.

Society of Friends

    Abstracts of Records of Bristol and Somersetshire, microfilms of Friends Collection in London at Swarthmore College.

    Archives of the Society in Ireland, Friends' Library, Dublin.

    Bucks County: Miscellaneous Records, with Index to Bucks County, Pennsylvania Monthly Meeting Records. HSP.

    Collection of Penn Papers, Friends' Library, London.

    Minutes of the Abington Monthly Meeting, Pennsylvania, 1682–1746, Transcribed from the original, presented by Joseph E. Gillingham, 1893.

    Minutes of the Philadelphia Monthly Meeting, MSS. Formerly at the Friends' Arch Street Library, now in the Haverford College Quaker Collection.

    Philadelphia County: Index to Miscellaneous Papers, Gilbert Cope Collection. Minutes of the Monthly Meetings at Orange Street, Pine and Orange Streets, and Fifteenth and Race Streets, Philadelphia.

Soderlund, Jean R. *William Penn and the Founding of Pennsylvania, 1680–1684.* Philadelphia: University of Pennsylvania Press and the Historical Society of Pennsylvania, 1983.

Sprigge, Joshua. *Anglia Rediviva*, MSS, BL. Published volume, London, 1649.

Stearns, Raymond Phineas. *The Strenuous Puritan: Hugh Peter, 1598–1660.* Urbana: University of Illinois, 1954.

Sturgess, H. A. C. *Register of Admissions to the Honorable Society of the Middle Temple from the Fifteenth Century to the Year 1944.* 1959.

Subsidy Roll I H no. 25., PRO D. Copy of the original by Philip Hore in notes for his *History of Wexford*, St. Peter's College, Wexford, Ireland.

Survey and Warrant Book. City of Philadelphia, Department of Records, City Archives.

Thomson, W. W. *West Chester County and Its History.* Chicago, 1898.

Tolles, Frederick B. *Meeting House and Counting House: the Quaker Merchants of Colonial Philadelphia, 1682–1763.* Chapel Hill: University of North Carolina Press, 1948.

Transactions of the Cumberland and Westmorland Antiquarian Society. Edited by Cory. N. s. 4, 1902.

Underhill, Sarah Gilpin. "Indians of Bucks County Two Hundred and Fifty Years Ago." *Friends' Historical Society of Philadelphia Bulletin* 23 (1976).

Venables, Robert. *The Narrative of General Venables.* Edited by Charles H. Firth. *Royal Historical Society Publications, 2: 61.* London, 1900.

Watson, Foster. *The Curriculum and Text-Books of English Schools in the First Half of the Seventeenth Century.* Transactions of the Bibliographical Society 16 (1903): 159–269. London.

Westropp, Johnson. "Cromwellian Account Books, Limerick." *Journal of the Royal Society of Antiquaries of Ireland. Papers and Proceedings* 29: 11.

Whitehead, William A. *Documents Relating to the Colonial History of the State of New Jersey.* Vol. 1, 1631–1687. Newark, 1880.

Whitelock, Bulstrode. *Memorials of the English Affairs from the Beginning of the Restoration of King Charles II.* New ed. Vols. 3 and 4. Oxford, 1853.

Whiteside, J. "The Holmes of Mardale." *Transactions of the Cumberland-Westmorland Archeological Society*, n. s. 2 (1902): 143.

Wight, Thomas. *A History of the Rise and Progress of the People Called Quakers, in Ireland, from the year 1653 to 1700 . . . afterwards revised, enlarged, and continued to the year 1751 by John Rutty.* 4th ed. London: Printed and sold by William Phillips, George Yard, Lombard Street, 1811.

Wills Proved in Philadelphia, 1682–1692. Publications of the Genealogical Society of Pennsylvania. Vol. 1 (1896), and 2 (1692–1697).

Winpenny, Thomas R. "The Nefarious Philadelphia Plan and Urban America: A Reconsideration." *PMHB* 101 (1977): 102-113.

Winstanley, Gerard. *Letter to the Council of State.*

Wolf, Stephanie Brauman. *Urban Village: Population, Community, and Family Structure in Germantown, Pennsylvania, 1683–1800.* Princeton, 1977.

Wood, Anthony á. *Athenae Oxoniensis. . . .* Edited by Philip Bliss. Vol. 1. London, 1813.

Glossary

Alienation: transfer of ownership.
Assign: to transfer property.
Barony: (in Ireland) division of a county.
Bill: draft of a proposed law presented to legislature for discussion and vote.
Bill of exchange: a written order by one person to another to pay a certain sum to the first or a third person by a given date.
Certificate of Marriage: a certificate given by a Friends' Meeting declaring that there is no impediment to the marriage of a couple who are members.
Certificate of Removal: a certificate given by a Friends' Meeting declaring that a member is in good standing and free to go elsewhere.
Charter: a document establishing a borough or corporation with stated privileges and rights.
Charter of Liberties: an alternate title for William Penn's *Frame of Government*.
Duffel: coarse woolen cloth with thick nap.
Enfeoff: to put in possession of the fee-simple or fee-tail of lands, tenements, etc.
Entail: to settle possessions on successive persons with exclusive rights thereto.
Factor: one who buys or sells for another.
Fee simple: absolute possession.
First Purchaser: a purchaser of a tract in the first five hundred thousand acres of land in Pennsylvania offered for sale by William Penn between July 1681, and April 1682, with rights to city lots and liberty lands.
Freeholder: a property owner free to sell, will, or give away land.
Fustian: coarse cloth made of cotton and flax.

Headright: fifty acres to be given to a settler who paid his passage to Pennsylvania but had not enough money to buy land.
Hereditament: any property that can be inherited.
Indenture: a deed or sealed agreement between two or more parties.
Indentured servant: a person contracted to a certain term of service in payment of a sum advanced.
Kersey: coarse narrow cloth woven from long wool, usually ribbed.
Lease and release: a lease of land for a very long term—e.g., from ninety-nine to several hundred years, followed by an agreement to convert the lease to absolute sale at the end of that period.
Letters patent/Patent: open letter or document granting ownership.
Liberty lands: ten thousand acres of land surrounding the city available to First Purchasers in proportion to the size of the purchase.
Manor: a landed possession from the holders of which the owner has the right to expect certain fees and within which he has certain privileges.
Osnaburg: coarse linen.
Penny: the smallest unit of English money: 1/12 of a shilling.
Pound sterling (£): 12 shillings, approximately the modern $100.00.
Proprietary: proprietor.
Quitrent: annual small feudal fee required of the purchaser in perpetuity by the proprietor. It could be purchased for a lump sum by the purchaser of the land and required by him of one to whom he sold the land.
Remission: payment or release from a debt.
Replevin: restoration to or recovery by a person of goods or chattels destrained or taken from him, upon his giving security to have the matter tried in a court of justice and to restore the goods if the judgment is against him.
Royalty: right of government over minerals.
Sachems/sachemakers: heads of Indian tribes.
Seignory: the authority, rights, and privileges of a feudal lord; relation of a lord to tenants of a manor.
Seisn: possession, as of freehold; turf or key handed over in "livery of seisn" as a sign of possession.
Shallop: small oar or sail-propelled boat.
Stroudwater: blue and red woolen cloth.
Surveyor's terms, instruments and procedures:
  Acre: 160 square rods.
  Chain (Gunters): a hundred links of sixty-six feet (of heavy wire), with every ten links marked off by a brass ring.
  Circumferentor: a flat brass bar with sights at each end and a magnetic compass over a graduated card in the center, mounted on a tripod.
  Compass: (1) "an instrument for taking measurements and describing circles, consisting (in its simplest form) of two straight and equal legs connected at one end by a movable joint"; (2) "an instrument for determining the magnetic meridian or one's direction with respect to it, consisting of a magnetic needle turning on a pivot" over a *compass card*, the

circumference of which was divided variously into degrees, minutes, and seconds.

Field book: a record book of convenient size to be used by all surveyors for accurate and uniform records of their surveys. It should be ruled in three columns for degrees, rods, and parts of rods.

Metes and bounds: the method of describing a surveyed tract according to linear measurements and outline identified by landmarks or marks made by the surveyor, such as trees, streams, or marks made with implements.

Overplus: land in excess of the stated survey included because too small or irregular or of too poor quality to survey practically.

Perch, pertch, pole: a statute rod of 16 1/2 feet.

Plane table: (as recommended by Leybourn) a flat square or rectangular surface over which a sheet of paper ruled to receive the surveyor's observations is held firmly in place by a tightly fitted frame. On one side of the frame were scales or indexes to help determine heights and distances; on the other, movable sights, sometimes with a magnetic compass mounted on a compass card at the center, or with a half-circle or protractor for measuring angles. The table was mounted on a sharpened stake or stakes that could be driven into the ground, or on a tripod.

Protractor: a graduated semicircle for measuring angles.

Quadrant: a graduated quarter-circle used for measuring angles and altitudes and ascertaining latitude and longitude, especially in navigation.

Royal paper: 24"x19" for writing, 25"x20" for printing.

Scale: graduated line indicating proportionate distances.

Sight: device for directing the eyes in making direct linear observations.

Station: a point from which observations are made.

Theodolite: a horizontal graduated circular plate with an index bearing sights, sometimes with the addition of a compass, level, vernier (a short, movable scale), etc.

Triangulation: division of a tract into triangles in order to determine the total acreage involved.

Index

Acrod, Benjamin, 177, 255
Act for the Satisfaction of Adventurers and Soldiers, 37
admeasurement, 37
admeasurers, 43, 44
Agreements Made in England, 97
Allen, Nathaniel, 76, 79, 80, 92, 261
Allen, Samuel, 261
A Narrative of the Cruel Sufferings . . ., 54
   title page photograph, 55
Andros, Sir Edmund, 146, 150
Arnold, Thomas, 76 n. 4
Articles of War, 15
Ashcom, Charles, 80, 97, 104, 118, 129, 160, 171, 180, 186, 195, 196, 205, 206, 207, 209, 210, 235, 240, 241, 244, 258, 259, 269, 292, 293
A Short Advertisement upon the Scituation . . ., 160
Assembly, 223–226
astrolabe, 39
Atkinson, James, 143, 144
azimuth compass, 39

Balaverhassett, John, 37 n. 4
Baldwin, William, 291
Baltimore, Lord, 89, 90, 91, 100, 101, 102, 110, 120, 123, 125, 133, 135, 141, 145, 147, 148, 150, 151, 191, 194, 195, 213
Barbados, 72, 77
   Quaker trade in, 77
Barclay, Robert, 146, 147, 152, 153
Barker, T., 271
Barry, William, 224
Beardsley, Alexander, 274
Berkeley, John, Lord, 145
Beverall, James, 37 n. 4
Bezar, John, 76, 79, 80, 92, 160
Biles, William, 136, 139, 175, 214, 215
Blackwell, John, 283, 287
Blakleach, Richard, 240
Blunston, John, 224, 226

boundary problems:
   claims, 104, 110–111, 195, 196–197, 203, 207, 209, 210, 233, 249–251, 257
   county, 169, 219, 220, 235, 277, 288
   40th parallel, 75, 100–101, 110, 123
   Lake Erie colony, 246
   New Castle, 86, 124, 141, 142, 288
   New Jersey, 145–148, 149, 150, 151, 152
   Pennsylvania and Maryland, 85, 91, 100, 101, 110, 123, 195, 212, 213
   Philadelphia, 112–114, 148, 220, 233, 234
Bowen, John, 118, 261
Bowman, Thomas, 98, 195, 249
Bradshaw, James, 244
Bradshaw, Rachel Penn, 76 n. 1
Bradshaw, Rebecca, 17, 76 n. 1
Brassie, Thomas, 105, 111, 120
Bridges, John, 223
Brown, Whitall, 37 n. 4
Browne, Robert, 16
Buckley, Samuel, 280, 281
Budd, Thomas, 274
Bullynge, Edward, 146

Calvert, Charles, 85
Calvert grant, 110, 124
Cann, John, 111, 221
Cantwell, Edmond, 136, 143
Carpenter, Samuel, 126, 127, 129, 130, 164, 165, 182, 192, 197, 198, 199, 209, 211, 212, 214, 228, 229, 237, 239, 263, 277, 278, 280, 288
Carr, Andrew, 104
Cart, Joshua, 234, 247, 274
Carter, William, 292
Carteret, Sir George, 145, 146
Carteret, Philip, 146
Cave dwellings, 107, 127, 163–164, 272, 288
Cecil, William, 97
Cerey, Thomas, 105
Chambers, Benjamin, 144, 238, 240, 264, 272, 273, 274, 281

Charles I, 13
Charles II, 54, 75, 89, 124, 141, 142, 145, 221
Charter of Liberties, 136, 140, 141
"Children of Light." See Society of Friends
circumferentor, 39, 40
Civil Survey, 37, 43, 44, 52
Clancy, Samuel, 78
Claridge, Samuel, 50, 57, 62, 66, 70, 77, 78 n. 7, 79, 98, 144, 203
Clark, William, 120, 121, 136, 137, 139, 140, 145, 176, 193, 194, 198
Claypoole, James, 76, 77, 78, 78 n. 8, 79, 80, 93, 126, 137, 147, 164–165, 180, 181, 198, 199, 207, 228, 230, 235, 237, 239, 240, 246, 254, 265, 269
Claypoole, John, 78 n. 7, 87, 207, 265
Claypoole, Norton, 76
Clayton, William, 136, 139, 140, 143, 174, 175, 193, 205
clergy, Catholic, 44
Clifton, Sir Richard, 58, 59
Clifts, Samuel, 99
coat of arms, 5, 20, 21, 21 n.11
Coburn, Thomas, 273
Cock, Lasse, 93, 136, 137, 156, 174, 175, 242, 252
Collyer, William, stepfather, 7
Commissioners of Estate and Revenue, 198
Committee for Elections and Privileges, 120, 121
Committee for Justice and Grievances, 120
Committee of Twelve, 105
Compendious View of some . . .Sufferings . . ., 50
Congregationalists, 16
Cook, Arthur, 240, 253, 254, 261, 287
Cook, John, 293
Corbet, Miles, 37
Corsley, Richard, 273, 290
Council for governing province, 136, 137, 139, 140, 144, 148, 164, 173, 176, 191, 193–194, 195, 197–198, 199, 219, 221, 223, 224, 225, 226, 231, 240, 241, 243–244, 258, 287
    bicameral government, 137
Council of East New Jersey, 135
Court, provincial, 199, 225
Coxe, Daniel, 246
Crefeld. See Germans
Crispin, Hester Holme, 128, 167, 168, 193, 293
Crispin, Mary, 255
Crispin, Rebecca, 255
Crispin, Sarah, 255
Crispin, Silas, 85, 97, 98, 126, 128, 155, 167, 168, 203, 266, 267, 293, 298
Crispin, William, 17, 38, 68, 75, 76 n. 1, 77, 80, 85
Croft, James, 105
Croft, Maudlin, 21

Croft, Sarah. See Sarah Holme
Croft, William, 21
Cromwell, Lord Henry, 45, 50
    attitude toward Society of Friends, 49
Cromwell, Oliver, chapters 2–3 passim
    army, 36
    death, 54
    nepotism, 36
Cromwell, Richard, 54
Cuppage, Mary, 67
Cuppage, Robert, 37, 52, 53 n. 8, 58, 59, 63, 67
Curles, Joseph, 110
Curtis, Joseph, 156

Dare, William, 125
Davies, Richard, 184
Day, John, 271
de la Grange, Arnoldus, 110, 111
Diamond, Richard, 80, 81, 87, 89, 106, 265
Dickinson, Allis, 79
Diggers, 17, 20
Discipline, army, 15
Dongan, Thomas, 152, 191
Down Survey, 40 n. 9, 44, 81
dragoons, 14, 35 n. 2,
Drogheda, 25, 26
Ducket, Thomas, 144, 291
Dungeare, 52
Durkin, Thomas, 160

Earl of Essex, 15
Eaton, George, 296
Eckley, John, 199, 274, 287
Edmundson, Grace, 70, 144
Edmundson, William, 62, 66
Edridge, John, 146
Ellis, Thomas, 272, 274
England, Christian, 217
England, Philip, 219
Everard, George, 17

Fairman, Thomas, 89, 93, 97, 103, 112, 129, 133, 142, 143, 145, 190, 203, 223, 232, 248, 249, 260, 272, 276, 279, 280, 281, 297
Farmer, Jasper, 233, 234, 239, 289
Farmer, Jasper, Jr., 234
Fenwick, John, 141, 146, 147, 149
Fifth Monarchy, 20, 48
Fleetwood, Charles, 37
Fletcher, Elizabeth, 49, 50
Fletcher, John, 50, 87, 126, 289
flood of 1687, 267
Flower, Enock, 174
Ford, Philip, 76, 77, 207, 276, 295
Forman, George, 110
Forrest, Walter, 261
Foster, Allen, 161
Foster, William, 161

Fox, George, 18, 48, 53, 61, 62, 153, 294
  portrait of, 19
Frame of Government, 135, 138, 140, 142, 143, 144
Frampton, William, 221, 233, 240, 244, 265
Free Society of Traders, 78, 87, 102, 110, 118, 120, 122, 126, 137, 140, 164, 177, 179, 181, 213, 216, 228, 229, 239, 264
  plans for development, 177–178
Fretwell, Ralph, 203–206, 207, 208, 209, 210, 215, 216, 228, 232, 236, 246, 270
"Friends of Truth." See Society of Friends
Fuller, Abraham, 50, 62, 65, 70
Furly, Benjamin, 182
Furnis, Henry, 273
fur trade, 151, 178, 191

Galloway, siege of, 30
Germans, 177, 180, 182–183, 185 (map detail), 187. See Pastorius
  Low, 164, 182
glasses, topographical, 39
Goodson, John, 164, 177, 215, 228, 245, 246, 272, 274, 280
Graham, James, 110
Gray, John, 232, 233, 248, 249, 250, 251, 260, 263, 264, 274–275, 280, 294
Gray, Samuel, 224
Griggs, John, 120
Groome, Samuel, 151–152
Gross Survey, 37
Growden, Joseph, 143, 195, 220, 226, 232, 233, 247, 260, 261, 275, 281, 294
Growden, Lawrence, 143
Guest, George, 111

Haige, William, 76, 79, 80, 86, 89, 91, 97, 98, 99, 100, 105, 111, 123, 136, 137, 174, 175, 196, 227, 230
Hall, Robert, 249
Hall, William, 37 n. 4
Hardiman, Hannah, 212
Hardin, Nathaniel, 261
Harrison, James, 79, 101 n. 11, 129, 136, 140, 148, 175, 194, 198, 199, 205, 206, 207, 209, 211, 213, 227, 240, 253, 254, 261 n. 5, 266
Hartford, Charles, 237
Hastings, Joshua, 158
Hawkins, Jeffrey, 118
Hawkshead Grammar School, 6, 8, 10, 44
Hawkshead-Coniston area, 3, 5, 6
Hazelgrove, John, 160
Hendrickson, Jacob, 175
Hendrickson, Yeshro, 175
Hermann, Augustine, 83, 91, 101, 123
Hermann, Ephraim, 83, 109
Hillyard, John, 136
Hodge, Samuel, 147
Hodgkins, Milissent, 291
Holcomb, Richard, 67

Holland, John, 161
Holme, Abraham, 17
Holme, Alice, 4
Holme, Christopher, 283
Holme, Elinor, 67, 71, 168, 171, 196, 265, 280, 293, 295, 296
Holme, Esther, 47
Holme family, record of deaths, 69
Holme, George, father, 4, 7, 8
Holme, George, grandfather, 5
Holme, Hester, 56, 71
Holme, Mary, 47
Holme, Michael, 5, 265–266, 285–286
Home, Sir Robert, 38
Holme, Samuel, 53, 68
Holme, Sarah, 21, 23, 29, 30, 31, 47, 48, 67
Holme, Sarah (daughter), 35, 47, 67
Holme, Susanna, 52, 65
Holme, Thomas,
  appointed surveyor general, 79
  begins Pennsylvania survey, 96
  boyhood, 7
  controversy with Gray, 250–251
  conversion, 18
  death, 296
  financial problems, 60
  hybrid map ?, 83
  insecurity, 278
  investment in Pennsylvania, 78
  letter to Penn, 170
  map, 130, 131, 257, 259, 260, see Map 1687
  marriage record, 22
  memorial obelisk, xvii, 296
  military career, chapters 2–3
  new commission, 284
  on Penn's council 136,
  parents, 4, 7
  payment for work, 165
  Penn's commission to, 81, 82
  Penn's accusations against, 297
  real estate dealings, 236, 237, 245
  relations with Indians, 94–96
  retirement from council, 245
  school desk, 9
    photograph, 10
  schooling, 8–10
  surveying methods, 130, 133; response to, 277
  will, 297–298
Holme, Thomas (son), 47
Holme, Tryall, 57, 104, 171, 196, 203, 236, 261, 266, 292, 298
Holme, William, 57, 65, 104, 133, 160, 168–169, 171
Hooten, Thomas, 126
Hopton, Arthur, 39
Howell, John, 168
Hudson, Thomas, 277
Hughes, John, 203

Independents, 16
Indians, 128, 143, 155–156, 157, 158, 174, 177, 191, 192, 213, 214–215, 231, 237, 238, 240, 242, 243, 244, 249, 250, 252, 253, 277
    Penn's letter to, 93
      copy of letter, 94
    Sectarius, 174
    Susquehanna territory, 237–239
    Upland purchase document, 243
Inglo, Richard, 221
Inquisition, 37
Ireland,
    civil government of, 37
    resettlement of, 36
Irish wars, 22, 25–30

James II, Duke of York, 110, 124, 141, 142, 145, 146, 150, 151, 152, 221, 283
James, John, 139, 292, 293
Jennings, Samuel, 147
John ap John, 86, 184
Johnson, Claus, 261
Johnson, Mons, 131
Johnson, Neels, 131
Jones, Charles, Jr., 233, 284
Jones, Edward, 184, 276
Jones, Griffith, 79, 99, 120, 121, 129, 139, 143, 144, 188, 230, 234, 253
Jones, John, 86, 87 n. 16
Jones, Michael, 27
Jones, Samuel, 296
jurisdiction, 111

King, Walter, 272

Lakin, Henry, 292
Lamb, F., 261
Lancashire, people of, 3
Land, Samuel, 110
Laurie, Gawen, 146, 151
Laws Agreed on in England, 178, 179
Laws and Ordinances of War, 15
Lawson, Neals, 240
Lee, Charles, 292
le Haes, John, 111
Lehnmann, Philip Theodore, 129, 147, 156, 188, 196, 198, 203, 207, 211, 213, 233, 267
Lenthall, Speaker of the Parliament, 25
Levellers, 17, 20, 21
Lewes, Henry, 144
Lewis, Henry, 246
Leybourn, William, 40, 97
Liberty lands (Philadelphia), 103, 107, 113, 114, 115, 125, 128, 130, 143, 162, 165, 168, 179, 180, 182, 186, 189, 196–197, 220, 230, 288
Lilburne, John, 17, 20
Limerick,
    Holme residence in, 30
    reconstruction of, 35
    siege of, 30
liquor laws, 192, 192 n. 31
Lloyd, Charles, 184
Lloyd, Thomas, 164, 191, 193, 194, 196, 197, 198, 199, 201, 208, 212, 213, 220, 221, 226, 227, 231, 234, 240, 244, 253, 254, 255, 264, 269, 287, 296
Loe, Thomas, 53, 57, 63
Logan, James, 284
Longshore, Robert, 131, 189, 275, 289, 292, 293, 296
Lower Dublin Academy, xvii
Lowther, Margaret Penn, 166
Lowther, William, 195, 270, 276, 280
Lucas, Nicholas, 146
Ludlow, Edmund, 37
Lundy, Richard, 76 n. 4

McVeagh, Edmund, 79, 87, 126, 171, 289, 296
magnetic compass, 39
Magson, Francis, headmaster, 8
Magson, Peter, headmaster, 8
Mann, Abraham, 121, 223, 224, 225, 226
Mann, William, 273, 274
Map, 1687, 99, 118 n. 13, 132 (detail), 133, 138, 161, 162, 166, 178, 179, 184, 185 (detail), 186, 187, 203, 232, 234, 241, 242, 247, 253, 259, 260, 261, 262, 275, 277, 280, 284; second version, 286
Map of Some of the South and East Bounds (Morden), 83, 84
Map of Virginia and Maryland, 83
Markham, Rebecca Penn, 76 n. 2
Markham, William, 75, 76 n. 2, 81, 85, 89, 91, 92, 93, 98, 99, 100, 101, 101 n. 11, 102, 105, 107, 109, 110, 123, 125, 136, 143, 145, 155, 191, 227, 239, 240, 242, 244, 245, 249, 250, 251, 253, 254, 260, 263, 264, 272, 274, 277, 280, 284, 294
Marsh, Robert, 215
Martin, John, 92, 105, 162
Mathews, Thomas, 147, 149, 150
Matson, Margaret, 175
Matson, Neels, 175
Mayne, William, 62
Meeting house, first, 188
Mettamicont, Richard, 196
micrometer, 39
Mildmay, Katherine, 247
Miller, Thomas, 163
Millnor, Nathaniel, 283
Moll, John, 109, 111, 121, 136, 140, 157
Moon, Samuel, 295
Morden, Robert, 83, 84
More, Nicholas, 77, 79, 110, 118, 120, 121, 137, 142, 143, 156, 177, 179, 194, 199, 206, 213, 214, 220, 223, 224, 225, 226, 228, 230, 236, 264, 265
Morris, Anthony, 274

Morris, Lewis, 91, 123,
Moss, Joseph, 261, 265, 266, 285
Mr. Penn's Patent, 75 n. 1

Neilson, Peter, 162
Nevill, James, 147
Newbold, Abraham, 54
New Castle, 109, 124, 141, 145
Newcourt, Richard, 115
New Mediterranean Sea Company, 246
New Model army, 14, 20
Noble, Richard, 80, 83, 97, 113, 123, 125, 130, 135, 136, 158, 160, 241

O'Byrne, Brian MacPhelim, 27
O'Derrick, "Blind Donough," 44
Osborne, Henry, 38
Osborne, John, 87, 126, 289
Osborne, Richard, 38
Ousley, Richard, 37 n. 4
Owen, Griffith, 184

Parliamentarians, 13
Parliament's Commission for the Civil Government of Ireland, 37
Paschall, Thomas, 103 n. 12, 130–131, 133
Pastorius, Francis Daniel, 156, 163, 164, 180, 182–183
Pearce, Richard, 233
Pemberton, Phineas, 79, 221, 225, 248
Penn, Gulielma, 147, 199
Penn, Gulielma Maria, 270
Penn, Letitia, 276
Penn, William, 53, 54, 57, 62, 63, 76, 77, 78, 81, 82, 83, 85, 92, 93, 98, 101 n. 11, 103, 104, 105, 107, 109, 110, 111, 112, 113, 114, 115, 117, 121, 122, 123, 128, 130, 135, 136, 137, 138, 142, 144, 147, 149, 150, 155, 156, 157, 158, 159, 175, 178, 179, 186, 188, 189, 190, 191, 192, 193, 195, 204, 210, 211, 213, 218, 227, 229, 232, 237, 239, 243, 246, 247, 250, 254, 255, 257, 259–260, 261, 262, 263, 264, 266, 267, 269, 278, 284, 287, 289, 293, 294, 295, 297
    arrest in England, 286; release, 293
    directive on cave dwellings, 272
    Farewell to Pennsylvania, 199
    Holme's map, 259
    manors of, 166, 167, 268
    portrait of, 64, 119
    return to England, 199–200
    seating land, 269–270
    will, 198
Penn, Springett, 198
Penn, William, Jr., 166, 276
Penn, Sir William, 53
Pennington, John, 276
Pennock, Christopher, 138, 219, 276, 291
Pennsylvania,
    constitutions, 122
    economy, 165
    Penn's tract, 75
    punishment for crimes, 175. See also witches
    rural tracts surveyed, 174
    whaling, 181
Pennsylvania Company, 78
Peter, Hugh, 22, 26
Petty, William, 39, 40, 42, 43, 83, 103
Philadelphia, 92, 111–113, 159
    bank property, 291
    boundaries and lots, 125, 176, 189, 190, 196–197, 216, 218, 248, 260, 261, 263, 264, 274–276, 280–281, 288, 289–290, 292
    charter made, 196
    English settlements, 179–180
    first meeting house, 188
    Free Society lots, 178
    German tracts. See Germans, Pastorius
    grid pattern, 115, 117
    Holme picks site, 97
    housing, 127, 159, 163, 230. See cave dwellings
    meeting house, 129, 216
    quays, 291
    roads, 273
    Society Hill, 117
    topography, 116
    Welsh tract, 179, 183–184, 185 (map detail), 260, 269, 271
    wharves, 290
Phipps, Joseph, 161
Pickering, Charles, 168, 240, 249, 250, 260, 261, 263, 264, 275, 276, 277, 280, 281, 292
Pierson, Thomas, 201, 202 n. 1
plane table, 40
Portraiture of the City of Philadelphia, 44, 115, 116, 116 n. 12, 126, 127, 160, 163, 178
    copy of, between pp. 116–117
Powell, David, 241, 253, 271
Presbyterians, 16
Presmall, Robert, 162
Pritchard, Edward, 184
protractor, 39, 43
Pusey, Caleb, 292

Quakers. See Society of Friends
quinquipartite deed, 146

Rambo, Peter, 162
Randall, Francis, 67, 72
Richardson, Francis, 234
Richardson, John, 136, 143
Richardson, Samuel, 249, 274
Rideout, Nicholas, 98, 190, 236, 266
Robeson, Andrew, 284
Robinson, Andrew, 236
Robinson, Patrick, 177, 221, 225, 226, 227, 247, 264, 290, 292, 293
Rocheford, Denis, 189

Rogers, Francis, 77, 78
Rogers, George, 78
Roundheads, 21
Royalists, 13, 15, 17, 21, 26
Rudyard, Thomas, 76, 80, 97, 98, 99, 135, 147, 151, 195, 197
Russell, Richard, 188–189

Salters, Hannah, 98, 161, 191
Salway, William, 292
Sample, William, 120
Sanderlin, James, 240
Sands, Sir Edwin, 21
Sandys, Bishop Edwin, 8
Sandys, Edwin, 6
Sawrey, Miles, 5–6
Scull, John, 240
Scull, Nicholas, 251, 252, 253
seal, Holme's, 42
Seller, John, 83
Separatists, 16
Shardlow, William, 208, 230, 276
ships, sailing,
   Adventure, 86
   Alexander of Inverness, 173, 174
   Amity, 76 n. 2, 78, 79, 80, 81, 83, 85, 86, 91, 92, 93, 105, 184, 265
   Bristol Factor, 76, 79, 110
   Edward and Ann, 71
   Elvis and Mary, 71, 76
   Endeavor, 197, 199
   Freeman, 91, 96, 105
   Friends' Adventure, 102, 139
   Friendship, 96
   Golden Hind, 102
   Griffith, 146
   Harp, 71, 173
   Hester and Hannah, 91, 96
   Hopewell, 102
   Jeffrey, 102, 110, 177, 178
   John and Sarah, 76, 77, 79, 86
   Kent, 147
   Lyon, 96, 184
   Mary, 96
   Mary of Southampton, 173
   Philadelphia Merchant, 293
   Providence, 102
   Riggin, 293
   Samuel, 102
   Society, 96, 103 n. 12, 105
   Submission, 79
   Unity, 78 n. 7, 265
   Welcome, 102, 110, 177
   Wren, 221, 239
Sibthorp, Mary, 292
Sicklemore, James, 49, 50
Simcock, John, 79, 111, 120, 121, 136, 137, 140, 175, 198, 199, 205, 206, 208, 209, 221, 225, 229, 230, 242, 287
Simpill, William, 111

Smith, John, 147
Smith, Ralph, 91
Society of Friends, 18, 20, 47, 48, 50, 51, 53, 54, 61, 62, 65, 66, 69, 70, 129, 144, 216–217, 226, 227, 229
Songhurst, John, 144, 188, 237, 246, 250, 274
Southerby, William, 194, 244,
Southern, Edward, 121, 143
Southern, John, 223
Spread, John, 79
surveying,
   instruments, 39
   system of, 38–43 passim, 97
surveyors,
   in Ireland, 36–46 passim
Susquehanna project, 289–290
Swedes, 111

Talbot, George, 191
Taylor, Christopher, 120, 121, 122, 126, 129, 136, 140, 143, 144, 148, 149, 156, 174, 175, 188, 193, 199, 206, 208, 209, 229, 234, 240, 264, 265
Taylor, Israel, 118, 248, 253, 258, 277
Telner, Jacob, 182
Tewkesbury, 20
   Holmes in, 23, 29
   war in, 21
The Compleat Surveyor, 40
   title page photograph, 41
theodolite, 39, 40
The Resurrection of John Lilburne, 20
The Souldiers Catechism, 14, 15, 25
Thompson, Robert, 246
Thomas, John ap, 184
Thornhill, Robert, 65
Thornton, John, 83
Tories, 44, 58
Tottenham, John, 98, 284, 285
Townstead, 187
Turner, Robert, 56, 57, 62, 65, 66, 77, 128, 129, 165, 198, 199, 203, 216 n. 29, 229, 230, 234, 237, 246, 248, 253, 254, 255, 269, 273, 274, 287, 288, 295, 296

Upland, description of, 87, 92
   boundary dispute, 100
Usher, Thomas, 224

vernier, 39
Vincent, Sir Mathias, 246

Wade, Robert, 83
Walker, Francis, 261, 274
Waller, Sir Hardress, 21, 22, 45, 50, 50 n. 6
Warner, Edmund, 146
Watson, Luke, 120, 121
Webb, Thomas, 233
Welch, William, 194, 195, 199, 201

Well Spring Plantation, xvii, 98, 167, 190, 196, 203, 236, 261
Welsh, 184–185, 186, 187, 191, 241, 259
Werden, Sir John, 150, 152
Weston, Anton, 175
Wexford,
 center of Quaker activity, 67
 conquest of, 28
 Cromwell's home in, 29
 Holme property in, 46, 56
 photograph of, 52
 restoration, 59
Wharton, William, 104
Wheeler, Gilbert, 214, 277
Wheeler, Henry, 37 n. 4
whipping. See Pennsylvania, punishment
White, John, 223, 226
Whitehead, Benjamin, 250

Whiteside, Alice, (mother) 6
Whitpain, Zachary, 217–218, 251, 252, 253
Whitwell, Francis, 120, 136, 201
Wilcox, Barnaby, 226
Wilkinson, Jonas, 293
Williams, Dunk, 248, 261, 274
Wilson, John, 37 n. 4
Winstanley, Gerard, 17, 18
witches, 175–176
Withers, Ralph, 120, 136, 137, 177, 230
Wood, William, 193, 194, 199, 208, 209, 216, 221, 230, 276
Worrel, Richard, 261
Worsley, Benjamin, 37, 38, 39, 40
Wynne, Thomas, 136, 144, 148, 149, 184, 188

Yardley, William, 120
Yocum, Peter, 131, 162

OF PENNSILVANIA IN AMERICA.

Begun by Wil. Penn Proprietary & Governour thereof Anno 1681.

THE CITY OF PHILADELPHIA.

A Map of THE PROVINCE OF PENNSILVANIA Containing the three Countyes of CHESTER PHILADELPHIA & BUCKS

NEW JARSEY.

www.ingramcontent.com/pod-product-compliance
Lightning Source LLC
Chambersburg PA
CBHW081113160426

42814CB00035B/307